Oxford Studies in European Law

General Editors: Paul Craig and Gráinne de Búrca

GOVERNING SOCIAL INCLUSION

Governing Social Inclusion

Europeanization through Policy Coordination

KENNETH A. ARMSTRONG

OXFORD
UNIVERSITY PRESS

OXFORD
UNIVERSITY PRESS

Great Clarendon Street, Oxford OX2 6DP

Oxford University Press is a department of the University of Oxford.
It furthers the University's objective of excellence in research, scholarship,
and education by publishing worldwide in

Oxford New York

Auckland Cape Town Dar es Salaam Hong Kong Karachi
Kuala Lumpur Madrid Melbourne Mexico City Nairobi
New Delhi Shanghai Taipei Toronto

With offices in

Argentina Austria Brazil Chile Czech Republic France Greece
Guatemala Hungary Italy Japan Poland Portugal Singapore
South Korea Switzerland Thailand Turkey Ukraine Vietnam

Published in the United States
by Oxford University Press Inc., New York

First published 2010

British Library Cataloguing in Publication Data
Data available

Library of Congress Cataloging in Publication Data
Armstrong, Kenneth A.
Governing social inclusion : Europeanization through
policy coordination / Kenneth A. Armstrong.
p. cm. — (Oxford Studies in European law)
Includes bibliographical references and index.
ISBN 978–0–19–927837–4
1. Social legislation—European Union countries. 2. European
Union countries—Social policy. I. Title.
KJE3275.A76 2010
303.3094—dc22 2010023729

Typeset by Newgen Imaging Systems (P) Ltd., Chennai, India
Printed in Great Britain
on acid-free paper by
CPI Antony Rowe,
Chippenham, Wiltshire

ISBN 978–0–19–927837–4

1 3 5 7 9 10 8 6 4 2

GENERAL EDITORS' PREFACE

Kenneth A. Armstrong's timely book on governing social inclusion in the EU brings together three important themes in EU policy and scholarship. The first is that of governance, and more specifically some of the novel modes of multilevel governance which have emerged in the context of European integration. The second is that of Europeanization, a theme which includes the 'top-down' question of the impact of the EU on national law and policy, as well as the 'bottom-up' impact of national structures and institutions on the development and implementation of European law and policy. The third substantive theme is that of the creation and evolution of EU social inclusion policy, social inclusion being the name which is given to EU anti-poverty policy.

The book is a rich source of information both on the development at the European Union level of social inclusion policy, but also on the interaction between EU and domestic norms and institutions through a careful case study of the adaptation and reaction of the United Kingdom to the evolving EU policy.

It contains many useful and interesting insights into the nature and operation of EU governance, and a range of thoughtful and critical reflections on the extensive literature on the Open Method of Coordination (OMC). Departing from some of the existing analyses, Armstrong cautions against easy assumptions about the relative effectiveness of 'hard' versus 'soft' law, or about the desirability in this field of harder rather than softer policy instruments. Instead, he advises that close attention be paid to the precise function (whether convergence, coordination, institutionalizing accountability, mobilizing and linking actors and policy-makers etc) of any given OMC process, and locates the weaknesses of the OMC on social inclusion in some of the failures of coordination within the policy, and in specific shortcomings in its institutional design, rather than in the absence of hard sanctions or 'stronger' legal rules. He also cautions against the assumption that the open method of coordination is a single coherent category, or policy mode, and takes care to distinguish the institutional mechanisms and instruments of the social inclusion OMC from those of other coordination processes.

This book is a thoughtful scholarly analysis of a complex and important area of EU policy. It is well informed by insights drawn from the political science literature while offering interesting reflections from a legal perspective on these much-debated modes of governing. There is an interesting chapter questioning some of the received wisdom about the relationship between the EU's legally-privileged 'economic constitution' and its weaker social policy dimension, and a chapter examining whether the process and discourse of constitutionalism has anything to offer the development of EU social policy in general, and social inclusion policy in particular. Finally, the book suggests some interesting lessons to be learned from its analysis of a decade of EU social inclusion policy, and makes a number of concrete suggestions as to how the governance of EU anti-poverty policy could be improved. Overall, it is a rich and nuanced work which should be of interest to all those concerned with EU governance or social inclusion, and to academics and students of law as well as from the social and political sciences.

Paul Craig
Gráinne de Búrca June 2010

ACKNOWLEDGEMENTS

This book started life as a smaller project, funded by the Leverhulme Trust through its research fellowship scheme, to explore the potential for civil society actors in the UK to engage with a new technique of European Union governance called the 'open method of coordination' (OMC). Out of that initial research, the project grew and developed to become the study presented here which analyses the capacity of the OMC to 'Europeanize' domestic strategies and policies to combat poverty and social exclusion.

Many people and numerous organizations have contributed to the realization of this study. As the interviews undertaken for the project were done on a non-attributable basis, I simply wish to think the officials within the European Commission, the civil servants of the UK Government and devolved administrations, and the secretariats of EU-level and domestic social NGOs for giving of their time and experience so generously. I would also like to thank colleagues and friends at the School of Law, Queen Mary University of London for their support and encouragement. I have been incredibly fortunate to have been able to discuss the ideas presented in this study with colleagues at Queen Mary and elsewhere. In particular I wish to thank the following for their comments on, and for their intellectual engagement with, this research: Richard Ashcroft, Iain Begg, Nick Bernard, Gráinne de Búrca, Marise Cremona, Tamara Hervey, Claire Kilpatrick, Deborah Mabbett, Imelda Maher, Joanne Scott, David Trubek, Louise Trubek, and Jonathan Zeitlin. Aspects of this study have been presented as papers in too many places to mention, and again I am incredibly grateful to have had the opportunity to develop the research in such stimulating intellectual environments.

Friends and family have lived with this project for as long as I have. Their support and encouragement has been invaluable. So many thanks to you all. I am especially indebted to Ian Druce for providing bubbles and confectionary as well as incredible support.

Finally, I am delighted that Paul Craig and Gráinne de Búrca were willing to include this book in their fantastic European law series for Oxford University Press. To the editorial team at Oxford University Press, as well as thanking them for their professionalism in taking this book from idea to manuscript to published work, I am also intensely appreciative of their patience. Trying to write on a subject that has been in a continual stage of development was very challenging, not least in terms of knowing when to draw a line. The editorial team at Oxford University Press were willing to trust my judgment and to accept my promise that I would deliver to them the best book that I could write. As to the quality of that book, it is now for others to judge. Any errors are, of course, the responsibility of the author.

London

March 2010

CONTENTS

TABLE OF CASES

EUROPEAN COURT OF JUSTICE

GENERAL COURT

GERMANY

TABLE OF LEGISLATION

EUROPEAN UNION

Regulations

Directives

Decisions

Recommendations

Resolutions

UNITED KINGDOM

LIST OF ABBREVIATIONS

BEPG	Broad Economic Policy Guidelines
COSLA	Convention of Scottish Local Authorities
CSR	Comprehensive Spending Review
DWP	Department of Work and Pensions
EAPN	European Anti Poverty Network
EC	European Community
ECHP	European Community Household Panel
ECHR	European Convention on Human Rights
EEC	European Economic Community
EES	European Employment Strategy
EMCO	Employment Policy Commitee
EMU	Economic and Monetary Union
EPC	Economic Policy Committee
ESC	European Social Charter
EU	European Union
FRA	Fundamental Rights Agency
HMT	Her Majesty's Treasury
MEP	Member of the European Parliament
NAPincl	National Action Plan on Inclusion
NGO	Non Governmental Organization
NIB	National Implementation Bodies
NRP	National Reform Programme
NSR	National Strategy Reports
NTSN	New Targetting Social Need
OECD	Organization for Economic Cooperation and Development
OFA	Opportunity for All
OMC	Open Method of Coordination
PSA	Public Service Agreement
SDS	Sustainable Development Strategy
SPC	Social Protection Committee
TEU	Treaty on European Union
TFEU	Treaty on the Functioning of the Union
UK	United Kingdom

LIST OF TABLES

1

Europeanizing Social Inclusion—Theory, Concepts and Methods

Introduction

In 1997, 18 per cent of the population of the European Union (EU) lived in a household below the relative income poverty threshold,[1] representing some 60 million people, half of whom had lived below this poverty threshold in the preceding three years (European Commission and Council, 2002). Forty years on from the 1957 Treaty of Rome and its promise of 'an accelerated raising of the standard of living' (Article 2, EEC Treaty), a sizeable proportion of the EU population appeared to have been left behind in the development of a Common Market, and not to have benefitted from subsequent initiatives to give that market a 'social dimension' (Rhodes, 1991; Wise and Gibb, 1993).

While many might find the levels of poverty in the modern EU unacceptable, it is, however, less than self-evident that tackling this issue ought to be a core mission of the EU rather than a fundamental responsibility of its constituent Member States who have traditionally been sovereign in the realms of personal taxation and social welfare. Yet, in 1997, new provisions were added to the then European Community Treaty to make action to combat social exclusion the joint responsibility of the EU and the Member States. The purpose of this book is to investigate the manner in which the problem of this economically and socially excluded population has been 'Europeanized'.

The aim of this book is to make a distinctive contribution to the literature on social exclusion in two related ways. The first is to give an explicitly

[1] Households with less than 60% of national equivalized median income.

'European' dimension to the discussion. Understandably, much of the literature on poverty and social exclusion has a national preoccupation as this is where the statistical evidence has been generated; relative poverty indicators situate households within national income distributions; and the main social policy levers are domestic. However, beginning in the 1970s and accelerating through the 1990s and the turn of the millennium, issues of poverty and social exclusion have come to the attention of EU policymakers. It is this 'Europeanization' of social exclusion that is the substantive focus of this study and it is intended to add to, and engage with, studies which are either explicitly or implicitly nation-state focused. However, as will be apparent from the opening discussion, the task is not simply one of scaling up a domestic analysis to an EU level. The 'European' nature of intervention demands a sensitivity to constitutional, policy and governance questions that are specific to the EU and which raise important questions as to the nature and identity of EU intervention.

The second contribution is to adopt a governance perspective. With notable exceptions (Newman, 2001; Daly, 2003), the governance context—typically that of the nation state—remains implicit and latent in studies of poverty and social exclusion. Here, explanatory value is attached to mapping structures, strategies and policies to tackle poverty and social exclusion onto an increasingly multi-level governance context. The connection to the Europeanization thesis can also be made. Once we identify the sub-national, national and European levels of governance acting upon the development of policies and strategies to combat poverty and social exclusion, it becomes possible to explore the extent to which 'Europe' is, or is not, an important causal factor in shaping domestic policies and strategies, and whether different levels of governance also play different roles.

However, the preoccupation is not merely with governance 'levels' but also with governance techniques and tools. The central focus of analysis in this regard is on the emergence of EU techniques of policy coordination intended to support and enhance domestic policy efforts to combat poverty and social exclusion. In particular, in 2000, the Heads of State and Government of the EU meeting in the European Council made a commitment to making a decisive impact on the eradication of poverty and to deploy a novel policy coordination technique—the 'Open Method of Coordination' (OMC)—to that end. This attention towards issues of poverty formed the social strand of the EU's overarching 'Lisbon strategy' launched in 2000, aiming to reconcile economic and employment objectives—'competitiveness' and 'more and better jobs'—with concerns about social cohesion and social protection.

Rather than transferring legislative competence to the EU in areas of social welfare, the EU sought to Europeanize domestic social policies through policy coordination. It is this deployment of the OMC as the governance mechanism of Europeanization that lies at the heart of this study.

As is explained in detail in chapter two, it is difficult and often misleading to try and give a simple, abstract and archetypal definition of 'the OMC'. For present purposes it suffices to say that policy coordination is oriented towards a variety of mechanisms of influence (vertical and horizontal) on the domestic strategic and policy environment. These influences range from the development of reporting and monitoring exercises oriented around common objectives, to the use of indicators and data as a means of facilitating problem-identification and problem-solving by Member States. Influences also emerge through 'peer review' processes and attempts to develop strategic governance processes that are open to non-governmental organizations and the voices of those experiencing poverty. In this way, the process of coordination does not impose a harmonized European solution on Member States but rather encourages a process by which states open their domestic systems of strategy-formation and policy-making to a range of influences from both within and without the state.

The key time frame under analysis is the ten-year period from 2000–2010; a period that began with the launch of the Lisbon strategy and the OMC to combat social exclusion and ended with the year in which a decisive impact on the eradication of poverty was to be made: 2010 was also designated European Year for Combating Poverty and Social Exclusion. Nonetheless, that time frame is contextualized both in the long-term development of EU engagement with issues of poverty, and in the period immediately prior to the launch of the OMC. Indeed, the period from 1997 is especially significant to this study for three reasons. First, as identified earlier, new provisions were agreed in the 1997 Amsterdam Treaty that made combating social exclusion a joint activity of the EU and its Member States. Secondly, the European Commission published a Communication on *Modernizing and Improving Social Protection* (European Commission, 1997) that can be seen as part of a process that led to the contextualization of EU actions to combat social exclusion within a broader process of the modernization of national social protection systems. Thirdly, in 1997 'New Labour' was elected to government in the United Kingdom (UK) with explicit pledges to tackle social exclusion and to end child poverty within a generation. Using a case-study of the Europeanization effects of the OMC on the UK, this book seeks to identify the extent to which sustained attention to issues of poverty and social exclusion, combined with significant changes to governance context both above and below the level of the nation state have shaped policies and strategies to combat poverty and social exclusion.

In developing a socio-legal account of the Europeanization of social exclusion, the book draws on a range of disciplinary backgrounds, particularly social policy, political science, and law. This poses challenges both for the author and for the reader. However, as far as possible, the book attempts to synthesize materials from these disciplines into an accessible narrative structure without doing violence to the richness and variety of scholarship within and across these disciplines. The study is both empirical—drawing on extensive analysis of documentary sources supplemented by interviews with key actors[2]—and normative inasmuch as it offers a critical perspective on debates around the use of novel techniques of governance and suggests ways in which the governance architecture might usefully be reformed.

These, then, are the general aims and objectives of the study. In the sections below, more precise meaning is given to the key concepts and methods deployed throughout the book.

Europeanization

Olsen has suggested that '"Europeanization" is a fashionable but contested concept' (2002: 921) and a term that is capable of being deployed to analyse very different phenomena. It is a term that suggests a process of change in a European context, but specification of what is changing, by what mechanism(s) and to what extent requires further elaboration. Olsen usefully distinguishes between five different phenomena that are often implicated in Europeanization studies (2002: 923–4):

- *changes in external borders*: the territorial expansion of European systems of governance;
- *institution-building*: the emergence of European institutions and actors with a governance competence and capacity;

[2] The project began life as research funded by the Leverhulme Trust through its Research Fellowships scheme and was developed in the context of a UK Economic and Social Research Council seminar series on the Lisbon Strategy. Both sources of funding are gratefully acknowledged.

- *penetration of national systems*: domestic adaptation to European governance;
- *exporting forms of political organization*: emergence of forms and structures of 'European' governance outside the territory of Europe; and
- *a political unification project*: the totality of change that signifies a deepening of integration within the territory of Europe.

In this project, the 'institution-building', 'domestic penetration' and 'political unification' meanings of Europeanization are explored.

In chapters three and four the 'institution-building' conceptualization of Europeanization is analysed. In particular, the emergence in 2000 and subsequent development of a process of policy coordination in the areas of social inclusion and social protection forms the core of the Europeanization analysis in these chapters. Chapter five looks to the nation-state level and considers domestic adaptation to this novel policy coordination process, with a particular focus on the UK. In this way, these three chapters together shed light both on what has been 'uploaded' to the EU system of governance, as well as to what is 'downloaded' into the Member States (on the use of the uploading/downloading metaphor, see Börzel, 2002). Chapters six and seven deal more specifically with the ability or inability of EU policy coordination to offer a credible contribution to the building of a European social policy which might, in turn, strengthen the integration project overall. In particular, chapter seven explores the potential of 'constitutionalism' to act as a vehicle for Europeanization in a manner that might strengthen the EU's social identity and its social policy interventions.

However, the analysis presented in these chapters also aims to make a distinctive contribution to the Europeanization literature through its focus on 'policy coordination' as a mechanism of Europeanization. At issue is how well theories and concepts of Europeanization—typically developed by reference to 'traditional' forms of EU governance—work in analysing the implications of a new technique of governance that relies less on imposing a new rule or institution on EU Member States and more on stimulating domestic policy-making processes to open out to new sources of influence.

As well as a need for definitional clarity and conceptual parsimony to avoid the problem that Radaelli highlighted of 'conceptual stretching' (2003a), any analysis of Europeanization also demands clarification of the theoretical and methodological implications of the analysis. As Bulmer highlights (2007: 47), Europeanization is the phenomenon which requires explanation: it is not itself a 'theory'. From a *theoretical* perspective, Europeanization analyses typically seek to explore issues of causation. However, one needs to be careful to identify the dependent and independent variables at issue. Thus, when seeking to analyse the process of institution-building at EU level, it is change in EU governance which is the *effect* to be analysed. When exploring domestic adaptation, it is EU governance which is one of the potential *causes* of change. This switching of variables is not itself a problem provided it is clear at any given point what it is that is being explained: indeed, by relating the two levels of change—EU and domestic—a relatively rich analysis of the dynamics of Europeanization can be made.

Nonetheless, as Exadaktylos and Radaelli (2009) note, an important *methodological* distinction can be made between 'top-down' and 'bottom-up' approaches to explaining domestic adaptation. One can take an approach which starts with 'Europe' as a cause and then seeks to explain variation in domestic adaptation to this cause. This is a 'top-down' approach in Caporaso's terms (2007) and for him it involves a three-stage analysis: European integration; adaptation pressure; and domestic mediation of adaptation forces. Different analyses may place more or less emphasis on one or more of these stages. For example, at the first stage, European integration may, in governance terms, product a range of instruments creating different mechanisms and pressures for domestic adaptation (see Bulmer and Padgett, 2005; Citi and Rhodes, 2007). At the second stage, authors like Caporaso (2007) and Börzel and Risse (2003) have sought to explain adaptation pressures in terms of the 'goodness of fit' between what has been 'uploaded' to the European level and the domestic level into which the European model is 'downloaded'. At the third stage, attention can be drawn to the role of domestic institutions and actors in mediating pressures (see in the social exclusion context Armstrong, 2006a). Importantly, the methodology of a top-down approach treats all variables as endogenous to the model (Caporaso, 2007: 27): it is concerned with tracing domestic effects to a European cause. Exadaktylos and Radaelli (2009) contrast this approach with a 'bottom-up' methodology which starts with a domestic effect and then seeks to explain 'Europe' as one of a competing range of independent variables that may have caused domestic change. This sort of approach, therefore, avoids tendencies of studies of 'Europeanization' to assume the very thing that they are seeking to explain, namely, whether domestic changes have a European cause.

In chapter five, both 'top-down' and 'bottom-up' methodologies are used to explore different facets of domestic change. As Zeitlin has noted (2005a, 2009), we need to be careful to tease out change in the form of adaptation to the OMC, and changes to domestic policies. This methodological clarification is significant because, as Zeitlin identifies, we need to consider separately the influence of the OMC on both policy *processes* and *substantive* policies. As regards the former, a more 'top-down' methodology is deployed to analyse how the UK has adapted to the OMC *qua* governance process, with an emphasis placed on changes to domestic processes, organizational structures and the role of domestic political and social actors in the elaboration of national plans and strategies to be reported back to the EU through the OMC. The aim of this analysis is to isolate a *potential* source of influence on domestic policy arising from procedural adaptation to the OMC. Its preoccupation is with whether the OMC destabilizes 'closed' mechanisms of domestic strategy-formation and policy-making by opening them out *vertically*—to include the influence of different levels of government to one another as alternative sources of interests, ideas and values shaping domestic policy—and/or *horizontally*—to the influence of non-state and out-of-state actors as sources of interests, ideas and values.[3]

However, governments can decide to continue along established policy paths or to learn outside the context of the OMC. There may be rival or competing sources of change operating within the domestic arena. Therefore, a more 'bottom-up' approach is appropriate when trying to trace specific changes to policy back to a European cause. Accordingly the analysis in chapter five will also consider whether changes in domestic policy and politics have variable and even competing causes. It does not privilege 'Europe' as a source of change.

Governance

In an echo of Olsen's comment (above) about the term 'Europeanization', Newman has observed that '[G]overnance has become a hard-working and somewhat overused concept' (Newman, 2001: 16). Like 'Europeanization' it is a term that can be given different meanings or different emphases within

[3] Hall distinguishes between two different types of policy learning: 'state-centric' and 'state-structuralist' (Hall, 1993). In the former, policy-making and learning remains internal to the 'state' (meaning the core structures of the political system) while in the latter, the state opens out to a broader range of societal interests. Adapting this distinction to the context of the OMC and EU influence on policy, the essential distinction that is made here is between learning which is essentially within a closed self-referential internal world of government—in the context of devolution this also implies that each level of government learns autonomously—and one that is open to other levels of government, to other societal actors and to influences external to the state.

and across a range of disciplines (see generally Pierre, 2000). It is not the intention here to either repeat or critique the abundant governance literature. Rather, and to facilitate an understanding of the governance approach adopted in this study, two specific issues will be addressed. First—and related to the discussion of Europeanization above—the 'governance turn' in EU studies will be explored. Second, the value of a governance approach to the study of social policy will be highlighted.

Governance and EU Studies

The European Union figures in a number of accounts of the rise of 'governance'. For some, the EU is an *effect* of a more general reconfiguration of state authority. Faced with new challenges and limited capacities, nation states have looked to transnational cooperation to maintain or enhance their influence over economic, political and social affairs. This account is closely allied to that other slippery term 'globalization'. Alternatively, the EU can be understood as a driver or *cause* of changes to domestic governance—a key preoccupation of the Europeanization literature discussed above. However, the EU is also a *subject* of governance, and much of what we think of as the 'governance turn' in EU studies is concerned with unpacking the EU as an evolving system of governance in its own right.

Kohler-Koch and Rittberger (2006) identify the period from the mid-1990s onwards as marking the 'governance turn' in EU studies. As their survey article identifies, this 'turn' is not exactly unidirectional in the sense that it encompasses a variety of preoccupations and orientations. A key feature they note is an increasing attention towards the study of policy-making processes at EU level (see also Pollack, 2005). This is consistent with Caporaso's description of a 'post-ontological' shift in the literature on European integration: from seeking to make sense of why European integration occurs to analysis of what European policy-making processes entail (Caporaso, 1996). An important characteristic of EU policy-making highlighted in this literature is its 'multi-level' nature. Attention is also drawn to the range of actors involved in the policy process: not just the EU's own institutions but also those of the Member States, and private as well as public actors. In this empirical style, the emphasis lies in mapping the shifting locus of political authority both vertically and horizontally.

Governance studies have also sought to identify more overarching characterizations of EU policy-making, whether in terms of identifying the EU as a form of 'network governance' or as engaging in 'regulatory politics' (Kohler-Koch and Rittberger, 2006: 34–6). Building on these characterizations, scholars like Helen Wallace have identified a range of 'policy modes' each of which signifies a different configuration of the distribution of competences, institutional roles, actor constellations and styles of decision-making (Wallace, 2005).

In one sense, the emergence of policy coordination as a governance technique can easily be brought within these characterizations of EU governance. The features of this governance tool can be identified and, indeed, significant variation in the styles of policy coordination across different policy areas can usefully be mapped (Laffan and Shaw, 2005). There is no doubt that studies of the OMC form part of an abundant literature on EU governance, with the OMC itself attracting a large amount of scholarly attention.[4] The approach adopted here is empirical—a detailed mapping and exploration of the emergence and evolution of the application of the OMC to combating poverty and social exclusion—critical and evaluative—orienting attention to the strengths and weaknesses of the processes—and normative—positioning the OMC within normative debates about how to ensure both effective and legitimate EU governance (especially those concerned with 'experimentalist governance': see Sabel and Zeitlin, 2008).

Nonetheless, policy coordination through the OMC can also be troubling for scholars of EU policy-making not least because policy-making remains within the nation state rather being transferred to EU institutions. The function of the OMC is not to make policy itself but rather to provide a framework within which states are encouraged to identify policy problems and to seek solutions either within their own domestic systems or by learning from the experience of others. Studies of Europeanization may need to adapt to this decentralized form of EU governance as those studies may have adopted explicit or implicit templates of EU governance that are challenged by this new instrument.

The displacement or decentering of the classic 'Community Method'—the adoption of binding legal rules by the EU legislature (the Council of Ministers and European Parliament) at the initiative of the EU executive (the European Commission) and authoritatively interpreted by an independent

[4] See indicatively: Hodson and Maher, 2001; de la Porte, 2002; Chalmers and Lodge, 2003; Regent, 2003; Borrás and Jacobsson, 2004; Szyszczak, 2006; Zeitlin and Pochet, 2005; Zeitlin, 2008.

court (the European Court of Justice (ECJ))—is also uncomfortable for characterizations of the EU as dominated by forms of 'regulatory politics' in which legislation and litigation are foregrounded as key drivers of European integration. Moreover, acknowledgment of alternative forms of governance other than those associated with regulatory politics is particularly challenging when that characterization is crucial to the defence of the EU's limited capacity to generate democratic legitimacy (see Majone, 1998 and Moravcsik, 2002).

This study also points to potential pitfalls in treating the OMC as just yet another tool or instrument of EU governance in an ever increasing taxonomy of mechanisms of EU intervention. In particular, in designing research projects which seek to compare the OMC to other tools or instruments of EU governance, scholars tend to give an overly singular identity to 'the OMC', thereby suppressing significant differences between policy coordination processes and tensions within any given policy coordination architecture. In chapter two, this problem is explored in detail.

Governance and Social Policy

Although scholars have written about 'governance' and EU social policy—including on the role of the OMC in reshaping the governance of EU social policy[5]—few have tried to make the connections between 'social policy' and 'governance' more explicit in terms of what each offers the other. Important exceptions are the work of Newman (2001) in respect of UK social policy under the 'New Labour' government, and Daly (2003) who has interrogated the utility of the governance literature for social policy analysis (Daly, 2003), and has also applied these insights to an understanding of the development of EU social policy—including the role of the OMC—in the context of the Lisbon strategy (Daly, 2006; 2008).

Newman's study is salient as it sought to explain developments in UK social policy in terms of a shift towards 'new modes of governance' and to use an 'institutionalist' framework to explain this change—an approach which animates this study and whose preoccupations are discussed below. This book is very much in that vein but it develops the point by giving a clear European dimension to the analysis of change.

[5] See generally de la Porte and Pochet, 2002; Wincott, 2003; Trubek and Trubek, 2005a,b; Buchs, 2007; Kröger, 2009.

Daly makes a similar point but for her, the issue is more directly one of how a preoccupation with governance relates to the study of social policy. As she observes, 'the over-riding tendency is for developments in the welfare state to be taken as examples of change (or not) in governance rather than analysed in their own right for their contribution to governance and as active in political settlements more widely.' (Daly, 2003: 118). While to an extent this observation holds true for this study in that EU intervention to combat social exclusion is a case-study of changes in EU governance arising from the advent of techniques of policy coordination, nonetheless, the intention has been not to write a book about 'the OMC', with the social policy context a mere convenient prop for the argument. This project very deliberately distances itself from generalized accounts of the role of 'the OMC' in EU governance (see chapter two). By a careful exploration of the emergence and development of policy coordination as a means of Europeanizing domestic policies and strategies to combat social exclusion, the intention is to make the constitutional, policy and governance dimensions of EU social policy intervention active elements of change. To be sure, the analysis presented here does seek to reflect back on the many claims and counter-claims about the legitimacy and effectiveness of the OMC as an instrument of EU governance. However, the evaluation offered is not a wholly decontextualized one but rather asks what experimental forms of governance like EU policy coordination offer those concerned to see poverty eradicated and social exclusion combated.

Institutionalism and Institutionalization

Among the many 'turns' in studies of the EU, the 'institutionalist' turn (see generally Schneider and Aspinwall, 2001) has been of some significance in bringing processes of institution-building and institutional change to the fore. As Heidenreich and Bischoff (2008) describe it, Europeanization entails a process of 'institutionalization', and not surprisingly, institutionalist theories have been deployed to provide a theoretical underpinning to Europeanization studies (Bulmer, 2007). Institutionalist theories—old and new—seek to give political, economic, and legal institutions explanatory roles in contrast to approaches which view societal variables external to the political, economic or legal systems as the fundamental factors shaping political, economic or legal life. Institutions play a role either because formal institutional structures are also actors (as with 'old' institutionalist studies of the legislative, executive or judicial organs of the state: Peters, 1999: 3 *et seq.*) or because other types of institutionalized practices—standard operating procedures, rules, norms, values—mediate and act upon the behaviour and choices of actors within the broader societal environment of the relevant system (typically the concern of the 'new' institutionalism). Institutionalist analysis has been applied with some success to studies of the EU. As an approach to understanding European integration, it has brought the formal institutions of the EU as political and legal actors back into accounts of how integration proceeds. As an approach to EU governance, the role of routine procedures for legislating and handling EU business; of formal and informal rules and codes of conduct; of the norms and values of the EU, have been highlighted in explanations of EU policy-making.

In this study an institutional approach to policy coordination is taken with a view to analysing processes of institution-building—the emergence and embedding of the OMC as a form of governance architecture; of institutional change—explaining changes within this governance architecture over time; and of institutional adaptation—the mediating function of domestic institutions in shaping responses to the OMC. Nonetheless, institutionalist approaches vary in their particular orientation and in the section below varieties of institutionalist theory will be briefly noted.

Varieties of Institutionalism

As there are varieties of 'Europeanization' studies so too are there varieties of institutionalism. While there may be common agreement on the now somewhat banal statement that 'institutions matter', how and why institutions matter is often more contested, with conceptualizations reflecting very different understandings of the role of structure and agency, stasis and change, exogenous and endogenous preference and the importance of time.

Three variants of 'new institutionalism' have tended to dominate analyses: *rational* institutionalism, *sociological* institutionalism, and *historical* institutionalism (Hall and Taylor, 1996). As Guy Peters puts it (1999: 44), rational institutionalism views institutions as 'collections of rules and incentives that establish the conditions for bounded rationality, and therefore establish a "political space" within which many interdependent political actors can function'. Of course, this approach can extend beyond the 'political' domain to the economic or legal, but the essence of the orientation is towards actors negotiating their way through and orienting their strategies around a set of institutions (including not just formal organizational structures but also systems of rules). If rational institutionalists tend to view institutions as strategic contexts or incentive structures epiphenomenal to the preferences of actors, sociological institutionalists seek to bring institutions to the fore as mechanisms of socialization and preference-formation. Whereas rational institutionalists may typically conceptualize institutions as the 'rules of the game', sociological institutionalists seek to enquire into the meaning of the game for the actors participating in any given process. Consistent with the 'constructivist' turn in political science and international relations, sociological institutionalism explores institutions as systems or streams of meaning through which a world is socially constructed and behaviour oriented. What historical institutionalism brings to the table is the temporal dimension (Bulmer, 2007: 50; Bulmer, 2009). In particular, historical institutionalism seeks to account both for continuity and change over time whether in terms of policy or in terms of the institutional structures themselves.

To these established varieties of institutionalism, Vivien Schmidt has suggested a fourth candidate variant: 'discursive' institutionalism (Schmidt, 2008; Schmidt and Radaelli, 2004). Her goal is to give both a clearer analysis of the role of ideas in policy-making—ideas expressed in discourse and exchanged either within the political system itself or communicated between the political system and its social environment—and to argue that discursive institutionalism offers a more promising reconciliation of structure and agency than the other 'older' new institutionalisms. Whether or not Schmidt is right on the latter point others can debate. This author's interest is more with her analysis of the role of ideas in policy-making. This is particularly significant in the context of a study of the OMC. Recall that EU policy coordination does not entail a transfer of policy-making to the EU. Rather, the intention is to open out the domestic political arena to new sources of information and ideas through which policy learning may take place. What ideas are 'uploaded' and institutonalized in EU discourses and how domestic political arenas adapt to such ideas are at the heart of the open coordination process. Accordingly, the role of discourse will be analysed more fully below. For the moment, it is enough to acknowledge both that discursive institutionalism may be a fruitful explanatory vehicle for studying the OMC and that more broadly, the analysis of Europeanization—the institution-building at EU-level and domestic adaptation—can be conducted within an institutionalist framework in order to give an integrated account of the role of actors and organizational structures, of processes, of substantive rules, discourses, frames and paradigms and their interaction over time.

Law, Legalism and Institutionalization

It is important to address a potential objection to the deployment of an institutionalist analysis to the study of EU social policy coordination. In EU studies, 'institutionalization' has often been associated with a process of 'legalization' (see Cichowski and Börzel, 2003) with resort to legislation and litigation signifying a dynamic process of law-led integration and institutionalization (Fligstein and Stone Sweet, 2001). Certainly, law making—especially the process surrounding the drive to complete the internal market—together with the longer-term process of creating an EU legal order with strong judicial mechanisms of enforcement, projects an image of EU law as an institutionalizing and integrative force: integrative of itself as an institution and—as a medium of integration—of economic and social spheres.[6] This conceptualization of institutionalization focuses particular attention on the regulatory techniques of governance associated with the 'Community Method' and the 'constitutionalization' of enforcement techniques. However, the more we treat institutionalization as a product of legalism, the less obvious it might seem to adopt an institutionalist approach to the study of phenomena in which traditional institutional forms of law are displaced or decentred. Indeed, for some the emergence of new tools of governance like the OMC constitute something of an unwarranted diversion of intellectual energies: an analytical 'red herring' no less compared with the institutionalizing forces of an apparent legalization of Europe (Idema and Kelemen, 2006).

If institutionalization is conceptualized as driven by a process of legalization, then 'lawness' itself may be signified by formal institutionalization (Walker and de Búrca, 2007). We end up with a highly reciprocal relationship between law and institutionalization and a concomitant contrast and distancing of law and institutionalization from 'new governance' forms in which traditional legal governance techniques are decentred or reformulated (Walker and de Búrca, 2007). Again, the result is one which tends to cast analysis of a governance technique like the OMC beyond the boundaries of institutional analysis and even beyond the concerns of law.

The approach adopted here is one which seeks to avoid such stark oppositions between, on the one hand, law and institutionalism and, on the other, new governance techniques. At a minimum, legalization and institutionalization

[6] The most comprehensive critique of the idea of EU law as inherently integrative can be found in Shaw, 1996. See also Armstrong, 1998a.

are not synonymous: the absence of legalization need not be an absence of institutionalization. More profoundly, but also more problematically, is the recognition that while lawness may indeed be signified by recognized and practised institutional structures—indeed law is a form of 'institutional normative order' (see del Mar and Bankoswki, 2009 and the discussion of the work of Neil MacCormack contained therein)—those institutional structures, particularly the role of legislation and adjudication, are undergoing change to meet emerging governance demands. Traditional instruments are changing and new forms of governance are emerging. At a maximum, law's institutional and integrative capacities may be under profound strain and this may be especially so in a context like the European Union, whose governing and legitimacy capacities may be in limited supply. Even without heralding a 'crisis' of law and government, and even if the experimentalism of some novel techniques does not stand the test of time, there is an interesting phenomenon to be studied and the question is simply one of how best to organize that study. It does not seem sensible to cut that study off from either institutional or legal analysis. As regards institutional analysis, picking up the thread of an earlier argument (Armstrong, 2003), notwithstanding the dominance of the idea of institutionalization as legalization, the sort of institutionalist framework outlined above can be used to shed light on the evolution of the OMC. Indeed, as Zeitlin observes, the development of the social OMC processes can be seen as part of a new compromise among Member States in which 'they would insist on institutionalization of a public-regarding process of agenda setting', but not in the form of the traditional 'Community Method' but rather through a form of 'experimentalist governance' (Zeitlin, 2005b: 213). The objective of this book is to deploy a range of institutionalist insights in studying the Europeanization of social exclusion and thereby to mainstream the analysis of something novel within a relatively familiar analytical framework. As regards legal analysis, the point is simply not to cast studies of the OMC beyond the realm of legal theory or EU legal studies. It is always the dilemma of law that it seeks some form of 'closure' by being able to stabilize expectations and order behaviour and yet at the same time retain an 'openness' to an understanding of the world that law does not yet know in order that it retains its capacity to order. That inherent tension within law is visible within new forms of EU governance. Moreover, lawyerly preoccupations with 'accountability', the protection of 'fundamental rights', and concepts of 'citizenship' can all be mustered in an analysis of the OMC. In any event the relationship between the forms and techniques of EU social policy governance and the adjudicative role of the

ECJ in applying EU economic law has raised questions of the balance of constitutional values in the EU and, indeed, has influenced constitutional and treaty reform. In short, there is hardly an absence of legal concepts, themes and preoccupations to be mined in a study of the OMC.

Navigating through these difficult theoretical waters is not without difficulties and it requires careful signposting. Nonetheless, new institutionalism and new forms of governance can fruitfully be explored together.

Social Exclusion—Language and Concepts

As has already been noted, it is easy to allow the substantive topic—social exclusion—to end up playing a rather subsidiary role compared to the elaboration of the concepts of 'Europeanization', 'governance' and 'institutionalism'. An important feature of this study, however, is its attempt to give EU social policy a more active and explanatory role in the shaping of EU governance.

One way of bringing the substantive area to the fore and to relate it to the institutionalist approach deployed is to analyse the role of 'discourse'. Discourse and its analysis has become a familiar feature of the study of public policy (Hajer and Laws, 2006). As already intimated, following Schmidt (2008), a discursive institutionalist perspective may be of particularly utility in the study of a governance process which generates and diffuses ideas about social exclusion—the phenomenon, its causes and effects, and potential solutions—through recursive cycles of policy coordination. The institutional context structures what discourses are communicated and how domestic systems adapt to the policy ideas contained within them. Over time, certain discourses may become institutionalized and reproduced or may change over time.

Discourses can also be concerned with what sorts of discourses are selected; how the issue of social exclusion is framed in these discourses; what paradigms are in use and what they entail. This can be illustrated by material contestation over the substantive ideas, priorities and goals contained within policy discourses. Moreover, discourses can also be about the utility of certain governance tools and techniques as the modality for achieving the goal of combating social exclusion. This is what Schmidt refers to as a higher order, 'meta' institutional discourse (Schmidt, 2008: 316). In this way we can do more than expose a background—albeit novel—institutional structure or deconstruct the discourses of social exclusion: the governance process can be viewed as a site for contestation over ideas about EU social policy and combating social exclusion as well as over the governance context itself. Patterns of institutionalization and institutional change can then be brought to light.

With this general orientation in mind, the sections below elaborate more fully the language and concept of social exclusion and the manner in which this study relates discourse to institutionalization and institutional change. It is useful to explore at the outset the manner in which the language of 'social exclusion' can itself be viewed as a project of Europeanization. Attention then turns to the influence of 'discourse' analysis and its potential application to this study. More specifically, the role of 'discourse', 'frames' and 'paradigms' will be explored.

The Europeanization of a Language

The concept of 'social exclusion' is in many ways a Europeanized concept in itself. It has its origins in French social theory and policy. It was not then inevitable that the language of 'social exclusion' would become of more general European usage and currency, let alone that in 1997 a new British government would feel comfortable in establishing a Social Exclusion Unit. A key explanation for this linguistic transplant is the European Union (Berghman, 1995).

Beginning in 1975, the then European Economic Community adopted decisions establishing 'action programmes' to combat poverty.[7] In essence these programmes funded studies and pilot projects investigating poverty in the Member States. The programmes were colloquially known as the 'Poverty Programmes'. However, there was a linguistic turn with the third programme adopted in 1989.[8] This five-year programme was concerned with 'the economic and social integration of the economically and socially less privileged groups in society'. Some months after the adoption of this

[7] Council Decision 75/458/EEC concerning a programme of pilot schemes and studies to combat poverty [1975] OJ L199/34 and covering the period from December 1975 to November 1981. Subsequently, the Council adopted Decision 85/8/EEC on specific Community action to combat poverty [1085] OJ L2/24 and covered the period from January 1985 to December 1988. Both decisions were based on Article 235 EEC Treaty.

[8] Council Decision 89/457/EEC of 18 July 1989 establishing a medium-term Community action programme concerning the economic and social integration of the economically and socially less privileged groups in society [1989] OJ L224/10, for the period from 1 July 1989 to 30 June 1994.

decision, the Council—under a French Presidency—adopted a Resolution on 'combating social exclusion'.[9] Point 6 of the Resolution declared that:

> ...social exclusion is not simply a matter of inadequate resources, and that combating exclusion also involves access by individuals and families to decent living conditions by means of measures for social integration and integration into the labour market.

We will return to the meaning and content of 'social exclusion' below. What is important is the simple emergence of a concept of 'social exclusion' within the language of the institutions of the European Union. This 'institutionalization' of the language was also advanced by the establishment of the European Observatory on Policies to Combat Social Exclusion. Coordinated by Graham Room and with an academic membership including Europe's leading social policy analysts—including Jos Berghman and Chiara Saraceno—the first annual report of the Observatory noted that (Room, 1991):

> The Observatory is charged with studying the efforts of the public authorities within each member state to combat social exclusion. On the basis of these studies, the Observatory is intended to assist the Commission in promoting a transfer of know-how between the member states and an improvement in the effectiveness of their interventions. This may in turn lead to a convergence in their national policies.

These ideas of promoting transfers of knowledge and enhancing domestic policy efforts were important precursors to the later OMC. But more immediately, the combined effect of funding action programmes and of establishing the Observatory was to create a means by which the very language of social exclusion might be diffused through a European academic research community and gradually taken up by political actors. It is difficult to imagine that the language of 'social exclusion' could have made the direct leap from French social policy into domestic policy contexts without the mediation of European structures and European programmes.[10]

[9] Resolution of the Council and the Ministers for Social Affairs meeting within the Council of 29 September 1989 on combating social exclusion [1989] OJ C277/1.

[10] One should perhaps note that while social 'exclusion' has generally been received as a useable term, its relationship to social 'inclusion' may be a little more complex. Kröger notes (2009) that in France, the idea of 'social inclusion' has little or no domestic resonance. In interviews with Scottish officials, by contrast, a certain amount of play was made of the devolved government promoting 'social inclusion' while English counterparts sought to tackle 'social exclusion'. However, in EU policy the languages of social 'exclusion' and 'inclusion' are both used: the

As Room suggests, the concept of social exclusion was politically useful for governments that did not want to admit that poverty was a problem. However, the ascendancy of the language of social exclusion has not wholly displaced concerns with poverty. If the advantage of the former is that it is broad, dynamic and multi-dimensional—ie it is more than about low income—the disadvantage might be that it draws attention away from low income as an important cause and effect of exclusion. Poverty can, therefore, be a useful language for bringing low income back into the analysis. It has also been used as a means of identifying certain target groups of which 'child poverty' has developed as an object of particular concern within the EU and Member States. Nonetheless, there can be a danger in using only the language of 'poverty' to describe certain vulnerable groups like children or the elderly if it results in a perception that anti-poverty strategies need not be addressed to those in the adult working age population (ippr, 2004).

In short, social exclusion entered the lexicon of official EU discourses and has been downloaded into the languages of domestic policy-making. However, it does not have a linguistic monopoly and the language of poverty remains a vital aspect of dialogue both within official government circles and in wider communication within the public and social sphere.

The Turn to Discourse

The emergence of a common language of 'social exclusion' is not the same thing as suggesting that this language has a common and shared meaning. Indeed, like so many other European concepts it is perhaps its flexibility which is a great part of its appeal. One way of trying to unpack the concept is to consider the language as containing—or even concealing—multiple 'discourses'.

The analysis of discourse has, indeed, played an important role in the exploration of the meaning, for example, of the turn from 'poverty' to 'social exclusion', and in the analysis of domestic social policy in general (see Levitas, 1998; Newman, 2001; Lister, 2004). A highly influential work was Ruth Levitas' study of the discourse of social exclusion in the making of 'New Labour' policy both in Opposition and then later in government in the UK. It provides a useful starting point for the orientation of this present study.

former tends to signify the problem while the latter is a convenient label for the OMC process designed to tackle the problem.

Levitas developed a tripartite taxonomy to guide her analysis based on three different social exclusion 'discourses'. Importantly, these discourses were understood as capable of being deployed simultaneously in policy debates. Levitas labelled the three discourses as 'RED', 'MUD', and 'SID'.

'RED' represents a redistributive approach to social exclusion that developed from debates about poverty but—building in particular on the work of Townsend who situated those in poverty and deprivation *relative* to the society in which they lived—saw social exclusion as being about more than income poverty. Levitas associates this 'critical social policy' perspective with an understanding of societal membership in terms of citizenship—following Marshall (1950)—and exclusion as a denial of citizenship rights.

If RED looked to structural causes of exclusion, MUD represents for Levitas a discourse that places responsibility for exclusion on the individual. It focuses on issues of welfare dependency, family breakdown, and anti-social behaviour. In this way, the 'underclass' are to be brought back into a social and moral order not by reliance on the state, but by personal behavioural change.

The 'social inclusion discourse' (SID) draws on French social policy and the work of Durkheim in his conceptualization of exclusion as exclusion from the social and moral order, but what is interesting about Levitas' analysis is that she viewed this contemporary discourse as encoded specifically in EU policy debates about the labour market as a mechanism of inclusion.

For the moment, attention is simply drawn to the recognition of multiple and competing accounts of social exclusion contained in these discourses. Each provides a different sort of mapping of problem and solution. They each represent a 'paradigmatic' discourse in their understanding of the causes, effects and approaches to social exclusion.

There is, however, a danger that in giving explanatory space to the role of discourses we end up saying little other than that different people might say and mean different things when discussing social exclusion. How discourses are organized and reproduced and how they impact on policy-making is left unexplored. Moreover, it is a weakness of Levitas' study that the discourses shift around in terms of their sources—political parties, academics, civil society, the media—and, therefore, the causal relationships between discourse and policy-making are not always very clear. That discourse matters to policy-making is largely an implicit assumption of the study rather than something to be explained. It will also be of importance to this study to highlight that, as in British political discourses, multiple paradigmatic discourses are present within and act upon European social policy discourses even if, as Levitas suggested, inclusion through the labour market often exerts a dominating influence on EU policy debates.

Newman drew attention to the link between discourses surrounding the reform of social welfare and an institutionalist analysis in her study of welfare reform in the UK (Newman, 2001). For Newman, discourses can become 'institutionalized' (Newman, 2001: 30):

> A shift in discourse produces new logics of appropriate action which are disseminated through policy networks, become embedded in government guidelines and legislation and are institutionalised through practices such as inspection and audit regimes. New discursive practices are adopted by organisations in order to establish or retain legitimacy in a changing policy climate.

An important aspect of this study is to map the parallel institutionalization of discourses alongside the institutionalization of the processes through which discourses are diffused through the operation of the OMC. Through the content analysis of documents produced within the context of the OMC—in the form of Commission Communications, joint reports of the Council and Commission and National Action Plans—the capacity of the OMC as a governance tool to diffuse, reproduce and institutionalize discourses can be explored. Alternative sources of discourse in the form of non-governmental organization (NGO) communications and those from a wider network of experts are also brought to the fore. The function of the analysis is to consider questions such as: what sorts of problems are identified; who is considered to be the object of concern; what kinds of solutions are considered appropriate? What is striking about the analysis presented in subsequent chapters is how seriously actors took the linguistic presentation of key aspects of the OMC: from the choice and even ordering of the common objectives to be pursued by the OMC to the very name of the process. Not least as part of the sociology of the OMC, discourse did appear to matter.

Methodologically, there are significant obstacles to this sort of content analysis when applied to the OMC. Unlike analysis of parliamentary debates, of legislation and of supporting official guidance, it can be hard to know just where to look for sources of language and text. Much of the analysis here will be conducted through discussion of official documentation and NGO position papers. Yet, even that can be difficult to find with many important documents not easily accessible even if in fact publicly available. As well as raising important normative issues about the transparent quality of governance through the OMC, there is, then, simply a risk of overlooking texts which are not formally published or whose existence is unknown.[11]

As Schmidt observes (2008), discourses can be of different 'types' and 'levels'. In terms of the 'type' of discourses at play, Schmidt distinguishes between 'cognitive' and 'normative' discourses. Cognitive discourses engage interests by specifying what is to be done. Such discourses are maps orienting actors in certain directions. Normative discourses engage values: they are suggestive of what ought or ought not to be done. The importance of the distinction is that cognitive discourses suggest what actors should do while normative discourses suggest why they should act in a certain manner.

Moreover, Schmidt distinguishes between 'coordinative' discourses among policy actors and 'communicative' discourses between governmental and non-governmental actors (Schmidt, 2008). Both these forms of discourse are important to this study not least when they illustrate contestation either within official policy circles or between policy-makers and other actors. For example, discourses that place emphasis on inclusion as labour market participation have been contested by academic commentaries that view the market as a means of exclusion (O'Brien and Penna, 2008) or as a normalizing practice that may be questioned within critical social policy circles (Bowring, 2000). From within the NGO community, greater emphasis may be placed on a 'citizenship' or 'fundamental rights' paradigm. Therefore, an important aspect of this study will be to look not just at the content of the official 'coordinative' discourses of EU and national governmental officials but also the 'communicative' discourses seeking to penetrate the official circles of discourse and communication.

As regards 'levels', Schmidt identifies a scale of abstraction with first order discourses operating at the level of the content of specific 'policies'; a second order discourse concerned with policy 'programmes'; and a third order discourse related to underlying 'philosophies'.[12] Later discussions will focus on the content of policy discourses and the different philosophies underpinning EU policy coordination.

[11] Continual reorganization of the EU's website and the transition across different generations of the OMC in the social sphere often led to web-links disappearing and 'archive' documents relating to earlier cycles of policy coordination being difficult to trace. Moreover, there was often no standardized way to reference some of the materials, particularly those documents generated by the Social Protection Committee.

[12] See also Hall's tripartite orders of change in British economic policy (Hall, 1993).

Programmatic Discourses: Policy Frames and Policy Paradigms

As Hajer and Laws note (2006), the concept of policy 'framing' has—much like discourse analysis—attained a certain maturity in studies of public policy. Indeed, it may be that the two are simply aspects of the same phenomenon: 'discourse framing' (see Bauer's analysis in the context of the European Commission's 'Poverty Programmes': Bauer, 2002). However, following Schmidt, a distinction can be drawn between first order 'policy discourse' and a higher order 'policy framing'. Policy framing can be said to be the act of demarcating and confining an area as a policy field or a sub-policy field. It draws a boundary around that field or sub-field and gives it a certain programmatic coherence. Much like a picture frame it sets a boundary of material inclusion and exclusion.

With regard to the object of this study, we can identify policy frames along two dimensions of analysis. There is an intra-EU social policy framing and an inter-EU policy framing process. Within EU social policy, it is possible to frame the OMC to combat poverty and social exclusion within debates about the need for, and identity of, EU social policy in a very general sense. This entails consideration of the material content and boundaries of EU social policy; the division of competence between the EU and the Member States and the range and choice of available tools and levers. More specifically within EU social policy, we can think of different social policy sub-fields which also frame the OMC. These include not only the development of action to combat social exclusion from the earlier 'poverty programmes' but also a more distinctive policy preoccupation with the modernization of 'social protection' systems. Developments within 'employment policy' might also be considered as a frame for the OMC, not least because of the modelling of the OMC on the European Employment Strategy (EES). In short, within EU social policy, the sub-fields of 'poverty/exclusion', 'social protection' and 'employment' policy, frame—and compete to frame—EU intervention.

However, action to combat social exclusion also has to be considered within policy frames that extend outside of EU social policy itself. After all, the OMC to combat social exclusion was launched as part of the overarching Lisbon strategy which was itself framed as a virtuous combination of 'competiveness' and 'social cohesion' (Borrás and Jacobsson, 2004). Therefore, of crucial significance is how the situation of EU social policy within that strategy—and the relative roles and weights of social, economic and later environmental policies—frames the development of the OMC. This point is particularly important in light of the relaunch of the Lisbon strategy in 2005 and contestation around the identity of EU social policy and of the shape and direction of the OMC at that time.

If policy frames simply refer to the broad substantive fields within which policies are elaborated, policy 'paradigms' are instances of attempts to draw cognitive and normative discourse into a more precise representation and understanding of the nature of a policy problem and its solution. The three discourses identified by Levitas, for example, are examples of paradigmatic discourses. Another example is the three social exclusion paradigms identified by Silver (1994): *solidarity*—associated with Durkheim and reintegration of the excluded back into the social and moral order; *specialization*—exclusion as a consequence of societal differentiation which, in the Anglo-Saxon tradition, emphasizes individual responsibilities and mutuality of citizenship rights and obligations; and *monopoly*—in suggesting that social inclusion demands egalitarian social democracy, this draws on Weber's notion of social closure as the interplay of class, power and status in serving the interests of the included. While, as Lister notes (2004), Silver did not intend these paradigms to represent specific national social welfare families, analyses often identify particular paradigms within different welfare state traditions. For example, a distinction has sometimes been drawn between a liberal Anglo-Saxon and a Continental paradigm (see Room, 1995; Silver and Wilkinson, 1995). The Anglo-Saxon tradition of social policy scholarship is said to be concerned with distributive issues, poverty lines and income inequalities, while the more Continental tradition concerns itself with relational issues—of power and social and economic status—and processes by which excluded groups might be reintegrated into the social order (Room, 1995). The concept of social exclusion as a European discourse might be seen to mediate between these paradigms.

There is a certain value in exploring such 'domestic' European paradigms of social exclusion as a means of trying to explain what has been Europeanized in the sense of what has been 'uploaded' to the EU. However, that approach does not do justice to the specificity and limitations of the EU governance context. The EU is not the mirror image of the nation state in social policy terms. Indeed, the study evidences the slow and often painful process of giving the EU a social identity. Therefore, the emphasis in this study is upon seeking to tease out the paradigmatic nature of social exclusion within EU social policy. Much like Levitas' strategy with regard to domestic policy, the goal is to unpack the social paradigm(s) at play and encoded within EU policy discourses.

For Szyszczak (2001) the Lisbon strategy represented a 'new policy paradigm for social policy'. In her analysis, this paradigm reflects visions of the relationship between the economic and the social; of the role of the EU and of the states in social policy; of the participation of social partners and civil society; and of the use of new tools and techniques of governance. Although useful in situating the OMC to combat social exclusion within a broader pattern of change encapsulated by the Lisbon strategy, it is less clear that there is a singular paradigm at play. Indeed, it might be suggested that the Lisbon strategy brought forth an assemblage of different kinds of policy paradigm acting across economic, employment and social policy domains: of 'sound money' and fiscal prudence (Hodson and Maher, 2001); of tackling joblessness and promoting labour market 'flexibility' (Ashiagbor, 2005); of combining flexibility with the security of social protection ('flexicurity'); of utilizing social policy as a 'productive factor' (European Commission, 2000a) and 'activating' those on welfare back into employment.

Specifically in terms of EU social policy, for the purposes of this study, three paradigms will be of significance. The first is a relatively narrow preoccupation with issues of income poverty, income adequacy and income inequality. It retains a more singular focus on poverty and deprivation. This is the 'redistribution' paradigm. The second paradigm is, by contrast, a much broader conceptualization of social exclusion as a denial of the fundamental rights of citizenship. While travelling much of the way with the redistribution paradigm it also looks beyond issues on income poverty to the whole range of barriers to inclusion and the power relationships that perpetuate exclusion. It is a paradigm that typically represents social exclusion as a 'multidimensional' phenomenon. This is the 'social citizenship' paradigm. The third paradigm has a less strong orientation towards the causes of social exclusion and instead places clear emphasis on employment as a mechanism of inclusion. But it also highlights the interconnection between the adequacy and sustainable of social welfare (increasingly under demographic as well as economic pressure) and the role of the labour market. This is the 'activation' paradigm.

Quite clearly, these three paradigms are not wholly original and have associations with the paradigms identified by Levitas and Silver. The ambition—especially for an EU lawyer—is not some reinvention of the social exclusion policy wheel. Rather, the argument is simply that multiple social policy paradigms are at play in EU social policy discourses: there is not a singular or unique EU social policy paradigm. These paradigms are not identical either to the discourses in any given Member State, nor are they a reflection of a specific European welfare tradition. Drawing from the wide resources of domestic social policy experience and welfare traditions but institutionally refracted through the EU governance system—its limited competence, its institutional architecture, its substantive policy preoccupations across time—there is something distinctive about the workings of these paradigms in an EU context. Returning to the institutionalist orientation utilized here and following Newman's insight, different discourses and paradigms can and do become institutionalized within the specific features of EU governance.

The point of analytical intervention, therefore, is one which views the governance architecture for policy coordination as a site for multiple discourses, frames and paradigms relating to social exclusion. Discourses, frames and paradigms are generated, diffused and institutionalized by, and within, different institutional aspects of the governance architecture of the OMC. However, the material content of these discourses, frames and paradigms is open to contestation either from actors within the governance process or outside of it. Moreover, the governance process itself may become the object of discourse and contestation. In this way, the governance process creates a space for a certain *reflexivity* in the interaction of both processes and the material content of those processes. In this way, as Daly urges us, contestation around the content of EU social policy and the governance context of social policy can make social policy a more active component in studies of EU governance.

Social Europe

As intimated above, one of Olsen's meanings of Europeanization refers to '[T]he degree to which Europe is becoming a more unified and stronger political entity.' (Olsen, 2002: 924). Framed in the context of this project, this raises questions concerning the relative importance of the EU's social identity in building European integration and the role of social policy coordination in developing that social identity.

Miguel Poiares Maduro—writing after the entry into force of the Treaty of Amsterdam—argued that it was time for Europe to face up to its 'social self' (2000). He highlighted in particular the manner in which the argument for there to be a social dimension to European integration tended to be cast in functionalist terms and oriented towards managing the consequences of market integration, especially as the reach of EU economic law extended into the social realm. Yet for Maduro, this provides a rather limited horizon upon which to build Europe's social identity.

Nonetheless, the functionalist style of reasoning has dominated our understanding of Europe's political and social identity. Perhaps the clearest example can be found in the work of Fritz Scharpf who described the original constitutional settlement of the EEC as entailing a 'decoupling' of the economic and the social (Scharpf, 2002). While economic constitutionalism at EU level grew and flourished, the 'deal' was that this ought not to be at the expense of the competence of Member States to enact social regulations with which to 'embed' the market (Joerges and Rödl, 2009). This 'social deficit' was not therefore a design flaw as such but rather an understanding of the relative roles of the EU and nation states. However, the argument for increasing the EU's social role on this account lies with the gradual erosion of this legal and spatial boundary between the economic and the social. Judgments of the ECJ in 2007 and 2008 have given new impetus to demands either to shore up domestic social defences or to rebalance constitutionalism at EU level through some new constitutional settlement. There may well be—as Maduro himself contends—arguments for a new constitutional settlement or 'social contract' in which EU social policy's identity is augmented and clarified. However, as is analysed in detail in chapter six, tethering a claim for a more social Europe to the apparent defence of domestic social policy is, as Maduro suggests, limiting as a conceptual space but also entirely yoked to EU economic law having the sorts of corrosive effects that those prosecuting this argument contend. It is suggested that Scharpf and others have tended to offer un-nuanced accounts of the impact of EU economic law on domestic social policy—in particular, no distinction is drawn between the realms of competition law and free movement—and lapse into a caricature of the relationship between EU economic constitutionalism and domestic social policy. As is explored in chapter six, the argument made here is not to deny that EU economic law interacts with national social policy but rather that it does so in more intricate ways, with the ECJ often finding mechanisms either to shelter solidaristic social institutions from EU economic law or, to balance economic and social objectives. But regardless of how one interprets the data, the central point remains Maduro's one that this style of argumentation frames Europe's social self within the very logic and space offered by managing the demands, or counteracting the effects, of market integration rather than by seeking to constitute some other basis for the EU's social identity.

The arguments put forward by Scharpf and by Joerges and Rödl are also more directly relevant to this study because they suggest that new tools of governance like the OMC cannot provide a basis for—to borrow the title of one of the first collections of essays on the OMC—'building social Europe' (de la Porte and Pochet, 2002). Even if Scharpf lauds the aspiration of the OMC to fill the governance gap between a wholly decentralized competence of Member States and a wholly centralized EU legislative competence, given his construction of the corrosive effects of EU economic constitutionalism, he ends up viewing the OMC as impossibly undermined by 'hard law' and only capable of being defended by legally strengthening the OMC. Once again, the potential and utility of policy coordination as one means of developing the EU's social identity is viewed through the lens of the insatiable functionalist demands of market integration.

In chapter seven the analysis turns to the capacity of European constitutionalism to facilitate Europeanization through the articulation of social objectives, social values and social rights. It explores the problems in giving the EU a more substantive social identity and considers different theoretical strategies through which to reconcile a desire to embed more concretely a European social vision while at the same time recognizing that the nation state remains the primary locus for the institutions of social solidarity.

The final chapter highlights proposals to strengthen EU policy coordination in the social sphere. While the EU may have resolved—at least contingently—its constitutional identity crisis by settling upon, and finally putting into practice, the Lisbon Treaty, thorny issues of governance—and the role of the EU in economic and social governance—would require resolution as the ten-year Lisbon strategy ended and the outlines of a new 'Europe 2020' strategy emerged. The analysis presented in this chapter looks to available resources, institutions and governance techniques in suggesting ways to build a governance architecture that can strengthen the EU's interventions to eradicate poverty and combat social exclusion while ensuring that the normative weight that this architecture is intended to carry is one that can sensibly and legitimately be borne by transnational institutions.

2

Policy Coordination in the EU

Introduction

The focal point for this study is a process of policy 'coordination' intended to stimulate Member States to adjust and adapt their domestic structures, strategies and policies in order to make a decisive impact on the eradication of poverty and to combat social exclusion. Launched in 2000, this process was one of the first of the so-called 'open methods' of coordination (OMC): a nomenclature that emanated from the Extraordinary European Council meeting in Lisbon in March 2000. At that meeting, the Heads of State and Government of the EU Member States committed themselves to a new strategic goal: 'to become the most dynamic and competitive knowledge-based economy in the world capable of sustainable economic growth with more and better jobs and greater social cohesion'. The OMC was to be one means of taking forward that goal.

The aim of this chapter is to reflect on the emergence of the OMC as a new tool of EU governance. The central contention put forward is that the OMC has a rather more ambiguous identity than is often admitted by scholars studying the EU's evolving governance architecture. Although the development of the Lisbon strategy 'constituted' policy coordination as a potentially generalizable form of EU governance, it is important to pay attention to the specifics of any given OMC process and the evolution of coordination processes over time. All too often, the OMC is decontextualized and abstracted, with no particular regard paid to the dimension of time. Moreover, it will be suggested that variations in the architecture of different OMC processes are significant and represent the outcome of the push and pull between competing rationales for policy coordination as well as different coordination philosophies. Ultimately, it will be argued that the OMC is a 'hybrid' form of governance within and across two important dimensions. It is a hybrid form of governance in the sense that different 'modes' of governance are at play within its architectural and methodological elements. It is also a hybrid in seeking a virtuous combination of actions intended to influence decentralized policy-making while also then seeking to hold Member States to account for their policy performance. The ambiguity of the OMC as a tool of EU governance lies in the tensions that arise within and across these two dimensions.

Constituting Coordination as 'The OMC'

At the Lisbon summit in 2000, a number of policy realms were identified as candidate fields for open coordination (see Rodrigues, 2001):

- information society (para. 8, Presidency Conclusions),
- research and development (para. 13),
- enterprise and innovation (para. 15),
- education (para. 27),
- social protection (para. 31),
- social inclusion (para. 32).

Although emerging as an apparently new governance technique, policy coordination was not unknown prior to 2000, especially in the realms of economic and employment policy coordination (discussed below). Even in the candidate areas identified at Lisbon, the EU was not initiating coordination from a standing start and had engaged in a variety of forms of coordinated action that might be described as nascent OMC processes (see also Wincott, 2003). This was particularly true in the areas of social inclusion and social protection.

As Ferrera, Matsaganis and Sacchi (2002) have noted, a pre-OMC type of EU policy coordination was initiated in the early 1990s in the area of 'social protection'. In 1992 the Council adopted a Recommendation (92/441/EEC) on common criteria concerning sufficient resources and social assistance in social protection systems,[1] recommending to Member States that they recognize a right to sufficient resources and to social assistance and to adapt their social protection systems to the principles and guidelines set out in the Recommendation. The 'Guidelines' set out a range of factors which Member

[1] Council Recommendation 92/441/EEC on common criteria concerning sufficient resources and social assistance in social protection systems [1992] OJ L245/46.

States should take into account: e.g. living standards and price levels in the Member State; adjustments to meet specific needs; ensuring incentives to seek employment for those of working age. References to appropriate indicators such as average incomes, data on household consumption and periodic review of the levels of sufficient resources based on these indicators was suggested. More significantly, Council Recommendation 92/442/EEC on the convergence of social protection objectives and policies[2] attempted to develop a convergence strategy by which national social protection systems would be guided by principles laid down in the Recommendation. De la Porte and Pochet refer to these recommendations as a 'premature version of OMC' (2002: 41). As is explored in chapter three, the later OMC process was constituted by rather different policy discourses, paradigms and frames but, nonetheless, the point is simply that later OMC processes often built upon earlier forms of EU intervention.

The significance of the Lisbon summit, therefore, was its discursive constitution of policy coordination techniques as 'the OMC'. As Radaelli has highlighted (2003b), the 'legitimating discourse' of the OMC provided a new opportunity for EU policy-makers to recast existing, or propose new, initiatives as examples of the OMC. It also created a new entity for scholars of the EU to study.

Nonetheless, this very act of naming and labelling techniques of policy coordination as *the* OMC has also had a rather more negative effect. It has tended to suppress differences between so-called OMC processes and also ambiguities and tensions within any given process. While this suppression is not especially troubling when engaged in by EU policy-makers keen to add impetus to their interventions, the argument made in this chapter is that all too often, academic scholarship has contrived to give policy coordination a rather more singular identity, typically for the purposes of comparing policy coordination to other apparent 'modes of governance'. This has often resulted in rather simplistic characterizations of EU policy coordination and ill-suited comparisons.

In the sections which follow, the intention is to reveal ambiguity and tension within the architecture of policy coordination rather that to suppress it. The point is not to declare '*ceci n'est pas OMC*', but rather to suggest that the act of labelling and naming policy coordination as the 'OMC' can also be an act of concealment and, in the spirit of Magritte and his inspiration of

[2] Council Recommendation 92/442/EEC on the convergence of social protection objectives and policies [1992] OJ L245/49.

Foucault (Foucault and Magritte, 1983), by a more careful exploration of the relationship between the label and the phenomenon, a more nuanced and less tidy image of the OMC can then be projected.

For the moment, it is worth noting two key ways in which policy coordination through the OMC across a range of policy fields can end up having a rather unitary and coherent identity. The first is the portrayal of some kind of 'ideal-type' OMC (see for example, ter Haar, 2008). Often this is based on the Presidency Conclusions of the Lisbon European Council. There, it was stated that the OMC consisted of (para. 37 of Lisbon Council Conclusions):

- fixing guidelines for the Union combined with specific timetables for achieving the goals set in the short, medium and long terms;
- establishing, where appropriate, quantitative and qualitative indicators and benchmarks against the best in the world and tailored to the needs of different Member States and sectors as a means of comparing best practice;
- translating these European guidelines into national and regional policies by setting specific targets and adopting measures, taking into account national and regional differences;
- periodic monitoring, evaluation and peer review organized as mutual learning processes.

While indicative of certain elements of the methodology of EU policy coordination, this is not a sufficiently robust definition of any extant OMC process. However, it can sometimes be treated as if it can, nevertheless, serve as a kind of 'archetypal' OMC, even when it is acknowledged that actual processes diverge from it (see Borrás and Jacobsson, 2004). The second way in which simplification occurs is to take any substantive OMC process and then treat it as a generalizable example of the OMC. Given the rather longer-term history of policy coordination in the employment sphere, the study of the OMC through the lens of employment policy has tended to be dominant (also because it has attracted attention from legal scholars as well as political scientists). However, as will be highlighted below, even the most superficial comparisons of employment policy coordination and the OMC to combat social exclusion reveals significant variation between these processes. Moreover, employment policy coordination itself has undergone substantial architectural evolution (Armstrong and Kilpatrick, 2007).

Not all scholarship falls into the traps and tendencies noted above. Zeitlin (2005), for example, highlights the difficulties of any empirical analysis of the OMC, due to the multiplicity and complexity of processes. Laffan and

Shaw (2005) produced a very careful empirical and comparative analysis of different OMC processes, albeit one that would need updating in light of subsequent changes. The study presented here is not a comparative one: neither comparing different policy coordination processes nor comparing an OMC to other tools of EU governance. Instead, the orientation of the analysis is towards revealing the specific governance architecture for policy coordination to combat poverty and social exclusion and its evolution over time.

Evolving Policy Coordination

Instead of thinking about an archetypal or abstracted OMC process, one way of orienting our understanding of the OMC to combat poverty and social exclusion is to explore the evolution of techniques of policy coordination over time. The more immediate inspiration for this OMC was the European Employment Strategy (EES)—formalized in the 1997 Amsterdam Treaty (Article 128 EC) though building on the 'Essen' process starting in 1994—and its governance architecture for policy coordination. The EES was itself inspired by the multi-lateral surveillance of Member States' economic policies (provided for in Article 99 EC), developed in the context of moves towards economic and monetary union in the EU.

The EES provided the template for the OMC to combat social exclusion in a double sense. First, employment policy is also a policy domain that remains within the legislative competence of the Member States. That the Member States were willing to open their employment policies to the influence of a European coordination process can be seen as paving the way to other policy coordination processes in areas where competence fundamentally remains with the Member States. Secondly, and more directly, the methodology of coordination under the EES was the inspiration for the form of the OMC process developed in the sphere of social inclusion. It was a methodology that European anti-poverty groups had pressed the EU to adopt in order to establish a process to take forward the Amsterdam Treaty's new provision on combating social exclusion (EAPN, 1999). In this way, what emerged was an OMC to combat social exclusion that had some of the key methodological features of the EES:

- a mechanism for setting common 'objectives' ('guidelines' in the case of the EES);

- national action plans (NAPs) through which Member States would report on their adaptation of national strategies and policies in light of the common objectives;
- monitoring and evaluation of the NAPs by the European Commission and the Council with publication of 'Joint Reports';
- statistical support for evaluation through the elaboration of common 'indicators';
- a more specific programme of 'peer review' in which individual states would suggest examples of good practice to be evaluated by other Member States.

Yet the OMC to combat social exclusion also diverged from the EES template. Under the EES, 'Recommendations' could be addressed either collectively to the Member States or to individual Member States. EU-wide targets for increasing rates of participation in employment were also set, whereas EU-level targets for a reduction in poverty levels were not agreed. In the early life of the EES the number of guidelines proliferated and were updated and sharpened with successive annual cycles of the coordination process (Armstrong and Kilpatrick, 2007). By contrast, the first cycles of the OMC to combat social exclusion were biennial with little or no iterative changes to the common objectives. The significance of differences in coordination methodology will be explored further below. It is enough to note for the moment that certain elements of coordination—recommendations, targets and initially increasingly prescriptive guidelines—were absent from the social inclusion OMC.

Both the EES and the economic policy coordination processes are treaty-based processes whereas subsequent OMC processes have emerged and evolved through institutional practices. The issue of whether to further anchor or embed the social OMC processes in the treaties coincided with the 'constitutional' debates surrounding the constitutional and later Lisbon treaties. Even without a constitutional or treaty-reform debate, the relationship between the treaty-based economic and employment coordination processes, and the non-treaty based OMCs, has also been contested within the context of debates about the shape and direction of the Lisbon strategy itself. These developments are explored in greater detail in subsequent chapters. The point that is being made here is that the OMC to combat social exclusion cannot really be understood either as an abstract archetypal OMC or merely as a useful indicative sample of an OMC process. Such an approach tends to give an overly general, static and ahistoric 'snap-shot' of the OMC process. To return to the institutionalist approach highlighted in chapter one, this study takes seriously the dimension of 'time' in the analysis of Europeanization (Bulmer, 2009) and in that way shares an historical institutionalist preoccupation with the evolution of institutions and governance structures over time. Thus, the better way of making sense of the object of this study is to place it in its historical context and to view it as an evolution from earlier coordination processes and also in continuing creative tension with those earlier processes. Moreover, it is a process whose methodological features have themselves changed over time. In the evolution of policy coordination techniques, while there is inter-generational familial resemblances between the different processes, there is also variation and mutation.

The OMC in the Context of the Lisbon Strategy

It is also important not to decontextualize the OMC from the substance and material content of the Lisbon strategy itself. When launched, the strategy was frequently referred to as encompassing a mutually reinforcing policy triangle of economic, employment and social policies (environmental policy was later added to this mix). The importance of the 'coupling' of these policies becomes apparent when one considers that it is also often said that as originally conceived, the European integration project involved a 'decoupling' of the economic from the social (Scharpf, 2002). As Ferrera notes, one interpretation of the original EEC project was to see it in terms of 'a virtuous circle between *open* economies and outward-looking economic policies on the one hand, and *closed* welfare states and inward looking social policy on the other' (Ferrera, 2005: 92). While the then EEC became active in processes of market integration—characterized by Majone as 'regulatory' policy-making (see inter alia, Majone 1996)—redistributive policies of market correction were considered to be a matter for the Member States. As Wincott cogently notes, this apparent division of responsibilities has supported a market liberal conceptualization of the EU as a form, in Majone's terms, of 'regulatory state' (Wincott, 2003): a limited transfer of non-majoritarian economic regulatory responsibilities to the EU while the more legitimacy-demanding realm of social policy remained with the Member States. This imagery is also consistent with the ordo-liberal vision of the EEC as a form of economic constitutional order (Streit and Mussler, 1995) operating principally through mechanisms of 'negative integration'—the judicial removal of obstacles to trade and distortions to competition—with a limited capacity for political intervention via 'positive integration'—legislative intervention—in the name of market regulation. While more of a normative vision of European integration than one that holds up to sustained empirical analysis—eg where does the common agricultural policy fit in this vision?—it projected an understanding of a spatial and legal decoupling of the economic and social spheres.

This understanding of a division of labour between the EU as engaging in market integration while Member States retained their competence in the provision of social welfare has come under significant pressure with the 'boundaries of welfare' (Ferrera, 2005) becoming more porous. In part these pressures come from the limited reach of EU economic law itself into the realm of national social welfare policies but also from more global economic pressures. Moreover, significant demographic challenges have also added to the problems facing Member States in the organization and delivery of their social protection systems. The Lisbon strategy and the use of the OMC, therefore, represent attempts by the EU to find a framework for policy re-integration to support a 'modernization' of domestic social welfare systems but in a manner which—in the absence of stronger legitimating mechanisms at EU level—can spread the normative weight between EU and national levels. Without replacing national social welfare systems with a single 'European Social Model', the Lisbon strategy does, nonetheless, seek to promote social—and economic—reform within a common European framework. The difficulty for scholars, however, lies in evaluating the capacity and legitimacy of the OMC to undertake the tasks expected of it in this context. In what remains of this section, four key positions are staked out by reference to the writings of Scharpf, Sapir, Offe and Sabel and Zeitlin.

The relationship between 'negative' and 'positive' integration has a virtually iconic status in EU legal studies not least through Joseph Weiler's contrast between limitations on national 'exit' imposed via 'normative supranationalism'—the founding constitutional doctrines of the ECJ as applied in the material context of EU economic law—and the more difficult attempt to restore national 'voice' via the mechanisms of 'decisional supranationalism'—the EU's norm-making processes (Weiler, 1991). For Scharpf, what is lost on the swings of negative integration is not, however, made up on the roundabouts of the EU's own decision-making processes: a problem he famously termed the 'joint-decision trap' (see Scharpf, 2006 for a reworked version of the original thesis). Thus for Scharpf (1999: 121), there are policy areas where:

> ...the legal force of negative integration and the economic pressures of transational factor mobility and regulatory competition have significantly reduced the problem-solving capacity of national political systems, and where this loss is not compensated by corresponding gains in European problem-solving capacity.

The OMC represents the apparent mechanism by which this problem-solving capacity is to be reinforced. However, for Scharpf, without a more robust legal basis the OMC's problem-solving capacities are limited by the constraints of EU economic law on domestic social policy autonomy: the very autonomy on which the OMC relies is, on this view, limited by the reach of negative integration. In this way, while Scharpf is not opposed to the OMC as a governance technique, for him, its capacity to work effectively is undermined by the substantive imbalance of economic and social values in European constitutionalism: a veritable constitutional asymmetry.

For Sapir, creating a new balance between the economic and the social is also the challenge facing Europe and the Lisbon strategy is intended to be the framework through which to reform economic and social institutional structures that have become 'dysfunctional' in the face not only of the pressures of globalization but also significant demographic challenges. Drawing on the work of his High-Level Group (Sapir et al, 2004), Sapir counselled the EU to adopt a 'two-handed' strategy of domestic social and labour market reform and EU-level action to complete the single market in product and services markets (Sapir, 2006). While Sapir has some confidence in returning to the regulatory policy-making of the Single Market programme to complete the market in products and services in Europe—something also urged by the later Kok report (Kok et al, 2004)—that confidence was noticeably lacking in his appraisal of the role of the OMC in reforming labour markets and social protection systems. Existing policy coordination mechanisms may not do enough to either incentivize states to reform their policies or to shame them if they do not. Either these processes themselves require to be reformed or indeed, other types of instrument may be a more suitable means of achieving reform. Thus Sapir's pessimism with policy coordination is more preoccupied with apparent inherent limitations of existing processes than it is with external constraints on policy autonomy.

Offe's negative assessment of policy coordination proceeds in a rather different manner to either Scharpf or Sapir. Offe (2003) shares with Scharpf an interpretation of European integration in which the original boundaries between the economic and the social sought to embed European market-making in domestic institutions of market-correction. But whereas Scharpf views the OMC as a noble—albeit flawed—attempt to connect economic integration to a domestic vision of social protection, Offe considers policy coordination as the medium of reforms that are destructive of a model of 'embedded capitalism'. For Offe, the kinds of 'cognitive' change which policy coordination seeks to produce through the generation, institutionalization and diffusion of policy discourses, paradigms and frames, may induce domestic 'unlearning' intended to render domestic institutional structures of social and labour market protection ripe for 'modernization' and reform. In this way, rather than the Lisbon strategy being a means of recoupling the economic and the social, it may represent the detachment of the economic from even its domestic social tethers. Or to the extent that it represents a new EU-level accommodation of the economic and the social it may be the mechanism of 'harmonization through the back door' but without even the limited levels of democratic legitimation that the EU can muster under its 'Community Method' of harmonization. Either way, Offe's pessimism lies not in the failures of the OMC to achieve its goals, but rather its success in recalibrating social welfare systems.

Others, however, offer a more positive account of the potential of new forms of governance to address the challenges facing labour market and social welfare systems and to do so in ways which mediate the boundaries horizontally between economic, employment and social spheres and vertically between centralized and decentralized institutional structures (see Zeitlin, 2003). Zeitlin views the emergence of new forms of governance, including the OMC as part of 'the progressive shift in both national and EU debates away from the goal of a single Social Europe as a regulatory counterbalance to the single market in favour of an alternative approach based on connecting welfare diversity with the European Social Model through policy coordination and mutual learning' (Zeitlin, 2005: 214). The intellectual roots of this claim lie in the viewing of the OMC as a species of an 'experimentalist' governance architecture (Cohen and Sabel, 2003; Sabel and Zeitlin, 2008). In this way the enduring domestic social and economic institutional pluralism which acts as a background condition for the emergence of EU policy coordination is also its experimental strength in acting as a policy laboratory from which Member States can engage in 'learning from difference' (Sabel and Zeitlin, 2008). Although not unique to the EU, coordinated policy learning may be an important means by which EU Member States seek solutions to common problems without resorting to a one-size-fits-all approach or which leaves them as unilateralist masters of their own destiny. Particularly in the EU context the OMC may be a more normatively satisfactory approach than either an attempt to recreate democratically legitimate social and economic institutions and structures at EU level, or some form of 'multi-speed Europe'. Nonetheless, for Kerber and Eckardt (2007), the institutional design of the OMC is a more 'top-down' architecture than is required for successful experimentation. Using the economic theory of 'laboratory federalism' as a comparison, Kerber and Eckardt suggest that the OMC is a more centralized process for policy learning (for support see Smismans, 2004), oriented towards the convergence of policies whereas in laboratory federalism, divergence in policies through policy innovation is as possible as convergence. Thus, in order for policy coordination to achieve the experimentalist dream of Sabel and Zeitlin, it may be necessary to hold the OMC up to more critical institutional examination rather than viewing it as simply one of a number of examples of this experimentalist architecture in action.

What this brief discussion illustrates is the contested nature of the OMC in terms of its apparent ability to manage the boundaries between the economic and the social and the EU and its Member States. Even if scholars agree on why the Lisbon strategy and the OMC emerged at a particular time in the trajectory of European integration—again a good reason for relating the OMC to combat social exclusion to its economic and employment policy predecessors—there is profound disagreement as to the implications of the turn to policy coordination in buttressing, reforming, demolishing or modernizing social welfare systems in the EU. Once again, this underscores the contested nature of the OMC.

Competing Rationalities for Policy Coordination

The role of the OMC in mediating the boundaries between centralized and decentralized policy-making may be more complicated than the discussion in the previous section suggests. Even if scholars diverge on the effectiveness and legitimacy of the OMC, they might all presume that the OMC has a singular function and rationale. However, as Begg has suggested (2008), there may be very different rationales motivating the turn to policy coordination in the EU. Begg identifies the following key rationales for coordination:

- Persuading national policies to swim in the same direction may help prevent damaging spill-overs arising from wholly unilateral action. This is

particularly significant in an economic context, especially for those countries for whom monetary responsibilities have been transferred to the European Central Bank but whose fiscal and economic policies are largely domestically determined.
- Even in the absence of spill-over there may be much to be gained from states acting in concert to define common solutions to common problems particularly if policy learning can be promoted from the experience of those states coordinating their activities.
- Coordinated activities in a European framework may facilitate reforms that would otherwise be blocked domestically.
- Coordination may simply enhance the capacity of individual states to puzzle through their own problems especially if the coordination processes enhance process of joined-up government or give new sources of information that help identify more precisely the challenges states face.

To put it a slightly different way, but essentially following the same approach, it can be suggested that there is a spectrum of justifications for coordination (a point well-illustrated by debates about EU economic governance in the aftermath of the financial crisis of 2008–09). At one end we find situations where unilateral action is likely to result in spill-over effects for other states, while at the other end, states are essentially capable of acting unilaterally but may benefit from mechanisms that enhance problem-solving capacity, policy coherence and policy effort. In the middle of this spectrum there are situations where all or many states face the same problem and may benefit from similar solutions and coordination allows them to achieve outcomes in a more efficient and more optimal manner that working alone.

However, if we think about this spectrum more directly within the context of the division of powers in the EU, then the polar ends of the spectrum pose rather different problems. As a *Notre Europe* paper argued (Collingon et al, 2005), the more there are real problems of spill-over in the EU, then the more this tends to argue for a greater centralization of authority in EU institutions and for instruments stronger than coordination. In this way, critics of the Lisbon strategy may be sceptical about too heavy a reliance on the OMC to achieve the aims and objectives of the strategy. This is apparent in the critical evaluations proffered by both the Sapir and Kok 'High-Level' groups in their reports (Sapir et al, 2004; Kok et al, 2004). At the other end of the spectrum, the issue is more one of whether there is a true commonality of experience to justify wholescale multilateral policy coordination processes rather than a more limited exhortation to states to learn from others (including non-EU states). In an EU where issues of competence and subsidiarity are always at issue, the mere resort to 'coordination' as a technique of governance does not itself resolve debates about the allocation and exercise of competence: coordination still demands justification. Accordingly, not only may we find that different policy coordination techniques have different underlying motivations, we might also discover that these motivations might demand either something more or indeed something less than EU policy coordination.

The 'Philosophy' of Policy Coordination

In chapter one, the role of coordination processes in generating, institutionalizing and diffusing policy 'discourses', 'frames' and 'paradigms' was identified. In her elaboration of 'discursive institutionalism', Schmidt identified a further category of organizing concepts, namely, 'philosophies' (Schmidt, 2008). In the context of this study, this could be given a substantive meaning, particularly by relating it to different political philosophies—liberal, conservative, social democratic—and their implications for the direction of policies to combat social exclusion. However, and partly to confine the more substantive analysis to issues of policy discourse, frames and paradigms, the use of the term 'philosophies' will largely be limited to the analysis of the functional properties of 'coordination'. The reason for this is a comment made by Marco Biagi in one of the early analyses of the European Employment Strategy.

Biagi (1998) drew attention to a fundamental 'philosophical' difference between policy coordination as 'co-operation' and coordination as 'convergence'. In broad terms, while 'co-operation' works with the autonomy of states to define their policies but promotes elective and selective learning across states, 'convergence' suggest that the process is not agnostic about what states can and ought to learn with a potential consequential reduction in policy diversity. In their handling of issues of policy autonomy and diversity, different policy coordination might appear to have different underlying philosophies.

Yet, the issue may in practice be more concrete and more complex than one of identifying the philosophy underpinning any given policy coordination process. The point that Biagi was making was not really a comparative one about different processes having different philosophies but rather that within the same process there might be a competition or tension between the philosophy of 'co-operation' and that of 'convergence'. That is to say, that different architectural features of a single coordination process might pull or push in different directions in their tolerance of policy autonomy and diversity.

Take, for example, the role of common objective or guidelines. The more prescriptive these become the less autonomy the Member States might have to project a different policy agenda. Add to this the possibility to address 'recommendations' to Member States or to 'name and shame' states by producing league tables of performance against common targets or indicators, then again, these elements of coordination act against the policy autonomy of states. By contrast, peer review processes may indicate a more open approach to policy learning. Common indicators on their own—without prescriptive guidelines or targets—can facilitate domestic processes of problem identification and enhance the capacity of states to exercise evidence-led policy autonomy. Indeed, even the same element, for example, common indicators, can serve two masters—as a basis for targets and league tables or as statistical support to domestic problem solving. Understanding what is to be expected of any given OMC process is, therefore, an intricate process of simultaneous 'deconstruction'—identifying the presence and absence of different elements of the coordination methodology, and 'reconstruction'—an interpretation of the interaction of these different elements. Aggregated, the result is that different processes can be expected to have greater or lesser tolerance of Member States' policy autonomy and of resulting policy diversity.

If both the philosophies of 'cooperation' and 'convergence' are at play within OMC processes, and if different elements of the architecture interact to either promote or inhibit policy autonomy and policy diversity, then this suggests that the 'convergence capacity' of different governance architectures will vary. This is the starting point for Citi and Rhodes (2007) in their analysis of the OMC. They compare OMC and OMC-type processes—and indeed forms of legislative intervention—in terms of their capacity to induce convergence. Thus, they identify the following possible mechanisms for achieving convergence:

- simple benchmarking and/or recommendations
- voluntary binding policy objectives and benchmarking and peer pressure
- voluntary binding policy objectives and benchmarking and peer pressure and structured coordination

- legally binding policy objectives (with sanctions) and benchmarking and peer pressure and structured coordination
- legally binding regulations.

All but the last of these mechanisms are described as forms of OMC. The implication of their model is that at one end of the scale—'hard law'—convergence capacity is highest with a gradual weakening of that capacity as OMC and OMC-like governance architectures are deployed—a shift towards 'soft' and 'softer' law.

Although a superficially appealing thesis, there are two problems with the Citi and Rhodes approach. The first problem is the assumption that each architectural or methodological element has 'convergence' as its goal and, therefore, that adding in more and more of these elements will ultimately increase convergence capacity. Yet, if we take the example of 'benchmarking' the literature identifies that even this single element of policy coordination can play rather different roles.

The Lisbon strategy has been interpreted as a process of structured learning via the diffusion of the benchmarking technique through the widespread use of objectives, indicators and mechanisms of review (Arrowsmith, Sisson and Marginson, 2004; Room, 2005). The OMC is often described either as a benchmarking exercise or at least a governance tool that utilizes benchmarking techniques. Nonetheless, 'benchmarking' and the associated process of 'learning' can be understood in rather different ways.[3] Arrowsmith, Sisson and Marginson identify three key variants of benchmarking operations. At one end of the spectrum we find highly constrained, disciplined 'top-down' benchmarking exercises where participants essentially are urged or even coerced into drawing particular lessons and adopting specific courses of action. This type of benchmarking might be described as 'convergent' in philosophy. In this approach, central institutions drive the process, ensure that participants are committed and engage in surveillance to ensure that decentralized institutions learn the appropriate lessons. This type of governance remains strongly hierarchical albeit associated less with direct 'command-and-control' and more with Foucaultian forms of 'governance at a distance'. At the other end of the spectrum, however, benchmarking allows a greater autonomy of the participants to choose what to learn via the information and data supplied by the benchmarking exercise

[3] Arrowsmith, Sisson and Marginson, 2004; see also Wincott, 2003 and Trubek and Trubek, 2005b.

and thus, operates in a more 'bottom-up' fashion. As Arrowsmith, Sisson and Marginson identify, the focus is upon problem-identification as a step towards best practice-identification. This is clearly more in the spirit of the philosophy of 'co-operation'. The third approach occupies an intermediate position: neither agnostic about what might be learned but driven equally by sustained and repeated efforts towards continuous improvement. Therefore, if benchmarking alone can be operationalized in radically different ways, it is too simplistic to posit a linear increase in convergence capacity premised on the assumption that the more elements one adds to benchmarking the more these elements will combine to produce policy convergence.

The second limitation is that even if we accept that any given OMC or any given aspect of OMC methodology is oriented towards 'convergence' we must consider more precisely what it is that might converge. Pollitt (2001) provides a useful categorization of 'convergence' in terms of 'debate', 'decisions', 'actions', and 'results'. Different instruments of EU governance may have different ambitions in terms of convergence across these four categories. To take one end of Citi and Rhodes' spectrum, an EU 'regulation' seeks convergence of both 'action' and 'results'. A directive gives rise to a uniform 'result' but in terms of 'action', Member States have discretion as to how to achieve the result prescribed by a directive. As was explored in chapter one, OMC processes are often more oriented towards the ideational category of 'debate'. At this level we may well find degrees of cognitive and normative convergence around certain discourses, frames and paradigms that are generated, institutionalized and diffused via the OMC. However, as Visser emphasizes (2009), this does not prevent a plurality of decisions, actions and results within the 'bounded rationality' created by cognitive or normative convergence. In this way, even certain constraints on autonomy at the level of changing logics of appropriate action need not be incompatible with degrees of policy diversity.

There is also a more general point to be made. It is easy to assume that there are global trends towards 'convergence' be it in public administration (the point of critical intervention for Pollitt, 2001), economics, politics or law. Regional integration projects like the European Union may appear to have convergence as their very *raison d'être*. Even while recognizing that the OMC is not the same as other forms of EU intervention like 'harmonization', it can be tempting simply to take for granted that its function is one of elimination of diversity. Yet empirically this may not turn out to be the case and normatively—particularly for those who view the OMC as a form of experimentalist governance—fostering diversity may be important to ensure the vitality of processes of public policy-making. There is, then, a danger in evaluating the OMC in terms of its ability to achieve convergence and concluding that if difference ensues, then, by implication the OMC has 'failed' as a governance technique. Whether or not resulting policy diversity is to be viewed as a failed attempt at convergence or as successful domestic policy innovation in light of new information and ideas rather depends on what policy coordination was meant to achieve in the first place. If it is simply viewed as essentially functionally the same as a comparator 'hard' legally binding regulation, then the presence of policy diversity may look like a bad thing. If on the other hand, its function is simply limited to stimulating policy experimentation, then diversity may be no bad thing at all. In short, research projects that seek to compare the OMC to other governance tools need to be clear on whether like is really being compared with like.

To return to Biagi's philosophical distinction, it is clear that this only gives us a useful starting point through which to seek to deconstruct the architecture of policy coordination. His distinction highlights key tensions within the governance architecture of the OMC: between working with or against the autonomy of states to match solutions to problems; between a desire to reduce or promote policy diversity; between 'top-down' benchmarking and constrained 'learning' and 'bottom-up' innovation in light of new sources of ideas and information. In this way, we can reformulate Biagi's initial philosophical distinction in terms of three propositions. First, different coordination processes may resolve the tension between top-down coercion and bottom-up influence in different ways, not least as a result of the different rationales which motivate any particular form of EU coordination in the first place. Therefore, we ought not to expect all coordination processes to operate in the same way. Secondly, the push and pull between the closure of coercive coordination and the openness of facilitative learning manifests itself more at the level of the particular elements of the OMC methodology. It is the presence and absence of different elements and their interaction which gives any process its identity. Therefore, within any given process, there is an architectural tension at play. To conceptualize the OMC in terms of an abstract archetype or to treat any substantive process as an exemplar of the OMC is, therefore, to miss this important point. Thirdly, we ought not to assume that any given process remains static across its life. For some, the aspiration may well be to make a relatively open coordination process more coercive. For others, the desire may be to loosen the constraints or to alter underlying paradigms and to increase the autonomy of the participants.

Modes of Governance

The idea that OMC processes constitute a 'mode' of governance is apparently an uncontroversial assertion. Nonetheless, and much like the label 'OMC', this nomenclature is more problematic than might at first be apparent. Indeed, it is important to distinguish between the language of 'technique' and of 'mode'. The essence of the distinction is the attempt to sever the particular instrument, tool or technique from its underlying governance mode(s) (Armstrong and Kilpatrick, 2007).

Defining ideal-typical 'modes' of governing is not entirely easy. Kooiman (2002), for example, distinguishes between 'hierarchy', 'self-regulation', and 'co-regulation' modes. Bulmer and Padgett (2005) distinguish between governance by 'hierarchy', by 'negotiation', and by 'facilitated coordination'. Colin Scott (2002) suggests a four-fold classification of 'control models'—'hierarchy', 'competition' or 'market', 'community', and 'design'—while Newman (2001) proposes a somewhat different classification of 'hierarchical', 'self-governance', 'rational', and 'open systems' models. While all agree on 'hierarchy' as a mode or model, the non-hierarchical candidates are differently categorized. This may explain why it is easier to position the OMC comparatively by what it is apparently not—typically 'hierarchy'—than it is to wrestle with its inherent identity or identities.

It is not necessary for the purposes of this study to seek to map and identify all potential modes of governance. Instead, Scott's ideal-type control models will be adopted and adapted. *Hierarchical* governance attains control through coercion. As the adoption of norms is not voluntary, the production of such norms places high demands on democratic processes of will-formation. Governance by *competition* refers to a market-driven process of choice and selection with norms set according to their ability to attract market participants. *Community*-based governance mechanisms develop norms and standards within a particular community usually distinct from the official circuits of power and control of the state. It is an activity that can be found within a whole range of organizations and communities and civil society broadly defined. The assumption of obligations is voluntary as is membership of the relevant community. Governance by *design* refers to spatial or time restrictions which induce alterations in behaviour.

Yet the experience of governance lies more often in the combination of these modes. This is what Scott (2002) refers to as 'hybrid' governance. The term 'hybridity' has attained some currency in the analysis of EU governance, including EU policy coordination.[4] But it can refer to different phenomena and three different instances of hybridity will be identified. The first is the hybridity which Scott identifies when pure modes combine. 'Co-regulation' for example, typically combines elements of hierarchy (eg non-voluntary standards) with community (the agreement of a group to devise a common means of attaining these standards). 'Self-regulation' may take place in the 'shadow of hierarchy': that is to say, participants adopt a standard which they would not otherwise adopt were there not a credible risk of a less desirable standard being imposed. This combines an anticipation of hierarchy with a community mode.

The second way in which modes combine is in the governance of a particular field or activity. As Newman identifies in her study of social welfare in the UK, multiple modes of governance can be brought to bear in governing a particular area of social life. In an EU context, Trubek, Cottrell and Nance note that (2006: 93): 'more and more scholars discover the simultaneous presence of "hard" and "soft" measures in the same policy domain'. Leaving aside the somewhat thorny matter of what might be meant by 'hard' and 'soft' law, the essential point can be recast in terms of the deployment of multiple modes of governance that combine to effect governance in a specific policy area.

The third aspect of hybridity lies in returning to the distinction between a governance 'technique' and a governance 'mode' and in suggesting that any given governance technique or tool may simultaneously deploy one or more governance modes. A directive, for example, can lay down a clear set of environmental obligations. It may, however, set different pathways to meet such obligations, for example, via market-based incentives. It may allow stricter standards to be set by particular groups or organizations. To simply label the directive as 'hard law' and hierarchical is, therefore, to over-simplify its contents. A single instrument can govern through multiple modes. The same is true for EU policy coordination processes. In the context of the OMC it is possible to see elements that seek to invoke hierarchy, competition and community engagement. Prescriptive common objectives or guidelines—even if not formally binding—aim to coerce states to follow them. The use of targets and indicators when accompanied by performance tables can induce competitive rivalry between states. The involvement of civil society and

[4] See in particular, the contributions of de Búrca, 2006a; Hervey and Trubek, 2007; Kilpatrick, 2006; Trubek, Cottrell and Nance, 2006.

social partners in OMC processes engages a certain 'community' aspect to governance. Indeed, the better way of thinking about the OMC may be not only to consider it as a technique which exhibits multiple modes of governance, but also to challenge the idea that the OMC is a singular instrument at all. Rather, it might be better thought of as an assemblage of practices and methodologies. Notwithstanding its discursive constitution as a new form of EU governance, the experience of policy coordination may be suggestive of a less coherent governance identity. Importantly, variation in methodologies across policy coordination processes ought not then to be constructed as offering more or less of the same thing as though one might turn up or turn down the power of an OMC as if it were a dial. The presence or absence of certain architectural features or methodologies relates more to the calibration of the coordination process and the interaction of its elements. To adapt an approach developed by Trubek and Trubek (2007), this combination of modes and methodologies can produce 'complimentarity', 'rivalry' or even a mutual 'transformation' of the elements of coordination, but it may also simply produce 'incoherence' and 'conflict' across the overall coordination architecture. The success or failure of different OMC processes rests in the ability of different architectural elements to work coherently in creating the cognitive and normative context for states to puzzle their way through policy problems.

Between Governance and Accountability

The aim of this chapter has been to argue for a more nuanced and complex understanding of EU policy coordination and, in particular, the need to avoid generalizations about 'the OMC'. EU policy coordination has been an evolving technique, with different processes exhibiting both similarity and variation from one another. The rationales for, and functional expectations of, policy coordination may be very different and therefore the institutional design of any given process will reflect those differences. How 'open' an OMC might be—the extent to which it works with rather than against the policy autonomy of states—and its tolerance of policy diversity will depend on the configuration of different methodologies. In this way, variation in policy outcomes is not simply a function of the domestic response to the OMC—in which the OMC is considered constant—but also a function of the extent to which any given OMC process is more or less tolerant of policy autonomy and policy diversity. Some OMCs are simply more open than others which often makes comparisons between an abstract or archetypal OMC and other governance tools a rather fruitless project.

However, there is another layer of complexity to add to the discussion. Thus far, we have treated policy coordination as a tool or mechanism of 'governance'. Although Member States remain competent to act in the relevant sphere of activity, EU institutional structures and mechanisms seek to govern at a distance by generating, institutionalizing and diffusing cognitive and normative policy discourse, paradigms and frames such that policy-making is simultaneously opened out to new sources of influence yet also bounded by those sources of influence. The capacity to govern is no longer to be viewed as a property that is wholly interior to the domestic political system but rather one which is in part shared with EU institutions. The domestic arena of decision-making is 'destabilized' by the OMC process.[5]

Nonetheless, the OMC also has another orientation, namely towards the monitoring and evaluation of the activities of the Member States in the area covered by the OMC. There are mechanisms for reporting and for evaluation. Conclusions are then drawn which are themselves publicly reported and in the case of the treaty-based coordination processes, collective and/or individual 'Recommendations' may be made. Together these mechanisms can be said to have the characteristics of a system of 'accountability'.

For Bovens, '[A]ccountability is a relationship between an actor and a forum in which the actor has an obligation to explain and to justify his or her conduct, the forum can pose questions and pass judgment, and the actor may face consequences' (Boven, 2007: 450). Bovens identifies different types of accountability: *political* accountability to parliaments, parties and voters; *legal* accountability to courts; *administrative* accountability to auditors and inspectors; *professional* accountability to professional bodies and peers; and *social* accountability to civil society and interest groups (ibid: 455–7). We

[5] The use of the term 'destabilization' is borrowed from Sabel and Simon's exploration of 'destabilization rights' in the context of public law litigation in the United States (2004). They define destabilization rights as 'claims to unsettle and open up public institutions that have chronically failed to meet their obligations and that are substantially insulated from the normal processes of political accountability' (ibid: 1020).The OMC may be regarded as a political form of destabilization—a destabilization regime—that performs an analogous function to the type of litigation which Sabel and Simon describe.

can use this approach to accountability as a way of exploring features of the OMC. In terms of actors providing accounts to a forum, we can conceptualize mechanisms of reporting by national governments with monitoring and evaluation carried out by EU institutions, networks of experts and social NGOs as engaging a range of types of accountability. More difficult, however, are the elements of 'obligation' and of 'sanction'. The non-treaty based processes of policy coordination are, strictly speaking, voluntary in nature. Yet all Member States have submitted their reports more or less on time and even candidate Member States engaged in a shadow OMC exercise prior to full membership. The very fact that 'Europe' has requested Member States to report is often treated by national administrations in much the same way as if the report were formally required. Socialized within a system in which states are expected to comply with European requests, the absence of a formal obligation to report is, in the end, of less significance than might first be apparent. The issue of sanctions is more problematic. For Bovens, the presence of some sort of sanction is what distinguishes an accountability mechanism from a mere information-gathering exercise (ibid: 451). Nonetheless, he prefers to view sanctions as 'consequences' to avoid limiting sanctions to very formal penal consequences. A whole raft of consequences may flow from the requirement to proffer an account. In the context of the OMC, the treaty-based processes do provide for consequences in the form of Recommendations addressed to states. Moreover, the multi-lateral surveillance of national economic policies may trigger the 'excessive deficit procedure' under the EC treaty with *potential* 'hard' consequences for states (see Hodson and Maher, 2004). Non treaty-based processes may have to rely more on naming and shaming and peer pressure as consequence though even these may vary across processes.

There may be a stronger objection to thinking of the OMC as an accountability mechanism. For Bovens, an accountability process is essentially a retroactive casting of a judgment on past action. The production of forward-looking national reports that are evaluated by EU institutions and other actors may simply be part of a Europeanized policy-making process. However, as Bovens notes, the line between accountability processes which seek to influence future acts and policy-making may be a fine one. Indeed, it may be a characteristic of new forms of governance that prospective 'governing' activities are informed by the lessons of past successes or failures. In this way, the OMC appears to be a hybrid form of governance in a double sense. In its governance dimension, the OMC is an assemblage of tools and methodologies underpinned by different modes of governance which create an architecture that represents a compromise between the competing philosophies of convergence and cooperation oriented towards a particular rationale for coordination. Elements of that architecture, however, are also oriented towards rendering Member States accountable for their policies and their policy performance.

The cyclical nature of the OMC process is also important to this dual identity and hybrid structure. At different times, greater or lesser emphasis may be placed on shaping the governance context—making revisions to the objectives, guidelines or targets, or the accountability dimension—development of narratives of domestic policy development that are then evaluated. This is particularly evident in chapter four where the move to a new three-year cycle of policy coordination has created more space for stronger evaluation of Member States' policies and strategies to combat social exclusion. Moreover, even at any given moment in time—especially where the OMC is the object of more fundamental reform pressures—the emphasis may shift away from increasing resort to centralized control in favour of more domestic ownership, coupled with enhanced accountability. To some extent this was the inspiration for changes to the economic and employment coordination processes with the relaunch of the Lisbon strategy in 2005.

For proponents of the OMC, this dual identity is a positive virtue. Indeed, it is noteworthy that Sabel and Zeitlin (2008) sometimes refer to experimentalist governance as 'dynamic accountability'. This speaks to a virtuous cycle of policy learning shaped both by new and fresh inputs of ideas diffused through policy coordination but also by critical evaluation of the policy performance of states. What might seem like a tension within the OMC is instead a productive cyclical yoking of decentralized policy-making to a centralized system for influencing and evaluating policy.

For critics of the OMC, this hybridity is a signifier of an identity crisis: a process that is caught between two identities. By trying to ride two horses, the OMC neither succeeds as a technique of EU governance—a 'red herring' when compared to more legalized forms of EU intervention (Idema and Keleman, 2006)—nor as a means of holding Member States to account. Moreover, as an attempt to govern without even the limited clothing of democratic decision-making in the EU, the OMC might better be thought of as an accountability problem rather than an accountability mechanism.

For present purposes, the intention is not to adjudicate between these two evaluations. Rather it is simply to highlight the apparent dual identity to the

OMC. More importantly, it is an issue to which the analysis returns in the final chapter when considering how to 'strengthen' policy coordination. For some, strengthening means making the OMC look more like 'hard law' by increasing its prescriptiveness, by limiting national autonomy and policy diversity and by centralizing authority in EU institutions (with a consequential need to make the OMC more democratically legitimate). This tends then to work solely along the 'governance' axis of the OMC. Yet, it is possible to argue that the alternative would be to strengthen the OMC's accountability function and to take decentralized policy-making—and responsibility for the resulting effects—more seriously and, therefore, to look less to the governance axis and more to the accountability axis as the dimension along which to make changes. These are the issues considered in the final and concluding chapter.

Conclusions

It is a difficult task to try and make sense of the emergence of the OMC as a technique of EU governance while at the same time challenging the very idea that the OMC is or might be a coherent and singular governance technique. There is a risk of appearing to be simply obtuse or contrary. Yet the alternative is to suppress the ambiguity and tensions which surround EU policy coordination. The argument put forward in this chapter is simply that we purchase the OMC as an object of scholarly attention at too high a price if we take it out of time and context. Scientific study of the OMC—whether legal science or political science—does not do justice to the exploration of the phenomenon of the OMC if it opts merely for abstract archetypes or assumes that any given example of policy coordination counts as a specimen of the species as a pretext for comparative analysis. Comparisons require like to be compared with like: this demands that we know what the OMC is like in the first place. As this chapter has demonstrated, on closer analysis policy coordination is a more ambiguous creature than might at first have been apparent. Moreover, as the chapters which follow indicate, policy coordination processes evolve and change over time. Studies which are sensitive to the context and time dimensions of EU policy coordination are more likely to better reflect the nature of the OMC and to reveal new possibilities for comparative analysis. In chapters three and four, the identity problems and potential tensions in the OMC governance architecture are explored in the context of the evolution of the OMC to combat poverty and social exclusion. Importantly, however, the intention is not to use this as a case study to reflect on the OMC per se, but rather to shed light on the utility of policy coordination as a mechanism for domestic adaptation in the social sphere. Consistent with the ambition set out in chapter one, the goal is to make EU social policy an active explanation for changes in EU governance.

3

Social Policy Coordination and the Lisbon Strategy

Introduction

At a meeting of the European Council in 2000 in Lisbon under the Portuguese Presidency, the Heads of State and Governments of EU Member States adopted the strategic goal of making Europe 'the most competitive and dynamic knowledge-based economy in the world, capable of sustainable economic growth with more and better jobs and greater social cohesion'. Member States also pledged to make 'a decisive impact on the eradication of poverty' by 'modernising the European social model, investing in people and combating social exclusion'. EU leaders agreed to apply the technique of policy coordination—the 'open method of coordination' (OMC)—in pursuit of this commitment. The aim of this chapter is to explore the initial phase of activity in which this OMC process was constructed. Returning to the themes identified in chapter one, it is a case study of a process of 'Europeanization' through 'institutionalization' (Heidenreich and Bischoff, 2008).

When we think of 'institutionalization', we usually have in mind a process by which something becomes regularized, made routine and given a certain continuity and fixity. When applied to 'governance', three key dimensions are brought into view. There is an obvious *procedural* dimension referring to the emergence and reoccurrence of certain ways of doing things, of standard procedures and of interactions structured by accepted and repeated practices, rules and norms. In more *material* terms, substantive policy discourses, paradigms and frames are generated and diffused which seek to influence and shape—cognitively and normatively—how an activity is to be conducted. Governance is an activity carried out by agents. Therefore, institutionalization also has an *actor* dimension referring to the development and embedding of new institutional actors, the interaction of officials as well as relationships between governmental and non-governmental actors. However, it is the interaction of these three dimensions which is of particular significance to the institutionalization of a governance process. Therefore, the analysis which follows does not seek to explain the emergence and evolution of the OMC process to combat social exclusion by reference to each dimension in isolation. Rather the better course of action is to deploy and rework these dimensions together with the broad institutionalist framework identified in chapter one as expositions of three key 'levels' of analysis.

The first level of analysis refers to institutionalization at the 'constitutional' or 'systemic' level. The identification of a 'constitutional' level is not entirely uncontroversial given the debacle over the use of this terminology in the context of the failed Constitutional Treaty and subsequent replacement Lisbon Treaty which consciously distanced itself from 'the constitutional concept'. Nonetheless, the point at issue—and one that is explored in much greater depth in chapter four—is the relationship between the emerging governance architecture of the OMC and the EU's underlying constitutional 'operating system', to borrow Joseph Weiler's famous metaphor (Weiler, 1997; see also Armstrong, 2008). The second level of analysis is concerned more directly with the substantive content of the governance process: from the broad framing of social exclusion as a policy problem through to more specific policy paradigms and policy discourses. Again, however, it is not just this material dimension in isolation which is significant but also the governance process as a site for contestation by governmental and non-governmental actors around the scope, content and trajectory of EU policy coordination. The third level of analysis is the governance architecture of policy coordination and the institutionalization of the elements of the OMC methodology. Necessarily this brings into focus the relationship between actors and processes but likewise it also investigates the relationship between contestation around the material content of EU intervention and the choice of governance tools and techniques.

As intimated, the focus of the analysis is upon the initial process of institution-building and, in particular, the first two cycles of policy coordination undertaken between 2000 and 2004. In the following chapter, subsequent developments are analysed with a particular focus on the issue of institutional change.

The Constitutional Context

The dominant constitutional language that frames and informs approaches to the OMC is that of 'competence' (see Szyszczak, 2006). In this section, the emergence of an OMC process to combat social exclusion is explored from the perspective of competence. Although often regarded as occupying something of a competence hinterland—a zone 'beyond' competence—a better way of approaching EU policy coordination is to view it as a product of the contested nature of EU competence: both constrained by limits on EU competence and yet simultaneously animated by the constitutional division of powers that has encouraged a search for alternative techniques through which to reconcile national diversity with European unity. The purpose of the enquiry is to evaluate the extent to which the OMC process to combat social exclusion has been institutionalized through a reconfiguration of competence to embed both the material objective of combating social exclusion and the process of coordination itself within the constitutional structure of the treaties.

The competence of the EEC in matters of social policy was originally highly limited and developments in this area have often been through the creative use both of the founding treaties as a legal basis for action and of a range of tools and instruments through which to seek influence upon Member States' policies (see generally Cram, 1993). The 'Poverty Programmes' of the 1970s and 1980s were a good example of this. The 1974 Social Action Programme[1] proposed 'the implementation, in cooperation with Member States, of specific measures to combat poverty by drawing up pilot schemes'. The European Social Fund was to play a leading role, particularly with regard to the promotion of inclusion within the labour market. However, other forms of action to tackle poverty were developed through Council Decisions setting up multi-annual action programmes financing projects designed to tackle poverty and social exclusion: the three 'Poverty Programmes'.[2] In terms of competence, the legal basis for these decisions was Article 235 EEC (now Article 352 TFEU) in recognition that while Article 2 EEC gave the Community the task of promoting an 'accelerated

[1] Council Resolution of 21 January 1974: [1974] OJ C13/1.

[2] Council Decision 75/458/EEC concerning a programme of pilot schemes and studies to combat poverty [1975] OJ L199/34; Council Decision 85/8/EEC on specific Community action to combat poverty [1985] OJ L2/24; Council Decision 89/457/EEC of 18 July 1989 establishing a medium-term Community action programme concerning the economic and social integration of the economically and socially less privileged groups in society [1989] OJ L224/10.

raising of the standard of living', nonetheless, the Treaty did not confer a specific legal competence for action in the sphere of poverty and social exclusion policy. With Article 235 EEC as a legal basis for action and its requirement of unanimous voting in the Council, the Commission faced potential deadlock in the Council when it encountered Member State resistance to the development of a fourth Poverty Programme. The Commission's attempt to 'stretch' Community powers by seeking to fund projects for which there was a line in the EU budget even in the absence of a legal act adopted by the Council, was frustrated by litigation brought by the UK—supported by Germany—against the Commission under Article 173 EEC (now Article 263 TFEU) (see also Bauer, 2002). The ECJ held that with the exception of non-significant expenditure, a basic legal act had to be adopted for the implementation of budgetary expenditure in addition to the existence of a budget line.[3] Although the Court preserved the legal effects of the contracts entered into, nonetheless, the decision highlighted the absence of a clear legal basis within the Treaty for action in the sphere of social exclusion policy.

However, with the Treaty of Amsterdam, a new competence context emerged for EU social policy. It will be recalled that during the negotiation of the Maastricht Treaty, attempts by a majority of states to agree a new social policy chapter of the EC Treaty failed due to the unwillingness of the UK government to accept further EU intervention in the social sphere. The result of the negotiations was that eleven of the then twelve Member States bound themselves to an Agreement on Social Policy annexed to the treaties via the Social Protocol allowing those states to adopt binding social policy measures: the UK would not be so bound. A key issue for negotiation in the intergovernmental conference preceding the Amsterdam Treaty was the continuing desire of the majority of EU states to end the Social Protocol and Agreement mechanism and to incorporate new social policy competences directly in the EC Treaty. The key to unblocking this negotiation was the change in government in the UK in May 1997. The timing could not have been more important. One of Prime Minister Blair's first acts as leader was to conclude the negotiations that produced the Amsterdam Treaty. While perhaps better known for its procedural changes in terms of the UK ending its social policy 'opt-out', the successful agreement of this Treaty was also of direct substantive significance to EU intervention to combat social exclusion.

Indeed, the Treaty heralded two important innovations for EU social policy. The first was the addition to the EC Treaty of a new Title VIII

[3] Case C-106/96, *United Kingdom v Commission (Social Exclusion)* [1998] ECR I-2729.

on employment policy, creating a mechanism through which employment policies—while remaining within the legislative competence of Member States—would be subject to the influence of a process of coordination at EU level. This gave a formal legal basis to the European Employment Strategy (EES); policy coordination under the EES would later provide a template for the design of the OMC to combat social exclusion. The second innovation was a new Title XI on social policy, education, vocational training and youth. As well as marking the end of the Maastricht Social Protocol and Agreement, this new social policy title made combating social exclusion one of the objectives to be pursued by the European Community and Member States (Article 136 EC). The European Commission, in its initial contribution to the intergovernmental conference negotiating the Treaty revisions (European Commission, 1996), had called for 'clearer provisions…concerning cooperation between Member States on matters of social policy, such as the fight against marginalization or against poverty'.[4] Support for this proposal was also maintained in the draft text prepared by the Irish Presidency in the latter half of 1996: a Presidency which was supportive of developing action in this area and which, as Lodge notes (1998), was able—even as one of the smaller Member States—to use its position as Presidency chair to obtain influence on the outcome of negotiations. This new provision marked a deeper material institutionalization of the EU's role in the sphere of action to combat social exclusion than the creative use of Article 235 EEC (now Article 352 TFEU) as a legal basis for the Poverty Programmes.

However, in process terms, the actual mechanism for fulfilling this new objective was not clearly specified. Article 137(2) EC Treaty envisaged the use of two possible techniques for advancing the objective to combat social exclusion. Inasmuch as 'exclusion' took the form of exclusion from the labour market, then legislative action by means of directives establishing 'minimum requirements for gradual implementation', could be adopted by the Council. But specifically as regard action to combat social exclusion more generally, Article 137(2) EC provided that:

> The Council…may adopt measures designed to encourage cooperation between Member States through initiatives aimed at improving knowledge, developing

[4] The European Parliament's resolution on the convening of the IGC stated that: '[T]he Treaty should provide a clear obligation on the part of the Union to develop a policy to overcome social injustice, exclusion, discrimination, and poverty, and give the Commission the necessary powers to implement it.' [1996] OJ C96/77.

exchanges of information and best practices, promoting innovative approaches and evaluating experiences in order to combat social exclusion.

In considering how this cooperative process might work, it is instructive to compare and contrast Title XI with Title VIII. For employment policy, Title VIII explicitly laid down a multilateral coordination process similar to that which had been developed in the sphere of economic policy (Title VII). Article 128 EC laid down an iterative process by which the Council would adopt employment guidelines, with the Member States reporting annually on the development of their employment policies in light of these guidelines. These reports would be evaluated by the Commission and Council and a report submitted to the European Council. The Council would then adopt new guidelines in light of conclusions reached by the European Council. Recommendations could also be addressed to the Member States either collectively or individually. The Belgian delegation had proposed to the 1996 IGC a similar style of policy coordination as regards 'social protection' policy to be facilitated by a new 'Social Protection Committee'.[5] This suggestion was not taken up and instead, under Title XI, for action to combat social exclusion there was a more vague exhortation to Member States to cooperate without any specific coordination methodology being expounded. In this way, the Amsterdam Treaty must be seen as a tentative and rather modest step forward in the legal institutionalization of policy coordination as a mechanism for taking forward the new material objective of combating social exclusion. Certainly the approach adopted was different from either that actually undertaken as regards the EES or that proposed by the Belgian government for a coordination process in the area of social protection.

However, a further round of treaty change took place with the Treaty of Nice. In particular, Article 137 EC was reorganized to provide a list of eleven areas in which the Community would 'support' and 'complement' the activities of the Member States, including action to combat social exclusion and a new objective of 'modernising social protection systems'. In this way, the Nice Treaty extended the material institutionalization of EU intervention into the area of social protection, and in doing so created a new formal institutional actor in the form of the 'Social Protection Committee' (SPC). Starting life originally as the High-Level Working Party on Social Protection, this group was later formalized by Council Decision made

[5] Note from the Belgian Permanent Representative to the IGC (26.11.96): CONF 3991/96.

under the new Nice provisions.[6] As will be indicated, this new institutional actor has occupied a central organizational role in mediating between the Commission and the Council (see Borrás and Jacobsson, 2004) in designing and managing the social policy governance architecture.

While the new Nice provisions extended the scope for policy coordination beyond the realm of action to combat social exclusion, nonetheless, the new provisions also made explicit that action by the Council excluded any harmonization of the laws in the areas of action to combat social exclusion and the modernization of social protection systems. Directives establishing minimum requirements could still be adopted in respect of the integration of persons excluded from the labour market. Thus, while the scope to utilize policy coordination as a technique of governance expanded, the ability to resort to harmonization was also more clearly circumscribed.

Even after the Nice Treaty revisions, it was evident that, comparing the EES to the OMC process to combat social exclusion, the former had a clearer legal institutional footing in the treaties than the latter. No attempt was made at Nice to elaborate further within the treaties the methodology or architecture of social policy coordination processes. Indeed, the OMC has had to rely on a range of textual resources including Presidency Conclusions and Council minutes as well as on repeated voluntary practices as institutional anchors of the methodology. Of course, the EES itself is not reducible to the bare bones of the Treaty and has also relied on a range of resources of greater or lesser legal status to inform its practices. Nonetheless, for some it is the treaty basis of the economic and employment coordination processes that distinguish them from the OMC: indeed, on this view, the 'openness' of the OMC is a reference to this absence of legal institutionalization and the essentially voluntary nature of coordination.[7] On the one hand, this absence of a legal institutionalization of process left political actors free to

[6] Council Decision 2000/436/EC established the Social Protection Committee as the successor to the High-Level Working Party: [2000] OJ L172/26. The legal basis for the measure was Article 202 EC. However, with the entry into force of the Treaty of Nice, the EC Treaty itself made provision for the creation of a Social Protection Committee. Council Decision 2004/689, establishing a Social Protection Committee and repealing Decision 2000/436, was adopted in October 2004, with a legal basis of Article 144 EC replacing the earlier decision: [2004] OJ L314/8.

[7] See the report by Working Group XI on Social Europe to the Convention on the Future of Europe: '...unlike the open method of coordination, the coordination procedures enshrined in the Treaty are compulsory and enable the Union institutions to make recommendations to Member States and even to impose sanctions on Member States which do not respect the line jointly adopted' (para. 41).

design their own methodology and to innovate and experiment with the governance architecture of the OMC as applied in different policy fields (see Laffan and Shaw, 2005 for a comparison of the different architectures of OMC processes). On the other hand—and as explored in depth in chapter four—non-treaty based processes have been rather more vulnerable to shifts in the political winds, raising question about the degree to which formal legalization may or may not be desirable.

In sum, and as noted in chapter one, the years 1997 and 2000 were both significant staging posts in the development of EU intervention to combat social exclusion. In both years, treaty revisions created a new constitutional context for EU activities. At the level of process, policy coordination emerged first as a specific means of advancing the objective of combating social exclusion and then later became a more generalizable instrument in the social sphere. Particularly in the sub-fields of social exclusion and social protection, policy coordination was the only show in town, albeit that when compared with employment policy, there was little institutionalization of the specific processes and methodologies of policy coordination. Nonetheless, in material terms, it was significant that action to combat social exclusion and then later the modernization of social protection emerged as new substantive social policy objectives. As regards the role of actors, influential Presidencies, persistent pressure from certain national delegations and changes in national governments, all created the political context for the development of new treaty provisions. Meanwhile new institutional actors like the SPC would emerge as influential drivers of the later OMC process.

The Policy Context

EU influences over social policy have historically had strong functional orientations towards market-building processes (see Streeck, 1995). That is to say, inasmuch as divergent social policies have created barriers to worker mobility or distorted market competition, they have been of concern to EU policy-makers. In this way, rules have emerged on social security coordination, on working time, and on discrimination.[8] Another field of EU social

[8] It would be wrong, however, to assume that EU intervention in these spheres continues to be solely dominated by this functionalist economic policy frame. Increasingly a conception of 'citizenship of the Union' is reshaping even familiar areas of past EU action, with developments being led by the ECJ. In this way, while Leibfried may be right to call attention to the

policy intervention has been in respect of labour law and industrial relations (Streeck, 1995). The Maastricht Treaty's Protocol and Agreement on Social Policy provided an enhanced competence not just for EU legislative powers but also for corporatist 'social dialogue' to result in agreements between management and labour (see Falkner, 1998). With the Amsterdam Treaty and the end of the UK 'opt-out' from these arrangements, a firmer treaty foundation for developments in this area was in place. On this basis a body of law and of cross-sectoral and sectoral agreements have emerged to structure industrial relations.

Nonetheless, even with these EU interventions, as Daly describes (2006), the 'core' of EU social policy has often been very different from the central preoccupations of domestic social policy. It is the Europeanization of these 'missing' domains of 'social protection, income redistribution, income adequacy' (Daly, 2006: 1) that is implicated in the Lisbon strategy through the OMC. The question that is explored here is the manner in which the Lisbon strategy 'frames' this new preoccupation with the missing domains of EU social policy. Consistent with the approach set out in chapter one, we can explore policy framing in two related ways. The first is in terms of the relationship between social policy, on the one hand, and other policy fields like economic and employment policies. The issue is really one of seeking to understand the contribution which enhanced EU social policy intervention is supposed to make to the broader policy objectives of the Lisbon strategy and in this way, to shed light on the manner in which economic, employment and social policies are welded together within the Lisbon matrix. The second concern lies with understanding more precisely the rationale for the OMC to combat social exclusion and the way in which, even with EU social policy itself, EU intervention via this OMC may be understood as bounded by different sub-policy frames.

EU Social Policy: From Missing Domain to 'Productive Factor'

For Daly and others, 'the underlying philosophy [of Lisbon] is of activation' (Daly, 2006: 466; Szyszczak, 2001; Wincott 2003). The idea of 'activation' is

role of judges in shaping EU social policy, his idea that this is motivated solely by aims of market integration is to ignore the significant reframing of judicial social policy intervention in terms of an emerging citizenship policy framework. See Leibfried, 2005. In this way, while action to combat sex discrimination was originally functionally oriented to distortions in labour costs, contemporary interventions on race, age, religion and sexual orientation also serve broader objectives relating to the political identity of the Union and the EU's relationship to nationals of the Member States *qua* citizens of a new polity.

strongly associated with the idea of social policy as a 'productive factor' which places its emphasis upon a harmonious mutual interaction of economic, employment and social policies (see especially, the European Commission's *Social Agenda 2000–5*: European Commission, 2000a). It refers to an articulation particularly of social protection and employment policies intended to encourage labour market participation while ensuring security for those outside of the labour market. This interpretation of Lisbon's social dimension pushes EU intervention beyond the sphere of 'social regulation' identified by Majone (1993)—associated with isolating national social redistributive policies from EU economic regulation—towards an attempt to connect and reconcile economic and social policies through EU action (see Wincott, 2003). It is this coupling or connection between economic, employment and social policies that has been presented as being the mutually reinforcing elements of the Lisbon policy triangle. In this way, the values associated with the 'European Social Model' are to be woven into the policy framework of Lisbon as much as the values of sound public finances and public expenditure prudence associated with 'Economic and Monetary Union' (EMU) (see Begg and Berghman, 2002).

Nonetheless, and as intimated in chapter two, analysts also offer contrasting interpretations of Lisbon's contribution to the relationship between economic and social goals. Offe's analysis of the Lisbon strategy is one that tends to view it less as a virtuous policy matrix and more as the vehicle through which 'embedded capitalism' cuts free from its national social tethers. Thus, Offe (2003: 463) concludes that while superficially remaining intact, national welfare systems are being 'hollowed-out':

> The national welfare state can no longer constrain the market and impose a regime of decommodification upon the market. To the contrary, now it is being left to the market to decide which arrangements are in fact affordable and employment-enhancing, and which ones must be dropped as a competitive liability.

On this reading, action to promote social cohesion and social inclusion is largely a cipher for removing obstacles to, and enhancing capabilities for work. In like mind, for Chalmers and Lodge, the 'strategy' of Lisbon is to create a 'strong neo-liberal policy dynamic' in which employment and social inclusion policies are simultaneously superficial and substantively limited by the constraints of EMU (Chalmers and Lodge, 2003).

There is every reason to take seriously concerns about the policy balance struck in the Lisbon strategy. After all, the provisions of the Treaty formalizing the EES make clear that employment guidelines are to be consistent with the Broad Economic Policy Guidelines (BEPGs). Moreover, the labour market has tended to be viewed as a key mechanism of inclusion and of mitigating the risk of poverty. The virtuous policy mix of Lisbon can quite easily be projected as a recipe that simply demands increased labour market participation and welfare reforms intended to push people into low-paid and insecure employment while states cut back on social expenditure in the name of budgetary prudence and fiscal discipline.

However, for Daly, 'Lisbon' can also be read as containing 'strong countercurrents' to the insistence on social policy as a productive factor, including: a focus not just on employment status but also on the situation of those outside the labour market; a vision of the 'good society' beyond the market through the provision of social goods and ties of solidarity; an emphasis on social policy beyond floor regulatory standards to encompass redistributive issues; and a specific and direct attention towards poverty and social exclusion as a matter of European concern (Daly, 2006: 469–70). In other words, for Daly, there is a distinctive social policy vision which is also at play within the Lisbon strategy. But as she is careful to note, one needs to be cautious in viewing the particular emphasis on social inclusion as 'either embedded or settled in the EU landscape' (ibid: 470).

Self-evidently, it is not enough to proclaim that the Lisbon strategy had a 'social' dimension. On the one hand, one can point to the materialization of EU social policy within an ideal of an 'active' welfare state with EU policy coordination attempting to reconcile competing social and economic demands. On the other hand, contrasting interpretations conceptualize EU social policy as either the handmaiden of market forces destabilizing domestic social protection systems or as the counterweight to such forces reinforcing European values of solidarity and social protection. The point of the analysis here is not to adjudicate between these different interpretations but rather to echo Daly's point that the launch of the Lisbon strategy did not clearly embed a singular EU social policy vision or settle its relationship with economic and employment policies. Indeed, as is explored in chapter four, as the Lisbon strategy evolved, the identity of EU social policy and its relationship to economic and employment policies became increasingly contested.

Social Exclusion and Social Protection

Much of the discussion in the previous section oriented our attention towards EU social policy via its relationship to economic policy imperatives. In this section, our focus is more particularly on the different policy frames and paradigms acting within EU social policy in its materialization of 'social exclusion' as a subject of concern and as an object of EU policy coordination. Of course, this discussion is not unrelated to the earlier discussion and indeed it will be indicated below that developments within EU social policy were being shaped by changes in the broader EU policy agenda. The point of intervention here is simply to tease out the dynamics of EU social policy itself in the framing of action to combat social exclusion.

As was highlighted in chapter one, the discourse of 'social exclusion' emerged through the 'Poverty Programmes' of the EU and this continued to be an important institutional path within EU social policy leading towards the OMC process to combat social exclusion. However, an alternative pathway began to emerge in the 1990s in which combating 'social exclusion' became intertwined with interventions to reform 'social protection'. Yet even this latter trajectory altered from one initially concerned with giving the single market a social dimension—alternatively framed in terms of protecting fundamental rights or removing obstacles to free movement—to one increasingly influenced by the relationship between social protection, employment policy and sustainable social expenditures within an 'activation' paradigm.

The reform of social protection systems has often been presented as instrumental to action to combat social exclusion. Recall that in 1992 the Council adopted a Recommendation (92/441/EEC)[9] on common criteria concerning sufficient resources and social assistance in social protection systems, recommending to Member States that they recognize a right to sufficient resources and to social assistance and to adapt their social protection systems to the principles and guidelines set out in the Recommendation. More significantly, Council Recommendation 92/442/EEC[10] on the convergence of social protection objectives and policies attempted to develop a convergence strategy by which national social protection systems would be guided by principles laid down in the Recommendation. The aim of coordination was to help states to face common challenges including those arising from social exclusion and demographic change. Commentators describe the 1992 Recommendations as forming a 'premature' or 'embryonic' OMC (de la Porte and Pochet, 2002; Ferrera, Matsaganis and Sacchi, 2002).

[9] [1992] OJ L245/46. [10] [1992] OJ L245/49.

Nonetheless, the material justifications for coordinated action drew on rather different sorts of policy frames than those which were later to animate social policy coordination within the Lisbon strategy. The 1992 coordination processes were embedded within two competing policy frameworks. On the one hand, the Recommendations formed part of the Commission's 'Action Programme' for the implementation of the (non-legally binding) 1989 Charter of the Fundamental Social Rights of Workers (European Commission, 1989). Chapter five of the Action Programme related to 'social protection' and suggested a two-pronged strategy for the implementation of the Charter—in particular, Article 10[11]—as part of 'a comprehensive and consistent drive to combat social exclusion'. Thus, a fundamental rights orientation to the development of EU social policy framed EU action to coordinate social protection systems.

On the other hand, policy development was strongly influenced by internal market policy. The 1989 Charter itself was not divorced from the economic objectives of the EU. In the Recitals to the 1989 Charter a connection was made between the goals of job creation and competitiveness—to be driven by the completion of the internal market—and the contribution of social policy as a means to 'the strengthening of the competitiveness of undertakings' and as an 'essential condition for ensuring sustained economic development'. The justification for coordination lay in managing potential externalities and spillovers within the internal market. Thus, the Commission was keen to highlight:

- the diversity of social protection systems as a barrier to worker mobility;
- diversity as potentially encouraging a form of undesirable mobility in the form of benefit tourism;
- a general fear of a lowering of standards of social protection as Member States sought to conform to the budgetary discipline of EMU (thereby increasing risks of exclusion) combined with a specific concern that states might use a lowering of social protection as a means of obtaining competitive advantage (as an alternative to monetary devaluation).

[11] 'Every worker of the European Community shall have a right to adequate social protection and shall, whatever his status and whatever the size of the undertaking in which he is employed, enjoy an adequate level of social security benefits.

Persons who have been unable either to enter or re-enter the labour market and have no means of subsistence must be able to receive sufficient resources and social assistance in keeping with their particular situation.'

Although the autonomy of the Member States to organize their social protection systems was affirmed, the linkages made to the internal market and EMU indicate that the unconstrained autonomy of Member States to respond to common challenges was conceptualized as undesirable and requiring to be disciplined.

As the 1990s progressed, the 'modernization' of national social protection systems grew as a preoccupation of EU policy. However, this was accompanied by a development in the policy context, described by Ashiagbor as a shift from 'social policy' to 'employment policy' (Ashiagbor, 2005: 89–100). Building on an earlier Communication (European Commission, 1995), the Commission's 1997 Communication on *Modernizing and Improving Social Protection* (European Commission, 1997) announced that the key issues for modernization were:

- social protection as a 'productive factor': viewed from the dual perspectives of the EES and the BEPGs, social expenditure should promote employment and shift from passive to active measures to support labour market inclusion;
- making social protection 'more employment friendly':
  - balancing flexibility and security by reforming tax and social protection systems to provide incentives for work and a safety net for those out of work;
  - enhancing support to find work;
  - reforming the funding of social protection;
  - managing transition from work to retirement;
  - promotion of social inclusion and guaranteeing minimum incomes;
- adapting social protection to demographic changes;
- adapting social protection to changes in the gender balance.

In this way, issues of modernizing social protection were increasingly framed in terms of their contribution to the development of employment policy (see Szyszczak, 2001).

Following up on this Communication, in 1999, the Commission produced a Communication on *A Concerted Strategy for Modernising Social Protection* (European Commission, 1999) which set out the framework for the development of EU policy in the sphere of social protection. In it, EMU was seen as reinforcing the case for a 'concerted approach' to the modernization of social protection systems, with the successful implementation of the EES considered as necessitating a 'parallel and complementary process' on the modernization of social protection. Thus, the Commission proposed a four-stranded strategy based around the objectives of:

- making work pay,
- making pensions safe and sustainable,
- promoting social inclusion, and
- ensuring a high quality and sustainable health care system.

In this way, by the time of the Lisbon summit, the promotion of social inclusion was constructed as part of a broader process of modernizing social protection, itself linked to and influenced by an ideal of reconciling social, employment and economic policies towards common objectives. Importantly, this approach to the reform of social protection policies also broke with the cross-border, free movement rationalization of the 1992 Recommendations. In other words, the justification for EU policy intervention no longer rested on promoting or managing the consequence of free movement and the undesirable consequences of unilateral exercises of policy autonomy, but rather on the common challenges facing states (particularly demographic changes) and the benefits of using EU cooperation as a means of problem-identification and problem-solving. EU governance would, therefore, have purchase within the boundaries of the state even in the absence of a cross-border issue.

We had, then, two rather different policy pathways along which action to combat poverty and social exclusion was materialized. On the one hand, a path grew out of a strand of EU social policy intervention that named and rendered visible social exclusion as a 'multidimensional' phenomenon to be combated through a wide range of interventions. This was the path that projected forwards from the earlier 'Poverty Programmes'. As Room notes, this had its roots in a continental tradition of social policy concerned more with relational issues of power, participation and integration than with distributional issues. Nonetheless, he also noted the potential for a synthesis of these approaches inasmuch as social exclusion could be considered to be a denial of 'citizenship' rights (Room, 1995: 7). On the other hand, action to combat social exclusion became framed by EU interventions to reform social protection systems. Developing originally in the Single Market context and rationalized in terms both of fundamental social rights and free movement issues, the later Lisbon strategy re-framed the modernization of social protection systems to give greater prominence to the role of employment policy through an emergent 'activation' paradigm.

To return to the theme of institutionalization, at the level of material institutionalization, 'social exclusion' certainly developed as a preoccupation of EU policy-makers in advance of, and in the context of the Lisbon strategy. However, as will be developed more fully below, coordinated action to combat social exclusion occupied an unsettled material and normative space; the subject of competing policy frames constituted by competing policy paradigms.

The Governance Context

As identified above, neither the Amsterdam nor the Nice Treaties settled the issue of the precise mechanism for policy coordination. Moreover—and reflecting the discussion in the previous section—it was not even wholly apparent that what would emerge would be a policy coordination process solely in the area of social exclusion. It is striking that the Commission's 1999 Communication on *A Concerted Strategy for Modernising Social Protection* (European Commission, 1999) requested the Council to endorse 'a framework for closer cooperation in the field of social protection, based on the exchange of experiences, mutual concertation and evaluation of ongoing policy developments with a view to identifying best practices'. The Commission would monitor progress through an adaptation of its *Social Protection in Europe* report to be examined 'in articulation' with the Joint Employment Report. This appeared to envisage parallel *employment* policy and *social protection* coordination processes. For social protection policy coordination, the EP had encouraged the Commission to adopt:

> a methodological model, along the lines of the Luxembourg process on employment, based on . . . objectives . . . , to include identifying bench-marking criteria, evaluation systems and guidelines to form a basis for national action plans.[12]

It was perfectly possible that what would emerge would be an overarching coordination process. Indeed, specifically as regards social exclusion, the Commission's Communication on *Building an Inclusive Europe* (European Commission, 2000b) proposed as its 'operational tools' a multi-annual programme of support for activities to develop understanding of issues of social

[12] EP Resolution on the Commission's Communication on Modernising Social Protection: [2000] OJ C339/154.

exclusion aided by exchanges of best practice, together with a framework instrument to promote the integration of people excluded from the labour market (on the basis of Article 137 EC). The emphasis lay on *mainstreaming* the analysis of issues of social exclusion into the policy domains and governance architectures of employment and social protection policies rather than creating a new process for social exclusion. In this way, it would have been perfectly possible to view the Amsterdam and Nice Treaties as simply creating a new legal basis for the development of the kinds of programmes and studies developed under earlier action programmes with the results fed into employment and social protection coordination processes.

However, the institution of a coordination process specifically related to social exclusion can be explained by reference to the contribution of a range of actors. Not surprisingly, social NGOs like the European Anti-Poverty Network (EAPN) campaigned for action to combat social exclusion and as early as May 1999 had called for a distinctive process modelled on the EES (EAPN, 1999). Interestingly, the issue of poverty and social exclusion coincided with the political preoccupations of EU leaders in the late 1990s and early 21st century. This was reflected in the ambitions of a series of EU presidencies of the European Council. Thus, a distinctive policy focus on combating social exclusion emerged under the Portuguese Presidency in the first half of 2000. In a Presidency background note in January 2000,[13] the Presidency noted that: 'Europe in the 21st century needs to have a systematic policy to combat poverty and social exclusion in their old and new forms.' The Lisbon summit itself highlighted that, '[T]he number of people living below the poverty line and in social exclusion in the Union is unacceptable' and called for a 'decisive impact on the eradication of poverty' to be made. The work of the Portuguese Presidency did, of course, capitalize on initiatives under earlier presidencies, including that of the Irish Presidency which, as the Presidency of the IGC in the second half of 1996, had been influential in drafting the provisions on combating social exclusion that were ultimately included within the Amsterdam Treaty. Subsequent presidencies—French, Swedish and Belgian—each kept up the momentum generated at Lisbon in terms of the political importance attached to combating social exclusion. As several interviewees described it, the OMC to combat social exclusion emerged through a 'lucky run' of presidencies.

In addition to the role of the presidencies, the contribution of organizational structures and of actors within those structures is significant. Following on from the 1999 Communication on *Modernizing Social Protection*, Member

[13] Doc. 5256/00 (12.1.2000).

States agreed to nominate high-level officials to facilitate this process. This group was later formalized as the 'Social Protection Committee' (SPC). Having decided to prioritize its work, the consensus within the SPC was to make the issue of social inclusion the main priority,[14] with work on the other strands of the modernization of social protection agenda—particularly pensions—to follow. In this way, notwithstanding the potential tension between the two different policy pathways and foci of these pathways, the decision of the SPC to prioritize work on combating social exclusion squared the circle: a specific focus on, and process to combat, social exclusion could emerge, but one that was not detached from a broader concern to modernize social protection systems. Indeed, as we will see in chapter four, profound institutional change later brought the distinctive OMC process to combat social exclusion within an overarching social coordination process. Nonetheless, the independent life of the OMC process for two cycles of reports from 2001–2005 created something of a path-dependency to that institutional change.

In the sections which follow, the different elements of the OMC governance architecture are explored. As noted previously, while this architecture drew on past forms of policy coordination in the economic and employment spheres, it also departed in significant ways from those templates. Moreover, as suggested in chapter two, close attention requires to be paid first, to individual elements of that methodology in terms of whether the orientation is towards a more 'top-down' steering or 'bottom-up' influencing of national strategies and structures; secondly, to the interaction of different elements as regards their complementarity or rivalry or simply ambiguity; and thirdly, to changes in the methodology between the first and second cycles of the OMC process.

Common Objectives

Following on from the Lisbon Summit, the task of translating the Presidency Conclusion into a concrete methodology fell initially to the High-Level Working Party on social protection, and subsequently the Social Protection Committee as its formal successor. This new institutional actor can be credited with defining much of the OMC architecture. A key contribution of the SPC was to propose a set of common objectives to guide the process. Adopted by the Employment and Social Affairs Council meeting in Luxembourg on 17 October 2000[15] and endorsed at the Nice

[14] Progress Report by the High-Level Working Party on strengthening of cooperation for modernising and improving social protection: Doc. 8634/00 (18 May 2000).

[15] Doc. 14110/00.

European Council, the four common objectives (the 'Nice objectives') were to:

1. Facilitate participation in employment, and access by all to resources, rights, goods and services.
2. Prevent the risk of exclusion.
3. Help the most vulnerable.
4. Mobilize all relevant bodies.

Member States were requested to submit National Action Plans on inclusion (NAPincls) by June 2001 incorporating these objectives into national strategies and programmes. These NAPincls would cover the period 2001–2003 and would be reviewed and evaluated jointly by the Commission and Council.

Table 3.1 The Nice Objectives

The Nice Common Objectives in Detail

To facilitate participation in employment and access by all to the resources, rights, goods and services

Employment

(a) To promote access to stable and quality employment for all women and men who are capable of working, in particular by:
  - putting in place, for those in the most vulnerable groups in society, pathways towards employment and by mobilizing training policies to that end;
  - developing policies to promote the reconciliation of work and family life, including the issue of child- and dependent care;
  - using the opportunities for integration and employment provided by the social economy.

(b) To prevent the exclusion of people from the world of work by improving employability, through human resource management, organization of work and life-long learning.

Access to resources, rights, goods and services

(a) To organize social protection systems in such a way that they help, in particular, to:
  - guarantee everyone has the resources necessary to live in accordance with human dignity;
  - overcome obstacles to employment by ensuring that the take-up of employment results in increased income and by promoting employability.

(b) To implement policies which aim to provide access for all to decent and sanitary housing, as well as the basic services necessary to live normally having regard to local circumstances.

(c) To put in place policies which aim to provide access for all to healthcare appropriate to their situation, including situations of dependency.

(d) To develop, for the benefit of people at risk of exclusion, services and accompanying measures which will allow them effective access to education, justice and other public and private services, such as culture, sport and leisure.

Table 3.1 Continued

To prevent the risks of exclusion

(a) To exploit fully the potential of the knowledge-based society and of new information and communication technologies and ensure that no-one is excluded, taking particular account of the needs of people with disabilities.

(b) To put in place policies which seek to prevent life crises which can lead to situations of social exclusion, such as indebtedness, exclusion from school and becoming homeless.

(c) To implement action to preserve family solidarity in all its forms.

To help the most vulnerable

(a) To promote the social integration of women and men at risk of facing persistent poverty, eg because they have a disability or belong to a group experiencing particular integration problems.

(b) To move towards the elimination of social exclusion among children and give them every opportunity for social integration.

(c) To develop comprehensive actions in favour of areas marked by exclusion.

To mobilize all relevant bodies

(a) To promote, according to national practice, the participation and self-expression of people suffering exclusion, in particular in regard to their situation and the policies and measures affecting them.

(b) To mainstream the fight against exclusion into overall policy, in particular by:

- mobilizing the public authorities at national, regional and local level, according to their respective areas of competence;
- developing appropriate coordination procedures and structures;
- adapting administrative and social services to the needs of people suffering exclusion and ensuring that front-line staff are sensitive to these needs.

(c) To promote dialogue and partnership between all relevant bodies, public and private, by:

- involving the social partners, NGOs and social service providers, according to their respective areas of competence, in the fight against the various forms of exclusion;
- encouraging the social responsibility and active engagement of all citizens in the fight against social exclusion;
- fostering the social responsibility of business.

For Lodge, the agreement of common objectives can be considered to be an aspect of 'standard-setting' which entails setting 'the overall objectives and goals of a particular system' and its 'normative intent' (Lodge, 2007: 347–8). One way of exploring this is to consider how prescriptive the objectives are in terms of establishing obligations for Member States or at least strong normative steers. However, and more particularly in the framework of this study, we can also analyse the common objectives as a form of political discourse in which social exclusion is 'framed' by reference to different policy fields, and through which different 'paradigms'—normative and cognitive—are conveyed.

In terms of prescription and obligation, it is noteworthy that the substantive objectives (1–3) were relatively broad and exhortative rather than particularly precise about the sorts of reforms that Member States might need to undertake. The fourth objective might similarly be said to be fairly open. Nonetheless, when combined with apparently critical messages within the first 'Joint Report' from the Commission and Council concerning the inadequacy of involvement of all actors, particularly of those experiencing poverty,[16] this objective was utilized by anti-poverty groups to seek greater involvement for themselves 'and for those experiencing poverty' in the OMC process. In this way, the objective to 'mobilize' took on a more prescriptive quality. Nonetheless, simply analysing the objectives on a scale of 'prescription' or 'obligation' is not wholly revealing about the material content of the objectives.[17]

In terms of policy frames, multiple policy fields acted upon the construction of the Nice objectives: from employment policy and modernizing social protection to fundamental rights, equality policy and even information technology policies. In this way, overall the objectives reflected both the influences of the wide-ranging policy discourses of the Lisbon strategy as well as different strands of social policy discourses, including those predating the Lisbon strategy. What is significant about these multiple policy fields framing the objectives is their depiction of the prob-

[16] 'The need for an integrated strategy to promote the participation of those experiencing poverty and social exclusion is widely recognised. Yet this objective is not clearly and systematically reflected in concrete policy measures in the NAPs/incl, despite evidence indicating that failure to involve excluded communities is a major weakness in policy delivery.' (European Commission and Council, 2002: 68).

[17] Proponents of the analysis of international relations in terms of a 'legalization' of those relations have utilized a hard law/soft law continuum based on variations in the levels of 'obligation', 'precision' and 'delegation' in an attempt to explain this 'legalization': see Abbott et al, 2000; Abbott and Snidal, 2000. Scholars of the OMC often describe elements like the common objectives as being a form of 'soft law'. Nonetheless, as the analysis here demonstrates this turns out to have much less analytical purchase than might be supposed: see chapter eight and also Armstrong and Kilpatrick, 2007.

lem of social exclusion as something that required a 'multidimensional' policy approach. This insistence on 'multidimensionality' within official discourses was particularly important in securing the support of NGOs for the Nice objectives and helped to underscore the idea that the process was not solely concerned with issues of low income and employment status. Nonetheless, it also served political purposes in the sense that the very broad framing of the policy issue also allowed states to project very different national policy strategies and performances as being compatible with the Nice objectives.

As regards policy paradigms, it is worth exploring in more detail the first of the Nice objectives. In reality, this singular objective was really two quite different objectives. The first placed emphasis on employment as the key mechanism of inclusion—in Levitas' terms a reflection of the 'Social Inclusion Discourse' in action (Levitas, 1998)—and was in line with the thrust of the Lisbon strategy to increase employment rates. It was consistent with an 'activation' paradigm of EU social policy. The second part focused on social protection but much less in terms of the preoccupations of the activation paradigm—typically a concern with reforming social protection to encourage welfare recipients off benefits and into work—and more informed by a vision of social protection as a fundamental right with the emphasis placed on 'access' to social protection rather than the 'sustainability' of social protection systems. This is more consistent with a 'citizenship' paradigm of EU social policy and one often articulated by social NGOs in terms of social exclusion as a denial of fundamental rights (see eg EAPN, 2000). Moreover, this was reinforced by the fourth Nice objective. Its orientation towards the participation in policy-making of those experiencing poverty reflected contemporary trends in social policy (Daly, 2008) which can also be viewed through the lens of a citizenship paradigm (see also Mabbett, 2007). Taken together, the Nice objectives can be interpreted as encapsulating elements of both an 'activation' paradigm—a paradigm that tends to emphasize the *obligation* of individuals to include themselves through labour market participation—but also something more like a 'citizenship' paradigm and a vision of the 'good society' (Daly, 2006), with its emphasis upon the *rights* of individuals flowing from their membership of a political community.

However, a further means of seeking to develop some kind of 'discipline' on the content of the NAPincls was through the 'common outline' agreed between the Commission and the SPC and intended to translate the objectives more concretely into the structure of the NAPincls. Thus, Member

States were requested to highlight:

- major challenges facing the Member State;
- the state's strategic approach and main objectives;
- policy measures planned for the period from 2001–2003;
- indicators used to measure progress; and
- examples of good practice.

Particularly as the process moved on from the first to the second cycle, the common outline assumed an important structuring role in attempting to push states beyond producing NAPincls that merely reported on past action (see further below).

By contrast with the employment strategy where the experience of its early development was for the guidelines and recommendations addressed to states to become more detailed and prescriptive with each iteration of the cycle (see Mosher and Trubek, 2003 and Armstrong and Kilpatrick, 2007), there was very limited amendment of the Nice objectives between the first cycle (2001–2003) and the second (2003–2005). An informal meeting of the Employment and Social Affairs Council under the Danish Presidency of the EU in July 2002 requested that the SPC report back on any suggested revisions to the objectives. Its report concluded that the Nice objectives had proved to be 'balanced, robust and viable' and that the emphasis ought to be on 'continuity' to consolidate and build on progress.[18] The only substantive amendment to the objectives themselves was to identify immigrants as a potentially vulnerable group in terms of the third objective. Other changes—an emphasis on gender mainstreaming and on setting targets (considered below)—were proposed for the common outline to guide the second generation of NAPincls. These changes were adopted by the Council in December 2002.

What is also noteworthy about the process of revising the common objectives was the openness of the process to influences from a range of actors. Indeed, the task of constructing the OMC architecture has departed from the normal inter-institutional processes of the 'Community Method' particularly in terms of the strong influence of the SPC and NGOs and the lack of any clear role for the European Parliament or EU courts. For example, the SPC gave a commitment to take into account the deliberations of the October 2002 Roundtable on Social Exclusion held under the Danish Presidency before submitting its proposals to the

[18] Doc. 14164/02.

Council on the revision of the Nice Objectives. The chair of the SPC also met with EAPN on the eve of the Roundtable to discuss the SPC's draft proposals. Together with the Commission, EAPN lobbied for some of the changes to be made. In this way, new institutional relationships—as well as older connections between the Commission and social NGOs (see Bauer, 2002)—can be seen to emerge (see de la Porte, 2008). Importantly, while European Council Presidencies have some significance in giving broad shape and direction to the OMC process, in terms of the construction of the methodology of the OMC process in its initial phase of development, it was at the institutional level of the Commission, Council and SPC that the main developments occurred. Indeed, the revisions to the Nice objectives for the second cycle of NAPincls were never endorsed at European Council level.

In sum, analysis of the common objectives reveals first, the very broad framing of the problem of social exclusion in terms of a range of policy fields acting upon the construction of the objectives ('multidimensionality'); second, the tension between the material institutionalization of an 'activation' or a 'citizenship' paradigm; and finally, the development of new ways of working both between governmental actors in the context of the SPC and between governmental and non-governmental actors.

Common Indicators

Within the OMC, social indicators are assigned a key role in mapping and representing the phenomenon of social exclusion. The Lisbon Presidency Conclusions highlighted the need to develop a common set of indicators to support work in combating social exclusion through the OMC. Establishing a portfolio of *social* indicators was not unrelated to the use of a broader portfolio of *structural* indicators being developed by the European Commission as support for its 'Synthesis Report': the annual report to the Spring European Council covering the main policy fields of the Lisbon Strategy. In September 2000, the Commission presented its first Communication on Structural Indicators (2000c). The six 'social cohesion' indicators covered income poverty, joblessness, regional cohesion and educational attainment. Data for the income poverty indicators came from the European Community Household Panel (ECHP) dataset. As is evident from Table 3.2, these indicators gave a rather narrow interpretation of 'social cohesion' rather than the more encompassing multidimensional vision of 'social exclusion' at play in the Nice objectives.

Table 3.2 Structural Indicators

Structural Indicators 2000

Social Cohesion Indicators

1. Distribution of income (income quintile ratio).
2. Poverty rate (50% and 60% of median income) before and after social transfers.
3. Persistence of poverty.
4. Jobless households.
5. Regional cohesion (coefficient of variations of GDP per capita).
6. Educational attainment (14–18 year olds with lower secondary education and not in education or training).

In February 2001, a sub-group of the SPC was established to work on the portfolio of inclusion indicators. Its work was influenced not only by the existing social cohesion indicators but also by a team of experts headed by Tony Atkinson and contracted by the incoming Belgian Presidency to provide a report to be discussed at a conference in Antwerp (the results of which were published as Atkinson et al, 2002). As Marlier—one of the members of the expert team—has highlighted (Marlier, 2003) the preparation and active support of the Belgian Presidency was a crucial factor in facilitating the SPC's agreement of a suite of primary and secondary indicators, endorsed by the European Council at Laeken: the 'Laeken indicators' (Table 3.3). The process once again also highlights the influence of non-institutional actors—in this case social scientists—on the SPC.

In the primary indicators, we find repeated the six social cohesion indicators supplemented by more detailed low income indicators, and health indicators. What is striking is how dominant are the indicators on low income and joblessness. The attention given to low income is perhaps more in keeping with what Room (2005) describes as the earlier focus of EU social policy intervention on 'poverty' rates than its later concern with a broader notion of 'social exclusion'.[19] The key indicator of low income is the 'relative' at-risk-of-poverty indicator (those with less than 60 per cent of median equivalized income). Significantly, this is a relative rather than an absolute poverty indicator and one that is based on national—rather than an EU average—income distribution. As Staunton notes (2003), there was a fear that setting an absolute EU poverty indicator might be viewed as implicitly setting an

[19] The choice and range of indicators is the product of many variables such as the availability of data or domestic rules on what kinds of data may be legally collected (see Staunton, 2003). Via Eurostat and the ECHP dataset, data to support monetary indicators had been developed but not indicators on important issues such as housing (see Atkinson, Marlier and Nolan, 2004).

Table 3.3 The Laeken Indicators

The Laeken Indicators

Primary Indicators

1. Low income rate after transfers with low-income threshold set at 60% of median income (with breakdowns by gender, age, most frequent activity status, household type and tenure status; as illustrative examples, the values for typical households);
2. Distribution of income (income quintile ratio)
3. Persistence of low income
4. Median low income gap
5. Regional cohesion
6. Long-term unemployment rate
7. People living in jobless households
8. Early school leavers not in further education or training
9. Life expectancy at birth
10. Self perceived health status

Secondary Indicators

11. Dispersion around the 60% median low income threshold
12. Low income rate anchored at a point in time
13. Low income rate before transfers
14. Distribution of income (Gini coefficient)
15. Persistence of low income (based on 50% of median income)
16. Long-term unemployment share
17. Very long-term unemployment rate.
18. Persons with low educational attainment

EU-wide minimum income threshold which states might consider as trespassing on their social policy competence.

For Mabbett (2007), the emphasis on issues of low income meant that the indicators encapsulated a 'redistributive paradigm' with a focus on national reforms to the tax and benefits systems. For her, this element of the OMC methodology was in tension with the stronger 'citizenship' paradigm manifested at the level of the Nice objectives. In this way, while Member States might respond in more procedural terms to the elements of mobilization and participation implicated in this citizenship paradigm, they might equally not engage with the more substantive 'redistributive' paradigm represented by the Laeken indicators.[20] In any event, the Laeken indicators were adopted *after* the Member States submitted their first NAPincls and, therefore, were only available to structure the second cycle of NAPincls.

[20] It is noteworthy that some Member States—including the UK—were resistant to the idea of the development of indicators that might measure Member States' performance in terms of participation and involving actors. See the European Commission's synthesis of responses to the consultation on the evaluation of the OMC: European Commission, 2006c.

Social indicators are intended to be of direct relevance to the process by which states engage in benchmarking and policy learning (Mabbett, 2007). This process can be more or less constrained and more or less 'top-down' or 'bottom-up'. Certainly, once an indicator is agreed, it can then form the basis of setting targets which might then discipline the process of domestic policy reform (Atkinson, Marlier and Nolan, 2004). However, EU level targets were not considered appropriate. Even in the absence of specific targets, indicators can be used to benchmark Member States' performance in terms of each state's performance over time; their performance relative to other states; and relative to an EU average. However, as Room highlights (2005), indicators like the Laeken indicators that focus on outcomes do not necessarily aid states in determining which sorts of policies produce better outcomes or which policies are more efficient (the relationship between input and output in shaping outcomes). Thus, even if intended to induce learning within a redistribution paradigm, the specific objectives on their own would be unlikely to support 'top-down' lesson-drawing and at best might facilitate some 'bottom-up' contextualized policy development.

After the agreement of the Laeken indicators, work continued on the development of data and indicators. In 2003, the Council and EP adopted a Regulation to establish a dataset on income and living condition to replace the ECHP (EU-SILC).[21] As well as working on the social indicators, the SPC sub-group had to develop indicators for the emerging coordination process on pensions, putting pressure on its limited resources. In its mid-year report in 2003, the sub-group chair also noted that there were problems with two of the Laeken indicators—persons living in jobless households (7) and self-perceived health status (10)—which required work. With the increased importance attached to 'making work pay' within the employment process, there was also a need to develop indicators on in-work poverty.

The problem of fully capturing the phenomenon of social exclusion through the development of common EU indicators can be mitigated by the use of national indicators and national data (tertiary indicators) but with correlative problems of comparison. The problem may lesson over time as new indicators and data are developed. However, the proliferation of indicators creates its own problems. Developing a fine-grained analytical understanding of the extent of poverty and social exclusion—useful for bottom-up contextualized learning—may come at the expense of more 'top-down' lesson

[21] Regulation 1177/2003 of the European Parliament and of the Council of 16 June 2003 concerning Community statistics on income and living conditions (EU-SILC): [2003] OJ L165/1.

drawing or at the least, the identification of key problems and priorities to be addressed by Member States. This was precisely the problem with the use of the social cohesion indicators within the Commission's structural indicators portfolio. In reducing the number of indicators down from 42 in 2002 to 14 in 2003 (European Commission, 2003a), the result was that only the headline 'at-risk-of-poverty' measure was retained (supplemented by a long-term unemployment measure). Although data to support the wider range of structural indicators would still be available, clearly the Commission's intention was to develop stronger political messages for Member States.

In sum, in terms of actors and procedures, the development of the social indicators introduced social scientific experts into the process and created a new organizational structure in the form of the indicators sub-group of the SPC. The material focus of the Laeken indicators gave prominence to issues of low income and in that way projected a rather narrower focus than the 'multidimensionality' of the Nice objectives. While a tool for policy learning, it has been suggested that the indicators alone would be unlikely to facilitate strong 'top-down' lesson-drawing and more likely to contextualize 'bottom-up' reform initiatives. However, in developing the suite of indicators a tension began to emerge between a desire on the one hand, for clearer EU-level political message and priorities to be reflected in a smaller group of indicators, and on the other hand, for the development of more and more indicators to reflect the multidimensionality of the problem of social exclusion and to facilitate more contextualized learning.

Targets

In its contribution to the Lisbon summit,[22] the Commission had proposed targets of halving child poverty by 2010 and of staged reductions in the at-risk-of-poverty rate (60 per cent of median income) from 18 per cent in 2005 to 10 per cent by 2010. Although the summit did not agree to these targets, the Presidency conclusions anticipated that the Council would adopt 'adequate targets' by the end of 2000. The June 2000 meeting of the Employment and Social Affairs Council repeated this, while indicating that targets (and indicators) could be selected by Member States themselves in developing their national reports. However, when the October 2000 Council adopted the common objectives, targets—whether EU or national—were not

[22] *The Lisbon European Council—An Agenda of Economic and Social Renewal*: Doc 6602/00 (28.2.2000).

proposed. Recall that at this time, there were no agreed common indicators which might form the basis for setting targets. The priority lay instead with developing the indicators rather than target-setting although, as Atkinson, Marlier and Nolan note (2004:66), for some, the social inclusion process 'may only be given the same weight as employment and macroeconomy in EU and national decision-making when such targets are in place'.

The utility or otherwise of setting targets to give direction to the process is another manifestation of the broader question of the underlying philosophy or rationale of the coordination process. If the goal is to work with the policy autonomy of Member States to facilitate an open process of learning, with states learning according to their needs and individual situations, then setting centralized targets might be viewed as curtailing the power to self-determine what to learn, how much and from whom. This is the 'bottom-up' interpretation of the rationale for multilateral coordination. If, however, the aim of the process is to drive individual states to improve their policy performance—benchmarked against their own performance over time and/or against the performance of the best performing states—then the process becomes more one of top-down bilateral steering. Member States have tended to repeat their preference for the former over the latter interpretation of the motivating rationale for coordination; hence, the absence of centralized target-setting.

There are other reasons for resisting centralized target-setting. Insofar as the target is an EU-wide one, then no individual state has any particular incentive to increase its policy effort to make progress on the target, and the good progress of some can easily be undermined by the poor performance of others. In any event, as with targets in the public sector more generally, there is always the danger that the wrong targets are selected with policy effort expended in the wrong direction or that short-term target achievement may take priority over longer-term strategies that might yield better results. Moreover—and this point was made particularly by social NGOs—the advantage of the broad Nice objectives over specific targets was that the objectives were flexible enough to cover the multidimensional phenomenon of exclusion. The setting of a target—particularly when attached to a specific indicator—tends to take the focus away from the multidimensional approach. In addition, there was also the fear expressed by the Platform of Social NGOs that a target focusing on the headline at-risk-of-poverty rate might lead to a narrow focus on lifting the group of people just below the 60 per cent level above this threshold, while doing little to help those in deeper poverty.

The Commission returned to the idea of setting targets in its Communication to the Spring Council in Barcelona in 2002 (European

Commission, 2002a) in calling for a halving of the number of people at risk of poverty by 2010 (taking the 1997 figure of 18 per cent as a baseline). This proposal was resisted by the SPC who felt that basing a target on a single indicator was not consistent with the multidimensional approach and the adoption of a portfolio of indicators.[23] Instead, and in order to inject more 'ambition' into the process the SPC proposed that Member States set their own national targets in their NAPincls to be submitted for 2003–2005. This was the approach adopted in the Barcelona European Council Conclusions and elaborated upon in an appendix to the Common Outline adopted to structure the second cycle of NAPincls. This outline strongly encouraged Member States to set 'ambitious but achievable targets' that were 'relevant', 'intelligible', 'quantified and measurable', and 'time specific'. There was a suggestion that Member States consider selecting a small number of headline targets to make a political impact accompanied by more detailed targets through which progress might be monitored. Member States were also encouraged to use the common Laeken indicators as a basis for setting national targets and to benchmark their performance against other states or the three best performing states (the approach which had been used under the EES).

Evidently, the debate about the role of targets within the OMC is a debate about how best to strengthen the process. As such it raises questions about whether the OMC ought to evolve in the manner in which the EES had evolved in its earlier phase or whether the inclusion process was following a different trajectory, motivated by a less 'disciplinary' rationale and instead focusing on the facilitation of 'bottom up' learning. This issue has recurred throughout the life of the social OMC, and as explored in the final chapter, formed part of the debate around the successor to the Lisbon strategy, 'Europe 2020'.

National Action Plans on Inclusion and Joint Reports

In chapter five, consideration will be given to the substantive content of the NAPincls and the extent to which they do or do not evidence a 'Europeanization' of national strategies and policies to combat poverty and social exclusion. Here, the task is to explore the role of the NAPincls together with the joint report reviewing the NAPincls within the OMC architecture. Together, these documents provide a wealth of information and data. The aim of this section is to explore the function of this data collection and information dissemination. Three key aspects are considered. The first is the

[23] Opinion of the SPC adopted on 20 February 2002: Doc. 6644/02.

manner in which the joint reports represent the problem of social exclusion. The second is the capacity of the reports to guide states in what they might learn in tackling problems of social exclusion. The third aspect introduces the 'accountability' dimension of multilateral surveillance.

As Daly describes, (2008) the joint reports serve a function of 'problem representation'. Different aspects of the reports may, however, represent the problem in somewhat different ways. Structurally, the first cycles of joint reports were very lengthy documents containing a political executive summary, a more analytical section on the situation in the EU, and then shorter analyses of each of the Member States' NAPincls. The chapter analysing the situation in the EU generally—in utilizing the data supporting the Laeken indicators—tended to reinforce the 'redistributive' paradigm highlighted by Mabbett (2007). In other words, its focus was on issues relating to low income, including the impact of social transfers. However, the more political assessment of the priorities and challenges facing EU Member States (Table 3.4) reflected other policy frames and paradigms indicating, once again, that rather different signals and steers might emerge within and across different elements of the OMC architecture and might change over time.

Table 3.4 2002 and 2004 Joint Reports: Challenges and Priorities

Joint Report on Social Inclusion 2002	Joint Report on Social Inclusion 2004
Eight Core Challenges: 1. Developing an inclusive labour market and promoting employment as a right and opportunity for all. 2. Guaranteeing an adequate income and resources to live in human dignity. 3. Tackling educational disadvantage. 4. Preserving family solidarity and protecting the rights of children. 5. Ensuring good accommodation for all. 6. Guaranteeing equal access to and investing in high quality services (health, transport, social, care, cultural, recreational and legal). 7. Improving the delivery of services. 8. Regenerating areas of multiple deprivation.	Six Key Priorities: 1. Promoting investment in and tailoring of active labour market measures to meet the needs of those who have the greatest difficulties in accessing employment. 2. Ensuring that social protection schemes are adequate and accessible for all and that they provide effective work incentives for those who can work. 3. Increasing the access of the most vulnerable and those most at risk of social exclusion to decent housing, quality health and lifelong learning opportunities. 4. Implementing a concerted effort to prevent early school leaving and to promote smooth transition from school to work. 5. Developing a focus on eliminating poverty and social exclusion among children. 6. Making a drive to reduce poverty and social exclusion of immigrants and ethnic minorities.

Comparing the two reports, one can discern shifts in the representation of policy problems and priorities. The eight core challenges of the 2002 report are consistent with the 'multidimensional' approach of the Nice objectives in which the problem of social exclusion is framed by reference to a range of policy fields and forms of intervention that are consistent with a 'citizenship' paradigm. The 2004 report signified a narrowing of focus. Changes include moving from 'inclusive' labour markets, to 'active' labour markets; from subjective income adequacy and a right to human dignity to the adequacy of social protection systems. Some issues are lost—the focus on public services and areas of multiple deprivation—consistent with a move to focusing on individuals and the identification of particular target groups. The 'multidimensional' framing of the problem is replaced by a stronger emphasis on labour market participation and reforms to social protection systems in 2004, consistent with the increasing emphasis of the 'activation' paradigm. The 2004 report also appeared to signify an increased preoccupation with the situation of specific target groups. The issue of whether to focus policy coordination on target groups had been raised as the OMC process was being constructed but had not been adopted as an approach. The 2004 report, however, highlighted the situation of certain vulnerable groups outside the labour market: children, early school leavers not in training or employment, ethnic minorities and immigrants.

If the joint reports were intended to reinforce or supplement other aspects of the OMC in developing certain thematic priorities to be pursued within or alongside the Nice objectives, its more fundamental function was to act as a mechanism for reviewing national policies and strategies reported in the NAPincls. In their 2004 joint report (European Commission and Council, 2004), the Commission and Council described the role of the NAPincls in the following terms:[24]

> The fundamental reason for Member States to develop National Action Plans is to enable them to review and further strengthen their policies and programs with a view to moving them on to a new level of effectiveness. Member States approach this task from very different starting points both in terms of the level of poverty and social exclusion, in terms of their very different welfare traditions and in the light of different structures of governance.

[24] Joint Report by the Commission and the Council on social inclusion (2004): Doc. 7101/04.

Thus, it was accepted that Member States were differentially situated, with the analytical emphasis lying on moving each state forward from its starting position. In that sense, Member States were primarily benchmarked against their own initial position with successive NAPincls intended to strategically advance the Member States policies and programmes. Not surprisingly, then, a key function of the joint report was to analyse what was new about national policies and strategies to combat social exclusion rather than to consider the overall effectiveness of those systems.[25] Indeed, the 2002 report stated that its role was not to assess the effectiveness of the policies and programmes in place in the Member States (European Commission and Council, 2002). Rather the intention was to review how well Member States used their NAPincls and the OMC methodology strategically to plan their social inclusion policies and programmes. This approach has a number of implications.

First, it implied that a fundamental function of multilateral surveillance was to review domestic adaptation to the OMC as a process with a particular emphasis on the process by which Member States constructed their NAPincls, selected what they choose to report in light of the common objectives and indicators, and how strategic the NAPincls were. In other words, it was not directly concerned with substantive policy effectiveness. This is evident when we consider the rather limited set of critical messages which originally emanated from the review process. States were criticized for not fulfilling the fourth Nice objective of mobilizing all relevant actors—civil society, regional and local authorities, the social partners—in the process of preparing the NAPincls. Member States were criticized for treating their NAPincls as reports of their situations rather than as strategic plans clearly benchmarking their progressive development. Certainly the first round of NAPincls were more in the nature of reports not least because of the relatively short period of time Member States were given to prepare them. The common outline produced for the second round of NAPincls, therefore, encouraged states to be more prospective and forward looking and to develop national targets, emphasizing a disciplinary aspect of the process. Failures to reflect the multidimensionality of social exclusion and its gender dimension were also highlighted. But these substantive concerns are really to do with their representation in the reports rather than direct criticisms

[25] '... the report will tend to privilege recent action and may neglect more structural policies or institutions that concur in a decisive manner to promote social inclusion': European Commission and Council, 2004: 7.

of the substance or effectiveness of policy. Instead the focus was simply on the analysis of how well the Member States appeared to be responding to the OMC as a process, not whether Member States' policies and strategies were effective.

The Member States also resisted any attempt to rank the quality of their NAPincls. Prior to the agreement of first joint report the Commission adopted a Communication (European Commission, 2001a). In itself, this was interesting as it indicated that the Commission did want to have an independent voice in the review process, mirroring to some extent its independent right of initiative in the legislative process. However, the Communication encountered criticism from Member States because it ranked states according to the strategic and integrated nature of their NAPincls. This produced a ranking of states: the first group—Denmark, France and the Netherlands—were said to have comprehensive, proactive and preventative approaches; the second—Portugal, Finland, Sweden and the UK—were considered to be strong on diagnosis but only Finland and Sweden were highlighted as having 'developed universal social protection systems' (the UK was said to have been offended not to have been included); the third—Belgium, Germany, Spain, Italy and Ireland—were generally criticized for the lack of a coherent overall strategy integrating different levels of government (while Ireland already had a National Anti-Poverty Strategy, it had not updated or refocused the strategy in light of the Nice objectives); with the fourth group—Greece, Luxembourg and Austria—presenting only a snapshot of current activities. This typology did not reappear in the finally agreed report. For the second round of NAPincls, the Commission agreed to discuss its draft Communication in the SPC but continued to publish a separate Communication in advance of the joint report.

Secondly, there was an attempt to generate more motivation or ambition in national strategies. Take the following statement in the 2004 joint report:

> What has already been achieved by some countries in terms of social development needs to be built on even further. Other countries need to aspire to the benchmark set by the most successful and to progressively close the gap.

States were exhorted to have the ambition to not only advance from their current positions (moving up) but also to benchmark that ambition in terms of 'successful' states (aiming high). But it is not clear how states should determine what it would mean to be 'successful' or what it is that makes states good performers. From a learning perspective, simply presenting a whole range of data and examples of practices and policies does not necessarily highlight which policies are the most efficient in tackling poverty and social exclusion; which examples might constitute 'best practices'; and which best practices might be usefully adopted by Member States, given their different welfare traditions and systems. Thus, in avoiding direct analysis of the policy performance of states and in recognizing that there was little basis on which to identify 'good' practices, the 2002 joint report retreated into simply providing disconnected examples of national practices (good or otherwise) and critiques of the NAPincls in terms of their scope and ambition.

Thirdly, the process is clearly intended to be inclusive in the sense that it is to be relevant for all states, including the best performing states. All states are encouraged to move forward from their starting position regardless of whether that could be classified as a poor or good performance. If we take a comparison with the implementation of an EU directive, if a Member State's laws already meet the standards required by the directive it need do no more to transpose the directive into national law. By contrast, the OMC methodology seeks to encourage a continual process of improvement even for 'high-performing' states. While laudable in making the process relevant for all states, it does raise the question of priorities: is it as important for successful states to do more or as it is for poorly performing states to do better? Moreover, as Daly highlights (2008) it can result in states being subject to criticism for preparing NAPincls which do little other than highlight how effective their current arrangements are. This could lead to a situation in which the poor performing states are applauded for their motivation and effort to be better, but the best performing states lamented for their lack of ambition to be even better.

In sum, the first cycles of review can be characterized as at best creating a context for decentralized and contextualized policy learning but without the process making it clear what states ought to learn from the elaborate information-gathering and information-dissemination exercise. The difficulty with a rationale for coordination premised on 'bottom-up' learning is, however, that it throws into question whether a multilateral free-for-all is actually an efficient way of structuring that process. In the absence of stronger lesson-drawing steers, there is a danger that the exercise descends into an overly elaborate 'show-and-tell' exercise, with the potential benefits of the exchange of information insufficiently directly attributable to the process of 'coordination' itself. Moreover, in its attempt to 'represent' the problem of social exclusion, rather mixed messages were projected: the statistical analysis tended to follow the Laeken indicators in representing a more 'redistributive' paradigm (Mabbett, 2007) while the more political analysis indicated a move towards the 'activation' paradigm at the expense of the 'citizenship' paradigm and the representation of social exclusion as a multidimensional problem.

Thinking back to the discussion in chapter two concerning the 'governing' and 'accountability' dimensions of the monitoring and evaluation of NAPincls it is apparent that in the first cycles of the process there was little by way of a strong accountability pressure placed on states. In a process in which those giving the account—the Member States—are also part of the forum to which the account is given, and in the absence of a more independent role for the European Commission, the result was largely an information-swapping exercise. Moreover, as regards 'passing judgment'—identified by Bovens as a key aspect of the accountability process (Bovens, 2007)—the structure of 'joint' reports allowed rather different judgments to emerge. For example, in the 2004 joint report emphasis was placed on the importance of 'high levels of investment in policies to promote social inclusion' and on 'high levels of social investment' as a means of achieving the Lisbon strategic goal leading to the conclusion that 'the most socially progressive countries within the Union are also among the most economically advanced' (European Commission and Council, 2004: 3). However, this had not been in the Commission's original draft text. In this way, with both the Commission presenting its draft and then the Commission and SPC bargaining out the joint report, it was inevitable that rather different conclusions might be drawn from, or different emphases placed on, the analysis of the national reports and the data. This might be considered to undermine the capacity of EU institutions to convey clear judgments to the Member States.

Of course, that the reviewing process shied away from strong critical assessments of domestic policy performance did not prevent other actors using the data presented in the NAPincls and the joint reports from so doing. These documents are resources for academics and for NGOs many of whom have carried out their own evaluation exercises either of the Lisbon strategy as a whole or of more specific processes. This highlights the extent to which the reporting function of the OMC can facilitate a process of accountability to a set of actors outside of the EU institutional framework (see eg Jacobsson's analysis of the EES and inclusion processes in Sweden and Denmark: 2005). How deep that accountability process extends outside a core of 'insider' outsiders—particularly to national parliaments—is, of course, debateable (Benz, 2007), as is its ability to generate critical feedback that might then produce changes in domestic policy.

The Community Action Programme

The analysis presented this far has concentrated on the three elements of the OMC architecture which are typically studied: the common objectives, indicators, and mechanism for multilateral surveillance. As indicated, within and across these different elements, the paradigmatic representation of social exclusion can be portrayed in rather different ways. Another dimension to the coherence of the governance architecture relates to the relationship between the elements identified and the 'action programme' intended to enhance the EU's intervention to combat poverty. The process described above has been supported by the multi-annual programme envisaged in the Commission's *Building an Inclusive Europe* Communication. Proposed by the Commission in June 2000,[26] the Community Action Programme would support the OMC through three strands of activities:

- understanding and quantifying social exclusion—indicators and statistics, thematic studies;
- policy cooperation, exchanges of information and best practices—transnational exchange projects, peer reviews, network of independent experts, awareness-raising projects;
- promoting participation and dialogue—core-funding of key networks, roundtables and Presidency events.

The programme was intended to run from 1 January 2001–31 December 2005 with an overall budget of €70 million. However, negotiations over the package took a year longer than anticipated. With a legal basis of Article 137 (2) EC (specifying the use of the co-decision procedure), the negotiations between the Commission, Council and EP went all the way through to a conciliation stage: an increasingly unusual phenomenon in EU decision-making. Particular sticking points were the size of the budget and what type of programme committee to establish. As regards the former, the EP had amended the proposal to raise the size of the budget to €100 million; the compromise reached was for a total budget of €75 million. As regards the latter, this was a manifestation of a familiar battle between the Council and EP over which type of comitology procedure to use: the Council's preference for a 'management' committee prevailed over the EP's preference for an advisory committee. The effect of the inter-institutional wrangling was to push the time frame for the action programme back a year to run from 1 January

[26] [2000] OJ C337E/130.

2002–31 December 2006. Thus by the time of the eventual adoption of the Decision[27] and the start of the programme, the first cycle of NAPincls had already been submitted.

However, the programme has been relevant to the development of the OMC process in a number of ways. First, the Programme 2002–2006 provided initial financial contributions for up to three years for five transnational NGOs—European Anti-Poverty Network (EAPN), European Federation of National Organisations working with the Homeless (FEANTSA), Eurochild, European Transnational Network for Social Inclusion (RETIS) and the European Public Social Platform (EPSP)—aiding their participation in the process. Related to this, it supported awareness-raising programmes at national level: for example, it funded the 'Get Heard' project in the UK that facilitated workshops intended to help those experiencing poverty get involved in the second NAPincl (on which see chapter five and Pemberton, 2008). In this way, the programme supported the fourth Nice objective to 'mobilize all relevant actors'.

Secondly, 'peer reviews' were conducted under the management of this programme, with research institutes tendering to organize the review process. These thematic peer reviews are intended to support and facilitate the exchange of best practice and mutual learning. Taking place usually over two days, the peer reviews take the form of seminars hosted by a state show-casing an example of its good practice. A discussion document is prepared by the host state, with comments from participating states (normally five to six self-selecting 'reviewing' states), and participation from thematic experts and the peer review managers as well as representatives from the European Commission. Each review is completed by the production of a synthesis report summarizing the review and identifying possibilities for lesson-drawing for other states. The emphasis, therefore, is on self-selection of topics and of participants 'opting-in' to any given seminar rather than the process being driven by the Commission.[28] The peer review process did not begin until 2004—with fifteen peer reviews held between 2004–2005—and therefore, the reviews drew on the NAPincls and joint reports rather than feeding into them.

[27] Decision 50/2002/EC of the European Parliament and of the Council establishing a programme of Community action to encourage cooperation between Member States to combat social exclusion: [2002] OJ L10/1.

[28] See the final report of the evaluation of the peer reviews in 2004 and 2005 available at <http://www.peer-review-social-inclusion.net/peer-reviews/results-of-the-peer-reviews-2004-and-2005-2/final_report_pr-2004_2005.pdf> (Accessed in March 2010).

While positively evaluated by those participating in the reviews—indeed one interviewee felt that the thematic peer reviews were more useful for contextualized mutual learning than the general coordination methodology—an evaluation of the action programme concluded that there was little evidence of a wider dissemination of the results of the peer reviews outside of this small group and that 'institutional learning is not systematically taking place as a result of the Peer Review Programme' (European Commission, 2006a).

Thirdly, the programme also supports a network of experts. Established in 2003, the network provides critical independent appraisals of Member States' NAPincls by drawing on the national expertise of its members. While the experts' critical analysis of the NAPincls 2001–2003 was intended to inform the 2003–2005 NAPincls, there was insufficient time between the establishment of the network in early 2003 and the submission of the second round of NAPincls in July 2003 for this to occur. However, the expert contributions were available to Commission staff in preparing the joint report 2004 and these reports can create a form of expert accountability beyond the political accountability function of the joint reports described above.

What emerged, therefore, was a hybrid process combining, on the one hand, an OMC methodology and, on the other, a supporting financial instrument funding strands of activities intended to feed into the coordination methodology. In some ways, this can be viewed as a marriage of a new governance tool with a somewhat older style of EU policy intervention in the social sphere. But this 'hybrid' approach also contained within it sources of potential tension and rivalry. Recall that the Commission's *Building an Inclusive Europe* communication had viewed this financial instrument as its primary operational tool with outputs from it likely to feed into other coordination processes rather than supporting a distinctive OMC to combat social exclusion. Moreover, even if it would feed into a specific OMC, the question of what would really drive learning—the general cyclical coordination process or the thematic and contextual approach of the action programme—would remain open. Finally, in institutional terms, we ended up with two different types of steering committees—the political SPC and the management programme committee—but with the boundaries of responsibilities, the setting of priorities and the general interaction between the two largely ill-defined, albeit moderated to some extent by the duplication of some personnel across the two committees.

Conclusions

The analysis presented here has focused on the emergence of the OMC to combat social exclusion as a process of institutionalization and institution-building operating at the constitutional, policy and governance levels. The process of institutionalization has been characterized here in terms of the process, material and actor dimensions of institutions. In light of that analysis, the following conclusions can be drawn.

The first reflection is that in terms of *process*, a relatively stable methodology of policy coordination developed and was applied across two initial cycles of the process. Unlike the economic and employment coordination processes, that stability was not referable to a treaty-derived process and, despite constitutional change in which action to combat social exclusion was made a material objective within EU law, no attempt was made to 'constitutionalize' the OMC at a procedural level. Rather it relied on repeated patterns of interactions between actors—including new formal institutional actors like the SPC—and the development of new processes of interaction between officials of the Member States and the EU's institutions, and between governmental and non-governmental actors. Nonetheless, the issue of legal institutionalization of process became of significance as the constitutional context changed and, as is explored in chapter four, in further rounds of treaty reforms the issue of 'constitutionalizing' the OMC was debated.

Secondly, the OMC process also departed from earlier attempts at social policy coordination under the 1992 Recommendations. The 1992 Recommendations created a textual and formal basis for coordination that was 'law-like but law-lite' (Armstrong and Kilpatrick, 2007). That is to say that the process of promulgating the Recommendations followed the normal legislative process of the EU involving the Commission, Council and Parliament. The form and language of the Recommendations was typical of EU directives: the point of departure was the non-binding nature of the Recommendations. By contrast the OMC process developed outside of the normal 'Community Method' of decision-making, with its textual sources ranging from Presidency Conclusions to SPC Opinions and Council minutes. In methodological terms, lawyers are familiar with interpreting legal texts. These texts assume a certain style in EU law and are published in particular forms. The task of the lawyer is not fundamentally one of uncovering the texts but rather of taking a given text and suggesting its meaning and its relationship to other similar texts. With the OMC, the researcher must discover and draw on a range of general texts—Commission 'Communications'; the 'Opinions' of supporting committees; 'Conclusions' of the Council of Ministers and European Council—as well as the specific texts generated through the policy coordination process—common objectives, indicators, national reports, peer reviews, joint reports. While the presence of an 'authoritative' legal text does not itself create a singular interpretation, the absence of such a text and the plurality of a range of documents serving a variety of purposes does make the discovery and interpretation of the development of social policy a rather more demanding exercise. Thus, when Szyszczak stated that 'Lisbon' was associated with the institutionalization of a new social policy 'paradigm', she was also careful to note that discerning the content of that paradigm required analysis of a wide range of documents and materials, both pre- and post-dating the Lisbon European Council (Szyszczak, 2001). As Borrás and Jacobsson (2004) highlight, the OMC process is, therefore, different from other examples of EU intervention typically described as 'soft law'. Indeed, the concept of 'soft law' is one so over-stretched as to exert very little analytical purchase on the emergence and evolution of the OMC.

Thirdly, in more *material* terms, the starting point has to be the new commitments made in the treaties to combat social exclusion, amplified and reiterated in the Lisbon Presidency Conclusions in the undertaking of the EU and Member States to make a decisive impact on the eradication of poverty. In terms of Europeanizing action to combat social exclusion, these statements underpin EU intervention in a new way. However, once we attempt to add more specific content to these commitments it quickly becomes apparent that competing policy frames and policy paradigms act upon the materialization of social exclusion as a subject of concern. In terms of policy frames, a depiction of social exclusion as a 'multidimensional' phenomenon allows a very broad range of policy fields to act upon the representation of the problem of social exclusion. However, it was also possible to view EU intervention as motivated by a somewhat narrower sub-policy field, namely modernizing social protection policies. Viewed from the latter perspective, the decision to focus initially on social inclusion was simply a means of prioritizing work with the ambition always being to focus more on the issue of reform to national social protection systems. As regards policy paradigms, three different paradigms can be detected within policy discourses: a 'citizenship' paradigm, an 'activation' paradigm and a 'redistribution' paradigm. In this way, the problem of social exclusion can be represented in rather different ways and the initial development of the OMC might best be described as an unstable institutionalization of all three paradigms within and across different elements of the OMC methodology.

Fourthly, unlike early episodes of EU social policy intervention the material justification for coordination in this area was not one functionally connected to managing the consequences of market integration (with its potential spillovers and externalities) but rather one based on the apparent positive-sum gains to be derived from policy learning. Nonetheless, the issue then is the degree to which the process seeks to structure what is learned. As was identified in chapter two, learning can be conducted within highly constrained 'top-down' benchmarking processes or relatively open 'bottom-up' and decentralized processes of problem and solution identification. The early cycles of the OMC tended to emphasize the latter, with top-down pressures exerted largely at the level of the adaptation of the national systems to the OMC process rather than at the level of the evaluation of the substance and effectiveness of domestic policy.

Finally, as regards *actors*, it is often said that the OMC has given a particularly central role to the European Council, to be contrasted with the exclusion of the European Parliament and the EU courts. Certainly, meetings of the European Council have been particularly significant at the constitutional and system levels, both in terms of treaty change—the amendments to the treaties creating the new employment and social titles—and in terms of the adoption of the Lisbon strategy and the launch of specific coordination processes. But while this impetus to coordinate can be attributable to this high level, the concrete process of building the institutional design of OMC has been conducted more at the level of the Commission and the Council with new actors—especially the Social Protection Committee—playing a key guiding and mediating role. What is also distinctive about the OMC in terms of its institutionalization is its openness to a range of actors. While it is clear that certain actors like the European Parliament have struggled to work out how to engage with and influence the OMC, other actors—social NGOs and academic experts—have found new channels of access within the process.

4

Relaunching the Lisbon Strategy and the Streamlining of Policy Coordination

Introduction

The emergence of a process of policy coordination to combat poverty and social exclusion in the EU was analysed in the previous chapter. This process developed out of the Lisbon strategy with its aspiration to promote economic growth and employment while safeguarding the European Social Model. Although Member States remained competent to decide upon their economic, employment and social welfare policies, the intention of the Lisbon strategy was that these policies would be increasingly Europeanized, including through the influence of mechanisms and institutions of policy coordination: the 'open method of coordination' (OMC). An OMC to combat poverty and social exclusion was launched in 2000 and, as was discussed in the previous chapter, two cycles of the coordination process were completed by 2004.

The period from 2005 onwards represents a time of significant development for the Europeanization of social exclusion. Adopting the same organizing framework utilized in chapter three, in this chapter, an evolving process of institutionalization—of procedures, of the role of actors and organizational structures, and of the material content of policy—is explored at the constitutional, policy and governance levels. However, of particular significance in this chapter is the dimension of institutional change and the analysis here seeks to account for change between the first and second generations of the OMC to combat poverty and social exclusion.

At the constitutional level, a process of treaty reform was underway that was couched in an explicitly 'constitutional' language (Weiler, 2005) and resulted in the adoption of a Constitutional Treaty. Whether or not to 'constitutionalize' the OMC was debated prior to and within the constitutional reform process. Any decision to embed or anchor the OMC—either as a generic EU governance tool or to make specific provision for a social OMC process analogous to the treaty-based employment and economic policy processes—would be expected significantly to raise the profile of EU action in this area. Of course, the Constitutional Treaty project failed when the text was rejected in referenda in France and the Netherlands. Nonetheless, this moment of potential institutional and constitutional change and the encounter between EU 'constitutionalism' and new tools of EU governance like the OMC, was revealing about the possibilities and limits to institutionalizing the OMC within a more clearly defined legal framework.[1]

At the policy level, significant changes took place that had both direct and indirect impacts on the OMC to combat poverty and social exclusion. In 2005, following on from critical evaluations of the Lisbon strategy from 'High-Level' groups chaired by Sapir (Sapir et al, 2004) and Kok (Kok et al, 2004), and with the appointment of a new European Commission, came a refocusing of the policy priorities of the Lisbon strategy to concentrate on 'growth and jobs'. Not surprisingly, this concentration of energy and attention on the economic and employment policy sides of the original Lisbon triangle, to the apparent exclusion of the social side, raised concerns as to the potential de-materialization of social policy from Lisbon's policy matrix. Simultaneously, within EU social policy itself, new policy coordination techniques had emerged or were emerging in the fields of pensions[2] and health and long-term care:[3] areas of activity which, together with social inclusion, had been identified as key to 'modernizing' social protection systems (European Commission, 1999). In policy terms, the association of efforts to combat poverty and social exclusion with an overarching agenda of modernizing social protection systems and ideas of 'active inclusion' could be interpreted as a dilution of the particular commitment to making a decisive impact on poverty as undertaken by the European Council in Lisbon in 2000 and as framing action in this field more directly towards the goals of economic and employment policy coordination, ie, of constraining social expenditure to the demands of budgetary discipline and of 'activating' welfare recipients into the labour market.

[1] See de Búrca, 2003; Zeitlin, 2005b; Walker, 2006; Armstrong, 2008.

[2] European Commission (2000d, 2001b); Social Protection Committee, *Adequate and Sustainable Pensions*: Doc. 8792/01; Social Protection Committee and the Economic Policy Committee, *Joint report on objectives and working methods in the area of pensions*: Doc. 14098/01; European Commission and Council Joint report, *Adequate and Sustainable Pensions*: Doc. 7165/03.

[3] European Commission and Council Joint report, *Supporting national strategies for the future of health care and care for the elderly*: Doc. 7166/03; European Commission (2004).

Changes at the policy level also translated into significant changes to the governance architecture of EU social policy coordination. In 2005 the European Commission set out the basis for an overarching 'Social Protection and Social Inclusion' OMC (European Commission, 2005a), covering the areas of social inclusion, pensions and healthcare[4] with new common objectives, indicators and a reporting cycle to run in parallel with the relaunched Lisbon partnership for growth and jobs. It is to institutional change at the constitutional, governance and policy levels that the analysis now turns.

The Constitutional Context

If the first phase of the OMC to combat social exclusion was largely a means of delivering on the treaty provisions relating to combating poverty introduced by the Amsterdam Treaty, the second phase of development took place in the shadow of the treaty reforms associated with the Constitutional Treaty. Although a relatively recent innovation in EU governance, the idea of the OMC as a tool of governance had gained some currency in political and academic circles and, therefore, attention turned to the issue of whether to 'constitutionalize' the OMC. Of course, the debates surrounding EU social governance were wider than merely the issue of whether to give a clearer treaty foundation to the OMC. It encompassed questions of social values and whether the EU needed a stronger legislative competence in the social sphere. Indeed, as Trubek and Trubek argue (2005b), while for proponents of the OMC, the constitutional 'moment' was an opportunity to advance the cause of decentralized policy coordination, for opponents, the debate was a distraction from the 'real' work of pushing for a greater centralization of EU political authority over social issues. For present purposes, the analysis does not concern itself with whether the EU needed a 'stronger' social dimension (an issue explored in depth in chapters six, seven

[4] As regards the fourth strand of action—'making work pay'—the Commission produced a Communication on this in 2003 (European Commission, 2003c). As a theme cutting across both the reform of social protection systems and the European Employment Strategy, this strand did not produce a distinctive coordination process but rather the issues were absorbed into the employment and social protection and inclusion processes. It is also worth noting that EU-level social NGOs raised objections to some aspects of the Communication: see Social Platform Press Release, *Making Work Pay: Stigmatising the non-employed and endangering the European Social Model* (15.1.2004).

and eight). Instead, it explores the very possibility of constitutionalizing the OMC.

As Walker has suggested (2006a), constitutionalism can refer to a range of different qualities—*nominalism* (the expansive scope of the constitutional concept); *textualism* (the use of law as a mode of recognition and coding); *hierarchy* (the priority to be afforded to that which is coded and recognized as constitutional); and *self-containment* (the autonomy and comprehensiveness of the constitutional claim)—and can generate a range of potential relationships between 'constitutionalism' and 'governance'—*subsumption* (absorption of one within the other); *instrumentalism* (using one towards the ends of the other); *non-correspondence* (an inability of constitutionalism to engage with forms of governance); *structural antagonism* (a contradictory relationship); and *transformation* (a reflexive mutual engagement of constitutionalism and governance). As will be suggested below, infusing the debates concerning the constitutionalization of the OMC were these quite different conceptualizations of the potential relationships between constitutionalism and new forms of governance. For proponents of the OMC, the Constitutional Treaty afforded an opportunity for an instrumental usage of constitutionalism towards governance ends (through both nominalism and textualism in Walker's typology). For sceptics, constitutionalization could serve the different instrumental goal of constraining the use of the OMC (subsumption), or it might hold the OMC at arm's length to the central constitutional preoccupation with defining and limiting the spheres of EU legislative competence (non-correspondence) or its accommodation might undermine the aspiration of competence clarity (structural antagonism). Not surprisingly then the encounter between constitutionalism and the OMC proved to be a difficult one to manage, with the OMC tending to occupy an unsettled constitutional and institutional space (Armstrong, 2008).

Even before the work of the Convention on the Future of Europe got underway, the role of the OMC within the EU's governance architecture had been explored in the European Commission's *European Governance* White Paper (European Commission 2001c). Governance Working Group 4a had given broad support to policy coordination as a governance technique but as a complement rather than a rival to EU law-making. It noted that the working methods of EU institutions were premised upon the Community Method rather than policy coordination. It highlighted the potential for the Commission's right of initiative to be usurped by the European Council and indicated a desire for parliamentary scrutiny of the OMC. The Working Group's report also highlighted wider concerns that the OMC might drive out 'hard law' or conversely might be a substitute for it but in areas where legislative competence had not been attributed to the EU.

In accepting a complementary role for the OMC to that of the Community Method, the White Paper itself sounded a stronger cautionary note in identifying the following as the preconditions for the use of OMC:

> The use of the open method of coordination must not dilute the achievement of common objectives in the Treaty or the political responsibility of the Institutions. It should not be used when legislative action under the Community method is possible; it should ensure overall accountability in line with the following requirements:
>
> - It should be used to achieve defined Treaty objectives.
> - Regular mechanisms for reporting to the European Parliament should be established.
> - The Commission should be closely involved and play a co-ordinating role.
> - The data and information generated should be widely available. It should provide the basis for determining whether legislative or programme-based action is needed to overcome particular problems highlighted.

What is instructive about the White Paper is that it reflected conflicting evaluations of the desirability of formally recognizing the role of the OMC as a new tool of EU governance. On the one hand there was a wish to formalize and acknowledge the mechanism, but on the other a desire to contain and constrain its use *vis à vis* the traditional Community Method, as well as to adapt and reform the OMC in line with the institutional elements of that method. In other words, and to use Walker's typology (2006a), constitutionalization of the OMC would have strong textual/nominal as well as instrumental connotations. In this way, the White Paper debate rehearsed arguments that were later to manifest themselves in the debates surrounding the Constitutional Treaty.

Within the Convention drafting the Constitutional Treaty, there was a broad consensus within the Working Groups on the desirability of including some form of horizontal treaty clause identifying the OMC as a tool of EU governance (see de Búrca and Zeitlin, 2003; Tsakatika, 2004). As Zeitlin notes, one of the Convention Vice-Presidents Guiliano Amato, prepared a draft text that would, in generic fashion, constitutionalize the OMC as a tool of EU governance (Zeitlin, 2005b). However, neither the draft nor the final Treaty establishing a Constitution for Europe[5] contained such a horizontal clause. What explains this failure to 'constitutionalize' the OMC?

[5] Treaty Establishing a Constitution for Europe: [2004] OJ C310/1.

First, even for proponents of the OMC, the difficulty with proposing any kind of horizontal definition of the OMC lay with how to define the process. The Lisbon Presidency Conclusions give a rather poor definition of the OMC process and would not be a suitable basis for a treaty amendment. Moreover, any attempt to define the methodology would simply expose the high level of differentiation evident across different policy coordination processes undermining the 'singular' identity ascribed to policy coordination through its labelling as 'OMC' (see Laffan and Shaw, 2005).

Secondly, if instead of trying to capture the essence of disparate extant OMC processes, the members of the Convention had tried to invent an ideal-type OMC, they would be faced with the choice of whether to make the OMC more or less prescriptive, more or less multilateral and more or less democratic and transparent. As Tsakatika observes (2004), the option of the status quo—an ad hoc and political control over the institutional design of OMC—trumped the alternative of having to make tough political and normative choices and then to embed that choice in law. One of the virtues of the OMC has been its relative non-legalization and its institutionalization through practice. Nonetheless, the decision not to develop a more prescriptive template for the OMC also meant that any impetus to animate the institutional design of the OMC through constitutional values—democracy and transparency, subsidiarity and proportionality—was either lost or rendered in an ad hoc manner (Zeitlin, 2005b).

Thirdly, if differentiation in design is interpreted as an experimental strength of the OMC then any attempt to prescribe the architecture of OMC would run the risk of strangling the very experimentalism from which the OMC draws normative strength. While avoidance of this 'rigidification' of the OMC (de Búrca and Zeitlin, 2003) argued in favour of a fairly loose stab at defining the OMC in the Constitutional Treaty, it did rather beg the question of whether the OMC would be better off as a form of institutionalized praxis rather than a constitutionalized ideal-type.

Finally, as Tsakatika notes (2004:97), '[O]pen coordination defies the logic of clear allocations of competence'. As de Búrca highlights, a central objective of the Constitution was to agree definitions of categories of competence, and then to allocate policy fields to these categories as part of a strategy of presenting European constitutionalism as one founded on 'limited EU powers, clarity in the division of competences between States and the EU, and the shaping of an effective and visible EU government' (de Búrca, 2003: 814). The Constitutional Treaty had identified three 'generic' categories of competence—exclusive, shared and supporting—and two 'sectoral' areas—coordination in the economic and employment spheres, and the common foreign and security policy competence. However, the OMC did not fit neatly into either the generic or sectoral categories of competence.

As regards generic competence, in addition to the familiar categories of 'exclusive' and 'shared' competence, the drafters sought to introduce a third general form of competence in respect of the Union's competence 'to carry out actions to support, coordinate or supplement the actions of the Member States, without thereby superseding their competence in these areas'.[6] This could have opened the door to treating the OMC as one species of this generic competence. However, the areas identified for the exercise of this competence—including human health, education and industrial policies—did not precisely match the fields where the OMC process was in operation, including the social policy domain.[7] In other words, while the 'category' of competence could accommodate the use of the OMC, the 'catalogue' of policy areas in which this competence could be exercised omitted the social policy domain in which OMC processes were operative.[8]

As regards the sectoral areas of competence it was noteworthy that only the treaty-based coordination processes for economic and employment policies were identified.[9] Nonetheless, the catalogue of areas in which this competence applied also made reference to social policy coordination.[10] However, whereas provision was made for the *mandatory* coordination of economic and employment policies, social policy coordination was presented as *discretionary*. The effect was not to treat economic, employment and social policy coordination as different species of the same genus, but rather to treat economic and employment policy coordination as if they were the genus of competence of which social policy would be a particular—subservient—species. This perpetuated a constitutional and legal distinction between the different coordination processes.

An alternative to the constitutional inclusion of a horizontal clause on the OMC would have been to make the institutional roles and processes of policy coordination more explicit in the substantive provisions of Part III of the Constitution. The model of the treaty provisions for the economic and employment coordination processes could have been used, thereby creating symmetry within the treaties in the treatment of policy coordination in different

[6] Article I-12(5) CT, now Article 2(5) TFEU.

[7] Article I-17 CT, now Article 6 TFEU.

[8] Note that Article III-210 phrased the Union's competence in the social field in terms of supporting and complementing the activities of the Member States.

[9] Article I-12(3) CT, now Article 2(3) TFEU.

[10] Article I-15 CT, now Article 5 TFEU.

substantive policy domains. Certainly, for Vandenbroucke—then Minister for Social Affairs and Pensions in the Belgian Federal Government and a key protagonist in the development of the EU's intervention in the social sphere—one way of 'anchoring' the social OMCs more firmly in the constitutional structure of the Union was to look more directly at amendments to the substantive social policy provisions of the treaty (see de Búrca and Zeitlin 2003). The difficulty, of course, is that this might rigidify the praxis of OMC in the social policy domain: a point to be kept in mind when we consider the substantial changes to the governance architecture of the social OMC processes below.

Vandenbroucke proposed a new treaty article that would, in broad terms, make provision for an OMC on Social Protection and Social Inclusion. Instead what the Constitution adopted—rather hurriedly at the last minute (see Zeitlin, 2005b)—was a very muddled set of social provisions. On the one hand, the Constitution more or less replicated Article 137 EC by making action to combat social exclusion and to modernize social protection systems specific objectives of EU social policy.[11] On the other hand, the Constitution introduced a new set of social provisions couched in more explicit OMC-type language which exhorted the Commission to 'encourage cooperation between the Member States and facilitate the coordination of their action in all social policy fields' covered by that chapter of the Treaty and, more particularly in a list of enumerated areas.[12] Importantly, it continued:

> To this end, the Commission shall act in close contact with Member States by making studies, delivering opinions and arranging consultations both on problems arising at national level and on those of concern to international organisations, in particular initiatives aiming at the establishment of guidelines and indicators, the organisation of exchange of best practice, and the preparation of the necessary elements for periodic monitoring and evaluation. The European Parliament shall be kept fully informed.

It is noteworthy that, in addition to casting social policy intervention more directly within the language and technique of the OMC, this new article would also institutionalize—albeit relatively weakly—an accountability function for the European Parliament. But equally striking is the indicative list of policy areas in which such policy cooperation was to be encouraged:

(a) employment;
(b) labour law and working conditions;

[11] Article III-210 CT, now Article 153 TFEU.
[12] Article III-213 CT, now Article 156 TFEU.

(c) basic and advanced vocational training;
(d) social security;
(e) prevention of occupational accidents and diseases;
(f) occupational hygiene;
(g) the right of association and collective bargaining between employers and workers.

Neither the fields of action to combat social exclusion nor the modernization of social protection are specifically identified in this list. The result is a rather unclear distinction between general policy cooperation—which would be a basis for the existing OMC to combat social exclusion—and the more explicit provision for social policy coordination which would apparently not provide a basis for the OMC to combat social exclusion.

Of course, the Constitutional Treaty was dealt a fatal double blow from the French and Dutch electorates. Nonetheless, the Lisbon Treaty replicated the substantive provisions of the Constitutional Treaty discussed above. A revised constitutional 'operating system'[13] for EU governance has, therefore, been installed. However, what is readily apparent is how reluctant that operating system appeared to be to allow the OMC as a generic governance technique to 'run' on this new constitutional architecture. The OMC encountered a constraining constitutionalism wedded to the aspiration of competence clarity with the result that the constitutionalization of a generic OMC was rejected (in Walker's terms, it demonstrated 'structural antagonism'). Indeed, the very fluidity of the OMC—acting across a range of levels of governance—could be seen as a corruptive Trojan virus to be 'quarantined' (Trubek and Trubek, 2005b), tamed and contained within the EU's constitutional operating system. As regards any more particular substantive treaty changes to institutionalize the social policy coordination processes, there is a sense in which drafters were both seeking instrumental ways to make provision for OMC processes—understandable in the wake of the diffusion of the OMC as a 'legitimating discourse' (Radaelli, 2003b) and as a governance tool—while hedging their bets against institutionalizing any particular OMC process lest it not stand the test of time—also understandable given the absence of clear empirical evidence as to the effectiveness of the OMC processes and the shifts in the policy environment of the Lisbon strategy itself (see below). Albeit a more explicit textual constitutionalization

[13] 'Constitutionalism is the DOS or Windows of the European Community... It is the operating system conditioning the process of governance itself ...' (Weiler, 1997: 97–8).

of the processes and institutions of social policy coordination, the resulting treaty changes, nonetheless, represented a relatively unsettled institutionalization of the OMC as a tool to combat poverty and social exclusion.

The Policy Context

If the constitutional debates about the institutionalization of the OMC were relatively abstract and indeed, unresolved, then it was at the policy level that the material institutionalization of the OMC—its substantive orientations and the relationship between social and economic concerns—became rather more concrete. In this part, two dynamics of institutional change are explored. The first relates to the changing context of the Lisbon strategy itself following its mid-term review and the decision of the incoming European Commission under President Barroso to relaunch and refocus the strategy. As will be indicated below, while the outcome was one in which the aims and goals of EU social policy were reiterated as remaining within the Lisbon strategy's balanced policy agenda, the governance architecture altered with social policy coordination conducted outside the Lisbon governance architecture. The second aspect of institutional change relates to the material focus of EU social policy coordination itself and the specific commitments to combating poverty and social exclusion. As was noted in chapter three, the launch in 2000 of an OMC process to combat social exclusion gave a distinct identity and focus to EU social policy coordination. However, a subsequent process of 'streamlining' reunited action to combat social exclusion with the policy issues of reforming pensions and health and long-term care: the policy strands identified in the Commission's 1999 Communication on *Modernizing Social Protection* (European Commission, 1999). The emergence of an overarching OMC on 'Social Protection and Social Inclusion' covering these three policy strands had important implications for the material focus of policy coordination in general and for action to combat poverty and social exclusion in particular.

The Relaunch of Lisbon

In 2005, with a new Commission and new Commission President in place, the EU announced a 'new start' for the Lisbon strategy (European Commission, 2005b) to give policy priority to economic growth and increasing employment.

Whereas the original Lisbon strategy (Lisbon I) had aimed for a mutually supportive material institutionalization of a triptych of policy priorities—growth, jobs and social cohesion—the relaunched Lisbon strategy (Lisbon II) initially appeared to be a return to a decoupling of the social from the economic with its emphasis on 'growth and jobs'. Indeed, the new start to the strategy was interpreted by many—and particularly by European social NGOs—as signalling a downgrading of the social dimension of the Lisbon strategy. However, behind the simple re-presentation of the material focus of Lisbon on 'growth and jobs' lies a more complex policy picture.

Even before the relaunch of the Lisbon strategy, the material focus of Lisbon I had changed. Starting with the Göteburg European Council in 2001, the policy geometry of Lisbon altered from the original policy triangle of economic, employment and social policies to become something more of a quadrilateral with the inclusion of environmental policy (Begg, 2008). However, with the relaunch of Lisbon, the precise relationship between the Lisbon strategy and the EU's 'Sustainable Development Strategy' (SDS) was not wholly clear. In its 'new start' communication, the Commission described the Lisbon strategy as 'an essential component of the overarching objective of sustainable development set out in the Treaty', thereby apparently treating Lisbon II as subsidiary to the SDS. However, elsewhere in the communication, the SDS was treated as a parallel process outside the Lisbon strategy. In many ways, this is instructive for thinking about the role of EU social policy within the Lisbon strategy in that it highlights a tendency to view certain broad policy objectives as being within the value system of the strategy, but with some of the mechanics of the policy process and governance architecture as 'orbiting' the strategy in a more 'satellite' fashion.

The mid-term review had been informed by certain critical evaluations of EU economic governance (Sapir et al, 2004) and of the Lisbon strategy itself (Kok et al, 2004). The Sapir High-Level group—composed of distinguished academics—had been commissioned by then Commission President Prodi to review the EU economic system and to make proposals for increasing economic growth while ensuring social cohesion in an enlarged EU. The Sapir group identified that while the objectives of growth, stability and cohesion could be met at the same time—the original goal of the Lisbon strategy—in practice, trade-offs could result as a consequence of failures to design and coordinate governance techniques and of failures of coordination across levels of governance. Although it had relatively little to say on EU social governance it was, nonetheless, apparent that social protection systems were understood as facing new challenges (not least from demography); that economic growth was viewed as the prerequisite to sustaining social protection systems; and that labour market flexibility and 'activation' policies were considered to be essential reforms (see also Sapir, 2006). In this sense, the authors of the report were not agnostic on the nature of EU social policy intervention: domestic reforms to social protection systems were to go hand in hand with domestic reforms to labour markets within an activation paradigm of EU social policy.

In many ways, the Sapir analysis was overshadowed by the influence of the Kok report. The Spring 2004 European Council had asked the Commission to establish a high-level group to evaluate the Lisbon strategy as a way of feeding into the mid-term review of the strategy. By contrast with the Sapir group, the high-level group chaired by Wim Kok contained stronger representation of senior business executives (it also included a number of economics professors and some representation from unions). Its report (Kok at al, 2004) echoed the sentiment of the Sapir report, that advancing growth and employment were key to securing the European 'social contract' in terms of underpinning social protection systems and public services as expressions of European values. It also echoed Sapir in identifying the need for a clearer allocation of responsibilities between the EU and Member States and for the strategy to be clearer about its substantive focus. It suggested a need to focus on five priorities:

- the realization of the knowledge society;
- completing the internal market and promoting competition, with a particular emphasis on opening up services markets;
- improving the business environment;
- building flexible and inclusive labour markets; and
- environmental efficiency and sustainability.

In the absence of any specific social policy priority and in adopting the metaphor that 'a rising European tide lifts every European boat' (Kok et al, 2004: 40), the Kok report was interpreted as viewing social progress as the dividend of economic growth rather than something to be pursued as a policy objective it is own right or even as part of an 'activation' paradigm.

Following the analysis in these reports, Commission President Manuel Barrroso put forward proposals for a 'new start' to the Lisbon Strategy relating to:

- a refocusing of the substantive priorities of the strategy;
- increasing domestic ownership of the strategy; and
- streamlining and rationalizing the Lisbon governance architecture.

For present purposes it is institutional change at the level of the substantive priorities of Lisbon—and the potential de-institutionalization of social policy from that material scope—that is of concern.

A central complaint of the Kok report was that Lisbon I had become too encompassing: 'Lisbon is about everything and thus about nothing' (Kok et al, 2004: 16). The idea of reprioritizing 'growth and jobs' was, therefore, to give a clearer focus and aim to the Lisbon strategy but with the risk of uncoupling social cohesion from Lisbon's material scope. However, this apparent narrowing of the focus of Lisbon II is more ambiguous than it appears.

While focusing on 'growth and jobs' implied a narrowing of the priorities of Lisbon II, the range of policy fields called upon to support these priorities was no less encompassing. This was wholly evident from the Commission's own (renamed) website for growth and jobs which gave the impression that achieving the strategy was dependent upon the virtual entirety of European substantive policy (at least those policy fields within the first pillar).

Moreover—and crucially for present purposes—Lisbon II appeared to signal a retreat from Lisbon I's commitment to a balance between competiveness and social cohesion. Although the European Commission produced a revised *Social Agenda* in 2005 (European Commission, 2005c) that attempted to highlight the complementarity between the social agenda and the mid-term review, overall the document was a rather lacklustre affair and in any event did not have the same high-level commitment that had been given personally by President Barroso to the relaunch of the Lisbon strategy. With both the 'new start' Communication and the Kok report interpreted as sidelining social policy as a positive priority of the Lisbon strategy, there was a concerted effort by a range of actors to reiterate the importance of the social commitments made in 2000 and maintain a balanced substantive scope to the strategy.

Not surprisingly, the relaunch of the Lisbon strategy was met with resistance from the European social NGOs active in this area. EAPN, for example, was more particularly vexed by the European Commission's 'new start' Communication. Whereas for EAPN the Kok report had simply ignored Lisbon's social dimension, EAPN accused the Commission of only listening to one voice—that of 'big business' interests said to have dominated the High-Level Group—and of ignoring the voices of NGOs in the mid-term review process (EAPN, 2005a).[14] The Social Platform President accused

[14] Note also Zeitlin's criticism that the communication did not sufficiently draw on the range of views which had been expressed in the Commission's own evaluation processes (Zeitlin, 2008).

the Commission President of 'killing' the balanced policy agenda agreed at Lisbon.[15] For President Barroso, it was more a case of tending to the 'sick child' of poor European economic performance.[16]

Criticism was not, however, limited to non-governmental actors and critical voices emanated from within the new organizational structures within which the OMC processes were embedded. In its Opinion on the Kok report—produced together with an Opinion from the Employment Committee and serving also as their contribution to the mid-term review of the Lisbon strategy—the Social Protection Committee made clear that:[17]

> The SPC feels strongly that modernising social protection and fighting poverty and exclusion are an indispensable part of promoting higher growth and employment and vice versa. Creating a balanced and mutually supportive interaction between these domains is an essential part of the Lisbon strategy. The report appears to underestimate the role of social policies as an investment which contributes to increased growth and employment.

As for national governments, successive European Council meetings reiterated Lisbon's social dimension as part of a balanced and integrated policy agenda. Significantly, the 2005 Spring European Council under the Luxembourg Presidency repeatedly made reference to social cohesion as part of the Lisbon process and, in particular, rearticulated the commitment of the EU and Member States to social inclusion policy. In presenting the priorities of its Presidency to the European Parliament in January 2005, the Luxembourg Prime Minister Jean-Claude Junker had personally warned against focusing solely on competitiveness to the exclusion of the social and environmental dimensions of Lisbon and argued that '[I]f Europe wants to be strong, she needs three things that go together: improved competitiveness, greater social cohesion and a more

[15] Platform of Social NGOs, 'Mr Barroso, you killed the European dream!': <http://www.socialplatform.org/News.asp?news=11761> (Accessed in March 2010).

[16] 'Let me say this. It is as if I have three children—the economy, our social agenda, and the environment. Like any modern father—if one of my children is sick, I am ready to drop everything and focus on him until he is back to health. That is normal and responsible. But that does not mean I love the others any less!': speech to the Conference of Presidents, European Parliament, Brussels, 2 February 2005. Speech 05/67, Rapid Press Release: <http://europa.eu/rapid/> (Accessed in March 2010).

[17] SPC, *Joint Opinion of the Employment and Social Protection Committee on the Report of the High-Level Group*, Doc. 15529/04.

balanced ecological environment'.[18] As Zeitlin notes (2008), subsequent European Councils reiterated the original strategy's commitment to social cohesion.

How then should we evaluate institutional change at the policy level? The controversy surrounding the relaunch of Lisbon was essentially concerned with the material content of the Lisbon strategy and the relative institutionalization of economic and social policy concerns. Looking back to the discussion in the previous section, the potential vulnerability of Lisbon's social dimension to shifts in the political winds and to the influence of different actors appeared to underscore a view that in the absence of a firmer anchoring of the OMC within the treaty system, Lisbon's social dimension would remain weakly institutionalized. Nonetheless, even in the absence of a more legalized institutionalization, we can identity a significant role for actors and organizational structures in maintaining social policy concerns within the material scope of the Lisbon strategy.

If we attempt to account for institutional change or stasis in terms of the role of actors, one difficulty lies in evaluating which actors are important and where leadership lies. There is an evident competition between the European Commission—with a tradition of the right of policy initiative under the Community Method—and the European Council in giving strategic orientation to the Lisbon strategy. Clearly, the incoming Commission in 2005 under a new President had an agenda to revitalize and refocus the Lisbon strategy. In doing so, it relied on the expertise in the Sapir, and perhaps more influentially, the Kok high-level groups. However, the 'Conclusions' of subsequent European Council meetings sounded a rather different note to that of the Commission's 'new start' Communication.

But even the role of the European Council is difficult to evaluate: is it the role of the European Council as an institution over time, or is the particular Presidency of the European Council more significant? Clearly, the European Council has little ability to micro-manage the Lisbon strategy and its meetings were in any event dominated by the bigger themes of the Iraq war, the fate of the Constitutional Treaty, and agreement on the EU budget. But, it was to the European Council that social NGOs and other actors looked for language and reassurance in its conclusions, that the social dimension still mattered. Given the stance taken by the Luxembourg Presidency in defending the social dimension of Lisbon it was timely that Luxembourg held the

[18] Speech of 12 January 2005 accessed from <http://www.eu2005.lu/> (Accessed in March 2010).

Presidency in the first half of 2005 as the debate surrounding the relaunch of Lisbon took off. But perhaps the importance of this particular Presidency was also to remind EU leaders of what the European Council had agreed in 2000: to make a decisive impact on the eradication of poverty. In that sense we might consider the 2005 European Council under the Luxembourg Presidency as an attempt to buttress Lisbon's balanced policy matrix against forces which might attempt to revisit social commitments. Those forces were not just unleashed by the appointment of a new Commission but potentially from the shift away from the social democratic governments in office in 2000. Thus, despite changes in government in Germany and France, their Presidencies of the Union stuck to the line adopted by the European Council in 2005 that social cohesion remained part of the Lisbon process.[19] In any event, with the rejection of the Constitutional Treaty in France and the Netherlands, Member States were perhaps mindful of a need to signal to domestic voters that further European economic integration would be balanced by a concern with social cohesion. In this way, publically recommitting to a social dimension to the Lisbon strategy was not unrelated to political leaders' desires to maintain momentum within the broader project of European integration.

Although it is tempting to look to the European Council as a source of high-level commitment to EU social policy, it is perhaps not a sufficiently reliable guide to the day-to-day practices of the actors and organizational structures that operationalize the social OMC processes. It is at this lower level that the material institutionalization of Lisbon's social dimension through institutional praxis might be better measured. We have already noted the role of the Social Protection Committee in seeking to defend the role of modernizing social protection and of combating poverty and social exclusion as 'indispensable' elements of Lisbon's policy orientation. It was joined by the Employment, Social Policy, Health and Consumer Affairs (ESPHCA) Council in reiterating the original objectives of the Lisbon Strategy and its balance between economic growth, employment and social policy dimensions. Indeed, in a statement made by the labour ministries of nine Member States in February 2007, the necessity of reinforcing the European Social Model, of relaunching social Europe, and of viewing social

[19] German Presidency of the European Union, 'Europe—Succeeding Together. Presidency Programme', <http://www.eu2007.de/includes/Downloads/Praesidentschaftsprogramm/EU_Presidency_Programme_final.pdf> (Accessed in April 2010). French Presidency of the European Union, 'Europe Taking Action to meet Today's Challenges', <http://ue2008.fr/webdav/site/PFUE/shared/ProgrammePFUE/Programme_EN.pdf> (Accessed in March 2010).

policies as also promoting economic growth and competitiveness within the context of Lisbon was repeated.[20]

In sum, if we take the relaunch of Lisbon as a moment of potential institutional change, we can conclude that the material decoupling of the economic from the social dimensions of Lisbon was successfully resisted and political actors recommitted themselves to maintaining a social dimension to the strategy. Nonetheless, this did not prevent a reprioritization of the policy elements of the strategy to focus on growth and jobs and, as will be discussed below, while the governance architecture of economic and employment policy coordination was integrated within the relaunched Lisbon strategy, social policy coordination developed as a more parallel process. In this way, the recommitment to Lisbon's social dimension is rather more ambiguous: on the one hand, this parallel or 'satellite' social policy coordination process operating outside of the governance structure of the new Lisbon partnership for growth and jobs might be considered to undercut the fine words of European Council conclusions claiming a commitments to Lisbon's social dimension, but on the other hand, retaining a certain distance between the social policy coordination process and the 'integrated' growth and jobs process may have been no bad thing for the distinctive identity and role of EU social policy coordination.

Reframing Social Policy Coordination: From Social Inclusion to Social Protection

In considering the relative roles of economic and social policy within the Lisbon strategy it is easy then to overlook the changing nature of EU social policy itself: or more precisely, the different ways in which EU intervention in the social policy sphere might be framed. After all, the issue may not simply be one of economic versus social policy, but rather one of what sort of social policy—what material and substantive content—is being institutionalized.

As was noted in chapter three, EU intervention in the social sphere developed along different paths. Historically, EU social policy developments were strongly imbued with internal market concerns: either as a means of promoting free movement or as a means of dealing with its consequences. That said, another historical path projected forwards from the Poverty Programmes of

[20] *Un nouvel élan pour l'Europe sociale* signed by the labour ministries of Belgium, Bulgaria, Greece, Spain, France, Italy, Cyprus, Luxembourg and Hungary. The text can be found on the website of the French Permanent Representation to the EU: <http://www.rpfrance.eu/> (Accessed in April 2010).

the 1970s and 1980s and was concerned with identifying and measuring the incidences and causes of poverty and exclusion within the Member States. As such, its justificatory rationales were rooted less in free movement issues and more those of citizenship, equality and fundamental rights. The EU's earlier intervention into the sphere of social protection systems combined these different historical paths and rationales but later moved more in the direction of an 'activation' paradigm focusing on the mutual interaction of economic, employment and social policies. The launch of the OMC process to combat social exclusion appeared institutionally poised between continuity with a policy path leading from the earlier Poverty Programmes—with social policy concerned with distributive issues—and a path which embedded action to combat social exclusion more firmly in the activation paradigm that was shaping the modernization of social protection systems. Of concern in this section is whether action to combat social exclusion was re-materialized in the course of institutional change in a way that altered the manner in which EU policy intervention was rationalized, framed or conducted. In many ways the answer to that question requires exploration more specifically of the different elements of the OMC's governance architecture. While that task is undertaken in the next section, here attention focuses more generally on the effects of a programme of 'streamlining' of policy coordination processes on the material focus of EU social policy coordination.

The initiative to 'streamline' policy coordination processes had its origins in a Commission Communication of 2002 (European Commission, 2002b) that proposed synchronizing and rationalizing the treaty-based economic and employment coordination processes. At that time, the Commission also intimated its intention to reflect both upon streamlining the social inclusion and pensions processes—two of the strands of work identified in its 1999 communication on modernizing social protection—and the linkage between these OMC processes and the treaty-based coordination processes. By the time of its 2003 Communication on 'Strengthening the Social Dimension of the Lisbon Strategy' through streamlining (European Commission, 2003b), the scope for rationalization had increased with the moves towards policy cooperation in the sphere of healthcare. It was readily apparent that an overarching 'social protection' OMC process was being suggested covering the three strands of social inclusion, pensions and healthcare.

While the desire to streamline and synchronize was broadly welcomed it was also resisted and criticized. Although many of the criticisms related to the nature of the future governance architecture—discussed in detail below—more broadly they reflected concerns both as to the relationship between Lisbon's social and economic/employment sides as well as to the identity of EU social policy coordination itself. For example, there was concern that the working methods and actors simply varied across the different social OMC processes. In pensions, a close working relationship had developed between the Social Protection Committee and the Economic Policy Committee. While there was agreement that this was necessary for developing work on pensions, for action to combat social exclusion it was less clear that there was as much enthusiasm for the influence of finance ministers in this domain of EU social policy.

More generally, there was a widespread concern that streamlining would lead to a loss of focus and momentum as regards action to combat poverty and social exclusion. The potential loss of specific NAPincls, together with the arrangements for involving NGOs and civil society were viewed not merely as procedural changes, but as weakening the substantive commitment to combating social exclusion. When coupled with a shift in focus towards 'social protection', it appeared as though the new social policy OMC would embed action to combat social exclusion more firmly within the activation paradigm motivating the 'modernization' of national welfare regimes. Indeed, as the Commission was launching its streamlined social OMC process, it was also initiating a consultation on 'active inclusion' (European Commission, 2006b). Although the content of this initiative will be explored in more detail in the final chapter, it is worth highlighting that this consultation—in referring back to the role of minimum income schemes that were originally the subject of two Council Recommendations in 1992—sought to frame that policy discussion more directly within the activation paradigm. Thus, the Communication noted that:

> The main challenge is thus to ensure that social protection policies effectively contribute to mobilising people who are capable of working while achieving the wider objective of providing a decent living standard to those who are and will remain outside the labour market.

Thus for Daly (2008: 7), 'active social inclusion' displaced the focus of the earlier phase of policy coordination on combating 'social exclusion'.

Nonetheless, while it is useful to attempt to articulate shifts in the framing of action to combat social exclusion within the general policy environment, it would be wrong to assume that the evolving governance architecture simply reflected those changes in an unmediated way. Rather it is important to look beyond and below the levels of general policy documents to discover the way in which the governance architecture itself evolved and how different elements of that architecture framed and articulated the problematic of social exclusion.

The Governance Context

It is at the level of the governance architecture of EU policy coordination that we would expect to find more specific examples of institutional continuity and change. As we have identified, a specific force for change emanated from the Commission's intention to 'streamline' the various social policy coordination processes as a spillover from the earlier streamlining and later integration of the economic and employment policy coordination processes. Yet, the prior existence of a governance architecture to combat poverty and social exclusion which had emerged and evolved through two cycles also created potential institutional resistances to change, or at least certain possible path dependencies to change. In this way, unlike the constitutional dimension where little ultimately changed, and to a greater extent than the policy dimension, we would expect change at the level of governance architecture to be more 'sticky'. The development of the governance architecture from 2005–2008 can be told as a story of an attempt to reconcile, on the one hand, a clear Commission desire to change the architecture to give greater overall visibility to social messages; to refocus policy coordination on issues of 'social protection'; and to reduce the administrative burdens of multiple coordination processes with, on the other hand, a resistance to the merging of different processes at different stages of development—with the more developed social exclusion OMC having a particular momentum—and with different methods and actors.

Before turning directly to the changed social policy governance architecture, some comment on the changes to the governance architecture of the relaunched Lisbon strategy are appropriate. Given the emergence of parallel streamlined coordination processes in respect of economic and employment policy on the one hand, and social protection and social inclusion on the other, developments on one side might serve as a useful counterfactual for how things could change on the other.

From Streamlining to Integration: The Economic and Employment Coordination Processes

Following on from the request of the Barcelona European Council in 2002, the European Commission proposed widespread rationalization and synchronization of the various policy coordination processes, beginning with the 'streamlining' of the treaty-based economic and employment coordination processes. These processes were synchronized to run on parallel three-year cycles and oriented by a common 'guidelines package' for both processes adopted after the Spring European Council (European Commission, 2002b). However, this was simply a precursor to the more radical institutional changes of the Lisbon growth and jobs partnership.

At the heart of the 'partnership' are the integrated guidelines covering economic and employment policies.[21] With each iteration of the coordination cycles, the tendency had been for the number of guidelines to increase. For example, the number of BEPGs had grown from the original three to twenty-three, supplemented by Eurozone-specific guidelines and country-specific recommendations (Deroose, Hodson and Kuhlmann, 2008). In the earlier phases of the EES, the number of guidelines had also increased, but, with the advent of streamlining, the number of employment guidelines was reduced by half (Armstrong and Kilpatrick, 2007: 666–8). This movement towards simplification and reduction of guidelines, combined with less iterative reformulation of the guidelines over time inspired the approach to the new integrated guidelines. The package adopted in 2005 (and re-endorsed in 2006) contained twenty-four general guidelines (sixteen pertaining to economic policy and eight to employment policy). Existing country-specific recommendations were stated to remain 'valid' but in the background. It was not until 2007 that the Council adopted new country-specific recommendations, described by Deroose, Hodson and Kuhlmann as aimed at 'a subset of Member States that were deemed to be facing the most acute reform challenges' (2008: 837). In its Strategic Report in advance of the 2008–2010 cycle of the process, the Commission indicated that the same guidelines would remain in place for the cycle 2008–2010 (European Commission, 2007b). The country-specific recommendations were also retained with a limited 'fine-tuning'.

The reporting structure was also overhauled. A range of reports under different processes were combined into a new single report—the 'National Reform Programme' (NRP)—covering economic (macro and micro) issues and employment policy, thereby marking the demise of the distinct National Action Plans on employment. Indeed, while much of the focus of attention may have been on the apparent demise of Lisbon's social dimension, it was the visibility of the employment process that was the greater casualty of

[21] The relaunched Lisbon strategy distinguished between those activities which would typically require action at EU level—the 'Community Lisbon Programme' (European Commission, 2005d)—and those within the responsibilities of the Member States in a new 'partnership' for growth and jobs. Analysis of the Community Lisbon Programmes lies outside the scope of this work.

Lisbon's relaunch. The new reporting structure operated on a three-year cycle. Member States produced NRPs in 2005 for the period 2005–2008 with annual implementation reports in 2006 and 2007. Member States were exhorted to take greater 'ownership' of their NRPs through nomination of a domestic Lisbon coordinator within government and by enhancing the role of national parliaments, social partners and civil society in the production and implementation of the NRPs (European Commission, 2005b: 31). For its part, the European Commission continued to produce annual reports for the Spring European Council, now referred to as annual 'Progress Reports' with a 'Strategic Report' prefacing a new three-year cycle. A new cycle of the process covering the period 2008–2010 began in 2008.

What is also significant about these architectural reforms was an apparent shift in the accompanying rationale for coordination. For Zeitlin, the Commission's emphasis on a 'bilateral' relationship with Member States under the new architecture represented—at least initially—a retreat from a 'multilateral', experimentalist and horizontal approach to policy learning (Zeitlin, 2008). Yet at the same time, the Commission shied away from the Kok report's demands for greater naming and shaming, and gave greater freedom to states to develop reform strategies in light of the integrated guidelines. Arguably, then, although the change in the governance architecture emphasized a more vertical dimension of the relationship between the EU and Member States, at the same time it placed more emphasis on rendering Member States accountable for their decisions than on iterative recalibration of normative steering. In other words, states were exhorted to exercise a responsibilized freedom but with the *quid pro quo* of enhanced accountability both in terms of increasing EU-level evaluation of the implementation of guidelines (Deroose, Hodson and Kuhlmann, 2008: 837) and in terms of governments' engagement with national parliaments and other stakeholders.

In this way, while treaty-based coordination—especially the EES—had been the model for many of the features of the initial OMC to combat social exclusion, that model had altered from one that initially emphasized iterative recalibration and densification of its objectives and recommendations to one that sought continuity and simplicity in its normative features with a greater emphasis on the accountability of Member States for their policy choices. For some, the ideal for the social OMC was to be more like the initial trajectory of the EES; yet, the experience of the EES made clear that institutional change within OMC processes was not uni-directional. Moreover, the loss of visibility of the EES within the integrated partnership for growth of jobs increased anxiety as to the visibility of action to combat social exclusion within a streamlined coordination of social protection and social inclusion policies.

The Streamlined Social Protection and Social Inclusion Process

In its initial 'streamlining' Communication (European Commission, 2002b), the European Commission signalled significant changes to the governance architecture of social policy coordination. In bringing together the three strands of activity—social inclusion, pensions, health and long-term care—a new 'social protection' OMC was being suggested. NAPincls and NSRs (pensions) would be integrated into a single report and the Commission and Council would agree a new Joint 'Social Protection' Report, replacing the pre-existing *Social Protection in Europe* reports. A single set of objectives was envisaged. In short, there appeared to be a radical shift away from a focus on social exclusion towards social protection. The ambition was to synchronize this reporting structure gradually by including the new EU10 states into the process from 2004 with the new social protection joint report appearing in 2005. The first cycle of the streamlined social protection and social inclusion process would begin in 2006 to run, exceptionally for a period of two years in order to enable the second cycle of the process to begin in 2008 and to run for an anticipated three years in parallel with the integrated Lisbon process.

From the initial proposal in 2003 to the launch of the new process in 2006, a number of influences and actors shaped the evolving governance architecture. Following discussions with the SPC and the adoption of its Opinion,[22] the Commission brought forward a Communication outlining its proposed governance architecture.[23] In turn, this was also the subject of discussion within the SPC and a further Opinion (jointly with the Economic Policy Committee) (EAPN, 2003). The organizational relationship between the European Commission and the committees—not just the SPC but also the Economic Policy and Employment Policy Committees—was key to negotiating institutional change and in the analysis below, the influence of the committees and of particular delegations within these committees will be noted. Social NGOs also continued to seek influence over the design of the governance architecture and groups like EAPN and the Social Platform were both active in producing

[22] Opinion of the Social Protection Committee (29 September 2003): Doc. 12909/03.

[23] Joint Opinion of the Social Protection and Economic Policy Committee (27 February 2007): Doc. 6801/06.

position papers. Importantly, both EAPN and the Social Platform identified 'continuity' and momentum in the OMC as positive virtues which streamlining threatened (EAPN, 2003). For both social actors, streamlining had to build on the Nice objectives, Laeken indicators and NAPincls rather than completely replace them.

Other influences were also at play. A presidency conference organized under the Luxembourg Presidency resulted in a report, *Taking Forward the EU Social Inclusion Process* (Atkinson et al, 2005) which emphasized the need for social indicators to play a more direct role in facilitating policy analysis. Two Commission evaluations were also significant: one evaluation covered the Community Action Programme—whose future was not mentioned in the Commission's initial streamlining communication—and the other, a specific evaluation of the OMC on social exclusion and pensions.

The evaluation of the OMC is perhaps more interesting as a record of views about the OMC than it was influential in shaping the future governance architecture.[24] In many ways, its insights were overshadowed by the furore surrounding the relaunch of the Lisbon strategy. Moreover, it was a look back rather than directly a look forward and the Commission was, in any event, more directly engaged in negotiations within the SPC on its concrete proposals for change. Nonetheless, responses to the evaluation—together with responses to the initial and subsequent Commission proposals—give us a picture of the dynamics of institutional change. The areas covered by the evaluation were:

1. the 'added value' of policy coordination,
2. the choice and relevance of objectives,
3. the role of indicators and targets in monitoring progress,
4. the mobilization of actors,
5. the ability of working methods to promote mutual learning,
6. the linkage between the social OMC and other OMC processes, and
7. how best to develop the OMC in a streamlined context.

[24] The OMC evaluation was guided by a questionnaire circulated to Member States with responses to the Commission by the end of June 2005. The intention was to present the evaluation report alongside the Commission's communication on the new streamlined process (European Commission, 2005a), but in the end, the communication appeared in December 2005 and the evaluation report in March 2006 (European Commission, 2006a).

In the analysis of the particular features of the governance architecture undertaken below, evaluation responses will be considered. However, a brief consideration of the issue of the 'added value' of the OMC is important given that it goes to the issue of the underlying rationale and function of the governance architecture.

Respondents were asked to distinguish between the added value of the process at EU and at national levels. In general, while there was enthusiasm for the role of the OMC in developing the EU's social dimension, when it came to identifying positive domestic impacts, the response of actors was vague, with a tendency to focus on processes (eg enhancing dialogue between domestic actors) over identification of particular substantive policy reforms. As regards the European dimension, for Member States, the added value of the OMC was both symbolic—highlighting that the EU had a social dimension at all, and functional—the potential value of policy exchanges and learning. Social NGOs tended to highlight the ongoing nature of the process allowing them both to critique its effectiveness while also remaining committed to the idea that the process could be strengthened (EAPN, 2005b). For EAPN, the launch of the OMC had prevented a policy hiatus following the demise of the earlier poverty programmes and argued that if the OMC did not exist something like it would have been invented to provide a framework for policy exchanges and mutual learning. In sum, the perception of respondents was that the rationale for, and added value of, EU policy coordination lay in keeping social issues on the EU's policy agenda (with potential incidental legitimacy benefits for the EU) and more tendentiously with the promotion of policy learning, notwithstanding the absence of particular examples and the sense that a stronger process was required in order for this to occur. In this way, at most the evidence of past experience was used to confirm a political commitment—a commitment reinforced by the European Council—to do something if not to suggest the concrete features of any revised architecture. It is to these specific features that we now turn.

(a) Revised Common Objectives

The very process of streamlining three policy coordination processes necessarily implied a change in the organization of common objectives. More significantly it posed a challenge to the substantive focus and direction of EU social policy coordination in three respects. First, there was a danger that the specific objective of making a decisive impact on the eradication of poverty by 2010, together with the consensus underpinning the broad Nice objectives would be lost in an overarching process. Second, the emergence of a new Lisbon partnership for growth and jobs integrating the economic and employment sides of the original Lisbon triangle raised questions as to whether this new context ought to be reflected in the common objectives and, if so, how ought that balance—a balance which was obviously contested as the discussion of the policy context above indicated—ought to be struck. Thirdly, even if action to combat social exclusion retained visibility within the common objectives, its substantive orientation and meaning might alter as a consequence of a renewed focus on social protection as the organizing framework.

The organization of new common objectives proved contentious. Given that the SPC was clear that social inclusion had to retain its visibility in the process—indeed, the new nomenclature for the process was agreed to be the 'Social Protection and Social Inclusion' OMC—and that social NGOs were keen to defend the existing Nice objectives, it would have been difficult for a single set of common objectives to emerge covering all three strands. Therefore, the idea of a 'pillar' structure emerged early on in the discussions. Nonetheless, the Commission was keen also to have a set of overarching objectives to bind the process together. On the one hand, these overarching objectives might simply have related to some of the process dimensions of coordination. On the other, they could seek to frame social policy coordination against a particular normative context. In this way, both the content of the individual 'pillars' and of the overarching objectives were the object of negotiation and discussion.

A set of common objectives for the social OMC was endorsed by the European Council in March 2006. The overarching objectives requested Member States to promote:

- social cohesion, equality between men and women and equal opportunities for all through adequate, accessible, financially sustainable, adaptable and efficient social protection systems and social inclusion policies;
- effective and mutual interaction between the Lisbon objectives of greater economic growth, more and better jobs and greater social cohesion, and with the EU's Sustainable Development Strategy;
- good governance, transparency and the involvement of stakeholders in the design, implementation and monitoring of policy.

As regards the presentation of the order of these objectives, the original draft of the Commission's proposal controversially gave primacy to the objective of 'supporting the achievement of the Lisbon objectives of creating greater economic growth and more and better jobs'. This was viewed by some Member States as treating the social OMC process as subservient to the Lisbon partnership rather than, as the EAPN put it as the 'social pillar' of Lisbon. Under pressure particularly from the Belgian and Luxembourg delegations—both countries submitted a joint response to the SPC—the order of the first and second objectives was symbolically reversed.

In terms of the substance of the objectives, it is noteworthy that with the exception of the third objective which is procedural, the other two objectives are substantive and seek to embed policy coordination within particular social policy frames and, in turn, to contextualize EU social policy within the wider Lisbon and SDS policy frameworks. Whether or not these are the right policy frames and contexts is, of course, open to debate but what is important is that they do attempt to articulate some kind of substantive vision: EAPN had been concerned that to 'propose a new set of objectives, which subordinate policy to procedural requirements, is to undervalue the Member States' 5-year experience of developing Plans built on mutually agreed objectives, based on common values and principles' (EAPN, 2005b).

As regards the substantive content of the new overarching objectives, the first objective located policy coordination within a range of social policy frames:

- social cohesion
- equality policies
- modernizing social protection
- social inclusion.

The Social Platform had argued for these common objectives to institutionalize policy coordination more firmly within an overall framework of the protection of fundamental rights, yet this is evidently missing. Nonetheless, it is to be noted that 'social protection' is but one social policy frame identified, with social cohesion—the key objective of the original Lisbon strategy—at the forefront.

The second objective then sought to embed EU social policy coordination within the wider framework of the relaunched Lisbon strategy and the Sustainable Development Strategy. This was essentially a question-begging exercise. While including this objective opened the way to building bridges between the social OMC and other policy processes, the quality of that interaction would be highly dependent on the connections made at both national and EU level between these different policy-making contexts. The practical implications of this objective were laid down in the Guidelines for preparing the national strategy reports, with Member States requested to give practical examples of the ways in which social policies enhance economic growth and employment ('feeding out') and conversely how growth and jobs strategies promote social inclusion ('feeding in').

A more detailed understanding of what is implied by this objective can be found in a report prepared by the SPC on the mutual interaction of the common social objectives and Lisbon II.[25] In recognizing that economic growth and employment are necessary but not sufficient conditions to ensuring social cohesion, the SPC noted that:

> Member States agree that sound public finances and higher employment rates under stable prices are the framework conditions for sustainable and wide-ranging social protection and inclusion policies; the latter aim at a fair and just society that guarantees equal opportunities for everyone and leaves no one behind. In Europe today well-designed social protection and social inclusion measures that implement the principles of gender equality and equal opportunities and encourage and reward work are indispensable to greater investment and growth and rising productivity.

At least for the SPC, the virtue of 'feeding in' and 'feeding out' was the apparent ability to marry a vision of the European Social Model—a 'fair and just society', equality of opportunities and other forms of substantive equality—with the post-EMU world of sound public finances and aspirations to full employment. Nonetheless, beneath that lofty aspiration, the practical guidance to Member States focused on more mundane institutional arrangements at domestic level such as ensuring 'joined-up' government and the 'poverty-proofing' of policies. In that way, the second objective sought not only to locate EU social policy coordination within a wider policy context it also provided a basis for the promotion of policy integration as a practical political art.

The third objective is a reformulation of the fourth Nice objective. On the one hand, it usefully identifies stakeholder involvement at different phases of the process: design, implementation and monitoring. On the other hand, the rather neutral verb—'involve'—does not have quite the same connotation as 'to mobilize' under the old objectives.

If the overarching objectives were largely there to contextualize social policy coordination, what then of the objectives underpinning the particular substantive pillars? As regards the objectives relating to combating social

[25] SPC Report on the mutual interaction between the common social objectives and the strategies for growth and jobs: Doc. 15444/07.

exclusion, social NGOs were consistent in seeking to hold onto the broad Nice objectives which they considered as an appropriate basis for a multidimensional conceptualization of poverty and social exclusion. Broadly this view was shared by Member States and as the Commission's evaluation synthesis document identified, proposals for change were largely limited to seeking adjustments rather than major revisions and with a greater emphasis on implementing the objectives than on changing them. That said, for some Member States there was a desire for a more particular focus to be given to certain target groups.

The result of the negotiations was that Member States committed themselves to making a 'decisive impact on the eradication of poverty' by ensuring:

- access for all to the resources, rights and services needed for participation in society, preventing and addressing exclusion, and fighting all forms of discrimination leading to exclusion;
- the active social inclusion of all, both by promoting participation in the labour market and by fighting poverty and exclusion;
- that social inclusion policies are well-coordinated and involve all levels of government and relevant actors, including people experiencing poverty, that they are efficient and effective and mainstreamed into all relevant public policies, including economic, budgetary, education and training policies and structural fund (notably ESF) programmes.

In its original draft, the Commission had formulated the first two of these objectives in the following way:

- Ensure the active social inclusion of all by promoting participation in the labour market and by fighting poverty and exclusion among the most marginalized people and groups.
- Guarantee access for all to the basic resources, rights and social services needed for participation in society, while addressing extreme forms of exclusion and fighting all forms of discrimination leading to exclusion.

As with the overarching objectives, objection was taken to the ordering of these objectives as it appeared to give central importance to labour market inclusion and again, at the suggestion of the Belgian and Luxembourg delegations, the first and second objectives were switched around. But there were also noteworthy substantive changes made. In particular, as originally conceived, the draft objectives placed a great deal of emphasis on tackling 'extreme' forms of exclusion and of fighting poverty among the most 'marginalized' groups. EAPN voiced strong objections to this formulation and complained that a focus on extreme poverty took attention away from all those experiencing poverty. EAPN also suggested that it set up a dichotomy between 'good' (active) inclusion in the labour market and 'bad' (passive) inclusion signified by reliance on social benefits (EAPN, 2006a). In this way, when presented in the manner initially envisaged by the Commission, it gave the activation paradigm a rather particular meaning: working age adults are expected to work, but even if they remain poor, they are not directly objects of concern as the emphasis of policymakers shifts to the most marginalized and those in extreme poverty. Although some of the sting was drawn by the revised formulation of the objectives and by their re-ordering, nonetheless, the centrality of the idea of 'active social inclusion' remained clear. The third objective builds on the previous cycles of the process in its emphasis upon gender mainstreaming and on integrating policies into budgetary planning and the use of EU structural funds.

How then, should we evaluate these changes? The changes appear to be attempts to manage three related tensions all of which relate to the way in which the objectives project competing policy paradigm or frameworks. The first is a broad tension between viewing social policy coordination as something that ought to articulate with the relaunched Lisbon strategy or viewing it as something that ought to develop according to its own distinctive social policy frameworks and even as a counter-weight of values. The second tension is a concretization of that broad tension in terms of whether the rationale for social policy coordination is premised on modernizing and activating social protection systems or embracing a broader perspective building on the original Lisbon and Nice consensus in focusing on social cohesion, on social inclusion and on access to rights. The third tension is a continuation of an older tension under the pre-streamlined process namely the extent to which employment is or is not viewed as central to social inclusion.

Although the drafting of the common objectives was not a legislative process, there was an interesting language game at play. Participants clearly believed that language and discourse mattered. While there is no obvious hierarchy to the objectives, participants in the process obviously felt that where an objective was placed on a list sent out some kind of message. In that way, political and social actors were contesting the materialization and institutionalization of the substantive norms and frames of EU social policy coordination. Of course, by adopting language that accommodated differences in perspective, the tensions are not resolved but rather simply absorbed into the process. Indeed, given their breadth and generality, it is clear that change at the level of common objectives is more in the nature of setting the overall policy context and collective conscience of the process, rather than as a means of more immediately directing the process. It can even be suggested that other elements of the OMC architecture—the common indicators and the reporting structures—generate more specific signals and steers for the process, and can direct the attention of political actors to particular priorities. In this way, while arguments over the content of the objectives are highly significant in terms of revealing competing discursive policy paradigms or frames, other elements of the OMC architecture have the capacity to steer the process in more specific ways and in ways which may even run counter to trends at this symbolic or discourse-framing level.

Finally, it is also noteworthy that in presenting its proposed new objectives, the Commission stated that, '[P]articularly for social inclusion, the more general presentation of objectives should allow Member States to focus on the policy priorities most important in each national context . . .'. In other words, the changes to be brought about by the revision of the objectives were neither intended to make the process more prescriptive nor top-down, but instead the emphasis lay on Member States setting their own priorities. This caused some anxiety among social NGOs who feared that such a decentralized elective and selective identification or priorities would 'reduce the possibility for comparison or mutual exchange and learning' (EAPN, 2006a). However, as will be discussed below that did not mean that other elements of the OMC architecture remained quite so agnostic as to priorities, with action to tackle child poverty and 'active inclusion' emerging quite clearly as key themes for activity under the new streamlined process.

(b) Revised Common Indicators

In its synthesis report on the evaluation of the OMC (European Commission, 2006c), the Commission reported that Member States generally viewed the commonly agreed indicators 'as doing a reasonable job' in 'underpinning EU-level exchange' and 'in animating national policy making'. Nonetheless, difficulties in the timeliness, reliability and continuity of EU data were reported by Member States with many delegations emphasizing the importance they attached to national data even if that limited comparability.

However, for some states, the EU policy coordination process was reported as having had a positive impact on national data collection; itself a form of Europeanization.

Even with broad support for common indicators, the context of streamlining together with other causal factors saw important changes to the portfolio of indicators used to support policy coordination. With streamlining came the challenge to adapt and adopt indicators to facilitate monitoring of a process covering three different strands of social policy. Clearly work on social indicators was more advanced than in healthcare and it is noteworthy that in the healthcare field there was a departure from the methodology guiding the selection of the original Laeken indicators in the use of certain commonly agreed 'national' indicators. Although these indicators lack direct comparability and may not have a common meaning they serve as a second-best alternative to common EU indicators.

More significantly, there was a particular desire not to let the list of indicators grow as a result of streamlining, but rather, 'to keep the list short and promote prioritization and concentration of the efforts at reform, improving transparency and public perception of policy outcomes'.[26] Yet, this was in tension with the use of a broad portfolio of social indicators to capture the multidimensional phenomenon of social exclusion and as an aid to mutual learning. In an attempt to resolve that tension somewhat, it was decided to mirror the new common objectives by having a set of overarching indicators as well as more specific indicators to underpin the social inclusion process. A portfolio of fourteen indicators—supplemented by twelve 'context information items'—support the overarching objectives of the process (Table 4.1).

The very idea of an overarching set of indicators is interesting as it begs the question whether there is anything that these indicators capture that the indicators for each strand do not. Indeed, the selected indicators tend to duplicate and overlap with those underpinning the separate strands of the process. What appears to drive the selection of overarching indicators is a desire to build an analytical bridge between the Lisbon and Sustainable

[26] Social Protection Committee and Economic Policy Committee Joint Opinion on the Commission Communication "Working together, working better: proposals for a new framework for the open coordination of social protection and inclusion policies": Doc. 6801/06.

Table 4.1 Portfolio of Overarching Indicators

Indicator	Definition	Type
1a at risk of poverty rate	% of persons with an income below 60% of median equivalized income	EU indicator
1b relative median poverty risk gap	The gap between the median equivalized income of those below the at risk rate and the threshold itself as a % of the at risk threshold	
2 Income inequality	Ratio of income received by top 20% of earners to that of the lowest 20%	EU indicator
3 Health inequality	Number of years of life expectancy at ages 0, 45 and 65.	Agreed national indicator
4 Educational outcomes (early school leavers)	% of 18–24 year olds with only lower secondary education and not in training.	EU indicator
5 Living in jobless households	% of people living in jobless households	EU indicator
6 Social expenditure	Projected total public social expenditure and projected change as a share of GDP	Agreed national indicator
7a Pension adequacy	Median equivalized income of people aged over 65 as a ratio of income of those <65.	EU indicator
7b Pension adequacy (replacement ratio)	Median individual pensions of persons 65–74 relative to median earnings of those 50–59	
8 Health inequality	Self-reported unmet need for medical care due to cost, waiting times or distance to travel.	Agreed national indicator
9 Improvement in standards of living from economic growth	% of persons with a disposable income below the at risk threshold anchored at a point in time (2005) and uprated in line with inflation.	EU indicator
10 Employment rate of older workers	% of those aged 55–59 and 60–64 in employment as a proportion of total population in each group.	EU indicator
11 In-work poverty rate	Those in employment but at risk of poverty	EU indicator
12 Activity rate	Share of employed and unemployed in total population aged 15–64.	EU indicator
13 Regional disparities	Regional variation in employment rates	Agreed national indicator
14 Health expenditure	Total health expenditure per capita.	Agreed national indicator.

Development Strategies and the streamlined social OMC process. In this way, these overarching indicators may support analysis of the mutual interaction of the processes. Nonetheless, by giving prominence to this aim, it runs the risk of inverting the priorities of the first and second overarching common objectives by giving priority to the contextualization of the process within the broader Lisbon policy agenda, thereby undermining the very specific changes to the order of these objectives agreed within the SPC (discussed above).

Two of the indicators in the overarching portfolio are also worth highlighting. The first is the indicator that takes 2005 as a baseline and measures the impact of economic growth on the at-risk-of-poverty rate. At one stage this would have been useful in measuring whether the economic growth strategy of Lisbon II was producing the promised social dividend to fund social protection systems. However, with recession hitting the EU as a result of the meltdown of global financial markets in 2008, the indicator's role may be more one in determining the effects of economic contraction on the risk of poverty. The other indicator which is noteworthy is that on 'in-work' poverty. As was noted in chapter three, work on the development of an indicator on in-work poverty had begun with a view to drawing a connection between the EES and work on combating poverty and social exclusion. The adoption of this new indicator within the suite of overarching indicators would be particularly relevant to 'feeding out' and 'feeding in' between the relaunched Lisbon process and the streamlined social OMC. Moreover, this indicator is especially significant in terms of what had been a normative presupposition of EU coordination to combat social exclusion, namely that employment is the best route out of poverty. The data generated by this indicator is revealing. While it supports the claim that when compared to the entire working age population those in employment are less likely to be at risk of poverty, if one looks at the population of those who are at risk of poverty over a third were in employment.[27] This indicates that for many EU citizens, work is poorly paid and not sufficient to provide resources to lift them above the at-risk-of-poverty threshold. In doing so it points to the need for Member States to adopt a mix of policy initiatives—from minimum wages to minimum income guarantees—to ensure that even for those included within the labour market, action is taken to combat poverty. The inclusion of this indicator is also important in light of the discussion above concerning the risk that, as originally conceived, the draft common objectives had

[27] See Eurostat's *Statistics in Focus*, 'Population and Social Conditions', 5/2005.

Table 4.2 Primary Indicators for Social Inclusion Strand

	Indicator	Definition	Comment
1	At risk of poverty rate	Same as overarching objective 1a.	Same as overarching objective 1a.
2	Persistent at risk of poverty	% of those below risk of poverty rate in current year and in at least 2 out of 3 preceding years	Only available data for all EU Member States from 2010 and so not available for 2006–2008 report.
3	Relative median poverty risk gap	Same as overarching objective 1b.	Same as overarching objective 1b.
4	Long term unemployment rate	Total long term unemployed as a proportion of active population >15	
5	Living in jobless households	Same as overarching indicator 5.	Same as overarching indicator 5.
6	Early school leavers	Same as overarching indicator 4.	Same as overarching objective 4.
7	Employment gap of immigrants	Difference between the employment rate of immigrants and non-immigrants.	
8	Material deprivation	To be developed.	Not available for 2006–2008 NSR.
9	Housing	To be developed	Not available for 2006–2008 NSR.
10	Self-reported unmet need for medical care due to cost, waiting times or distance to travel.	Same as overarching objective 8.	Same as overarching objective 8.

a more particular focus on those excluded from the labour market and the most extreme forms of poverty.

In terms of the indicators selected to underpin each substantive strand of policy coordination, a set of eleven primary, three secondary and eleven context indicators were adopted for policies to combat social exclusion (Table 4.2). This represented a reduction from the original list of eighteen Laeken indicators. Moreover, the list includes indicators which had not yet been developed and indicators for which there would not be data for the 2006–2008 reports, for example, the persistent at-risk-of-poverty rate. These changes tend to reinforce two concerns about the evolution of policy coordination to combat social exclusion. The first relates to the scope of the process. The reduction in the number of indicators might signify a move away from the multidimensional representation of the phenomenon of social exclusion with a consequential limitation of the scope for mutual learning. Moreover, the inclusion of new indicators on immigrant employment and on child well-being reinforces a preoccupation with particular groups as being at a particular risk of social exclusion: a significant trend identified by Daly (2008). While it may be important to identify specific risk groups, there is always a danger that in the process the experience of poverty and exclusion of working-age individuals will be decentred.

The second concern is with 'drift'. While changes in the overarching objectives are often more symbolic than substantive, it is the indicators that form the basis for quantitative and qualitative measurement and evaluation of domestic policies. Changes at the level of indicators can result in a rather episodic approach to the setting of national plans with issues coming on then off the political agenda. Overall this can result in plans that drift between cycles rather than systematically building on earlier iterations and project an image of EU policy coordination as being in perpetual transition.

Regardless of whether streamlining had occurred or not, there is an inherent source of change related to the very nature of the definition and redefinition of social indicators. As we noted in chapter three, the work of social scientists—Tony Atkinson and his collaborators—was important in defining the methodology and approach to the original Laeken indicators developed with the support of the Belgian Presidency. Under the Luxembourg Presidency, Atkinson and his team were again requested to produce a report for a presidency conference (Atkinson et al, 2005). Their report highlights the ongoing nature of the process of defining and refining indicators. The formal task of developing indicators remains with the Social Protection Committee Indicators Sub-Group (ISG). Its membership typically includes civil servants from national ministries with expertise on statistics but can vary to include non-departmental experts—for example, Eric Marlier who collaborated with Atkinson is the core Luxembourg representative and is employed by a research institute—to sociologists and economists—the Italian delegation includes economists attached to the Prime Minister's office. The Chair of the sub-group from its inception—David Stanton—is the UK representative and former head of the Department for Social Security (now DWP) Analytical Services Division. In this way, not only has the SPC been open to experts outside of its own membership, through the Indicators Sub-Group, there is strong social science expertise within the sub-group membership. That expertise has been harnessed to a process of institutional change as social scientists seek better means of mapping the phenomenon which indicators are intended to capture (on the role of social science in EU social policy more generally, see Atkinson, 2003).

Although in general the revised common indicators followed the methodology developed by Atkinson and his collaborators for the suite of Laeken indicators, they also departed from it particularly by including not just 'outcome' indicators but also 'input' indicators, for example, the level of social expenditure in Member States. This change was a response to the identification of a gap between the policy outcomes monitored by indicators and the policy initiatives reported by Member States in the first two cycle of NAPincls (Atkinson et al, 2005: 80). That is to say, it was not always apparent how changes in any given policy reported by Member States in their NAPincls produced or affected policy outcomes, compared to, for example, more general changes in the domestic economy (see also similar criticisms made by Room, 2005). The inclusion of a limited number of input indicators in the new portfolio might go some way to addressing this issue. But the more significant point made by Atkinson et al was the need for indicators to be better integrated into 'policy analysis': the generation of clearer narratives concerning the effect of specific policy initiatives on particular policy outcomes (Atkinson et al, 2005: chapter four). Detailed policy analysis is key to the sort of 'lesson-drawing' which is at the heart of mutual learning. As will be noted below, the SPC Indicators Sub-Group did become directly involved in this type of policy analysis in their work on child poverty reported in the 2008 joint report. This does, therefore, represent an important change from the use of indicators prior to streamlining and indicates an attempt to strengthen the use of indicators to support mutual learning (see Mabbett's criticisms of the earlier cycles of the process: Mabbett, 2007).

(c) National Strategy Reports and Joint Reports

A key justification for streamlining the various EU social policy coordination processes lay with the desire to reduce the reporting obligations on Member States. Yet from the very launch of the Commission's initial streamlining communication, the potential loss of specific National Action Plans on Inclusion (NAPincls) was resisted by social NGOs and indeed by many Member States.[28] However, somewhat different signals

[28] The UK was especially vocal in its defence of the retention of the NAPincls both during the streamlining discussions and again in 2008 when the Commission floated the idea of dropping the nomenclature of the National Action Plans on Inclusion.

were initially sent from the SPC and the EPC. The approach of the SPC was one that tended to emphasize streamlining as a means of bringing together, while retaining the autonomy of, the three strands of social policy coordination. However, for the EPC, its starting point was that merely combining the three processes would not of itself reduce the number or length of reports. Meanwhile for social NGOs, they continued to argue that the issue was not one of reducing the bureaucracy of 'reporting' but of making the national documents proper strategies to tackle poverty and social exclusion.

Member States were asked to draw up 'National Strategy Reports' (NSRs) with distinct chapters on each of the three substantive areas of policy coordination. In order to maintain the distinctiveness of the individual strands of the coordination process, the guidelines prepared by the Commission and SPC to facilitate the preparation of new strategic reports made clear that each substantive chapter of the new reports 'will serve as a national plan for the specific policy field'.

Recalling that this first cycle of the new reporting framework was, exceptionally, to run for a two-year period and that the Member States had already submitted detailed strategy reports on pensions in 2005, the focus of the 2006–2008 NSRs submitted in September 2006 was very much to remain on social inclusion issues, supplemented by Member States' first plans on healthcare and long-term care. Thus, in this transitional phase of streamlining, policies and strategies to combat social exclusion continued to dominate the OMC and the content of the national reports.

As to the joint reports, the first joint report on 'Social Protection and Social Inclusion' was produced in 2005 (European Commission and Council, 2005) with a subsequent joint report produced in 2006 (European Commission and Council, 2006). In many ways, these reports were something of a false start as they were adopted prior to the adoption of new streamlined national reports on the full three-year cycle. The 2005 report drew on a range of earlier reports including a 2005 'Update' report by ten of the EU15 Member States on the implementation of their 2003–2005 NAPincls as well as the first NAPincls of the new EU10 Member States submitted in 2004 (analysed in European Commission, 2005e). This was, then, the first joint report to cover both 'old' and 'new' Member States. Although covering social inclusion, pensions and healthcare, the report had little new material on pensions as Member States were submitting pensions reports in 2005. Indeed, the content of the report was dominated by the analysis of the social inclusion situation across the EU, thereby highlighting the more developed OMC process on social inclusion even within the new governance architecture. The 2006 report drew on 'implementation' reports submitted by the EU15 states and 'updates' from four of the new Member States, but as one report acknowledged, the timing of the national reports was less than ideal.[29]

The structure of the joint reports evolved from the two cycles of reports in 2002 and 2004. The 2005 joint report was the first to adopt a new presentational style consisting of a short fifteen-page 'key messages' report based on a Commission 'COM' document accompanied by a much longer technical statistical annex containing quantitative and thematic analysis and published as a Commission staff working paper 'SEC' document[30] (European Commission, 2005f; 2005g). This style of presentation is noteworthy for two reasons. First, the adoption of a shorter report can be interpreted as part of the ambition of streamlining to develop more visible social policy messages to be fed into the Spring European Council meeting. With the report covering three processes and an enlarged Union, there were understandable anxieties that the overall reduction in size of the report would diminish its potential for elaborating strong policy analysis. However, the production of the distinct technical annex and, significantly, the capacity to develop a more thematic analytical report in the years between production of national strategy reports (see below) in many ways met those concerns. Secondly, and more pragmatically, publishing the technical analysis in a 'SEC' document obviated the need for translation of this document into all the official languages of the EU. Clearly, this would inhibit the ability of a wide range of social and political actors to use this analysis either as a basis for learning from experience or as means of holding Member States to account for their policy performance.

The presentation of the joint report developed further in 2007 with the emergence of a clearer tripartite structure based around the key messages report, the technical statistical analysis, and a distinct 'country fiche report' (European Commission, 2007c, 2007d, 2007e). Importantly, whereas the Commission had held bilateral meetings on the content of the country fiches, this gave way to a more routine email correspondence with Member States

[29] 'The reports were prepared by Member States during an interim period. Discussions were still taking place on the future integration of the social inclusion process with the parallel processes on pensions and health and long-term care. The arrangements for implementing the revised Lisbon goals of economic growth and jobs were still being put in place and the relationship of the social inclusion process to this revised strategy was still being worked out. This uncertainty may have affected the ability of some Member States to report effectively on progress so far' (European Commission, 2006d).

[30] This also contained the 'country fiche' reports.

largely reviewing the Commission's comments for accuracy. Moreover, the presentation and 'peer review' of the NSR/NAPincls became formalistic with states only having fifteen minutes to present what were now reports covering three large policy domains.

The NSR/NAPincls for 2006–2008 were noted as being 'more strategic that in previous years, focusing on a more limited set of priorities' (European Commission and Council, 2007: 8). As discussed more fully in chapter five, Member States had been encouraged to report on a sub-set of priorities that had been identified in the 2005 joint report. An emerging focus on issues of child poverty was also apparent. Prior to the launch of the OMC in 2000, it had been suggested that the process focus on particular target groups but such an explicit strategy was displaced in favour of the multidimensional analysis of the problem of social exclusion. However, the European Council in 2006 called on Member States 'to take necessary steps to rapidly and significantly reduce child poverty, giving all children equal opportunities, regardless of their social background'. The 'key messages' part of the 2007 joint report and the analysis contained in the accompanying technical paper gave particular prominence to child poverty. Similarly the theme of 'active inclusion' also emerged strongly in the 2007 joint report and followed a consultation on the issue launched by the European Commission in 2006 (European Commission, 2006b).

No new NSRs were due in 2007 which created an opportunity for a more thematic 2008 joint report with the analysis focusing again on child poverty. Within the SPC, the ISG had established a task force to review child poverty within the EU27. Together with national reports on child poverty from the network of independent experts (financed through the action programme supporting the OMC), and replies to a questionnaire sent to Member States, the analysis of the ISG Task Force was discussed within the SPC in October 2007. The technical annex to the joint report drew on this work in presenting some 'main lessons'. But as well as undertaking the usual statistical analysis, the report explicitly assessed the policy performance of each Member State in respect of three factors influencing the risk of child poverty—children in jobless households, in-work poverty, and the impact of social transfers on child poverty—and then ranked Member States in terms of four groupings (from those states that scored well on all three factors to those that scored the least well). This produced the following rankings and diagnoses:

- Group A states performed well on all three factors: Denmark, Finland, Sweden, Austria, Cyprus, Netherlands and Slovenia. Continued monitoring of developments encouraged.

- Group B states achieved relatively good to below average outcomes: Belgium, Czech Republic, Germany, Estonia, France and Ireland. Policies aimed at reducing jobless households by access to 'quality jobs' considered as making a potential contribution to reducing child poverty.
- Group C states had average or below average outcomes: Hungary, Malta, Slovakia and the UK. Different policy mixes considered appropriate to include not only parental access to the labour market (including second earners) but also measures to support the income of parents at work.
- Group D states had average or relatively high child poverty outcomes: Greece, Spain, Italy, Lithuania, Luxembourg, Latvia, Poland and Portugal. States encouraged to adopt 'comprehensive strategies to provide better support for family income, and to facilitate access to quality jobs, especially for second earners'.

Two things are noteworthy about this grouping of states. First, if we call to mind the furore surrounding the ranking of Member States in the Commission's first Communication on the 2001 joint report, it is striking that this grouping of states emerged. The new reporting structure—its time frame and also its presentation—created space for a more specific thematic analysis of child poverty and for a more critical appraisal to emerge than had hitherto been the case. Moreover, that criticism was not of how the Member States had used the OMC to report on domestic performance but directly to evaluate the effectiveness of domestic policies in terms of their impact on child poverty outcomes. In this way, the process moved from one that formally claimed not to be making direct assessments of policy performance—a claim that was never wholly sustainable given that the common indicators could be used as a basis to judge policy performance—to one that did.

Secondly, the focus of diagnoses upon employment tends to reinforce the prescription of employment as the best route out of poverty and social exclusion. However, as the EU's own evidence indicates, work is not a guarantee of a reduction in child poverty unless it is quality, well-paid work and unless work can be reconciled with affordable and accessible childcare. Social transfers continue to play a significant role in reducing child poverty.

A further cycle of NSR/NAPincls for the period 2008–2010 were produced in a very different economic climate to the preceding reports. Not surprisingly, the social impact of the recession emerged as a key theme of the 2009 and 2010 joint reports. Importantly, the thematic analysis of the joint reports clearly relied on information other than that generated by the cyclical reporting mechanism. In particular, the SPC and the Commission produced joint reports analysing the social impact of the recession. Taken together with the deeper analytical work done on child poverty, it is evident that the NSR/NAPincls are simply one type of input into the monitoring and evaluation undertaken at EU level. Indeed, and perhaps supported by the openness of the SPC to engagement with experts, more detailed thematic work is being undertaken by the SPC which is then fed into the joint reports. That said, the strength of that analysis may vary. While the 2010 joint report had a strong focus on the impact of the recession it also had a thematic focus on housing and homelessness. However, one interviewee concluded that the discussion of housing and homelessness had been one of the less successful exercises undertaken by the SPC.

(d) From 'Action Programme' to 'PROGRESS'

One of the complaints from social NGOs and Member States about the Commission's initial streamlining communication was that it omitted any discussion of the future of the action programme intended to support the social exclusion OMC process. In part this was because the programme was due to end in 2006 in any event and would have its own evaluation undertaken. Nonetheless, even this highlighted the tendency to view the OMC and the action programme as somewhat distinct activities rather than as mutually supportive aspects of the overall governance architecture.

The funding of activities beyond 2006 was streamlined into a single financial instrument and programme—the Community Programme for Employment and Social Solidarity (PROGRESS)[31]—which brought together action programmes to promote equality as well as the employment and social inclusion programmes. The overall budget for PROGRESS was set at €743.25m for the period 1 January 2007–31 December 2013 to support five strands of activity:

- Employment policy
- Social protection and inclusion
- Working conditions
- Anti-discrimination and diversity and
- Gender equality.

[31] Decision 1672/2006 of the EP and Council establishing a Community Programme for Employment and Social Solidarity—PROGRESS: [2006] OJ L315/1.

The social protection and inclusion strand of activity was allocated 30 per cent of this funding—approximately €220 million across seven years—representing an increase in funding from the previous programme.

The activities funded under PROGRESS are intended to support the policy coordination architecture described above. Nonetheless, the articulation between the priorities developed within the reporting and monitoring process of the OMC and those within the action programme is often not clear with two distinct committees underpinning each aspect. For example, the peer review process continued with seven reviews conducted in each of 2005 and 2006, nine in 2007, seven in 2008, and nine in 2009.[32] Yet, the selection of areas for review is not necessarily correlated strongly with the priority themes emerging from the OMC, and it is noteworthy that the peer reviews are often compared to the OMC, with participants commenting favourably on the former as being 'more concrete' than the latter.

As the Decision establishing PROGRESS makes clear, one of the functions of the programme is:

> monitoring and evaluating the implementation of the OMC in the field of social protection and inclusion and its impact at national and Community level as well as analysing the interaction between this OMC and other policy areas.[33]

A good example of this evaluation of the OMC and its interaction with other policy areas can be found in the reports of the network of independent experts. In the earlier cycles of the OMC, the published reports of the experts were focused on the NAPincls of the Member States and assisted the Commission in the evaluation of the NAPincls. From 2006, however, these reports were no longer published but remained as confidential advice to the Commission. However, the experts also undertook thematic reports and as we saw above, the child poverty reports were used to inform the analysis and evaluation of Member States' policies to tackle child poverty. In addition the reports developed a more critical orientation towards the social OMC itself with one set of reports analysing the interaction between the social OMC and the Lisbon partnership for growth and jobs and another focusing on how to strengthen the social OMC. Both these reports are interesting commentaries on the state of the OMC after the changes made by streamlining.

In chapter eight, the issue of how to strengthen the OMC is considered in detail. For the moment, what is interesting is the analysis of the perceived weaknesses of the method. In their synthesis of the experts' reports, Frazer

[32] It is to be noted that the consortium organizing the peer review process changed when the contract was re-tendered.

[33] Article 5(b) Decision 1672/2006.

and Marlier (2008a) highlighted the following 'key findings':

- Awareness of the OMC is limited to s small group of involved actors and has not spread more widely within the national and sub-national polity.
- NGOs tend to evaluate the process more negatively often because they have high expectations of the process whereas participating officials are more positive but do not expect it to play a fundamental role within their policy-making processes.
- Less than a quarter of participating states view it as more than a means of exchanging practice and actually positively use the OMC in policy-making.
- Criticisms of the process include low visibility; low political status; low levels of integration into domestic policy-making; and the lesser status of the process compared to the growth and jobs agenda.
- Positive evaluations include improving governance arrangements and policy coordination; keeping issues of poverty and social exclusion on the political agenda; developing common conceptualizations of problems; generating a body of knowledge and data about problems and potential solutions.

What is striking is that these comments are not vastly different from those reported in the Member States' own evaluations of the process *prior* to streamlining.

Similarly, the report on 'feeding out/feeding in' (Frazer and Marlier, 2008b) emphasized the *potential* for productive synergies while reporting very limited positive mutual interaction between the social OMC and the Lisbon II partnership for growth and jobs. This was consistent with the SPC report on the mutual interaction of the processes and highlights that although the commitment to a balanced policy agenda had been re-established, by the launch of the 2008–2010 parallel cycles of the Lisbon II partnership for growth and jobs and the social policy coordination process, it was not apparent that the governance architecture at either EU or national level was capable of implementing a virtuous engagement between the 'integrated' economic and employment process and the 'streamlined' social OMC process.

Conclusions

The transition from the first generation of the OMC to combat social exclusion, to the second generation of the OMC on Social Protection and Social

Inclusion evidences both institutional continuity and institutional change. At the constitutional level, we saw an abortive attempt to 'constitutionalize' the OMC both as a general governance technique and more specifically as a means of institutionalizing the commitment to combat poverty and social exclusion through policy coordination. In any event, with constitutional reform stalled until the final ratification of the Lisbon Treaty and its entry into force on 1 December 2009, the OMC continued to evolve without formal legal change.

Where the social OMC encountered more turbulent air was in the evolving policy context of the Lisbon strategy. The relaunch of the strategy as a growth and jobs partnership and the development of an integrated governance architecture for economic and employment policy coordination had left the fate of the social OMC up for grabs. A combination of a campaign by social NGOs and rather fortunate timing in the run of EU presidencies ensured a reaffirmed commitment to the original social goals of the Lisbon strategy. Nonetheless, the governance architecture of the social OMC was left outside of the Lisbon integrated process and while expected to engage in mutual interaction, the two processes struggled to either 'feed in' or 'feed out'.

However, the forces acting on the social OMC were not wholly external to it. Within EU social policy itself, the agenda of modernizing social protection reasserted itself and subsumed the work on social inclusion within a more diverse social policy coordination process. That said, it is striking that the work on social inclusion continued to dominate the new 'streamlined' social OMC. Notwithstanding the reporting changes which led to National Strategic Reports being produced, distinctive NAPincls remained. While the common objectives were revised, they retained some of the original substantive multidimensional orientation, albeit that the paradigm of activation emerged more strongly and specific target groups—children and ethnic minorities—appeared as particular concerns. Changes in the common indicators brought in new possibilities for measuring in-work poverty and the effectiveness of social protection systems in providing an adequate income, yet at the same time data gaps were apparent and the move to EU-SILC created breaks in the run of data.

Amidst other technical changes to the governance architecture, what is noteworthy is that the periodical cyclical national reporting and EU monitoring evolved from a process that was itself largely about process in the first generation of the OMC to one that was increasingly capable of delivering substantive policy analysis. This we saw with the work on child poverty and later with the work on the social impact of the recession. In part, this was a function of the design change that meant that in intervening years between national reports, the joint reports could develop a more thematic focus. However, it was also related to the work of the Social Protection Committee and its relationship both to the work of the Network of Independent Experts and the Indicators Sub-Group. This capacity for enhanced assessment of the risks of poverty and social exclusion is interesting, but it equally calls into question the relationship between this sort of technical data collection and analysis and the more political messaging undertaken through the cyclical reporting and monitoring.

Taking the constitutional, policy and governance levels together, it is suggested that EU intervention to combat poverty and social exclusion occupied an unsettled institutional space in this second phase of development. Whether or not to constitutionalize the OMC and whether or not to treat social policy as inside or outside the Lisbon strategy were highly contested during this period. Elements of the governance architecture were strengthened but at the same time, across and within different elements, a range of not entirely consistent or coordinated signals and steers were being generated as the architecture evolved.

5

Europeanization through Policy Coordination

Introduction

In the previous chapters, the analysis explored Europeanization as 'institution-building' through an exploration of the emergence and evolution of policy coordination as a technique of EU governance. The concern of this chapter is to analyse Europeanization in terms of 'domestic penetration' by the EU (Olsen, 2002). In doing so, the evidence presented here very deliberately seeks to bring to the fore the theoretical, conceptual and methodological difficulties in conducting Europeanization analysis (see Bulmer, 2007; Radaelli and Pasquier, 2007; and Haverland, 2007). It is suggested that these problems are apparent when studying the OMC given both its open-textured natured and the continual interaction between EU and domestic institutions. The first part of the analysis, therefore, explores issues relating to conducting Europeanization research on EU policy coordination.

Analyses of Europeanization typically explore the relationship between membership of the EU and domestic *polities*, *politics* and *policies*. It is that tripartite structure of analysis that is utilized here. Of particular significance for a study of the OMC is the capacity of policy coordination to influence domestic policy. As will be explored further below, this is also where some of the more pressing methodological difficulties arise. As regards the polity and politics dimensions, changes at these levels may be something that a Europeanization analysis attempts to explain, ie, it is changes in the polity or politics of a Member States that is the dependent variable. Yet it is apparent too, that these dimensions are also mediating variables that explain the extent to which change in the policy dimension occurs. It is this mediating role which will be a particular point of focus, although changes to the polity itself will be noted where appropriate.

The analysis adopts a single case-study of adaptation by the UK to the OMC to combat poverty and social exclusion, spanning the first (2001–2003; 2003–2005) and second (2006–2008; 2008–2010) generations of reporting, monitoring and evaluation discussed in chapters three and four. The decision to take a single case-study requires explanation. There is every good reason to take a case-study approach to the analysis of the OMC but understandably, it might be thought better to adopt comparative case-studies across a number of Member States, or to compare the OMC to different governance techniques or to compare different OMC processes (see Haverland's discussion of case-studies in Europeanization analysis: 2007). Certainly, scholarly work on the OMC has often sought to draw comparisons across a number of Member States.[1]

Nonetheless, attempts to explore the effects of EU policy coordination through comparative research often has the effect of giving the OMC an overly singular and coherent identity. Even comparisons of the same OMC across different states—except perhaps as book length projects in their own right—run the risk of losing some of the detail and nuance that a single case-study can provide. The aspiration of this study is to draw out the issue in applying Europeanization analysis to a governance technique like the OMC and to develop a robust methodological approach which may guide future singular and comparative studies.

Mechanisms of Change

In Caporaso's (2007) three-stage Europeanization model a process of European integration occurs, that results in adaptation pressures, which are mediated in the domestic context. Yet, we cannot treat European integration as a singular phenomenon characterized by a unique governance technique. Adaptation pressures and domestic mediation are, therefore, related to the governance tool deployed. New forms of governance may produce different effects from those previously analysed in studies of European integration (see Radaelli, 2008). In this way, an initial point of clarity relates to paying particular attention to the governance technique at issue, especially when—like the OMC—its emergence is an aspect of change within the European

[1] See the studies in Zeitlin, 2005a; Heidenreich and Zeitlin, 2009; Kröger, 2008 and de la Porte, 2008.

integration process itself, whether characterized as evidence of the limits of the Community Method or as an alternative means of reconciling diversity within a common European framework.

This point is of particular salience because of the position of 'goodness of fit' explanations of Europeanization (see Börzel and Risse, 2003; Radaelli, 2003a). The essence of this hypothesis is that the greater the gap between the domestic situation and the EU norm, the greater the adaptation pressure. The hypothesis has been critiqued in the literature leading to responses that either goodness of fit is a necessary but not sufficient condition (Börzel and Risse, 2003), or that it is not even a necessary condition (Mastenbroek and Kaeding, 2006). Moreover, as Bulmer identifies, the hypothesis is problematic in the context of the OMC where '[T]he whole point of the OMC is to avoid imposing policy templates from the supranational level.' (2007: 52). Nonetheless, it will be apparent in the discussion below that different elements of domestic strategies and policies are more or less commensurate with aspects of the OMC methodology creating adaptation pressures. Moreover, because of the capacity of the domestic level to penetrate and project into the EU level—the influence of domestic actors on EU institutions not least through the mediating role of the SPC—sates may consciously seek to upload aspects of their domestic practices in order to limit the need for domestic adaptation. In this sense, the goodness of fit explanation is not wholly inappropriate in the context of the OMC but rather needs to be nuanced to manage its specificities and is subject to the overriding caveat that adaptation pressures *per se* are not a sufficient basis for explaining the effects of the EU on Member States.

An obvious approach is to compare different governance modes or techniques and hypothesize about their expected comparative influence on Member States. As discussed in chapter two, Citi and Rhodes (2007) sought to examine the domestic effects of different types of governance instrument including the OMC. Nonetheless, in focusing directly on outcomes—'policy convergence'—their analysis was less concerned to unpick the different dynamics and mechanisms of domestic change, preferring instead to hypothesize about the anticipated effects of 'hard' law—convergence—and then to extrapolate across the spectrum of 'soft' law and a scale of potential convergence effects. This gives us an overly simplistic account of the force of adaptation pressures emanating from different instruments; tells us nothing about the trajectory of such forces; and is not all that revealing about what it is that may be converging.

A more nuanced approach concerned with analysing the mechanisms of policy transfer was developed by Bulmer and Padgett (2005). In their analysis of policy transfer via coercive and non-coercive governance processes, Bulmer and Padgett compared governance by 'hierarchy', by 'negotiation' and by 'facilitated coordination'. For Bulmer and Padgett, their 'general hypothesis is that hierarchy will generate the strongest form of policy transfer' with facilitated coordination producing 'a diffuse form of mutual *influence* between states, or in the worst case, *abortive* transfer' (2005: 106). The strength of this analysis lies in its capacity to identify multiple trajectories and different intensities of adaptation pressure and their relationship to different modes of governance. The difficulty with their analysis and their treatment of the OMC is the tendency of the comparative approach to give the OMC a rather singular identity associated with a single 'mode' of governance and anticipated adaptation pressure, to be compared to other governance tools similarly understood as having a singular identity and association with a particular mode of governance. Rather stylized contrasts and dissimilarities between the OMC and other instruments emerge while at the same time, differences between OMC processes or even differences within the architectural elements of the OMC or changes across time are suppressed. The point that can be made then, is that one ought not to purchase a more variegated understanding of the different Europeanization effects of different approaches to EU governance by treating the OMC as an overly coherent singular governance tool for the point of view of comparison.

Therefore, in this study, the intention is not to seek to compare the OMC to other governance tools, nor to compare domestic adaptation to the OMC in different states. Rather the intention is to explore the responsiveness of the UK to EU policy coordination to combat poverty and social exclusion but in doing so, to be sensitive to the idea that different elements of the coordination architecture may generate adaptation forces of different trajectories and of different intensities.

In terms of the trajectories of forces for change, Radaelli (2003a) has suggested that there are essentially two directions of travel: vertical and horizontal. For Radaelli, the former is typically identified with 'hierarchy' as a mode of governance while the latter may be associated with 'competition' or processes of socialization. In this study, a somewhat broader conceptualization is offered of the range of modes of governance—and consequential trajectory of forces—operating within the OMC. Indeed, the approach adopted here reinforces the claim made previously that the OMC is not only an assemblage of methodologies, but also of governance modes. Colin Scott has identified four 'control models' which, for present purposes can be equated to 'modes' of governance as explained in chapter two. These consist of:

- hierarchy
- competition
- community
- design.

The hierarchical mode identifies the trajectory of adaptation as top-down, whereas competitive adaptation or selection assumes a more horizontal axis of influence (see Olsen, 2002; Bulmer, 2007). Community models emphasize bottom-up and horizontal processes of adaptation and 'experiential learning' (Olsen, 2002). Design models impose physical constraints on adaptation. In the context of the OMC this would include things such as the time given for, or the timing of, a reporting obligation, or the space constraints on the size of reports. The forces exerted by such constraints are top-down, bottom-up and horizontal. What is suggested here is that the OMC—rather than conforming to a single mode—contains a mix of methodologies which together exert adaptation pressures in all four of the modes depicted by Scott, acting along different trajectories and with different intensities. It is important then to tease out the responses of Member States in respect of particular aspects of the OMC methodology. This is the task undertaken more fully below. Before doing so, however, the analysis adopts the tripartite distinction common in the Europeanization literature that looks to the relative roles of polity, politics and policy as explanatory variables for domestic adaptation.

Polity

The mediating effect of the polity relates not only to the way in which European issues are specifically handled within the political system but also the way in which general features and changes in the polity affect the capacity and opportunities for the EU to influence domestic policy. In the discussion below particular emphasis is placed on the division of powers and institutional structures of the polity. In the context of a case study of the UK, an important preliminary point to note is the obvious historic absence of a written constitution for the UK. With a 'political constitution' (Griffiths, 1979), the role of the courts and the vindication of constitutional rights has been less of a defining feature in shaping social policy as might be found in other states (Fabre, 2005).[2] However, it is worth highlighting that in the period under study, the UK did experience an important European influence on its constitutional arrangements but not one emanating from the EU. The Human Rights Act 1998 incorporated the civil and political rights of the European Convention on Human Rights into domestic law. Nonetheless, the social and economic rights of the 1961 European Social Charter were not similarly incorporated. Indeed, although the Labour Government elected in 1997 signed the revised 1996 European Social Charter in 1997, it did not subsequently ratify the Charter. As such, social rights as fundamental rights have not been a defining aspect of constitutionalism in the UK. Accordingly the focus of the discussion of the polity is more directly concerned with the contours of political power and the relationship between governmental and non-governmental actors.

Central Government

Within central government, the Department of Work and Pensions (DWP)—as successor from June 2001 to the previous Department for Social Security—is of particular importance to this study. DWP had responsibility for publishing *Opportunity for All* as central government's statement of strategy and policies to combat poverty and social exclusion. This annual report contained indicators and targets to measure progress in achieving UK government goals. It was also within DWP that responsibility for preparing the National Action Plans on Inclusion fell (together with the early National Action Plans on Employment under the European Employment Strategy). Representatives from DWP are also members of the EU Social Protection Committee and in this sense, were important vehicles for the UK to project into EU governance (see Bulmer and Burch, 2005) as well as the means of mediating pressures from the EU. In this way, central government responses to EU coordination were mainstreamed within the normal business of the DWP rather than hived off to a distinct European unit or department.

The role of the Cabinet Office—as coordinator of government business—is also worthy of note. In the summer of 1997, following the election of the Labour government to office, it was announced that a new

[2] An important qualification to this has been the growing influence of judicial review of administrative action. Particularly in cases concerning discretionary resource allocation—a not unimportant area especially in respect of long-term case issues covered by the OMC—litigation has played an important role.

Social Exclusion Unit would be located within the Cabinet Office to report directly to the Prime Minister. The Unit was then transferred to the now defunct Office of the Deputy Prime Minister but responsibility was later transferred back to the Cabinet Office. The Unit itself was replaced in 2006 by the Social Exclusion Task Force which remained within the Cabinet Office. It is important to note, however, that the territorial scope of the Unit was England rather than the UK and its task was to develop thematic reports on different aspects of social exclusion that would then be taken forward by other government departments. Neither the Unit nor the Cabinet Office assumed a general coordinating role in respect of UK-wide policy on social exclusion nor a role in respect of responding to the OMC. In respect of the relationship between central government and the devolved administrations (discussed below), the Cabinet Office briefly played a coordinating role in respect of the Joint Ministerial Committee (Poverty). However, this structure fell into abeyance with coordination taking place at department level within DWP, including coordinating the involvement of the devolved administrations in respect of the UK NAPincl. In this way, DWP emerged as the key interlocutor both upstream in terms of handling EU policy coordination and downstream in coordinating the input of the devolved administrations.

The title of Minister for Social Exclusion has sometimes been used in respect of ministers of state within the Cabinet Office. In 2006, the then Prime Minister Tony Blair appointed Hilary Armstrong as Minister for the Cabinet Office and Social Exclusion as part of a renewed commitment to tackling social exclusion. The minister would have a seat in the Cabinet and chair a new Ministerial Committee on Social Exclusion with terms of reference:

> To develop an Action Plan for tackling persistent social exclusion; to ensure mechanisms for delivering the Action Plan are put in place; and to oversee longer term strategy development.

The *Reaching Out* Action Plan was adopted in September 2006. With the transition to Gordon Brown as Prime Minister in June 2007, Hilary Armstrong left office and by 2010 the social exclusion portfolio was once again held by a Cabinet Office minister of state—the Minister for the Third Sector—who would not attend Cabinet, with the chair of the Cabinet Committee on Life Chances (Social Exclusion) taken by the Minister for the Cabinet Office and the Olympics.

What this identifies is that notwithstanding the coordinative role of the Cabinet Office and notwithstanding that a specific Social Exclusion Unit was housed within it, in organizational terms, the Cabinet Office was not the institutional home of either strategies or policies to combat social exclusion, nor can its ministers be said to be their champion. Rather, DWP has been the institutional home of the UK's anti-poverty strategy—subject to the influence of HM Treasury discussed below—and certainly played the key role in coordinating UK government reception of the EU coordination process.

An important feature of UK central government has been the system for performance management of spending departments within the context of periodic 'Spending Reviews' undertaken by HM Treasury (HMT). Public Service Agreements (PSAs) are entered into with government departments that contain specified objectives and targets over the period of the spending review (typically a three-year cycle). The first Comprehensive Spending Review (CSR) 1998 created PSAs for the period from 1999 until 2002. The PSAs and the objectives they contain represent key strategic commitments by government. Responsibility for achieving these objectives rests with individual departments or is shared across departments.

PSA 2000 set out four main objectives for the then Department for Social Security (later DWP) that are relevant to this study:

- ensure the best start for all children and end child poverty in 20 years;
- promote work as the best form of welfare for people of working age, while protecting the position of those in greatest need;
- combat poverty and promote security and independence in retirement for today's and tomorrow's pensioners;
- modernizing welfare delivery so as to improve the accessibility and accuracy of services.

A fifth objective appeared in PSA 2002:

- improve rights and opportunities for disabled people in a fair and inclusive society.

The 2004 PSA reformulated the objective on modernizing welfare reform to:

- ensure customers receive a high quality service, including high levels of accuracy.

Within this largely stable set of objectives, the density and focus of individual targets changed over time. However, the broad objectives were reformulated in CSR 2007 to set thirty PSAs for the period 2008–2011. Of particular relevance here are:

- PSA8: maximize employment opportunity for all;
- PSA9: halve the number of children in poverty by 2010–2011, on the way to eradicating child poverty by 2020;
- PSA15: address the disadvantage that individuals experience because of their gender, race, disability, age, sexual orientation, religion or belief;
- PSA16: increase the proportion of socially excluded adults in settled accommodation and employment, education or training;
- PSA17: tackle poverty and promote greater independence and well-being in later life.

PSAs 10–14 also set objectives in respect of the health, safety, educational attainment and skills of young people. In this way, these objectives tend to take a lifecycle approach, with interventions focused on children, young adults, working age adults and older persons but also identifying that individuals and groups may be vulnerable to specific types of discrimination. The particular significance of the child poverty target will be noted further below. For the moment, it is enough to note that objective-setting and target-setting have been very familiar aspects of UK central government policy-making and budget-setting processes.

The role of HMT is not reducible to the system of spending reviews and performance management described above. The Treasury and its Chancellor were to play key substantive policy roles in the development of policies on tax credits as a central plank of the UK government's strategy to make work pay and to seek to avoid the dangers of poverty traps arising from moves from benefits to work. Moreover it was the Chancellor of the Exchequer that in 2003 announced a review into child poverty, reporting in 2004 (HM Treasury, 2004). In this way, the role of the Treasury was not confined to setting the broad parameters of macroeconomic or microeconomic policy but was very much part of the policy process in the reform of welfare policies.

Scrutiny of the executive rests with the committee structures of the Houses of Parliament. The European Scrutiny Committee of the House of Commons and the House of Lords European Union Committee have responsibility for sifting EU documents for their implications for the UK. Very little discussion of the OMC has taken place in these committees, although both committees have taken the opportunity—defensively—to seek to protect the prerogatives of the UK Parliament from encroachment by EU institutions via the OMC, particularly by resisting calls for EU-level targets in the social sphere. Scrutiny by departmental select committees has tended not to consider matters relating to OMC processes although they have been actively engaged in reviewing domestic welfare reforms. One example—scrutiny by the Education and Skills Select Committee—is however, instructive, with the Committee seeking assurances that the European Commission was not seeking to expand its involvement in higher education through the OMC by exploiting the absence of a firm treaty basis for EU policy coordination.[3]

Notwithstanding devolution of powers to the nations that constitute the UK, both the House of Commons Scottish and Welsh Affairs Committees monitored the implications of UK policy for these nations and, during the period of this study, published reports on poverty. It is, however, to the implications of devolution that the discussion now turns.

Devolved Government

One of the most significant structural changes within the UK polity has been the process of devolution of powers to Scotland, Wales and Northern Ireland: a change that was consequent upon the election of the Labour party to government at UK level in 1997.[4] The process of devolution has been asymmetric in a number of ways. First and most obviously, while devolution of powers to Wales and Scotland has been continuous since the first elections in 1999, the Northern Ireland Assembly was suspended in October 2002. Although new elections were held in Northern Ireland in 2003, the Assembly remained suspended and a new 'Transitional Assembly' was constituted as a non-legislative body to prepare for the resumption of devolved powers.[5] Devolution of powers to the Northern Ireland Assembly was resumed in May 2007 following new elections to the Assembly in March 2007. Secondly, the legislative and executive responsibilities of the devolved institutions varied from the outset. In Scotland, legislative and executive responsibilities were devolved to a Scottish Parliament and a Scottish Executive (later changing its name to the 'Scottish Government'). The Scottish Parliament has full

[3] House of Commons Select Committee on Education and Skills, Fourth Special Report (Session 2006–2007), HC 788.

[4] The Scotland Act 1998, Government of Wales Act 1998 and the Northern Ireland Act 1998 make provision for the establishment of the devolved institutions.

[5] Northern Ireland (St Andrews Agreement) Act 2006.

primary legislative authority in areas of devolved competence and a limited tax-raising power. Legislative and executive powers are devolved to the Northern Ireland Assembly, with the Office of First Minister and Deputy First Minister leading an Executive Committee of ministers. The devolution settlement was different for Wales in that the Welsh Assembly was not vested with primary law-making powers, but acted principally as an executive body, albeit with certain delegated law-making functions. Nonetheless, the issue of the legislative competence of the Assembly remained in issue and the Government of Wales Act 2006 introduced important changes. These changes including a formal legal separation of the National Assembly for Wales from the Welsh Assembly Government with the former acquiring a new right to adopt 'Assembly Measures', a legislative power conferred on the Assembly by a clause in a UK Act of Parliament. Thirdly, the areas of devolved competence vary across the nations.[6] Importantly, however, the key policy levers of income taxation and welfare benefits remained within central government control.

It is not possible in this study to do justice to the evolution of the governance of social inclusion within and across the devolved regions. Nonetheless, we can give a flavour of developments within the devolved administrations by highlighting two issue of relevance to this study. The first is to use the example of developments in Scotland to illustrate the diversification of strategies to combat social exclusion in the UK. This diversification had consequences for what it would mean to have a UK 'national' action plan (discussed more fully below). The second issue relates to a more direct effect of the OMC on strategies within the devolved administrations and here the example of Northern Ireland is used to highlight a very specific potential Europeanization effect.

In Scotland, the approach of Scottish Ministers was initially to follow the style of their colleagues in Whitehall, by producing annual *Social Justice* reports with targets, milestones and indicators based around a life-cycle approach. However, one of the problems with this approach was that key levers through which to make progress against these targets lay with central government through the tax and benefits system. The last *Social Justice* annual report appeared in 2002 and 2003 saw the last indicators of progress report using the original milestones. The *Social Justice Strategy* was reviewed and in 2004 replaced by a new strategic framework—*Closing the*

[6] Table 3 of the UK National Strategy Report 2008–2010 attempts to identify the different policy competences of the devolved administrations.

Opportunity Gap—with six objectives and ten targets. The objectives were consistent with a multidimensional understanding of social exclusion with a focus on employment, skills, financial exclusion, deprived communities, health status and access to services.[7] With the election of a minority Scottish National Party (SNP) Government in 2007, the policy framework shifted once again. The Scottish Government set out a new economic framework with new government 'purposes' including a specific solidarity commitment to raise the overall income and proportion of income of the bottom three income deciles. A new framework document—*Achieving Our Potential*—was published in November 2008 in collaboration with COSLA, setting out the Scottish Government's goal to tackle income inequality but also highlighting the desire for full devolved control over tax and benefits.

The point of setting out the changing Scottish position is to highlight two things. First, that devolved administrations would understandably seek to utilize their new powers and competences including putting in place distinctive strategies and policies to combat poverty and social exclusion. As such, the *Opportunity for All* annual report to the UK Parliament prepared by DWP could not be said to represent a UK-wide strategic document: it was increasingly a report on central government and English activities with the diverse strategies and policies developing within the devolved administrations reported elsewhere. The second point is that, as noted below, changes in the politics of the devolved institutions might, in any event, make the idea of a coherent and consistent UK strategy less tenable. Up until 2007 this was less significant given the degree of continuity in Labour domination of both UK and Scottish politics. This changed with the election of the SNP

[7] The new objectives were:

- To increase the chances of sustained employment for vulnerable and disadvantaged groups—in order to lift them permanently out of poverty;
- To improve the confidence and skills of the most disadvantaged children and young people—in order to provide them with the greatest chance of avoiding poverty when they leave school;
- To reduce the vulnerability of low income families to financial exclusion and multiple debts—in order to prevent them becoming over-indebted and/or to lift them out of poverty;
- To regenerate the most disadvantaged neighbourhoods—in order that people living there can take advantage of job opportunities and improve their quality of life;
- To increase the rate of improvement of the health status of people living in the most deprived communities—in order to improve their quality of life, including their employability prospects; and
- To improve access to high quality services for the most disadvantaged groups and individuals in rural communities—in order to improve their quality of life and enhance their access to opportunity.

Government with the emphasis shifting to the autonomy of Scottish policies and strategies including a new 'solidarity' objective of increasing overall income and the proportion of income earned by the three lowest income deciles as a group by 2017. While the SNP did seek to position Scotland comparatively to other similarly-sized northern European states—the 'arc of prosperity'[8]—this was about setting the case for the economic autonomy of a small state in Europe. It did not necessarily suggest a greater willingness to engage with an EU coordination process mediated through UK central government.

The case of Northern Ireland was different. In 1998 under direct rule, *New Targeting Social Need* (NTSN) was put in place as a replacement strategy to *Targeting Social Need* as the framework by which individual government departments would seek to skew resources towards social inclusion goals. However, evaluations of NTSN identified weaknesses in the framework and, again under direct rule, a consultation document on a new anti-poverty strategy was produced in April 2004 (OFMDPM, 2004). What was striking about this document was its explicit modelling of a Northern Ireland anti-poverty strategy on the EU policy coordination process. The emphasis was on setting targets and using indicators (including EU indicators) in a regional plan that would be consistent with what would be reported through the NAPincl.[9] Nonetheless, the intermittent nature of devolution in Northern Ireland made adoption of a new strategy difficult. Two rounds of consultation took place in 2004 and 2005, during which time, direct rule remained in place. In November 2006, under direct rule, the UK Northern Ireland Secretary launched *Lifetime Opportunities* as a new anti-poverty strategy for Northern Ireland (OFMDPM, 2006). Although this made reference to working in a European context and highlighted the role of the OMC, the document did not propose an anti-poverty strategy modelled on the EU process. Indeed, there was a certain continuity with NTSN in the sense of linking budgeting with policymaking,[10] while combining elements of the life-cycle approach used in central government reports—but with broad objectives and no clear targets or indicators—with a regional focus on

[8] The reference to an 'arc of prosperity' was referred to by the SNP leader in a speech in August 2006. The arc included Ireland and non-EU states Norway and Iceland.

[9] Nonetheless, there was criticism that the reporting structure of the OMC did little to recognize the relationship between social exclusion and conflict in Northern Ireland (Hillyard, Rolston and Tomlinson, 2005: 168).

[10] In the context of direct rule, this would mean skewing resources through the spending review and PSA process.

deprived areas. In this way, and perhaps as consequence of continuing direct rule, the potential transfer of a European model was somewhat abortive. One other important distinctive feature of the Northern Ireland situation is worthy of note. As well as establishing a transitional assembly, the Northern Ireland (St Andrews Agreement) Act 2006 gave express statutory authority to the Executive Committee of the assembly to adopt an anti-poverty strategy for Northern Ireland.[11] Whereas anti-poverty strategies emerged within the other devolved regions as expressions of political desires, in the Northern Irish example, it is a matter of statutory obligation. Devolution of powers to the Northern Ireland Assembly was resumed in May 2007 and in November 2008, the Executive adopted the 'broad architecture and principles' of the *Lifetime Opportunities* strategy as a basis for implementing its new statutory obligations to develop an anti-poverty strategy.

Local Governance

Local governance is vital to the implementation of social exclusion policies in the UK. However, the structure and organization of local governance varies across the UK. For example, in Wales, *Communities First* was launched in 2001 as the Welsh Assembly Government's key strategy for tackling poverty and social exclusion in the most deprived areas of Wales. 'Communities First Partnerships' bring together representatives of local communities, local statutory bodies—local government, health, schools, police—and local businesses in developing strategies to regenerate areas. This partnership approach is also evident in 'Community Planning Partnerships' under the Local Government in Scotland Act 2003 or the non-statutory 'Local Strategic Partnerships' for neighbourhood renewal in England. Local partnerships were also important to delivering the 'Sure Start' programme aimed at pre-school children in England (discussed further below).

The detailed local implementation of social inclusion strategies and policies is beyond the scope of this chapter. Nonetheless, aspects of these evolving governance relationships will be noted in the analysis below.

[11] Section 16 of the 2006 Act inserts the following provision as section 28E of the Northern Ireland Act 1998:

(1) The Executive Committee shall adopt a strategy setting out how it proposes to tackle poverty, social exclusion and patterns of deprivation based on objective need.

(2) The Executive Committee—

(a) must keep under review the strategy; and

(b) may from time to time adopt a new strategy or revise the strategy.

Politics

An analysis of the effects of the EU on UK anti-poverty strategies and policies cannot ignore the role of national politics, not least when changes in domestic politics lead to changes in government. This is particularly so in the UK given the transition to a new Labour Government in 1997 after eighteen years of Conservative rule. The Labour Government was comfortable in embracing the new discourse of 'social exclusion' (Levitas, 1998) and as Lister noted, was a 'rare example in recent years of adoption by a UK government of a European rather than a North American policy discourse' (Lister, 2004: 761). Yet, as Stewart and Hills noted (2005:9–10), there were fears that identifying social exclusion as being about more than poverty tended to sideline issues of income poverty and inequality. Moreover, for Levitas (1998) the attention shifted from inequality to 'opportunity', particularly the opportunity to take up paid work. Yet as the Institute for Public Policy Research (ippr) were also to note (2004), the language of poverty did not disappear. Indeed, the Labour Government made a pledge to eradicate child poverty and set targets to achieve this in its PSAs. In this way, the discourses of social exclusion and poverty have coexisted in UK politics, in part a reflection of a political shifting of the feet in terms of the extent to which politicians have or have not wished to address issues of income poverty and inequality.[12]

Politics and polity are also interrelated. Devolution of powers created a differentiated politics of social policy in the UK: a process also fuelled by changes in the voting systems for elections to the new institutions.[13] In Scotland, elections to the Scottish Parliament resulted in two Labour-dominated coalition governments with the Liberal Democrats.[14] The election of 2007 saw a shift to an SNP minority government. In Wales, the Labour party also entered into coalition governments, first with the Liberal Democrats in 1999 and then with the Welsh nationalist party Plaid Cymru in 2007, but with Labour's Rodhri Morgan holding the position of First

[12] Interestingly, the Conservatives in Opposition were willing to talk of poverty in taking on the Labour Government's record on poverty reduction. See David Cameron's speech of 8 October 2009 to the annual Conservative Party Conference.

[13] In Scotland and Wales, first-past-the-post constituency voting is topped up through an 'additional member' regional list.

[14] As James Mitchell described it: 'This was a gentle introduction to the consequences of multi-party, multi-minority politics facilitated by the continuation of the legacy of Labour-Liberal Democrat collaboration in the old Scottish Constitutional Convention.' SPICe Briefing, 07/21: <http://www.scottish.parliament.uk/business/research/briefings-07/SB07–21.pdf> (Accessed in March 2010).

Minister from 2000–2009. The situation in Northern Ireland is different as the composition of the Northern Ireland Executive is not solely determined by electoral success but also by a power-sharing structure which has seen the Unionist parties and Sinn Féin working together, not least by holding the offices of First Minister and Deputy First Minister respectively.

Leaving aside the Northern Ireland example for a moment, it is evident that the Labour party was the dominant political force in UK politics from 1997 until 2010, even under conditions of devolution. In this way, we would expect that the fundamental influence on UK strategies and policies to combat poverty and social exclusion would initially have been the change in central government control from Conservative to Labour. With devolution we would also expect there to be differentiation in policies with some elements of continuity of approach—given Labour party dominance even within sub-state polities—mitigated principally by the demands of coalition government (with a break emerging in Scotland after the 2007 election of a minority SNP Government). Nonetheless, across thirteen years of Labour UK Government, we would also expect to see changes within domestic policy and here the issue becomes one of seeking to trace sources of influences and to consider the role of both domestic and EU influences.

Policy

The extent to which domestic policies are the primary target of EU 'policy' coordination is rather more ambiguous than might at first be apparent. To the extent that policy is influenced, it is as a consequence of a more immediate desire to influence the domestic *strategic* environment. Indeed, the principal concern of the analysis below lies in evaluating the extent to which a Member State like the UK was responsive to EU pressures and influences on its anti-poverty strategies rather than with direct influences on the diverse policies which might be harnessed towards these strategic ends. Nonetheless, the density, stability and performance of the policy environment conditions the opportunity structure for external influence at a strategic level. Therefore, a brief overview of the domestic policy environment is required.

The election in 1997 of a Labour Government brought with it significant policy changes. As McKnight observes (2005), a key policy priority was to raise employment levels and tackle joblessness. An important initiative towards achieving this goal was the development of the New Deal programmes offering a new integrated approach to benefits and job-seeking—through new

Jobcentre Plus structures—with an emphasis on personalized support to move individuals off benefits and into work. This programme underpinned the Government's approach to modernizing social protection, 'transforming it from a passive benefits payment machine to an active system that tackles poverty, creates opportunity, and helps people become self-sufficient and independent' (UK NAPincl, 2003–2005: 12). Different 'New Deals' were developed for different target groups. Voluntary New Deal programmes were targeted at lone parents (on Income Support Benefit) and the disabled (those on Incapacity Benefit), while other New Deal programmes aimed at the working adult population emphasized the conditionality of unemployment benefits and the responsibility to take up opportunities of paid work.

Lone parents are a particular issue for the UK as they are overly represented in the number of workless households. Given the correlation between workless and poor households, tackling poverty and joblessness among lone parents has been a priority for the UK. Similarly, the number of persons claiming Incapacity Benefit in the UK has been of particular concern, with the UK NAPincl (2003–2005) reporting 2.7 million people of working age claiming this benefit. The UK NAPincl (2006–2008) announced a target of reducing this figure by one million over a decade. Following on from the Freud report on welfare reform commissioned by the UK Government (Freud, 2007) and a consultation Green Paper (DWP, 2008), new welfare legislation was introduced[15] which moved work-capable lone parents with older children off Income Support and onto Jobseeker's Allowance and introduced a new Employment and Support Allowance (ESA) to replace Incapacity Benefit. The issue of conditionality of benefits had been addressed in the Gregg report (Gregg, 2008) commissioned by the UK Government. The report recommended adoption of a spectrum of conditionality, with certain groups not subject to any conditions for receipt of benefits (eg those claiming ESA and lone parents with very young children), while for others a 'personalized' conditionality approach tailored to individual situations was suggested. Significantly, welfare reforms were introduced just at the point when economic recession made it harder to find work and pressures to reduce the post-recession budget deficit might make this sort of personalized support services harder to afford.

Making work pay underpinned two key policy initiatives. While often criticized for the bureaucracy associated with them, nonetheless, the introduction of tax credits was a flagship policy for the Labour Government. The

[15] See especially the Welfare Reform Acts of 2007 and 2009.

introduction of a minimum wage also marked a clear break with the policies of previous governments. Issues of income adequacy have, therefore, been closely related to participation in paid work.

Tackling child poverty has been a particular concern given the UK's very poor comparative record. The Treasury review initiated in 2003 resulted in a new child poverty measure composed of three related indicators: relative low income, absolute low income and material deprivation. Progress against this measure forms the basis for the child poverty target contained in the PSAs. In addition to the Treasury review and the subsequent Harker review (Harker, 2006), in 2009 the Government published a consultation paper *Ending Child Poverty: Making it Happen*. This was followed by the Child Poverty Act 2010 to put the child poverty targets on a statutory footing and to place consequential obligations on central and devolved government to develop strategies to meet the target and to report on progress. This legislative approach underscores the stress which has been placed on tackling child poverty within UK policy.

If we take together the domestic machinery for target-setting (with associated indicators for measuring progress) and the main reform initiatives highlighted above, it ought to be apparent that the issue in the UK has not been the absence of policies or initiatives to feed into policies to combat poverty and social exclusion but rather the capability and effectiveness of these reforms to deliver better outcomes. This has significant implications for the capacity of the OMC to influence the domestic strategic and policy environment as will be explored in more detail below.

Adapting to the OMC: A Case-Study of the United Kingdom

Identifying, measuring and categorizing the impact of the OMC on UK strategies to combat poverty and social exclusion are complex tasks. We can look for evidence of responsiveness to different elements of the OMC eg the production of National Action Plans on Inclusion; the use of the common objectives and common guidance for the preparation of NAPincls; responses to messages found in joint reports and council conclusions; the use of EU data and indicators; issues raised by non-governmental actors. Nonetheless, responsiveness to the OMC does not necessarily translate either into inputs into domestic strategies or policies to combat poverty and social exclusion.

We need to engage in exercises of policy-tracing that look to alternative explanations and rival sources of influence to determine the extent to which Europe really matters both for strategies and for policies to combat social exclusion.

The individual sections below seek to identify domestic adaptation to different elements of the OMC methodology. More than that, the analysis attempts to both measure domestic adaptation and to categorize the nature of the adaptation pressure. In terms of measuring domestic responses, once again, the Europeanization literature has supplied a variety of taxonomies with which to evaluate the extent of the domestic response. Radaelli (2003a) identifies four key responses:

- Inertia—no response;
- Absorption—the domestic system responds by accommodating the EU influence but within the standard operating processes and values of the domestic system;
- Transformation—this connotes a paradigmatic change;
- Retrenchment—there is active resistance to the attempted influence.

One other type of response might be considered to be relevant to a study of the OMC:

- Projection—this is where the Member State responds to EU influences by seeking to project back into EU governance its own models and values, hence reducing the extent of adaptation pressure.

As for categorizing adaptation, using the different models of governance discussed above, the analysis seeks to identify whether any domestic adaptation is the result of hierarchical, competitive, community or design influences.

As a means of organizing the analysis, responses to the different elements of the methodology will be grouped under three headings. The first section explores the dynamics of reporting and monitoring within the OMC with a particular focus on responsiveness to a range of sources of political coordinative communications between governmental actors at EU and national levels. This entails examination of responses to four sources of influence: (1) the general exhortation to develop a strategy in the form of a national plan; (2) the common objectives for the social OMC process; (3) the cross-EU issues identified in joint reports and the specific points raised in the country fiches accompanying the joint report; and (4) peer reviews. The second section looks to the more technical discourses surrounding common indicators and data. The third section explores responses to the role of non-governmental actors. By organizing the analysis in this way, the intention is to consider whether adaptation is different in response to different types of influence and discourse: political, technical, non-governmental.

Reporting and Monitoring

The discussion below focuses upon the UK's response to the request to report on its strategic plans to combat poverty and social exclusion and the use of common objectives as a means of structuring those strategic plans. More dynamically it considers the political communication and discourse emanating from the joint reports which, while not sanctions, nonetheless constitute a political accountability feedback loop which may itself trigger a response from Member States. The capacity for peer reviews to facilitate policy learning will also be explored.

(a) National Action Plans on Inclusion

Within the time frame of this study, four national plans were produced by Member States. The first generation of NAPincls (2001–2003; 2003–2005) were produced in response to the original set of common objectives and indicators on a biennial reporting cycle and within the context of a standalone OMC process to combat social exclusion. The third and fourth reports (2006–2008; 2008–2010) were formulated within the context of the National Strategy Reports (NSRs) covering the three areas of social exclusion, pensions and healthcare and in light of revised objectives and indicators.[16]

As a starting point, we can note that notwithstanding the absence of hierarchy, the UK—along with other Member States—voluntarily complied with the request to produce NAPincls.[17] Even states not then part of the EU were involved in producing inclusion 'memorandums' prior to EU accession. In terms of explaining this formal compliance, one obvious candidate explanation—compliance in the shadow of hierarchy—is not convincing as there was no plausible threat to mandate states to produce such reports. The idea of a competitive pressure to report is also not

[16] The 2006–2008 report was on a transitional two-year reporting cycle to allow the social OMC to align with the Lisbon growth and jobs coordination process. The 2008–2010 reports were intended to cover a three-year period up until 2011 and thus some commentaries refer to these as 2008–2011 reports.

[17] Member States were asked to produce 'update' reports in 2004: ten of the then fifteen Member States chose to do so (the UK did not do so). In 2005, a request was made for an 'implementation' report on the 2003–2005 NAPincl and all Member States submitted this including the UK, albeit that it submitted the report late.

wholly convincing although there might have been a reputational pressure to comply. A more convincing explanation would be to view this as a form of socialization within a community of officials operating at both national and EU levels: in the UK case, the DWP officials producing the NAPincl were also working with colleagues from other Member States in the Social Protection Committee. Moreover, national civil servants and ministers are now familiar with the need to comply with EU obligations. Even without the NAPincl being a matter of obligation, one UK official interviewed for this study highlighted the fact that the EU provenance of the request to produce a NAPincl was enough to provoke a compliance response. This is less of a shadow of hierarchy and more of a shadowy hierarchy: a learned response from doing business with Brussels.

The aspiration of EU officials was that Member States would produce strategic plans while the objective of monitoring was largely to evaluate how well that task had been achieved. Where Member States did not already have such strategic plans, then self-evidently, production of such a plan would indicate a strong Europeanization effect. Where states already possessed a strategic plan, then the Europeanization effect would be measured not just in terms of the mere adoption of the NAPincl but more in terms of the mutual interaction between the NAPincl and the existing domestic strategy. One effect could be the coexistence of the NAPincl and the domestic strategy. A more dramatic effect would be if the NAPincl replaced existing domestic plans and strategies. Again, the point to emphasize is that the initial effect to be judged lies at the level of adopting a NAPincl and its consequential impact on the domestic strategic environment rather than looking immediately for an effect directly on substantive domestic policy.

As regards UK policy, from 1999 the DWP produced the annual *Opportunity for All* (OFA) report to Parliament on central government policies and strategies to combat poverty and social exclusion. The first UK NAPincl was effectively a restatement of this document. This was hardly surprising given the design constraints of time—in terms of the short timeframe for producing the NAPincl—and timing—the recent adoption of OFA.[18] In this way, the response to the OMC was simply to absorb the request to produce a plan by switching the content of OFA into the first NAPincl

[18] Stewart and Hills (2005) also note that as the Labour party in Opposition had pledged to keep to Conservative spending plans for the first two years of its administration, it was only in 1999 that the Labour Government shifted its political discourse more explicitly towards tackling social exclusion. The publication of the first OFA report signalled this development.

and to detail a wide array of strategies and policies. Nonetheless, it was always ambiguous whether OFA was itself a strategy rather than a summary to Parliament of strategies that were contained, for example, in the objectives and targets set in the context of spending reviews and PSAs.

Whatever its precise status, changes across time were evident in OFA. The early OFA reports identified policies and strategies based around a life-cycle approach but from 2002 this changed to focus on the core elements of the UK Government's strategy. The EU process has not used a life-cycle approach but the change in OFA may simply have been a consequence of the annual report becoming repetitious and new ministers wanting to do new things with the report. Moreover, there was something of a later return to the life-cycle approach with a focus on children, working age adults and older persons, combined with a new focus on communities. It is difficult to conclude that these changes in focus and style within OFA derived from the influence of the NAPincls.

More significant evidence of an influence from the OMC was the 2005 OFA report. Coinciding with the UK's Presidency of the EU, OFA 2005 contained a 'Europe' chapter to highlight the OMC process. OFA 2005 also contained a specific chapter on 'Women' which was also significant given the impetus through the OMC to have a stronger analysis of gender in the national reports. A third important innovation in OFA 2005 was that it highlighted the activities of the devolved administrations. As discussed above, with devolution, it was apparent that OFA was a UK government document with each of the devolved administrations developing their own strategies and reports. The NAPincl created an opportunity for the work of the devolved administrations to be reflected in a 'national' plan. In an early analysis of the OMC, Bradshaw and Bennett noted (2003), '[T]he NAPincl process has in a way required the different jurisdictions to get back together again, a process which may eventually lead to a much less detached and more productive relationship between the UK government and the devolved administrations—both in policy and monitoring.' The extent to which the devolved administrations wanted an active role in the NAP process is open to question. Certainly they wanted representation of their activities within it but probably saw their own new strategic documents as the primary reference point for their activities. Nonetheless, the NAPincl did create a new space to bring together central and devolved strategies in one place and the section in OFA 2005 on partnership within the UK itself reflected that new working relationship.

This may all have been a one-off though due to the particular circumstances of the timing of the publication of the OFA report under the UK Presidency of the EU and coinciding with the annual Presidency 'Roundtable' being held in Glasgow in October 2005. OFA 2006 returned to a format of structuring the report around the life-cycle approach supplemented with a specific chapter on child poverty. Although the issue of child poverty became a key preoccupation of the OMC around this time, as noted above, the UK was already developing strategies and policies to tackle its high levels of child poverty. Indeed, this may be an example of issue transfer from the UK to the EU rather than the other way round.

Importantly OFA 2006 was the last OFA report. From that point on, the UK NAPincl became one of three strategic documents (the other two being the 2006 *Reaching Out* 'Action Plan' and the the 2007 pre-budget report and CSR). Yet of these three documents the UK NAPincl stands out because it was a report of both central and devolved activities and because of its relative continuity over time (its existence does not depend on the vagaries of the domestic political process). Thus, if the initial response to the OMC was to absorb the request to produce a NAPincl by transferring material from OFA into this new report, by the 2008–2010 cycle of reports, the NAPincl had effectively replaced OFA. Nonetheless, whether it be OFA or the NAPincl, the issue remains whether either of these documents can truly claim to constitute a strategy rather than a report of diverse strategies and policies. The impetus to replace OFA with the NAPincl may simply have been one of a desire to avoid duplication rather than to give the NAPincl a more visible or more strategic role.

(b) Common Objectives

The common objectives agreed at Nice and then reformulated from 2005 under the streamlined OMC process set out the framework within which Member States were requested to set out their strategies and priorities for action. The first UK NAPincl (2001–2003) structured its report around the substantive Nice objectives.[19] Given that the substance of what was being reported was drawn from OFA, the objectives were largely used as a reporting template rather than as a means of establishing new or revising existing

[19] The Nice objectives were to:

- facilitate participation in employment, and access by all to resources, rights, goods and services;
- prevent the risk of exclusion;
- help the most vulnerable;
- mobilize all relevant bodies.

strategic goals. Indeed, UK policy was stated as being based around four strategic objectives, to:

- eradicate child poverty;
- help working age people into work;
- provide older people with security in retirement; and
- narrow the gap between deprived communities and the rest.

These objectives drew more specifically on the objectives contained in the PSAs and which also framed the OFA reports.[20] As Stewart and Hills note (2005), these themes recurred within a broad multidimensional analysis of the causes and effects of social exclusion, albeit with a key emphasis on employment as the primary route out of poverty. In this way, UK strategies could be presented as broadly consistent with the multidimensional approach to social exclusion underpinning the Nice objectives, albeit without the overtones of a more rights-based social citizenship paradigm (this can be contrasted with the first French NAPincl: see Kröger, 2008: 88).[21]

The second UK NAPincl (2003–2005) also continued to use the Nice objectives as a template albeit that the objective of protecting the most vulnerable no longer constituted a theme in its own right in the UK report but rather was absorbed into discussions of the other substantive Nice objectives. And as with the first NAPincl, UK strategy was instead identified in its own thematic terms, this time as a three-pillared strategy based around:

- maintaining a strong economy;
- flexible labour markets to ensure that work is available for those that can work;
- accessible and accountable first class public services.

As a basis for an anti-poverty strategy this would appear to place emphasis much more on the objectives of economic and employment policy coordination than on the social policy objectives of the OMC to combat social exclusion. It gave the impression that growth and employment were the key drivers of domestic policy. Yet the remainder of the NAPincl faithfully reported a range of policies and strategies based around the Nice objectives of facilitating access to employment, access to resources, rights and services

[20] Curiously the objective of reforming welfare systems identified in PSA 2000 does not appear here but instead is substituted by the reference to deprived communities.

[21] De la Porte does suggest that rights-based approaches were introduced into debates within DWP but that these did not materialize in policy decisions (de la Porte, 2008: 242).

and preventing the risks of exclusion. There was, therefore, a certain tension between what the UK Government was stating as the basis for its strategy—growth and jobs—and what it reported as its actual social policies and tools to combat social exclusion.

What is also significant is that the UK Government's objectives reflected the priorities set out in its spending reviews and its PSAs, not least because the cycles of budgetary-planning and objective-setting were in advance of the OMC cycle. Thus, the second UK NAPincl stated that:

> Priorities for the period of this NAP must be set within the context of the domestic objectives set at all levels of government. This might include the time necessary for consultation, or existing budgetary or spending review cycles. These may not coincide with the timeframe of this NAP.

In this way, we could fairly conclude that any top-down pressure to develop priorities around the common objectives met with resistance from the structure and timing of domestic objective-setting. As such the role of the common objectives was largely to act as a design template for reporting. Moreover, it was not difficult for the UK to project a multidimensional approach to combating social exclusion in line with the Nice objectives, while at the same time placing a strong emphasis on economic growth and employment as drivers of policy.

In one important respect, however, the Nice objectives had a profound effect on the practices of DWP. The objective to 'mobilize' all actors and the perceived criticism in the first joint report that the NAPincls had not been developed in a participative manner was seized upon by social NGOs looking for new avenues of influence within the domestic political process. As documented elsewhere (Armstrong, 2005; 2006a), in the UK a self-conscious decision was taken within DWP to develop a more participative approach to the development of the second NAPincl. A Social Policy Task Force (SPTF) brought in social NGOs in dialogue with DWP around the NAPincl.[22] Since its inception the SPTF has been engaged in regular dialogue with the DWP. Importantly, seminars and awareness-raising sessions were held with grassroots organizations and a Participation Working Group emerged to feed the views of those experiencing poverty into discussions around the second NAPincl. The development of a participative approach to the NAPincl had

[22] Formally, the SPTF is a joint working group of two networks: the network of devolved social NGOs in the UK organized as the national member of EAPN; and the Coalition Against Poverty acting as an umbrella organization to give a UK focus to anti-poverty campaigning.

an important knock-on effect not just for the UK but for other Member States. When the Commission floated the idea of losing the distinct identity of the NAPincls for the second generation of streamlined reports, the UK pointed to the processes it had developed around the NAPincl and argued strongly for their retention within the context of the NSRs. With NAPincls retained as a distinct entity, the UK continued to publish in hard copy its NAPincl while only disseminating its NSRs in online form.

Under the streamlined objectives for the second generation of NAPincls, a procedural objective was maintained within the social inclusion strand requiring the involvement in social inclusion policies of governmental and other actors, including those experiencing poverty. The UK's 2006–2008 NAPincl—the first under the new streamlined approach—turned out to be the highpoint of the UK's informal participative approach. Building on the work of the Participation Working Group and the idea of developing a participation 'toolkit' to feed in the views of those experiencing poverty and grassroots organizations, funding from the EU's action programme was obtained for the 'Get Heard' project. As will be explored in more detail below, workshops and seminars were held around the UK and the views expressed were reported in the subsequent NAPincl. A DWP-sponsored Stakeholder Group also brought together central government departments, devolved administrations, local authorities and social NGOs in dialogue around the NAPincls. Yet despite all this activity, the participative process was weakly institutionalized in formal terms and highly reliant on the willingness of particular civil servants within DWP to put time and energy into fostering this dialogue between government and non-governmental actors. When a key civil servant was moved to another task, and with other pressures on staff within DWP, the experience of the fourth NAPincl (2008–10) was wholly different. As the EAPN assessment of the 2008–2010 reports identified (EAPN, 2008a), the SPTF only saw a draft of the NAPincl late on and without an opportunity to comment on it. The planned meeting of the Stakeholder Group was cancelled. One interviewee described the report as a 'rush job'. While not intending to signal a withdrawal from participative processes—indeed DWP moved to formalize its consultation process by recasting the Stakeholder Group as an 'advisory group' with an appointed Chair[23]—it did highlight the fragility of these processes and their reliance on personal rather than institutionally embedded commitments.

[23] The model for this was the Ethnic Minority Advisory Group.

In addition to the participation objective under the social inclusion strand, a new 'good governance' objective was introduced as an overarching objective. In chapter one of the UK's NSR—the overview chapter—the UK responded to this objective by identifying the governance process of the spending reviews and the PSAs together with the mechanisms for monitoring and evaluating progress in achieving these objectives. In this way, good governance was interpreted as 'evidence-led' rather than 'participatory' governance. Therefore, the participative approach outlined above remains limited to the NAPincl rather than to the NSR as a whole, which again reinforces the distinctive identity of the NAPincl in the UK.

Two new substantive overarching objectives and revised common objectives for the social inclusion strand were agreed for the new 'streamlined' OMC (see chapter four for further discussion). At the same time, design constraints limited the space available for Member States to report their strategies and policies, with the result that the UK opted to append multiple annexes to its reports. As noted above, one means of responding to the OMC objectives was to treat them as a thematic design template through which to structure the national reports. Looking at the UK NSR and NAPincl for 2006–2008, a distinct trend emerged. The first part of the UK NSR used the new overarching common objectives as a general reporting template. However, the NAPincl departed from that approach. While common objectives were set to normatively frame coordination, it was also to the priorities and themes emerging from Council Conclusions and joint reports that the Member States were asked to respond. In particular, the guidance given to Member States for the preparation of their 2006–2008 reports requested Member States to select certain priorities from those identified in the 2005 joint report (see Table 5.1).

Table 5.1 2005 Joint Report Priorities

1. increase labour market participation
2. modernize social protection systems
3. tackle disadvantage in education and training
4. eliminate child poverty
5. ensure decent accommodation
6. improve access to quality services
7. overcome discrimination and increase integration of people with disabilities, ethnic minorities and immigrants.

(European Commission and Council, 2005)

The UK NAPincl structured its report around four themes from this list:

- elimination of child poverty
- increasing labour market participation
- improving access to quality services
- tackling discrimination.

In this way, while the common objectives served a purpose as a means of normatively framing EU intervention, it is to responses to rival sources of EU influence—more specific policy messages emanating elsewhere in the process—that one has look to measure domestic adaptation. Given the strong correlation between the objectives of domestic policy and the priorities identified in the 2005 joint report, the UK had no difficulty in adapting to the streamlined process by structuring its report around the objectives set within its own domestic policy process.

This difficulty in isolating domestic adaptation to the common objectives increased with the fourth cycle of NAPincls. In particular, the guidance given to Member States became more detailed and in addition to the objectives of the OMC, Member States were asked to take note of the country-specific recommendations of the Growth and Jobs strategy; a note on setting targets; a voluntary planning tool for the preparation and monitoring of the NAPincls; a manual for gender mainstreaming; and a discussion paper on disability mainstreaming. Member States were asked to explore the mutual interaction of social interventions on the one hand, and the Growth and Jobs strategy, on the other. Thus, while the objectives of the process never became more prescriptive, the normative environment embedded within the broad governance architecture became more crowded and somewhat more demanding.

As in its 2006–2008 report, the UK NSR 2008–2010 utilized the overarching objectives as a template for the first part of its report and only loosely used the objectives for the social inclusion strand for its NAPincl, preferring instead to update progress on the four priorities identified in its 2006–2008 NAPincl. Notwithstanding the deteriorating economic climate in which the report was produced, the tone of the UK NSR was rather bullish and suggested that the UK economic fundamentals were sound and that the UK faced the economic challenges 'from a position of strength'. The possible effects of the recession on public expenditure, taxation, joblessness were not explored and what was presented in 2008–2010 was a relatively business-as-usual approach consistent with the priorities identified in 2006–2008. Recession and rising unemployment notwithstanding, labour market inclusion remained at the heart of UK strategy with ongoing welfare reforms aimed at moving certain target groups—particularly lone parents and the economically inactive—off income support and incapacity benefits and into reformed or new welfare benefits with greater conditionality attached as described above. Framed as a new balance between 'rights and responsibilities', the normative framework for these policy developments was less one of a rights-based citizenship paradigm and more squarely within the activation paradigm. Moreover, as Bennett and Bradshaw (2008) noted, while championing the concept of 'active inclusion' at EU-level—a concept partly framed as an expression of the right to adequate resources sufficient to live in human dignity—it was not a concept utilized in the 2008–2010 UK NSR.

How then ought we to characterize the role of objectives within EU governance and domestic adaptation to these objectives? While some may have thought that over time, and with revisions, the objectives would become more prescriptive that proved not to be the case. In that way, the influence of hierarchy as a mechanism of adaptation did not increase over time and indeed, in the second generation of NAPincls, Member States were encouraged to develop their own priorities within the overall context of the common objectives. At the same time, rival sources—from the guidance given to Member States in preparing their NAPincls to messages emerging from the joint reports—began to exert more influence.

The objectives also act as a mechanism of socialization in the sense of developing a common normative and cognitive framing of EU intervention. Nonetheless, that framing placed greater or lesser emphasis on a multidimensional understanding of social exclusion over time with employment policy acting as a continuing influence.[24] Within this broad framing of the OMC, for the UK, it was perfectly possible to identify problems from the perspective of a multidimensional analysis of social exclusion, yet in the analysis of policy solutions, to repeatedly emphasize the centrality of the labour market as a mechanism of inclusion. The evidence of the participative approaches

[24] For Daly (2008), if the Nice objectives sought to contextualize employment as a route out of poverty within a broader multidimensional analysis of the causes and effects of social exclusion, the streamlined OMC appeared to narrow the focus by emphasizing particular groups that were vulnerable to social exclusion and by giving greater prominence to active 'inclusion'—the connection between reform of benefits and employment activation—over social 'exclusion'. It is perhaps less evident that this was a function of the revision of the objectives themselves which broadly maintained a multidimensional framing of social exclusion and, as the discussion in chapter four illustrated, sought to place greater emphasis on issues of access to rights and services over labour market inclusion.

developing around the NAPincls did, however, engage something of the participative aspects of a social citizenship paradigm albeit without presenting this in terms of a fundamental rights perspective. Indeed, inasmuch as rights figured at all in the UK NAPincls it was as the stepping stone to a focus on correlative responsibilities to take up opportunities of paid employment.

Overall, however, it is far from evident that the substantive objectives of the OMC—when compared to the objectives set through the domestic spending review and PSA process—directly influenced UK strategies to combat poverty and social exclusion. Moreover, it is not even evident that it is the objectives that are the focal point of EU influence within the coordination process.

(c) *Joint Reports*

As Daly notes (2008), the joint reports play a dual role in the reporting structure of the OMC. First, and as noted above, these reports over time gradually became a means of elaborating political priorities—whether general common challenges or more thematic concerns like child poverty or active inclusion—to which Member States were asked to respond. A level of focus and prioritization emerged that was absent from the common objectives with the effect that the joint reports became a rival source of influence on the domestic strategic environment. Secondly, the reports—as analyses of the individual NAPincls—acted as potential feedback loops to the Member States. It is important to recognize that at least for the first generation of reports, the emphasis of the joint reports was generally on monitoring the quality of the NAPincls, and not a review or analysis of the effectiveness of policy (see also Daly, 2008). In this regard, it is also worth highlighting that the strategy of the European Commission in the first joint report of ranking the states in terms of the quality of their NAPincls was never repeated after the furore this created. Indeed Member States resisted naming and shaming exercises that might create a competitive pressure to enhance the quality of their strategic reporting. In the discussion which follows, attention is paid to the evolution of this dual identity to the joint reports in terms of domestic adaptation both to the general political messages generated by them and to the specific issues identified in the country fiches accompanying the reports.

If we look to the general messages of the first joint report (European Commission and Council, 2002), certain core challenges were identified (discussed in chapter three). In many ways, these challenges were elaborations of the first Nice objective in the sense of their focus on inclusion through the labour market combined with a broader articulation of a right of access to resources and to public services. It was not then difficult for the UK Government to accommodate these challenges in its responses by suggesting in its 2003–2005 NAPincl that UK policy was based around a three-pillared anti-poverty strategy founded upon a strong economy, flexible labour markets and first class public services.

Looking more specifically at responses to concerns or criticisms made of UK strategies, as was noted above, criticism of the degree of participation in the production of the first NAPincl did elicit a response from the UK. The 2002 joint report had also been critical of the gender dimension of the first NAPincls—including the UK's report—and the common outline for the second NAPincl requested Member States to 'mainstream gender at each stage of the plans'. The 2003–2005 UK NAPincl did make more explicit the connection in particular between women and social exclusion (and as noted above the 2005 OFA report also reflected this issue). That the UK had a problem with its above EU-average relative poverty rate emerged as a more substantive criticism in the 2002 joint report: a problem which the UK NAPincl 2003–2005 acknowledged but then absorbed by noting that for those in work, the relative poverty rate was on a par with the Netherlands and Austria and below that of France and Germany.

The 2004 joint report (European Commission and Council, 2004) was in much the same vein as the 2002 report in its tendency to avoid generating particularly critical messages. Again the focus tended to lie on the quality of the NAPincls—their multidimensional approach to social exclusion; the setting of national targets; strengthening institutional arrangements and improving participation in the NAPincls—with exhortations to keep up progress. However, with the move to streamlining coordination, the next round of NAPincls did not simply respond to the preceding 2004 joint report. Member States were requested to submit 'update reports' in 2004, but only ten of the then EU15 states chose to submit reports (the UK did not submit a report). An 'implementation' report was produced by Member States in 2005, but it was not until 2006 that Member States produced full NAPincls as one chapter of the new NSRs for the period 2006–2008. By this time, two further joint reports had been produced in 2005 and 2006. Alongside these reports the Council has also highlighted other priorities in Council conclusions, not least the new focus on child poverty.

Thus, in its 2006–2008 NAPincl, the UK did not respond directly to the points highlighted in the 2005 joint report. As well as highlighting the comparatively poor performance of the UK in terms of relative poverty, the 2006 fiche was critical on the issue of inequalities, and while noting that the UK was meeting its Lisbon targets on economic growth and employment it also highlighted risks of in-work poverty and rising levels of personal indebtedness. Two specific challenges were identified for the UK:

- to continue efforts to reduce persistent inequalities such as those in income, health, skills and 'life chances';
- to tackle levels of economic inactivity by engaging those people traditionally hardest to reach via a holistic and tailored approach.

Certainly there is a formal responsiveness in the 2006–2008 NAPincl to the issues raised in the 2006 country fiche. These responses ranged from acknowledging and absorbing the concerns to qualifying them, for example, noting that income inequalities had grown but were stabilized; or that high levels of home ownership exacerbated debt levels. Although it can be suggested that the country fiches moved beyond concerns with the quality of the NAPincls to begin to address policy problems more directly, it is perhaps less clear that the joint reports were identifying issues unknown to the UK. That is to say, there is a sense in which the dialogue between the Member States and the EU institutions conducted through the political reporting mechanism took on something of a therapeutic nature with Member States themselves identifying problem issues which the country fiches then echoed back to the Member States. That said, on the issues of in-work poverty and income inequalities, the EU was, nonetheless, highlighting that growth and jobs alone were not sufficient to tackle poverty and social exclusion in the UK. Indeed, given that the UK was already meeting its Lisbon targets on growth and jobs, the relatively poor position of the UK on certain key indicators of poverty and social exclusion could be used as a means of creating pressure for further national action.

The 2007 joint report was the first to analyse the new generation of reports covering all three strands of the OMC on Social Protection and Social Inclusion. Although the 2007 country fiche repeated the same two challenges for the UK as identified in the 2006 report, the narrative aspects of the fiche were generally more willing to be critical. Issues of inequality and concerns about the quality and sustainability of employment in the UK were particularly highlighted. Even measures that were viewed positively such as tax credits were criticized for being overly complex. Problems of combining administrative efficiency savings with activation strategies that relied upon more personal tailored solutions were noted (important given the thrust of welfare reforms for lone parents and the disabled). Indebtedness was again identified as a concern. The response in the subsequent UK NAPincl (2008–2010) was curt:

> The 2007 Joint Report on Social Protection and Social Exclusion identified the need for the UK Government to continue its efforts to reduce persistent inequalities, such as those in income, health, skills and life chances. Tackling levels of economic activity by improving engagement with vulnerable groups, whilst adequately supporting the transition to quality and sustainable work was also highlighted.

While this demonstrates that formally the UK heard the message conveyed in the joint report, nonetheless, on important issues like income inequality, the UK report had very little to say beyond an acknowledgment of the issue and the claim that changes to the tax and benefits system had 'arrested' the rising trend in inequality. The section of the UK NAPincl that focused on the priority of 'Tackling Inequality' identified gender pay gaps as an issue but not income inequality more generally. This response—veering somewhere between inertia and retrenchment—provoked a somewhat harsher critical message in the 2009 joint report:

> Despite the challenges identified in the 2007 Joint Report, the inequalities in terms of income and wealth are largely neglected; a different approach is taken by Scotland, which is committed to increasing the total income and proportion of income earned by the poorest three income deciles by 2017. Income inequality remains a persistent problem and is closely related to inequalities in health, education and life chances.

Not only was this a critical assessment of UK policy, the joint report used the context of devolution in the UK to point to the Scottish Government's new approach to tackling poverty and income inequality. This, perhaps, evidenced an interesting new strategy of using differentiation within the domestic strategic environment as a means of leveraging a greater horizontal adaptation pressure than might be achieved by mere top-down critique by the EU itself.

If the discussion above is suggestive that the system of political reporting and joint monitoring by the Commission and Council either produced little that was novel or sufficiently critical to incur a stronger response from the UK, or when critical, was largely ignored, then perhaps the best summation of how the UK Government treated the joint reports can be found in a rare example of engagement by the UK House of Common European Scrutiny Committee with the OMC. In concluding its scrutiny of the draft 2008 joint report and in clearing the document, the

Committee endorsed the position adopted by the UK Government. It is worth citing in full.

The Parliamentary Under-Secretary of State at the Department for Work and Pensions (Mr James Plaskitt) tells us that the draft joint report 'represents a sound synopsis of, and sign-post to, detailed study of some important issues by member states in the SPC. The Report's messages are unsurprising, but nevertheless identify issues worthy of further attention to support sharing of information and good practice'. He also tells us that Member States have contributed to and agreed the draft; and that the document has no direct policy, legislative or financial implications for the UK.

(d) Peer Review

Peer review has two distinct manifestations within the OMC. On the one hand, it refers to a process by which the national reports are presented by a Member State and reviewed by other Member States. Given that Member States are only given fifteen minutes to present their reports, this process has been devoid of any real meaning and in the case of the 2008–2010 NSR, the UK was only asked to present on pensions and healthcare and not inclusion. On the other hand, thematic peer reviews are conducted in the context of the action programme supporting the OMC. These peer reviews—hosted by a Member State that either seeks input into the design of a policy that is changing or seeks to propose a model of good practice—introduce a more horizontal dynamic to adaptation. During the period of this study the UK hosted three reviews all of which were projections of good practice rather than examples of a search for new policy ideas. Overall, on the experience of the reviews undertaken up until the end of 2009, comparatively the UK was moderately more inclined to review another state's practices (fifteen examples) than to host (three examples), with France, for example, moderately more inclined to host (five examples) than to review (eleven examples).

The three reviews hosted by the UK were on its Rough Sleepers Unit in 2004; on its 'Sure Start' strategy in 2006; and in 2009, its 'City Strategy' for tackling unemployment and child poverty. The selection of the Sure Start strategy is worth considering for a moment. The aim of the strategy is to support the UK Government's policies on child poverty by focusing on the integrated provision of a range of services at local level for pre-school children in England. It is an area-based approach with responsibilities devolved down to local level. Given the specificity of the structure of local government in England and of the governance of Sure Start itself—initiated as Sure Start Local Programmes (SSLPs) and then later transforming into

Sure Start Children's Centres—it was perhaps not an obvious example of a strategy that might easily be replicated in other Member States with different internal divisions of power and welfare traditions (after all it was not even a UK-wide strategy).

Moreover, whether or not Sure Start was an example of good practice was debateable. The UK Government had not authorized a randomized control trial for an evaluation of the programme. The early evaluation that took place was equivocal. While it found some 'small and limited effects of SSLPs' even these effects varied, with children in less socially deprived families achieving more beneficial effects than those in more socially deprived families (Belsky et al, 2006). A synthesis of the evaluation was used as the basis for the UK's host country report. Yet it was evident that even for the evaluators, it was too early and too difficult to evaluate the success of SSLPs given their diversity. More importantly, however, Sure Start was a programme in transition, with new Sure Start Children's Centres developing as the key vehicle for the strategy, with new governance arrangements and with an increased focused on supporting parents back into work (see Pemberton and Mason, 2009).[25] Given the annual spend of £1.8 billion on Sure Start reported in the 2006 NSR/NAPincl, it might have been better to know whether or not this programme really was an example of good practice from which other EU states might learn. Indeed, what is striking about the discussion paper used during the peer review to comment on the UK's practice was its exhortation to the UK to look less to the American experiences of its 'Early Head Start' programme[26] and instead to learn more from the experiences of Nordic and continental welfare traditions in their early years interventions.

The UK also participated in reviews hosted in other states. For example in 2009, it was very active in participating in four reviews: Denmark (social services); France (home care of people with Alzheimer's disease); Germany (healthcare in regions with ageing populations); and Norway (active inclusion of vulnerable people). There is no overarching pattern that emerges

[25] It is worth noting that the 2004 joint report had been critical of earlier UK policy aimed at term-time nursery school provision of childcare as not being a particularly effective as a way of helping lone parents into work.

[26] On the extent to which policy transfer from the US to the UK was evident see Welshman, 2010. The extent to which UK social policy has been Americanized or Europeanized is explored in Annesley, 2003. There is, of course, a debate over whether the OMC is a mechanism for Europeanization at all, or whether one of its dangers is that allows states like the UK to seek to upload a liberal Anglo-Saxon model of welfare and then to seek to transfer that model to other European states: the fear expressed by Claus Offe (2003).

from UK participation in peer reviews and while no doubt laudable and potentially very valuable it is difficult to see how issues of election to host or selection to review are in any way driven by the reporting and monitoring elements of the OMC. Moreover, as the Commission's own evaluation noted (European Commission, 2006a), there was little evidence of the capacity of the peer reviews to disseminate ideas and practices beyond the immediate group of participants. In this way, the peer reviews afford an opportunity for a horizontal dynamic of Europeanization—contextualized learning rather than competitive selection—but the evidence suggests that the force exerted was weak and was not amplified by the other elements of coordination described in the preceding sections.

Policy Assessment and Analysis

An important feature of the OMC is its use of indicators and data to identify and map the phenomenon of poverty and social exclusion as a basis not only for problem identification but also for analysis of the relationship between policy instruments and outcomes (Mabbett, 2007). In doing so in a comparative European context, indicators can facilitate a process of domestic policy change either as a competitive response to comparatively poor performance or as a contextualized learning response in which states simply seek to improve their level of performance by looking for examples of more successful practice elsewhere. The UK has tended to seek to emphasize this latter aspect of the OMC in line with a philosophical understanding of the OMC as a vehicle for policy learning. Nonetheless, what is significant about the use of indicators is their capacity to reach more directly into the analysis of policy and policy performance than was evidenced by the use of common objectives.

Before turning directly to examining Europeanization as domestic adaptation to common indicators, it is important to highlight that the evolution of EU indicators has also been an example of Europeanization in the sense of institution-building at EU level. This was discussed more fully in chapter four but is of relevance here given that for the first cycle of reporting and monitoring under the OMC, common EU indicators had not been agreed. Moreover, with the move to streamlining, important changes occurred in the portfolio of indicators.[27] The evolution and development of statistical

[27] The original 'Laeken' common indicators agreed for the OMC consisted of a set of ten primary and eight secondary indicators. Member States were free to supplement their analysis

capacity and the agreement of new indicators is an example of EU-level learning, or what Radaelli (2008) terms 'learning at the top'. This process is, of course, a function of the engagement of national representatives within the SPC Indicators Sub-Group and so, again, it is problematic to conceptualize the effects of, and responses to, indicators purely in a top-down fashion.

In her analysis of 'learning by numbers' Mabbett identifies different potential effects of EU indicators: *reviewing*, *translating*, *targeting*, *agenda-setting*, and *benchmarking* (Mabbett, 2007). A reviewing effect engenders a similar type of compliance response to that which we identified for the use of common objectives: the indicators act as a template through which to review and portray the domestic situation. This is an absorption response that may have no wider impact on the domestic strategic environment. Translation involves the interpretation of both national and EU indicators and data. Divergences between these two sources are likely to produce either transformation responses—where the authority of the EU data and its portrayal of an issue are accepted—or retrenchment responses—where the national indicator and data are preferred measures. Indicators can form the basis for the setting of national targets with the potential for transforming the domestic strategic environment. The agenda-setting quality of indicators can work at different orders. A single EU indicator may show that a state has a poor performance in a particular respect in a manner that may form the basis for concerted action for a policy response to tackle this problem. Yet as Mabbett notes (2007), a higher order of agenda-setting may occur when together indicators institutionalize a particular paradigm. Finally, indicators can facilitate two types of benchmarking: a state's own performance over time or a state's comparative performance in an EU context. Although it is understandable to focus on the latter as a driving force of competitive pressure to adapt, the OMC has placed an emphasis on the need for each state to seek to move on from its initial starting position and, therefore, to be of relevance even to those states with historically lower levels of poverty.

with tertiary (national/sub-national) indicators. With streamlining, while there was a certain continuity with the Laeken portfolio, important changes took place. A set of headline indicators underpin the overarching objectives of the OMC. Within the social inclusion strand, a new distribution of primary, secondary and context indicators was agreed. Importantly, a new typology of indicators emerged that distinguished between common EU indicators, commonly agreed national indicators (which would not permit direct comparison) and context information. A list of eleven primary, three secondary and eleven context indicators was agreed in 2006 for the social inclusion strand of the streamlined OMC. Not all the indicators in the portfolio agreed in 2006 were in place for the third cycle of NAPincls and in 2009 the definition of indicators on material deprivation and housing were adopted.

Moreover, inasmuch as a state has continuity of data over time and insofar as the evolution of EU data produces 'breaks' in the series of data, it may be that states learn more about the effectiveness of their policies by looking at national indicators and data over time than they do from comparative EU-wide snapshots. Benchmarking may, therefore, produce a range of responses from absorption, transformation or retrenchment.

In the analysis which follows, Mabbett's typology of the effects of indicators will be used, supplemented by the typology of domestic responses typically used in the Europeanization literature. While the analysis presented here lacks Mabbett's cross-national comparison, it aims to develop in some more detail the impact of indicators in the UK across a longer time frame.[28]

In terms of the use of indicators in a reviewing capacity, the UK had developed national indicators and data through which to review and monitor the domestic situation not least as part of the performance review mechanisms underpinning the PSAs. Thus, even without the common 'Laeken' indicators for the first NAPincls, the UK was able to provide detailed statistical analysis to underpin its NAPincl using the data and indicators derived from OFA. Once common EU indicators were agreed, the UK did then review the data in a separate annex to the 2003–2005 NAPincl. This response was largely one of absorption with UK-derived objectives and indicators—reported in OFA—driving domestic policy. Nonetheless, in terms of its use of EU and national indicators in a reviewing capacity, the 2007 joint report highlighted that the 2006–2008 national report was 'an example of good practice on how indicators can be used for policy making' with the UK monitoring its situation not only through national indicators and data but also linking this with a 'thorough assessment of the newly adopted EU indicators . . . thereby assessing the UK performance in the EU context' (European Commission and Council, 2007: 71). The UK's reports give useful summaries of which indicators are moving in positive or negative directions as well as highlighting any differences between EU and national data.

Given the coexistence of national and EU indicators and data, the issue of translation between these two sources becomes highly relevant. In the 2003–2005 NAPincl there is evidence of the UK using 'tertiary' national indicators to give a more up-to-date review of its median equivalized low income situation than that expressed by EU primary indicators. More significantly, however, the EU data on low income anchored at a point in time was directly

[28] The focus of Mabbett's analysis is the 2003 NAPincl and the use of indicators in Sweden, Spain and Germany as well as the UK.

contested. According to EU data (based on the old ECHP survey) the trend on this indicator showed a deteriorating situation in the UK. The UK's own tertiary indicator—based on a bigger Family Resource Survey—showed an improving picture. The 2006–2008 NAPincl again used national data. With the introduction of EU-SILC as a replacement to the ECHP, the baseline date as well as the data for the indicator changed making the EU indicator of relevance only to the period after 2005. In this way, while there may now be a basis for a commonly accepted interpretation of this indicator for cross-EU comparisons after 2005, the UK's own data may still be of more significance in determining the longer term trend in relative income poverty since 1997. If this episode evidenced a certain retrenchment response, other examples of translation indicate transformation responses.

Although the EU measure of relative poverty—60 per cent of median equivalized income—had itself become an accepted measure in the UK, the methodology of equivalization used in UK and national statistics differed. While Eurostat had adopted the modified OECD equivalization scale, the UK had since the 1970s used the McClements scale to measure incomes both before and after housing costs. As a result of its review of its child poverty measure, the UK Government decided to move to the modified OECD scale as a basis for measuring progress against its child poverty target even though this changing scale would show a larger number of children in poor households. It was argued that changing scale would facilitate comparisons with other EU countries and would better reflect UK Government strategies targeted at children in poor households. However, as a UK House of Commons select committee report identified,[29] this move was not without controversy not least because the new scale would be on a 'before housing costs' basis and ministers were urged to retain an 'after housing costs' measure at least for UK purposes. The adoption of the new scale to measure child poverty had a wider impact and from 2007, DWP moved to use the modified OECD scale in its Households Below Average Income statistics. While there clearly remains controversy about which type of equivalization to use, that all EU states use statistics derived from the same equivalization scale clearly provides a stronger foundation for cross-national comparisons.

During the period of this study, the use of indicators to form EU level targets was resisted and instead Member States were encouraged to adopt their

[29] House of Commons Work and Pensions Committee, *The best start in life? Alleviating deprivation, improving social mobility and eradicating child poverty*, Second Report (session 2007–08), HC42-1.

own targets. As already noted, targets based on national indicators have been a key aspect of UK policy-making. Apart from the specific child poverty pledge, the objectives and targets laid down in central government PSAs have tended not to focus specifically on issues of low income which are typically measured by EU indicators. There is no specific UK target to reduce the numbers of people living in household below average income or to seek to reduce income inequalities.

The issue of income inequalities was highlighted in the joint reports discussed earlier. It is a good example of an area where performance in respect of a single indicator might be used in an agenda-setting manner. Certainly, it is significant that the overarching portfolio of headline indicators for the streamlined OMC included an inequality indicator (the ratio of income of the top and bottom income quintiles). That indicator showed that the UK had a consistently higher ratio (5.4) than the EU25 average (4.8). The UK figure spiked at the end of the 1980s but then remained relatively flat and even fell slightly allowing the UK to present the situation as one of arresting the rise of income inequality. Notwithstanding the critical assessments in the joint reports and the adoption in Scotland of a 'Purpose Target' to tackle inequality—albeit one that is not based on the EU quintile ratio—it is not evident that the OMC was capable of pushing this issue onto the domestic policy agenda.

A different way in which indicators might act in an agenda-setting manner is where they are used in problem-identification within a particular paradigm. Mabbett (2007) has suggested that the original Laeken indicators—with their dominant focus on issues of low income—encapsulated a 'redistributive' paradigm. This could be contrasted with the common objectives for the OMC which sought to portray social exclusion as a multidimensional phenomenon within a broader social citizenship paradigm. As the UK has a tradition of measuring income poverty it is not all that obvious that the low income focus of the EU indicators had a specific agenda-setting role. That said it might be argued that given the tendency of domestic political discourse to slip between discussions of poverty and social exclusion and to downplay income inequality, the EU indicators have kept the issues of income adequacy and inequality on the agenda. Nonetheless, even if this effect of the indicators could be evidenced, employment has remained the paradigmatic solution to tackle low income in UK policy. What is interesting, however, is that the indicators have evolved in a manner that allows issues of in-work poverty to emerge;[30] important for the UK given both its

[30] Overarching indicator eleven measures in-work poverty.

disappointing record on poverty combined with its comparatively high historic levels of employment. In this way, there may be scope for EU indicators paradigmatically to frame a problem—low income—and evaluate the effectiveness of a solution—employment—in tackling that problem.

Perhaps the greatest hurdle to the use of EU indicators in an agenda-setting capacity is not just the rival sources of national and international data but also competition from different national organizations in their interpretations and analysis of data. The Joseph Rowntree Foundation has funded highly visible research on poverty and supports *The Poverty Site* as an online review of key indicators. The Institute for Fiscal Studies has also been active in this area, with reports on poverty and inequality in the UK (Brewer et al, 2007). The UK Government has itself commissioned research and reports. Significantly the UK Government established a National Equality Panel whose 2010 report, *An Anatomy of Economic Inequality in the UK*, was widely publicized in UK media. In an environment where the UK polity is richly populated by social scientists and civil society organizations with sophisticated analytical capacities matched by access to media outlets, it is simply not apparent that the EU as an agenda-setter is able to make its voice heard as clearly as it might.

This somewhat negative view of the capacity of EU indicators and their analysis to reach into the domestic strategic environment is also borne out in terms of the use of indicators to benchmark the UK's comparative performance. Although it is true that the change in the equivalization scale used for UK statistics will enhance the capacity to generate cross-country comparisons, it is striking the extent to which key policy reviews have often drawn their international comparisons from sources other than the EU, particularly the OECD. The Freud report on welfare reform relied extensively on OECD data (Freud, 2007), while the subsequent welfare reform Green Paper (DWP, 2008) used a mix of OECD and EU data. It is true that the analysis of child poverty in the UK has frequently highlighted this issue in a European context. Nonetheless, it is also striking that the international report on child poverty that attained high levels of media interest was the Unicef report on child well-being that used primarily OECD data (Unicef, 2007).[31] In this way, the responses found in the UK are suggestive of inertia or at best absorption of the EU as one of a range of potential international benchmarks. With the dominance of OECD data and indicators, it may be

[31] That the UK was bottom of a list of countries on a measure of the subjective well-being of children ensured that the report attained significant publicity.

that Europeanization gives way to internationalization in respect of comparative benchmarking.

We should not, of course, ignore the potential for the OMC to facilitate a state's capacity to benchmark its own performance over time. In the UK, with a long history of data collection this is of marginal significance. Indeed with EU-SILC only operational from 2005, the trend in data would not be all that revealing.

Governance and Participation: Responding to Non-Governmental Actors

The participation of non-governmental actors in the UK NAPincl—described above—was facilitated by the ability of domestic NGOs to leverage funds from the supporting EU action programme. While this programme did not core fund the work of national networks, it did support 'awareness-raising' projects. Two projects—'Get Heard' and 'Bridging the Policy Gap'—obtained funding. The 'Get Heard' project facilitated 146 workshops across the UK to feed the views of those with experience of poverty into the 2006–2008 UK NAPincl. Using the model of peer reviews at EU level, the 'Bridging the Policy Gap' project undertook three peer reviews of projects in England, Wales and Scotland with a focus on improving local services.

Nonetheless, what remains to be considered is what effect these projects had on UK strategies and policies to combat poverty and social exclusion. Given that the focal point for much of this activity was the preparation and production of the 2006–2008 and 2008–2010 NAPincls, then one source of evidence of a response lies in these documents. Certainly, the 2006–2008 NAPincl reviewed and reported some of the issues raised in the 'Get Heard' project by reflecting them in the text of the report and in an Annex. The 2008–2010 NAPincl also included a report of the 'Bridging the Policy Gap' project. Nonetheless, merely reviewing and reporting these views is not evidence of a causal effect of these participative process on the strategic or policy environment.

However, non-governmental actors like the SPTF do point to the capacity of dialogue around the NAPincls to not only put issues into the NAPincl but also to put issues onto the political agenda. As early as the 2003–2005 NAPincl, issues surrounding debt and financial inclusion were given prominence in OMC awareness-raising workshops and interviewees typically identified this as something that became of interest not just to DWP but to other government departments. Issues of in-work poverty were also cited in the SPTF's 'shadow' 2008–2010 NAPincl. Yet there are counter examples where strong NGO pressure on issues of income adequacy and active inclusion—as well as income inequality—simply are not reflected in what the UK Government projected in its 2008–2010 NAPincl. It is self-evident that central government in the UK—while undoubtedly developing new relationships and dialogue with civil society actors—nonetheless, remains the gatekeeper of what is or is not presented in the NAPincl.

There is, of course, the possibility that the participative processes and discussions around poverty and social exclusion in the context of the OMC have wider effects within domestic politics. Consultations on the substance of welfare reform may be able to draw on the enhanced capacities of domestic NGOs to feed views into consultative processes. Certainly the SPTF made a submission to the Freud Review into welfare reform. The Scottish Poverty Alliance—a sub-national NGO closely involved with the SPTF and linked to EAPN—drew on its experiences of the OMC, the 'Get Heard' and 'Bridging the Policy Gap' projects in its responses to a Scottish Parliament poverty and inequality discussion paper; to the UK House of Commons inquiry into poverty in Scotland;[32] as well as the DWP Green Paper on welfare reform. What is much more difficult to answer is whether or not these consultations, reviews and reports value non-'expert' knowledge of the experience of poverty or how these voices compete with the competitive market in social science expertise in the UK discussed in the previous section.

In terms of looking for evidence of Europeanization, the OMC has itself Europeanized UK civil society actors within the domestic polity. The NAPincls were a focal point and opportunity structure for national and sub-national NGOs to coordinate their own activities in seeking to influence the content of the NAPincls. As described above, new working relationships were developed with civil servants within DWP. National and sub-national groups were assisted by direct EU funding and indirectly through the funding of EAPN which was able to facilitate the capacities of its national members to engage with the OMC process. The transfer of the EU model of peer reviews used in the 'Bridging the Policy Gap' project was itself an interesting example of Europeanization.[33] In this way, non-governmental organizations within the UK polity became a potential force for wider Europeanization effects.

[32] House of Commons Scottish Affairs Committee, *Poverty in Scotland*, Second Report (Session 2007–2008), HC 128ii.

[33] Another example was the UK People Experiencing Poverty conference held in 2007 modelled on the EU's annual people experiencing poverty events.

The trajectory of that force is both horizontal—the developing relationships between social NGOs in the UK, and vertical—the 'bottom-up' channels of communicative discourse oriented toward governmental actors. For Pemberton, these vertical and horizontal linkages resonate with a 'multi-level governance' approach to European integration (Pemberton, 2008).[34] Nonetheless, this did not have the effect of being able to bypass central government and, indeed, DWP's role as a facilitator of communication between governmental and non-governmental actors was crucial, evidenced not least by what happened when key personnel within DWP were changed. As regards measuring the response to EU influences, certainly there was a transformation in processes and working relationships between a group of civil servants working within DWP on the OMC and non-governmental actors. But in terms of the substantive effect on the strategic and policy environment, concrete effects appear limited.

Conclusions

The evidence presented in this chapter confirms the capacity to use concepts and methods associated with the Europeanization literature as modes of analysis of EU policy coordination. Nonetheless, it also highlights the thesis of this book that we need to move beyond treating the OMC as a singular and coherent governance technique and to instead explore the operation of different elements of the coordination methodology. EU policy coordination creates adaptation pressures of different strengths operating along different trajectories as expressions of the different modes of governance at play.

Consistent with other studies of Europeanization, adaptation pressures are not a sufficient explanation of the domestic effects of the OMC. Domestic polities, politics and policies remain core to understanding the influence of the EU on its Member States. Indeed for critics of the OMC it is this domestic context which is very much at stake, though sometimes for contradictory reasons. For Offe (2003), it is the very fragility of the national institutions of social welfare—their liability to be 'demolished' through the OMC—that makes the OMC appear dangerous. Yet for Chalmers and Lodge (2003) it is the robustness of national institutions that is liable to make policy influence

[34] For a useful discussion of the literature on multi-level governance see Pollack, 2005: 39–41.

weak. What the evidence of this study suggests is that these sorts of generalized interpretations of the OMC and its effects are not wholly enlightening. A finer-grained analysis is required that pays attention both to the different functions of the OMC architecture—monitoring and reporting; policy assessment and analysis; governance and participation—as well as its individual methodological elements.

In looking at the cyclical process of reporting and monitoring, it is apparent that the UK NAPincl largely retained its status as a report of strategies and plans rather than acting as a strategy in its own right. Thus, while it may have displaced the incumbent domestic report—Opportunity for All—and while its territorial scope is both state and sub-state levels, its character remains principally that of a mechanism for reporting to EU institutions. This tends to suggest that the OMC acts more strongly as an accountability mechanism than as a direct means of influencing domestic strategies or policies.

The evidence also suggests a highly limited role for the EU common objectives, acting as a general normative context generating little adaptation pressures, and as a formal template around which Member States might review and report their strategies and policies. The objectives set in the domestic policy planning process are more immediate drivers of policy. In terms of problem identification, the early cycles of reporting operated in a quasi-therapeutic manner with the EU often simply echoing back problems self-identified in the UK NAPincl. Over time, the EU political messages—particularly around income inequality—became harsher but without generating strong domestic responses. Looking beyond the top-down dynamics of reporting and political monitoring, the peer review process introduced a more horizontal dynamic to European influences. Yet, the evidence suggests that it is not clear how this element of the methodology is functionally integrated into the overall coordination architecture. While of interest to the participants in the reviews it is also less evident that this extends out to government more generally. In short, the coordinative discourses of governmental actors are suggestive of a formal responsiveness to the OMC within a culture of compliance rather than evidencing either a retrenchment or transformation of the domestic strategic or policy environment.

It is in the relationship between EU and national indicators and data that we find some of the more interesting examples of adaptation pressures and responses. Moreover, with the development and evolution of a set of common indicators, stronger messages relating to the policy performance of Member States began to emerge, enhanced by the changes in architectural design that created a space for thematic issues like child poverty to emerge.

In the context of the UK, it already had a sophisticated set of indicators and data through which to assess and analyse policy and the issue of child poverty was very clearly already a domestic political priority. There was also extensive rivalry from domestic and international sources of policy analysis. In this sense, the influence of the EU on the UK was probably weaker than might be evidenced in other Member States and in this regard, it is clear that cross-country comparisons would be highly beneficial.

Finally in terms of governance and participation, there is clear evidence of domestic change in the relationships between governmental and non-governmental actors. If all we were to assess were changes in vertical and horizontal relations within and between political and social actors then we might happily speak of a strong Europeanization dynamic at work. Yet the capacity of that change to have a consequential impact on the domestic strategic or policy environment proves to be much more elusive and difficult to quantify and measure.

6

Economic Constitutionalism and Social Policy Coordination

Introduction

In the previous chapter, the capacity of EU policy coordination to reach into, and seek to influence, the domestic sphere was explored from the perspective of the responsiveness of states to the OMC as a governance technique. Particular attention was paid to the roles of the polity, politics and policy in shaping those domestic responses. In this chapter, the analysis takes a distinctly legal turn. It explores the thesis that while the OMC attempts to work with and through the social policy autonomy of Member States to manage processes of change, that autonomy is itself constrained by the forces of EU economic law.

As the European Court of Justice (ECJ) has observed on numerous occasions, while competence—including exercises of social policy competence—may remain with the Member States, the exercise of that competence must, nonetheless, remain compatible with the states' obligations under the treaties—including the economic freedoms—observance of which the ECJ will ensure. Moreover, these freedoms have been elevated to a constitutional status—they are 'fundamental freedoms',[1] directly effective and take precedence over inconsistent national law—and are capable of being enforced by litigants and lawyers through the European judicial architecture. Thus, Leibfried and Pierson (1995) have talked of 'semisovereign welfare states'. For Fritz Scharpf (2002), what began as a workable division of responsibilities between supranational economic integration and national social welfare has ended up with the former being turned against the latter with a

[1] Case C-112/00, *Eugen Schmidberger, Internationale Transporte und Planzüge v Republik Österreich* [2003] ECR I-5659.

resulting constitutional asymmetry between the higher economic law of the treaties and national laws intended to enshrine principles of social solidarity. Moreover, in the absence of a more extensive competence for social re-regulation at EU level and in the absence of a substantive EU constitutionalism that balances economic and social objectives, domestic social policy measures remain open to construction within the economic logic of market integration as interpreted by the ECJ. All of this raises the spectre of a court-driven process of market liberalization undermining the social policy competence of Member States (see Leibfried, 2005).

If correct, this thesis has profound implications for social welfare in the EU and the constitutional framework for social solidarity. It adds fuel to the fire of social democratic discontents with the decline of the capacities of nation states to form the boundaries of welfare, with a consequential desire to see the constitutional and democratic structures of the EU reformed to conserve a European social model of welfare and to prevent a 'drift' to the political right (see Follesdal and Hix, 2006).[2] This aspect is explored in depth in chapter seven. The concern here is with the implications of the thesis for the social OMC. For Scharpf, whatever the merits of OMC as an attempt to develop an alternative governance strategy to the traditional techniques of 'negative' and 'positive' integration, its capacity to function relies on the very policy competence and autonomy which he believes is systematically threatened by the reach of EU economic constitutionalism (1999; 2002). In this way, not only would national social welfare systems be open to 'Europeanization' pressures, and influences (see also Martinesen 2005a) these systems would actually be under threat as courts deployed the market logic of economic freedoms to trump social protection in ways which policy coordination processes would be powerless to resist.

There can be no doubt that EU economic law—not just free movement law but also competition law—has been invoked in litigation concerning the laws, institutions and practices of Member States, including in areas within social policy broadly defined. Yet to shift from this simple recognition of the capacity to invoke EU economic law in such circumstances to then claiming that the OMC is fundamentally constrained is to go too far. First, it tends to assume that the mere capacity to apply EU economic law to social situations

[2] Of course, for some, the EU's self-conscious attempt to adopt a 'Constitution' was less the moment when economic liberalism would be reined in, but rather the moment when market freedoms would truly attain a constitutional status. This is certainly one explanation for the rejection of the Constitutional Treaty in France and the Netherlands (see Howarth, 2007).

is itself proof of a marketization of welfare. This tells us nothing about what courts actually decide and what modes of analysis they use. The examination of case law presented here suggests that the real test of the impact of EU economic law on social welfare lies in the structured processes of justification and interest-balancing developed by the ECJ over time. Importantly, the ECJ has recognized a principle of 'solidarity' which can, under certain conditions, 'buttress' or insulate national social welfare systems from the influences of EU economic law. There are also important differences in the effects of EU economic law between, on the one hand, the competition rules and, on the other hand, the rules on free movement, with the EU courts willing to accept a more limited application of competition rules to 'solidaristic' social services,[3] than may be evident in its application of free movement principles. This asymmetry *within* EU economic law,[4] between competition and free movement rules, is simply not captured in much of the literature which either treats EU economic law as a monolith or alternatively looks only to the impact of competition law *or* free movement law on national social protection systems. The analysis offered here is a far more subtle and nuanced account of the effects of EU economic constitutionalism than a mere declaration that EU economic law trumps domestic social welfare.

Secondly, even if there were to be good examples of domestic practices being found to be incompatible with EU economic law, the more specific concern is with whether these practices are in fields of activity covered by existing OMC processes. Yet even this approach requires to be qualified in that whereas we might find examples of the application of EU economic law in some OMC areas—eg pensions and healthcare as provision of these services is extended to market actors—we might find significantly less intervention in core areas of social protection typically provided by the state.

The objective of this chapter is, therefore, to offer a balanced assessment of the extent to which the OMC process on Social Protection and Social Inclusion is constrained or undermined by the effects of EU economic law. It does not pretend to be the first analysis of the impact of EU economic law on national social protection systems.[5] But in examining a range of interactions

[3] Boeger, 2007, argues that the Court accepts two different types of solidarity rationale to exclude or limit the application of competition rules: (1) where public services are organized in such a manner as to provide a different distribution of goods and services than might be attained by a competitive market and (2) where public services are organized to reflect a public spiritedness or public ethos.

[4] On which see Baquero Cruz, 2002.

[5] See eg Bernard, 2005; Barnard, 2006; Hervey, 2000; Ferrera, 2005; Giubboni, 2001, 2006, 2007.

between EU competition law, free movement law and social law it attempts to provide a sustained analysis of the thesis that the OMC is undermined by the legal constraints of EU economic constitutionalism.

The Structure of EU Economic Law

While the non-lawyer may find case law analysis esoteric and abstruse, nonetheless, it is important to understand the way in which problems are articulated within the conceptual schema of European law. Of particular importance in this chapter is the role played by the ECJ as a gatekeeper in bringing social issues within or excluding them from, the scope of EU law.

The treaty rules on free movement are principally concerned with state measures which create obstacles to the exercise of those freedoms. Of particular relevance here will be the free movement of workers (Article 39 EC, now Article 45 TFEU); freedom of establishment (Article 43 EC, now Article 49 TFEU) and freedom to provide/receive services (Article 49 EC, now Article 56 TFEU). In terms of competition law, the anti-trust rules on anti-competitive agreements (Article 81 EC, now Article 101 TFEU) and abuses of a dominant position (Article 82 EC, now Article 102 TFEU) regulate directly the behaviour of 'undertakings'; typically private market actors. As Baquero Cruz highlights (2002), there is a basic public/private divide underpinning EU economic law.

However, under certain circumstances the activities of the state can trigger the application of the competition rules. Where the behaviour of the state would render ineffective the application of the competition rules, then the state itself breaches EU law. This involves reading the anti-trust rules in combination with Article 10 EC (now Article 4(3) TEU) which prohibits states from acting in a manner which would frustrate the achievement of the aims of the treaty. Secondly, the idea that Article 10 EC prevents Member States from acting in a manner that undermines the application of treaty rules is given concrete and specific expression in Article 86(1) EC (now Article 106(1) TFEU). Article 86(1) EC identifies the potential application of the treaty rules on free movement and competition to 'public undertakings' and 'undertakings to which Member States grant special or exclusive rights' (see Temple Lang, 2005). Nonetheless, Article 86(2) EC (now Article 106(2) TFEU) contains an important proviso, namely that where undertakings provide 'services of general economic interest', EU economic law is applicable 'insofar as the application of such rules does not obstruct the performance in law or in fact, of the particular task assigned to them.' In other words, activities which might otherwise fall foul of the treaties may be brought outside the application of EU economic law because of the (social) interest pursued by the state. Finally, the state is evidently the subject of the rules on state aid (Article 87 EC, now Article 107 TFEU *et seq.*).

Conversely, there are examples of the activities of 'private' actors being evaluated from the perspective of free movement law. There is an increasing horizontalization of the economic freedoms (see Van den Bogaert, 2002) and in the important rulings of the ECJ in *Viking Line*[6] and *Laval*[7] (discussed further below), the ECJ considered the Treaty rules on freedom of establishment and freedom to provide services applicable to obstacles to the exercise of these freedoms arising from the activities of trade unions as private actors.

The potential applicability of EU law to a social situation is not the end of the matter. Crucially, what may determine the legality of a domestic practice is whether it can be justified as pursuing a legitimate objective—eg a social goal—in a manner that does not disproportionately hinder the exercise of the economic rights conferred by the Treaty. Ultimately it is this interest-balancing exercise, carried out through the prism of proportionality which tends to be the focal point of analysis.

Before considering in detail the approach of the ECJ to the application of the competition rules and free movement law over time, the following section considers the manner in which the ECJ has handled suggestions that either the social domain should be considered to be immune from the application of EU economic law in the first place, or, that fundamental social entitlements should 'trump' economic freedoms.

The Applicability of EU Economic Law to the Social Sphere

The possibility of a zone of immunity for Member States social policies could arise in a number of different ways. First, it could be contended that

[6] Case C-438/05, *International Transport Workers' Federation and Finnish Seamen's Union v Viking Line* [2007] ECR I-10779.

[7] Case C-341/05, *Laval un Partneri Ltd v Svenska Byggnadsarbetareförbundet and others* [2007] ECR I-11767.

where the EU lacks or has limited legislative competence in a domain—typically the case in the areas in which OMC operates—then its courts do not have the competence to apply treaty-derived economic freedoms to those domains. However, in a consistent mantra, the ECJ has made clear that the legality of the manner in which Member States exercise competences not transferred to the EU still remains to be tested in light of treaty rules including their compatibility with the fundamental freedoms contained in the Treaty. That the EU lacks power to enact rules or measures in a field does not immunize the Member States' exercise of powers in that field from judicial scrutiny. As the ECJ made clear, for example, in its ruling in *Laval*,[8] that the EC Treaty did not confer legislative competence on the EU in respect of the right to strike did not mean that the exercise of that right at national level fell outside the scope of free movement rules. Accordingly, activities within the social realm are in principle within the material scope of EU economic law. Any potential immunity from review recognized by the ECJ, as will be seen, is specific rather than general, and highly qualified.

An alternative approach would be to suggest that in case of conflict, economic freedoms must yield to fundamental social rights. The relationship between economic freedoms and fundamental (social) rights has been explored in a number of important cases. In *Albany*, the issue was whether compulsory affiliation to a collectively-bargained sectoral pension scheme breached EU competition law.[9] It was argued that recognition of a fundamental right to collective bargaining ought to render such 'agreements' immune from scrutiny in light of EU anti-trust rules. In his Opinion,[10] Advocate General Jacobs considered whether a right to bargain collectively—as expressed in international legal instruments such as the European Social Charter (Article 6)—was recognized as a fundamental right within EU law. His conclusion was that the mere expression of the right within the European Social Charter did not automatically lead to the conclusion that it was recognized as a fundamental right by the European

[8] ibid.

[9] Case C-67/96, *Albany International BV v Stichting Bedrijfspensioenfonds Textielindustrie* [1999] ECR I-5751. Two central issues were at stake in *Albany*. The first was the liability of the state in terms of requiring compulsory affiliation to a collectively-bargained sectoral pension scheme. The other issue was the liability of the pension fund itself as an 'undertaking' which is discussed further below.

[10] Advocate General Jacobs Opinion was a joint Opinion encompassing two other cases: Cases C-155–157/97, *Brentjens* [1999] ECR I-6025 and Case C-219/97, *Drijvende* [1999] ECR I-6121.

Court of Human Rights or ought to be recognized as such by the ECJ. Moreover, given the ECJ's own case law on the recognition of fundamental rights within the EU legal order—in which such rights must be read having regards to the objects and purposes of the EU Treaties—the recognition of collective bargaining as a fundamental right would not automatically result in a trumping of the social over the economic. Jacobs concluded that: '. . . the mere recognition of a fundamental right to bargain collectively would therefore not suffice to shelter collective bargaining from the applicability of the competition rules.'[11] The ECJ did not consider the fundamental rights dimension to collective bargaining, ruling instead on the basis that the Treaty itself sought to promote social dialogue as a means of furthering the Treaty's social objectives.[12] However, in its 2007 rulings in *Viking Line* and *Laval*, the Court expressly acknowledged that strike action taken in defence of collective negotiations was a fundamental right to be protected as a general principle of Union law by the Court. However, and as predicted by Jacobs in *Albany*, this constitutional status did not then have the effect of sheltering strike action from the scope of application of the EU economic law. Indeed, unlike its substantive determination in *Albany* in which the Court gave a limited immunity to collective agreements from competition law scrutiny, in both *Viking Line* and *Laval* the Court proceeded on the basis that obstacles to the exercise of economic freedoms arising from the action of trade unions to defend collective agreements were in breach of the Treaty. It is readily apparent that the mere recognition of an activity as an expression of a fundamental social right neither immunizes that activity from the application of EU economic law nor does it necessarily lead to economic freedoms being trumped by fundamental social rights. Rather what the Court has developed in a series of cases (and supported by its Advocates General) is an approach in which economic freedoms and fundamental rights are required to be balanced. In other words, fundamental social rights are absorbed within the Court's analysis of internal market issues at the level of justification for actions which restrict free movement

[11] ibid, para 163.

[12] Having regard to the importance attached to social dialogue in the treaties, the ECJ did give a restricted immunity to the application of competition rules to pension schemes that were collectively bargained and had as their object improvement in the conditions of work and employment. Nonetheless, it was clear from later cases that this limited immunity only applied to collectively-bargained sectoral pension schemes. In *Pavlov*, the ECJ ruled that its approach in *Albany* was not applicable outside the context of collective bargaining: Joined Cases C-180/98 and C-184/98, *Pavel Pavlov and Others v Stichting Pensioenfonds Medische Specialisten* [2000] ECR I-6451.

rather than sheltering social goals from the gaze of EU economic law in the first place.

Three important conclusions can be drawn. The first is that the ECJ has confined its ruling in *Albany* and it is not authority for a general proposition that collective bargaining, or collective action to defend collective bargains, fall outside the zone of application of EU free movement rules. Secondly, the treatment of the right to strike as a fundamental right protected as part of the general principles of Union law, while superficially revolutionary, tends not to alter the legal treatment of the claim. In *Viking Line* and *Laval*, the ECJ's analysis of justification is motivated more by the Treaty's own social policy provisions and social policy objectives than by the metaphysical recognition of a fundamental right. The analysis focuses instead on the dual objectives of the Union—the pursuit of social and economic goals—and the need to balance the two. This suggests that proponents of a substantive rebalancing of European constitutionalism to give greater prominence to social rights as fundamental rights are in danger of chasing pyrrhic victories. The third conclusion is that the real test of the implications of EU economic law for the protection of social objectives lies in how the ECJ carries out its balancing function in any given example of litigation. Of particular significance will be the role of the proportionality principle in controlling the extent to which any restriction on economic freedom in light of social goals will be accepted.

In the sections that follow, the applicability of EU economic law to the realms of pensions, healthcare and social protection will be considered. In the course of testing the hypothesis that the OMC is undermined by the legal constraints of EU economic law, the analysis pays particular attention to the evolution of the ECJ's approach over time; to differences between the Court and its Advocates General; and to variances between the application of competition law and free movement law. The intention is to suggest that accounts of the law which tend to impute motive to the ECJ in terms of having a market liberalization agenda, often fail to acknowledge the extent to which the ECJ is not in control of the litigation processes which produce references to the ECJ.[13] Moreover, the ECJ has often struggled to develop coherent analytical tools which are fashioned in response to the welfare systems of one state yet require to be applied across the other Member States.

[13] Much of the ECJ's case law arises from requests from the national courts for interpretations of EU law: see Article 234 EC (now Article 267 TFEU).

Competition Law and Social Protection

The analysis below focuses on two issues that are key to determining the impact of EU competition law on the practices and institutions of social protection. The first issue is the extent to which the rules are applicable in the first place, particularly in terms of the definition of an 'undertaking' for the purposes of EU competition law. The second issue is the capacity to mitigate the application of the competition rules where the economic activity pursues a social goal in the general interest. It is the combination of these two aspects of EU competition law that will provide any evidence of a restrictive effect of EU law on the social policy autonomy of Member States.

The Concept of an 'Undertaking'

EU anti-trust rules apply to 'undertakings'. The definition of an undertaking is therefore central in defining the scope of the competition rules and their potential application to national social protection systems. The EU courts have consistently stated that 'the concept of an undertaking encompasses every entity engaged in an economic activity, regardless of the legal status of the entity and the way in which it is financed'.[14] This has become known as the 'functional' approach to interpreting the scope of the term 'undertaking' in that it focuses not on the legal status or mode of financing of an entity but on whether its activities can be functionally characterized as 'economic'. This also implies that for certain purposes and in respect of certain activities an entity will be an undertaking but not for others.

The practice of the ECJ has been to identify a range of indicators which show when activities are economic and when they are non-economic because of their solidaristic and redistributive nature. As regards the indicators of economic activity, these typically entail (1) the provision of goods and/or services; (2) risk-bearing by the entity as to the success or failure of the activity; and (3) the *potential* for the realization of profit (Odudu, 2004–5). The indicators of solidarity are somewhat harder to state as generalities given the different contexts of solidarity and the different modes of organization of social protection systems (eg insurance or non-insurance based). Nonetheless, typical aspects of solidarity in social protection systems (particularly insurance-based systems) include: (1) contributions proportionate

[14] See para 77 *Albany* (above n. 9), referring to Case C-41/90, *Höfner and Elser* [1991] ECR I-1979 and Cases C-159/91 and C-160/91, *Poucet and Pistre* [1993] ECR I-637.

to income; (2) benefits that are unrelated to contributions; (3) absence of the 'capitalization' principle for determining the level of benefits; and (4) cross-subsidy and redistribution. The Court's analysis proceeds on the basis of seeking to characterize the national social protection system according to the degree to which these indicators are present. Nonetheless, the difficulty for the Court is what to do when situations present with a mix of both types of indicator.

A useful starting point is the Court's ruling in *Poucet and Pistre*.[15] At issue was whether organizations managing sickness and maternity insurance schemes as part of the social security system (and for which compulsory contributions were payable) were to be considered to be 'undertakings' within the meaning of the anti-trust rules. The legal challenge was not to the compulsory nature of social insurance per se but rather the absence of a freedom of choice of provider and, thus, it was alleged that the funds managing the schemes were in a dominant market position contrary to Article 82 EC (now 102 TFEU). The Court of Justice concluded that the schemes were organized in accordance with the principle of 'solidarity' and did not, therefore, constitute economic activities.

A number of elements of solidarity in the scheme were highlighted: (1) contributions were proportional to income, but benefits were identical for all recipients; (2) benefits were maintained for a certain period for those no longer covered by the scheme; (3) pensions were not proportional to contributions and the contributions of those in employment paid for those in retirement; and (4) surpluses in funds could be used to off-set structural difficulties in other funds. In this way, the Court appeared to suggest that the presence of solidarity elements in social security systems ensured that they fell outside the scope of application of the competition rules.

In later cases, however, the Court concluded that activities within the social security field were indeed economic activities and the organizations managing these activities were to be considered as 'undertakings'. In *FFSA*,[16] the issue was whether an organization managing an optional supplementary pensions scheme could be considered to be an 'undertaking'. The scheme was not compulsory and supplementary pensions could be provided by life insurance companies. It was alleged that the fund was in a monopoly position given that it provided the basic old-age insurance to its members and

[15] ibid.

[16] Case C-244/94, *Fédération Française des Sociétés Assurances v Ministère de l'Agriculture et de la Pêche* [1995] ECR I-4013.

contributions made to it were tax deductible. However, it was contended that, following *Poucet and Pistre*, the scheme should be considered as falling outside the scope of the competition rules because of the presence of elements of solidarity.[17] The Court of Justice concluded, however, that the funds were to be considered as 'undertakings'. It pointed to the operation of the funds in accordance with the principle of *capitalization*: the extent of benefit conferred depended on the investment decisions made by the funds in respect of the contributions they received. While legal limitations on the use of the resources of the fund might make them less competitive when compared to private insurance firms, this did not render the activity non-economic. Equally the presence of elements of solidarity did not change the conclusion that the activity was economic, although the Court held open the possibility that these elements might come into play when considering whether the exclusive right to provide pensions for which contributions were tax-deductible was nonetheless compatible with the Treaty because of its social goal. In short, the Court appeared to be signalling that insurance-based social security systems would be capable of falling within the scope of the competition rules after all, despite the presence of elements of solidarity in the operation of the scheme.

The baton passed to the Dutch courts to raise questions about the compatibility of compulsory affiliation to pension schemes with the anti-trust rules. In *Van Schijndel and Cornelis*,[18] the ECJ avoided a ruling on the substantive questions concerning compulsory affiliation to a sectoral supplementary pension scheme, but the later case of *Albany*[19] brought the issue back to the Court of Justice. The Court had to resolve whether the pension funds ought to be considered as 'undertakings' and if so, whether the funds were abusing their dominant position contrary to Article 82 EC.

In *Albany*, legal action was brought by a textile company challenging the organization of the applicable sectoral pension scheme. The Dutch pension system comprised three elements: (1) a basic state pension; (2) supplementary

[17] As Advocate General Tizzano noted in his Opinion, these elements comprised: (1) contributions paid by active workers funded the pensions of retired workers (and hence no direct link between contributions and benefits); (2) financial solidarity between funds in that surpluses in one balanced deficits in others; and (3) certain minimum benefits payable even if contributions not made (or in any event not proportionate to contributions. The French Government also highlighted that the resources of the funds could only be used in accordance with rules established in decrees.

[18] Joined Cases C-430/93, C-431/93, *Van Schijndel and Cornelis v Stichting Pensioenfonds voor Fysiotherapeuten* [1995] ECR I-4705.

[19] Above n. 9.

pensions organized by sectoral pension funds; and (3) individual pensions and life insurance provided by private companies. The collectively-bargained sectoral supplementary pension scheme at issue had been in existence since the 1950s and Albany had complied with the obligation of compulsory affiliation since 1975. At that time the scheme provided fixed-sum benefits according to the number of years in service. Considering this to be insufficiently generous, Albany arranged a further supplementary pension with a life assurance firm to ensure that combined benefits to workers would amount to 70 per cent of final salary for those working for forty years. Although the sectoral scheme was reorganized in 1989 along the lines of ensuring benefits equivalent to 70 per cent of final salary, Albany considered its own arrangements to be preferable and sought exemption from participation in the scheme. The Fund declined to permit an exemption. At issue, then, was whether the Fund itself was an 'undertaking' for the purposes of EU competition law.

Advocate General Jacobs noted that in the organization of pension schemes Member States have a broad 'spectrum' of possibilities, from state-run social security systems through to private provision by commercial insurers. The difficulty was locating any given system along this spectrum. While the Court had appeared to suggest in *Poucet and Pistre* that the non-profit making nature of an activity, coupled with a social objective might bring an activity outside the scope of the competition rules, he considered that the approach adopted in *FFSA* suggested that these two elements would not suffice to exclude the application of the competition rules. His conclusion was that the elements of solidarity identified in *Poucet and Pistre* were not sufficient in *Albany* to deprive the pension funds of the character of economic undertakings. It is the presence of indicators of economic activity which prevail when determining whether an activity is economic: the mere existence of social objectives, non-profit-making and certain elements of solidarity are not themselves sufficient to change the characterization of the activity. For the Court of Justice, that the funds operated on the principle of capitalization and were free to determine both contributions and benefits (together with the possibility of firms seeking exemption from compulsory affiliation by reaching appropriate agreements with private insurers) indicated that the funds were undertakings within the scope of the competition rules. Following the approach in *FFSA*, while the non-profit-making and solidarity elements of the activity were not sufficient to deprive the funds of their economic character, they might be relevant in justifying the exclusive rights granted to the funds. In other words, the solidarity elements would be re-considered in terms of determining the extent to which the application of the competition rules applied to services of general economic interest might be mitigated (Article 86(2) EC, now 106(2) TFEU).

Subsequent cases can be seen as attempts by the European courts to apply the broad indicators developed in *FFSA* and *Albany* to national social protection systems organized in rather different ways. At one end of the spectrum is the *Poucet and Pistre* situation where the elements of solidarity are sufficient to persuade the Court that the situation falls *outside* the scope of the competition rules.[20] At the other end, are the *FFSA* and *Albany* situations where the elements of solidarity are insufficient to deprive the activity of its economic character, but, nonetheless, are relevant to determining the degree to which the application of the competition rules to services of general economic interest may be mitigated (discussed further below).[21] Given the range of possible ways of organizing the provision of social security, pensions and healthcare, it may be difficult to identify in advance which types of entity will be considered as engaged in an economic activity and, therefore, within the scope of the competition rules. Moreover, given the diversity of national systems, the result will be a relatively variegated pattern of potential application of the competition rules depending upon how the state organises its social protection systems.

Of course, once it is determined that an entity is an undertaking, the Court must then consider whether there is any actual restriction on competition. In *Albany*, the ECJ avoided any detailed factual or economic analysis of the restriction on competition created by the exclusive rights, but it did consider that the inability of firms to entrust their pension schemes to a single insurer resulted in a restriction of competition derived directly from the exclusive right granted to the pension funds. In *Pavlov*,[22] the Court noted that there was no evidence on the file that the fund had abused its dominant position on the market. In *FFSA*, the ECJ simply noted that there was a question 'still to be examined' as to whether the exclusive right to permit tax deductions

[20] Case C-218/00, *Cisal di Battistello Venanzio v Istituto nazionale per l'assicurazione contro gli infortuni sul lavoro (INAIL)* [2002] ECR I-691; Joined Cases C-264/01, C-306/01, C-354/01, C-355–01, *AOK Bundesverband et al* [2004] ECR I-2493.

[21] See *Pavlov* above n. 12. It is important then to recognize that subsequent cases did not overrule *Poucet and Pistre*. In Case T-319/99, *Federación Española de Empresas Instrumentación Científica, Médica, Técnica y Dental (FENIN)* [2003] ECR II-357, at para. 38 of its ruling, and after considering the case law following *Poucet and Pistre*, the CFI concluded that: 'Those cases thus leave the principle posited in *Poucet and Pistre* intact'. See also Case C-205/03P, *FENIN v Commission* [2006] ECR I-6295.

[22] Above, n.12.

for contributions to a pension scheme was compatible with the competition rules. It made no substantive finding on the point, leaving it to the national court to resolve.[23]

Thus, either because the entity was not an undertaking or because there was no impermissible restriction on competition, many of the cases simply would not fall foul of the competition rules. In the rare instance of a potential breach of the rules, attention would then focus on whether their social goal justified mitigating the application of the competition rules as discussed in the section which follows.

Services of General Economic Interest

The interpretation of Article 86(2) EC (now 106(2) TFEU goes to the very heart of the question of whether EU economic law prevails over national social services. Indeed, scholars have explicitly used this provision as a testing ground for Scharpf's thesis that economic norms are hierarchically prioritised over social values (Baquero Cruz, 2005; Soriano, 2003). As well as being relevant to the *Albany* situation—the role of pensions in social protection—the provision is also applicable more generally to the provision of public services as mechanisms of social protection and social inclusion. In this way, the issue of how to protect 'services of general economic interest' (SGEI) has come to symbolize contemporary concerns about the impact of EU economic law on national social sovereignty and alleged asymmetries of substantive constitutionalism.

Article 106(2) TFEU (ex 86(2) EC) provides that:

> Undertakings entrusted with the operation of services of general economic interest or having the character of a revenue-producing monopoly shall be subject to the rules contained in this Treaty, in particular to the rules on competition, in so far as the application of such rules does not obstruct the performance, in law or in fact, of the particular tasks assigned to them. The development of trade must not be affected to such an extent as would be contrary to the interests of the Union.

Its effect is to limit or mitigate the application of EU economic law (more particularly the competition rules) when the economic activity in question is one of providing a service of general economic interest. In essence, EU economic law is applicable only to the extent that it does not 'obstruct the performance, in law or in fact, of the particular task' assigned to the

[23] The Conseil d'Etat later found that there was an abuse of a dominant position: see Giubboni, 2001.

undertaking. By definition, a service which is not 'economic' but 'social' will not engage EU economic law in the first place.

Drawing clear conclusions for social protection policies is problematic given the very different sorts of cases that have come before the ECJ for an interpretation of Article 86(2) EC (now 106(2) TFEU). As Temple Lang suggests: '[T]he legal principles which have emerged have . . . never been authoritatively stated as a single set of rules in a clear conceptual framework' (2005: 46) and have not been developed specifically in relation to social welfare systems. Categorizing the ECJ's approach is, therefore, open to debate both in terms of what the ECJ has done and what it ought to do. Moreover, the approach of the ECJ has evolved over time.

Writing in the mid-1990s Gardner (1995) concluded that the ECJ viewed the interpretation of Article 86(2) EC in terms of a conflict between market and state planning with the Court adopting a narrow interpretation to give priority to the treaty-enshrined values of an 'open market economy with free competition' over competing models of economic organization. For Ross (2000) and Soriano (2003), this early case law was indeed preoccupied by a central economic question of whether the application of competition principles and market values would 'obstruct the performance' of the public service obligation by the undertaking. The focus of analysis turned on the extent to which the economic viability of the undertaking (and thus its ability to perform services of general interest) was threatened by competition. In adopting a narrow approach, this early case law might indeed be seen as supportive of the thesis that EU economic law restricted social sovereignty.

Nonetheless, there is broad agreement that the ECJ's judgment in *Corbeau*[24] was indicative of a shift in judicial strategy towards a greater willingness on the part of the Court to take seriously arguments that restrictions on competition were necessary in order to enable undertakings to perform services of general interest. The case concerned the extent to which it was permissible to create a postal monopoly which restricted competition but nevertheless performed a service of general economic interest (including public services obligations of universal service across the national territory at uniform rates). The Court made clear that in the absence of an exclusive right to provide postal services, it was conceivable that other economic undertakings would concentrate only on the economically profitable sectors, while the presence of an exclusive right recognized the extent to which there was cross-subsidy between more and less profitable elements of the service (necessary to ensure

[24] Case C-320/91, *Criminal Proceedings Against Paul Corbeau* [1993] ECR I-2533.

universal coverage). It did, however, indicate that where the 'economic equilibrium' would not be compromised in respect of a particular element of the service—it could be disassociated from the SGEI—then the restriction on competition would not be justified. So on the one hand, the Court makes clear that it is contrary to the Treaty to exclude from competition elements of postal services unrelated to the provision of services of general interest, but on the other hand, the elements of cross-subsidy to ensure the economic equilibrium required to provide services of general interest may justify the grant of exclusive rights. Which side of the line different elements of the service fell down on was left to the national court to determine.

Turning specifically to the area of pensions in *Albany*, for Advocate General Jacobs, it fell to the national court to determine whether the application of the competition rules would obstruct the provision of an SGEI. The ECJ, however, took matters into its own hands. It appeared to accept that there was a restriction of competition—the inability of companies to arrange their entire pension arrangements with a single insurer—flowing directly from the exclusive rights conferred on the pension funds. It then turned directly to whether Article 86(2) EC, nonetheless, required undertakings to be granted exclusive rights because, in their absence, they would be unable to perform the task assigned to them, or would not be able to do so under 'economically acceptable conditions'. Here, the solidaristic elements of the scheme were important. The potential departure of 'good risks' to private insurance companies (leaving the pension funds with 'bad risks') combined with the other elements of solidarity created constraints that rendered the services provided by the funds less competitive. Echoing *Corbeau*, the removal of exclusive rights would, therefore, 'make it impossible for it to perform the tasks of general economic interest entrusted to it under economically acceptable conditions and threaten its financial equilibrium'. Any restriction on competition was therefore to be accepted in light of the public service tasks to be performed by the pension funds and accordingly, the Member State was not precluded from making affiliation to the sectoral pension fund compulsory.

In terms of the proportionality analysis, the Court in *Albany* was noticeably unwilling to consider whether there was a better way for the Member State to organize its social protection system with fewer restrictions on competition as would be implied by a strict proportionality analysis. Thus, by contrast to its strict approach to derogations from free movement, the Court adopted a less intrusive proportionality analysis of domestic policy looking not to whether the public service ends are met by the means least restrictive of competition, but, as Baquero Cruz (2005) suggests, a lighter test of whether the means were suitable to achieve the public service goals. Thus in *Albany*, as regards the argument that the social objectives might be achieved by the Member State laying down minimum requirements to be met by the pension funds, the ECJ referred to the 'margin of appreciation' left to Member States in the organization of their social security schemes, leaving it to the state to consider whether minimum requirements would ensure the level of pension guaranteed by the existing system.[25]

Given the very limited data—the very few cases that ever get to court let alone raise competition issues applicable in the area of social protection—one needs to avoid making sweeping statements. But as regards core aspects of social protection there is almost no evidence that the anti-trust rules are systematically undermining the policy autonomy of Member States in areas covered by OMC processes on social inclusion, pensions or healthcare.

State Aid

The use of public funds to support entities to carry out public service obligations having a social inclusion objective—for example subsidized transport services or universal postal provision—may mean that such activities fall to be scrutinized in respect of the Treaty rules on state aid (Article 107 TFEU (ex 87 EC)). As Biondi and Rubini note (2005), the social purpose of aid does not of itself exclude it from being characterized as state aid. But nor is its social purpose irrelevant. The difficulty lies in determining at which level of analysis social aims are to be considered: at the level of defining the *scope* of application of the state aid rules in any given case or at the level of consideration of whether otherwise unlawful aid might be *justified*: a theme that has recurred throughout this chapter. As Biondi and Rubini have noted (2005: 91), the case law relating to the financial support of undertakings performing services of general interest has generated something of a 'jurisprudential clash' between advocates of a pure 'state aid' approach that tends to treat financial support as 'aid'—subject to notification and potential clearance by the European Commission—and those of a 'compensation' approach which seeks not to bring such support within the scope of the rules in the first place. Although

[25] An almost identical formulation of the point was made by Advocate General Jacobs in *Cisal di Battistello* (above n. 20), although again he emphasized that it was for the national court to determine whether an alternative approach of laying down minimum standards would achieve the same guarantees.

the Court of First Instance (now called the 'General Court' following the entry into force of the Lisbon Treaty) had in earlier cases approached the issue by considering Article 86(2) EC as a derogation for 'aid' which would otherwise have been considered to violate Article 87(1) EC,[26] the ECJ adopted a 'compensation' approach. In *Ferring* a tax was levied on direct sales by pharmaceutical companies to retail pharmacies.[27] Wholesale distributors were not the subject of the tax but were under a range of public service obligations to ensure continuity of provision of certain medicines. The issue was whether this effective exemption from the tax constituted 'aid'. The ECJ's conclusion was that it could not be considered as aid but rather as 'consideration' for the public service obligation intended to put the undertaking on an equal footing with those undertakings not covered by such obligations. There would only be state aid insofar as an advantage was conferred over and above that required to compensate for the public service obligation.

In his Opinion in *GEMO*,[28] Advocate General Jacobs noted that while the 'compensation' approach of *Ferring* has the advantage of avoiding the need for such aid to be notified and supervised by the European Commission, it tended to undermine the practical effect of Article 86(2) EC (now 106 TFEU). That is to say, if the financial support merely 'compensates' to the extent necessary for the performance of the public service obligation then it will not be aid and no issue of 'justification' arises. Conversely, any assistance which is not 'compensatory' but confers an advantage of an undertaking, by definition, will not be necessary for the performance of a public services and therefore will not be capable of justification. Treating financial assistance as *prima facie* state aid, but subject to clearance, would, however, render applicable the full EU supervisory system for state aid. For Jacobs, the appropriate solution would be to apply the compensation approach where it was clear from the outset that there was a direct and manifest link between the conferral of public service obligations and the receipt of a form of financial assistance.

Advocate General Jacobs opinion appears to have influenced the ECJ in its important ruling in *Altmark* concerned with subsidies to local transport.[29] Despite the urging of Advocate General Leger not to apply a 'compensation' approach, the ECJ adopted the mode of analysis deployed in *Ferring*

[26] See Case T-106/96, *FFSA v European Commission* [1997] ECR II-229.

[27] Case C-53/00, *Ferring SA v Agence centrale des organismes de sécurité sociale* [2001] ECR I-9067.

[28] Case C-126/01, *Ministère de l'Économie, des Finances et de l'Industrie v GEMO SA* [2003] ECR I-13769.

[29] Case C-280/00, *Altmark* [2003] ECR I-7747.

but with certain caveats: (1) the public service obligation must be clearly defined; (2) parameters on compensation must be determined *ex ante* in an objective and transparent manner (rather than an *ex post* compensation for losses suffered); (3) compensation must be proportionate and not exceed costs or create an advantage that would distort competition; and (4) where the service has not been the subject of public procurement, compensation must be determined in respect of typical costs for carrying out the public service. In this way, the Court established certain ground rules permitting compensation for public services without triggering scrutiny by the European Commission. The Commission later adopted Decision 2005/842/EC,[30] together with an explanatory framework document,[31] spelling out the circumstances in which, following *Altmark*, aid in support of public service obligations would not require to be notified to the Commission.

In this way, while Member States remain competent to entrust public service obligations to entities and to financially support entities in their execution of their obligations, the manner in which they do so must meet the conditions of *Altmark* as refined by Decision 2005/842. As regards the extent of EU control of those conditions—whether by the Commission or the EU courts—it is evident, as we have already seen with the ECJ's ruling in *Albany*, that the approach of the EU courts has been to exercise a rather limited reviewing function when compared to its approach under free movement law. Member States remain competent to determine the nature and scope of SGEI obligations, and as the General Court made clear in a judgment concerning the organization of private health insurance in Ireland on whether payments to equalize risks between insurers constituted state aid, 'the control which the Community institutions are authorized to exercise over the use of the discretion of the Member States in determining SGEIs is limited to ascertaining whether there is a manifest error of assessment'.[32] Moreover, in that case, notwithstanding that the private health insurance service was not 'universal' and could be seen as an 'optional' choice beyond

[30] Commission Decision on the application of Article 86(2) of the EC Treaty to State aid in the form of public service compensation granted to certain undertakings entrusted with the operation of services of general economic interest: OJ L312 (29.11.2005) p. 67.

[31] Community framework for state aid in the form of public service compensation: OJ C297 (29.11.2005) p. 4.

[32] Case T-289/03, *BUPA v Commission* [2008] ECR II-81. This case is relevant for this study given that the 'risk equalization scheme' at issue was intended to prevent private insurers targeting their services only towards good risks and so introduced a certain level of 'solidarity' into the scheme.

the state-provided health service, the Court, nevertheless, considered this as constituting a second pillar of the Irish health system under conditions operating in the general interest. As regards the necessity and proportionality of compensation paid for the SGEI, again, we see the review function limited to one of examining for manifest error: the Commission and courts are confined to examining the 'plausibility' of the compensation, looking only for compensation activities that are 'manifestly inappropriate'.[33] Whether or not this judicial reticence is itself a reaction to political responses (considered in the following section), it is evident that these are not the tests that would be readily adopted by an activist judiciary intent on infiltrating competition law into the national social protection systems.

Political Reponses to Safeguard Services of General Economic Interest

Notwithstanding the limited judicial imposition of competition rules to services of general economic interest, there can hardly be any doubt that Member States have been anxious to preserve the role of SGEIs in their national systems or at least exercise control over any liberalization of public services (not least that promoted by EU political institutions). Beginning with the Amsterdam Treaty, Member States have used treaty reform as an opportunity to seek to further safeguard their powers to endow undertakings with public service obligations: interpreted by Scharpf as an attempt to place limits on 'negative integration' (Scharpf, 1999:160–1). The Amsterdam Treaty added a new Article 16 to the EC Treaty intended to protect SGEIs.[34] The significance of this provision and its impact on the judicial *acquis* is, as ever, open to interpretation. It may simply underscore the importance attached by states to services of general economic interest which is, in any event, already recognized in the case law described above. As Ross notes (2000), Article 16 EC could also have been seen as acknowledging the fundamental social value attached to services of general economic interest as a shared *European* and not just a *national* value. In this way, it could contribute to the rebalancing of economic and social values within the treaties. With this in mind, it is noteworthy that

[33] Ibid, paras 220–2.

[34] Article 16 EC provided:

> Without prejudice to Articles 73, 86 and 87, and given the place occupied by services of general economic interest in the shared values of the Union as well as their role in promoting social and territorial cohesion, the Community and the Member States, each within their respective powers and within the scope of application of this Treaty, shall take care that such services operate on the basis of principles and conditions which enable them to fulfil their missions.

the importance attached to SGEIs was also expressed in Article 36 of the EU Charter of Fundamental Rights. It provides:

> The Union recognises and respects access to services of general economic interest as provided for in national laws and practices, in accordance with the Treaties, in order to promote the social and territorial cohesion of the Union.

With the entry into force of the Lisbon Treaty, Article 14 of the Treaty on the Functioning of the Union replaces Article 16 EC with the following:

> Without prejudice to Article 4 of the Treaty on European Union or to Articles 93, 106 and 107 of this Treaty, and given the place occupied by services of general economic interest in the shared values of the Union as well as their role in promoting social and territorial cohesion, the Union and the Member States, each within their respective powers and within the scope of application of the Treaties, shall take care that such services operate on the basis of principles and conditions, particularly economic and financial conditions, which enable them to fulfil their missions. The European Parliament and the Council, acting by means of regulations in accordance with the ordinary legislative procedure, shall establish these principles and set these conditions without prejudice to the competence of Member States, in compliance with the Treaties, to provide, to commission and to fund such services.

In addition, a new Protocol attached to the Treaties deals with services of general interest setting out what is meant by 'shared values' in the context of services of general *economic* interest, while also stating that:

> The provisions of the Treaties do not affect in any way the competence of Member States to provide, commission and organise non-economic services of general interest.

The extent to which this legalization of SGEIs is of more than symbolic significance is debateable. What is significant is the new competence to create a legal instrument at European level to give greater certainty and legal clarity to the application of EU economic law in this area. This will build on the approach developed in the realm of state aid following the *Altmark* ruling and state more generally the conditions for reconciliation of competition law and SGEIs.

Free Movement and Social Protection

At least as far as competition law is concerned, judicial review of exercises of national social sovereignty has been rather more sensitive to the policy choices of Member States than proponents of the economic constitutionalism-as-threat thesis would suggest. As Advocate General Poiares Maduro noted in *FENIN*,

> ... the Court is entering into dangerous territory, since it must find a balance between the need to protect undistorted competition on the common market and respect for the powers of the Member States [footnote omitted]. The power of the State which is exercised in the political sphere is subject to democratic control.[35]

Given that competition law is addressed primarily to the private sphere and given that Member States remain competent to design their social protection systems—including endowing entities with public service obligations—the EU courts have, in general, trodden rather carefully on the national territory. For Boeger (2007), this is a function of the democratic legitimacy of domestic social policies that reflect a principle of solidarity to which competition law must yield. What remains to be examined is whether that explanation stands scrutiny when we compare the ECJ's approach to the interaction of free movement law and national social protection systems.

In the sections below, the implications for national social sovereignty of EU law on free movement is explored. The objective is to determine the extent to which domestic social policy autonomy is constrained or limited by EU law, particularly in fields to which the social OMC is applied. In this regard, of significance will be the Court's approach to issues of 'justification' for measures found to inhibit these freedoms, and of the proportionality of the measures adopted to defend social interests. The analysis begins with the implications of the free movement of workers for domestic social welfare. Attention then turns to the issues concerning the right to receive cross-border health services and to have the costs reimbursed by the 'home' state. Finally, the discussion closes in on what has become the focal point for claims that judicial activism is undermining national solidaristic institutions, namely the effects of the law on freedom of establishment and freedom to provide services.

Free Movement of Workers

The migration of the economically active has the potential to reshape the boundaries of inclusion within the welfare systems of Member States

[35] Case C-205/03P, *Federación Española de Empresas de Tecnología Sanitaria (FENIN) v Commission* [2006] ECR I-6295, para. 26 of his Opinion.

(Ferrera, 2005). Two aspects of this reshaping will be considered below. First, the analysis highlights the application of EU rules on the coordination of social security benefits. Secondly, attention turns to the substantive entitlement to broader social advantages for the migrant EU national.

(a) Social Security

A key function of EU law is to facilitate coordination of social security systems. Without harmonizing substantive entitlements, EU law establishes rules concerning: equal treatment in terms of access to the social security system of the state in which the migrant resides; aggregation of periods of social insurance; the portability of benefits accrued in a Member State when the insured person moves. In this way, the boundaries of welfare extend to citizens of other Member States, while the state also has continuing responsibilities where its own nationals export their benefits outside the territory of the nation state (see Martinsen, 2005b). Member States do, however, remain competent to determine the nature and extent of their social security benefits. The coordination regime operates against the background of this pluralism and this policy autonomy.

The point of intervention here is not to engage in an elucidation of the complexities and intricacies of the social security coordination regime as initiated by Regulation 1408/71 (repeatedly amended, with a new consolidated regime taking effect from 1 May 2010).[36] Nonetheless, the case law surrounding the scope of the benefits covered by the coordination regime and case law on the exportability of benefits does highlight a degree of friction between the Member States and the ECJ which is of relevance to this discussion.

A distinction was drawn in the Regulation between those 'social security' benefits paid in respect of insured risks and covered by the coordination regime[37] and the realm of 'social protection'—the provision of social and medical assistance benefits that are typically non-contributory and often means-tested—that fell outside the scope of the Regulation. But rather than

[36] Regulation 883/2004 of the European Parliament and of the Council on the coordination of social security systems: [2004] OJ L200/1; Regulation of the European Parliament and of the Council 987/2009 laying down the procedure for the implementation of Regulation 883/2004: [2009] OJ L284/1; Regulation 988/2009 of the European Parliament and of the Council amending Regulation 883/2004 on the coordination of social security systems, and determining the contents of its annexes: [2009] OJ L284/43.

[37] Sickness and maternity benefits; invalidity benefits; old-age benefits; survivors' benefits; benefits in respect of accidents at work and occupational diseases; death grants; unemployment benefits; and family benefits: Article 4(1) Regulation 1408/71.

operating as a clear dichotomy, this distinction has been more of a fault line capable of creating conflict and tension between the ECJ and the Member States. The dichotomy reflected the Regulation's central preoccupation with a social welfare model based on employment-based insurance of social risks. As Martinsen highlights (2005a), the application of the Regulation outside of the context of the employment and insurance-based welfare systems of the founding Member States—in particular its application to residence and taxation based welfare systems—could be expected to create problems and tensions.

The ECJ sought to control the definition of social security benefits within the scope of the coordination regime in two ways. First, the identity of a benefit as a 'social security' benefit could not depend on it being treated as such within the law of the individual states.[38] The test the ECJ uses is an EU-wide test covering all the different welfare 'families' present across the EU's Member States. For the ECJ, 'a benefit may be regarded as a social security benefit in so far as it is granted, without any individual and discretionary assessment of personal needs, to recipients on the basis of a legally defined position and provided that it relates to one of the risks expressly listed in Article 4(1) of Regulation No 1408/71.' Within the realm of the OMC on Social Protection and Social Inclusion, whereas, social assistance by way of minimum income schemes like the *minimex* in Belgium have been held not to be social security benefits,[39] the provision of allowances to support long-term care such as the German or Austrian *Pflegegeld* are considered to be 'sickness benefits' within the scope of Article 4(1) of the Regulation (Martinsen, 2005b).[40]

The second way in which the ECJ controlled the material scope of the Regulation was in limiting collective attempts by Member States to categorize certain benefits within the scope of the Regulation itself. While respecting the principle of non-discrimination on grounds of nationality, Member States sought to ensure that certain sorts of benefits ought only to be capable of being claimed by those actually resident in the territory. This has been particularly evident in respect of benefits which appear to have both the characteristics of 'social assistance' (often because they are non-contributory) and 'social security' (because of their non-discretionary nature): so-called 'special non-contributory benefits'. As Martinsen

[38] Case 249/83, *Vera Hoeckx v Openbaar Centrum voor Maatschappelijk Welzijn, Kalmthout* [1985] ECR 973.

[39] Ibid.

[40] Case C-160/96, *Molenaar* [1998] ECR I-843.

highlights (2005b), as a result of ECJ judgments treating certain types of non-contributory benefits as social security benefits,[41] the Council responded by revising the Regulation to ensure that such benefits could only be claimed by those resident in the territory. The Member States successfully revised the Regulation to create an exception that while maintaining 'special non-contributory benefits' within the scope of coordination, nonetheless, prevented their exportation by permitting Member States to make receipt of the benefits conditional on residence. The sorts of benefits covered by this exception were laid down in Annex IIa to the Regulation.

Nonetheless, the ECJ itself responded by ensuring that the specific national benefits listed in Annex IIa met the definition of special non-contributory cash benefits according to the substantive provisions of the Regulation and to the principles which it had elaborated.[42] Thus in its ruling in *Jauch*, the ECJ determined that the Austrian *Pflegegeld*—which had been listed in Annex IIa—was not a special non-contributory benefit but rather a sickness benefit as per its ruling in *Molenaar* (and capable of being exported). It became apparent, therefore, that certain benefits were not validly listed in Annex IIa. When the Commission presented its proposals for the revision of Regulation 1408/71 to revise (and limit) the list of national benefits derogating from the principle of exportability, the Council amended the proposal at the request of the Finnish, Swedish and UK Governments to retain certain of their benefits on that list. While the Commission accepted the changes, it did hold open the possibility of future Court action. And indeed, the Commission brought an annulment action against the EP and Council contending that benefits listed in Article IIa—the Finnish child care allowance, the Swedish disability and care allowance for disabled children and the UK disability living allowance (DLA), attendance allowance (AA) and carer's allowance—did not meet the conditions necessary to be classified as special non-contributory benefits.[43] Not only did the ECJ annul the Regulation in respect of the Swedish and Finnish allowances, it also did so in respect of the UK's DLA and AA benefits, notwithstanding that in earlier case law, the

[41] Eg, the characterization of certain French supplementary allowances as old-age benefits within the scope of the Regulation, notwithstanding their non-contributory nature and their funding out of taxation: see Joined Cases 379–381/85 and 93/86, *Giletti et al* [1987] ECR 955.

[42] Particularly in Case C-215/99, *Jauch* [2001] ECR I-1901 and Case C-43/99, *Leclerc and Deaconescu* [2001] ECR I-4265.

[43] Case C-299/05, *Commission v EP and Council (Special Non-Contributory Benefits)* [2007] ECR I-8695.

Court had characterized both allowances as being covered by the exception for special benefits.[44]

There has, then, been an obvious tension between, on the one hand, the desire of Member States to limit the types of benefits covered by the coordination regime and to restrict the portability of certain of those benefits, and on the other, the ECJ expanding the boundaries of inclusion to protect migrants who have either paid specific contributions or otherwise paid into the taxation systems of states. The discussion above is, however, also a useful testing ground of Scharpf's related claims that not only is social sovereignty curtailed but Member States may be powerless to respond collectively because of 'joint decision traps' (for an updated version of his original formulation see Scharpf, 2006). A particularly significant constraint in this regard would be unanimous voting, applicable both to treaty change and to the adoption of EU social security legislation. Yet as we witnessed with regard to special non-contributory benefits, Member States did manage to amend Regulation 1408/71. They have not, however, had the last word as evidenced by the ECJ's 2007 ruling annulling the wrongful inclusion of certain benefits in Annex IIa to the Regulation. There can be no doubt that there is an interesting interplay of law and politics going on here. But it is a more nuanced and subtle interplay than that captured either by blunt assertions of EU economic law trumping social sovereignty or even of the joint decision trap thesis.

(b) *Social Advantages*

EU law has conferred on migrant workers and their family members rights to equal treatment in terms of access to the social advantages which a host state provides to its own nationals. That right to equality of treatment derived initially from the status of the migrant as a worker (who, after all, was paying into the host state's tax and benefits system), but was extended to the non-economically active through the 'Citizenship Directive'.[45] As the discussion here is solely concerned with the impact of EU economic law on social sovereignty it will not concern itself generally with the impact of EU citizenship.

[44] Case C-20/96, *Snares* [1997] ECR I-6057 and Case C-297/96, *Partridge* [1996] ECR I-3467. Without further justification, the ECJ held that these cases had to be analysed in the 'post-Jauch legal context'. However, the ECJ did limit the temporal effect of its judgment as regards the DLA's 'mobility' component.

[45] Directive 2004/38 of the European Parliament and of the Council on the rights of citizens of the Union and their family members to move and reside freely in the territory of the Member States: [2004] OJ L229/35.

Nonetheless, one example usefully illustrates both the manner in which the 'social' status of citizenship has reshaped even the rules applicable to workers, but where the ECJ has also shown itself more sensitive to demands that migrant EU nationals have some connection with the state from which they claim financial assistance.

In its judgment in *Collins*[46] the ECJ was asked to determine the lawfulness of the denial of financial assistance to a migrant EU national residing in the UK and seeking employment. The Jobseeker's Allowance (JSA) claimed by Collins formed part of the UK Government's strategy to make the benefits system 'activate' those not in employment by making short-term financial assistance conditional on the active search for work combined with a range of obligations and sanctions related to the behaviour of the applicant. In order to claim JSA the applicant had to be 'habitually resident' in the UK, or an EU national who is (or had been) a 'worker'. It was not in dispute that Collins was genuinely seeking employment as required by UK law: the issue was whether the denial of JSA to him on the ground that he was not 'habitually resident' constituted discrimination prohibited by EU law. Collins had only been resident for one month before making his claim. Not surprisingly, the UK Government was fearful that to expand the boundaries of inclusion to permit a non-economically active EU migrant to access social security benefits while resident for only a short period would have rather negative consequences for its social security system: the spectre of benefits tourism.

The case law of the ECJ was, however, not entirely favourable to Collins. Hitherto, the ECJ had held that while someone seeking work has the right to equality of treatment as regards access to the labour market, a distinction was to be drawn with regard to 'social and tax advantages' within the meaning of Article 7(2) of Regulation 1612/68. The right to invoke the non-discrimination principle in Article 7(2) was restricted to those already in employment.[47] However, the Court looked beyond EC legislation to the Treaty itself (Article 39 EC, now 45 TFEU), considering that an EU national was entitled to move freely and reside in another Member State for the purposes of seeking employment and was entitled to equal treatment in the host state. In light of the development of the concept of citizenship of the Union and the right to equality of treatment in matters falling within the material scope of the Treaty, the ECJ held that it was no longer possible to exclude from the

[46] Case C-138/02, *Collins v Secretary of State for Work and Pensions* [2004] ECR I-2703.

[47] Case 316/85, *Lebon* [1987] ECR 2811.

scope of application of that principle, access to financial benefits intended to facilitate access to the labour market of the host state.

While conceptually expanding the boundaries of inclusion within national welfare systems, the Court, nonetheless, qualified the practical effect of this boundary shift in an important way. Although it concluded that an habitual residence test introduces a difference in treatment between nationals and non-nationals (by disadvantaging migrant EU nationals who are less likely to meet the test than nationals who have never moved), it left it open to the Member State to justify its restriction on access to a benefit by requiring that there be a genuine link between the person seeking work and the employment market of the host state. That link could be established by a need to show that for a reasonable period the applicant was genuinely seeking work. While a residence requirement was potentially an appropriate means of evidencing that link, it had to be proportionate: the residency period could not go beyond that which was required for the national authorities to satisfy themselves that the applicant was genuinely seeking work.

What this example highlights is that it is certainly the case that the provision of benefits such as the JSA is not something within the complete discretion of a Member State to refuse to provide to a migrant EU national. Nonetheless, the ECJ does recognize that Member States may legitimately refuse to provide such benefits in the absence of a real link between the individual and the Member State as evidenced, for example, by the length of the time the individual has been present on its territory. It is the proportionality principle that mediates the relationship between the interests of the EU—in supporting free movement—and the interests of the state in preserving the integrity of its social assistance mechanisms. What is crucial, therefore, is how the Court—but more especially the national court—applies this analytical framework. In *Collins* the Social Security Commissioner, in applying the preliminary ruling of the ECJ concluded that the habitual residence test was justified and proportionate to ensure a real and genuine link between the claimant and the UK employment market. The test was, therefore, compatible with Community law; a conclusion upheld on appeal to the English Court of Appeal. Accordingly, Collins was not entitled to claim JSA.

Two conclusions can be made from this analysis. While the social status of 'citizen of the Union' is reshaping the boundaries of inclusion within national welfare systems, it does not of itself guarantee access to substantive benefits if the Member State has a legitimate reason for making access to benefits conditional on a residency requirement. Secondly, in practice it will be national courts and tribunals that will act as gatekeepers in their application of national and Union law. Therefore, while there are EU-imposed limits to the discretion of the Member States in the operation of their social welfare systems, there are equally limits to those limits insofar as Member States can justify the exercise of their policy autonomy. Once again, this neither supports the thesis that Member States have lost their social sovereignty nor does it suggest that the OMC is prevented from operating because of constraints imposed by EU free movement law.

Freedom To Receive Services

There is a parallel to be drawn between migration for work and the effects of migration in order to receive services, namely the fear that Member States' ability to organize core aspects of their social welfare systems or social services is undermined by the need to accommodate the right of citizens to access services beyond the national territory. As is well known, this has been of particular significance with regard to the cross-border provision of health services. Indeed, Article 22 of Regulation 1408/71 (discussed in the previous section), provided for a system of prior authorization (the 'E112' form) by which an individual could obtain treatment in another Member State and have the 'home' Member State pay the cost of that treatment. However, the ECJ created greater autonomy for itself, by increasingly basing its judgments not on the Regulation, but directly on Article 49 EC (now 56 TFEU) and the right of patients to receive services. Regardless of whether an individual founded their EU law right to cross-border treatment and reimbursement on the Regulation or directly from the Treaty, the approach of the ECJ was to treat requirements of 'prior authorization' by the home state or refusals to reimburse as *prima facie* obstacles to the receipt of a 'service' which would require justification by the Member State.

The identification of health services as 'services' within the meaning of the Treaty was itself a bold step by the ECJ.[48] In its ruling in *Kohll*,[49] the ECJ made clear that notwithstanding that health services fall within the ambit of a state's social security system, this fact alone did not immunize the service from the reach of Article 56 TFEU. Moreover, Article 56 TFEU is not only applicable to non-hospital healthcare services which are typically paid for by the patient (hence 'remuneration' as required for an activity to be a 'service') but also, as was made clear in *Geraet-Smits and Peerbooms*[50]—further clarified

[48] For more extensive analysis see especially Hatzopoulous, 2002, 2005; Bernard, 2005; Hervey and McHale, 2005.

[49] Case C-158/96, *Kohll* [1998] ECR I-1931.

[50] Case C-157/99, *Smits and Peerbooms* [2001] ECR I-5473.

in *Müller-Fauré*[51]—to hospital treatment in systems characterized as 'benefits-in-kind' systems. That reimbursement is sought from a state-funded, free-at-point-of-delivery system like the National Health Service in the UK, does not have the effect of taking the situation outside the scope of the free movement rules where, as in *Watts*,[52] the patient pays for the health service in another Member State.

The contrast with the ECJ's approach to the application of the competition rules in cases like *Poucet and Pistre* and in *Albany* is highlighted by Hatzopoulos (2005). The contrast lies not only in the extent to which social services fall within the scope of the Treaty in the first place, but also with the role of the Court in then analysing attempts by Member States to justify the rules found to pose obstacles to free movement. The ECJ has been willing to recognize a range of public interest justifications which Member States may seek to invoke when seeking to restrict free movement such as avoiding serious risks to the social security system's financial balance; maintaining a balanced medical and hospital service open to all; and the maintenance of treatment capacity or medical competence on the national territory. Nonetheless, there is an important difference in the application of these justifications to the issue of prior authorization as between hospital and non-hospital treatment.

In its rulings in *Kohll* and in *Dekker*,[53] the ECJ found that as regards non-hospital treatment, there were effective protections for the migrant patient provided either by the law of the host state or by EU law to ensure the protection of public health without the need for a prior authorization rule. However, as regards hospital treatment in *Geraet-Smits and Peerbooms* and subsequent case law, the Court considered prior authorization rules to be, in principle, necessary and proportionate to their aims. But—and importantly—the Court has sought to prevent the discretion to refuse authorization being used in an arbitrary manner and to that end, has proceduralized the exercise of powers by Member States by requiring that:

> ... in order for a prior administrative authorization scheme to be justified ... it must, in any event, be based on objective, non-discriminatory criteria which are known in advance, in such a way as to circumscribe the exercise of the national authorities' discretion, so that it is not used arbitrarily ... Such a prior administrative authorization scheme must likewise be based on a procedural system which is easily accessible and

[51] Case C-385/99, *Müller-Fauré and van Riet* [2003] ECR I-4509.

[52] Case C-372/04, *Watts* [2006] ECR I-4325.

[53] Case C-120/95, *Dekker* [1998] ECR I-1831.

capable of ensuring that a request for authorization will be dealt with objectively and impartially within a reasonable time and refusals to grant authorisation must also be capable of being challenged in judicial or quasi-judicial proceedings.[54]

In its ruling in *Watts*, the ECJ was particularly critical of the lack of a transparent legal framework for prior authorization within the UK's NHS.

Moreover, the Court has laid down a substantive test: the right to refuse authorization only if the same or similar treatment could be obtained within the national system without 'undue delay'. The Court will not permit an authorization to be refused merely on the grounds that the time the patient would wait was consistent with national waiting times and instead demands 'an objective medical assessment of the patient's medical condition, the history and probable course of his illness, the degree of pain he is in and/or the nature of his disability at the time' in order to determine whether the delay arising from the waiting list exceeds an acceptable period.

These and other cases do indicate that, in the words of Advocate General Geelhoed in *Watts*:

...there is an emerging transnational market for health care services which gives rise to problems, not so much in respect of the right to leave the Member State of residence or the right to enter another Member State to receive medical treatment, but in respect of the terms of financing such treatment.

In its *Watts* ruling, however, the ECJ was at pains to state that the necessary adjustments to the national systems did not undermine their sovereign powers in this domain. The Court also stated that the approach it has taken to prior authorization was not likely 'to lead to an exodus of patients.' As Bernard suggests, the freedom to receive health services is only likely to be of use as an additional resource for the mobile middle classes (2005: 274).

Nor does the *Watts* ruling toll the bell for waiting lists: only where there is an evident disjuncture between the waiting time for treatment and the patient's clinical need will the issue of authorization to seek treatment abroad arise. Crucially, judicial analysis turns not on whether the treatment could be obtained faster in another Member State, but rather whether the home state's treatment would be unduly delayed. That Member States organize their healthcare differently and offer treatment on different time-scales is accepted by the Court and rather than foreclosing the possibility of policy coordination in this domain, judicial intervention can be seen as a potential

[54] Smits and Peerbooms, above n. 50, para. 90.

exhortation to Member States to better coordinate supply and demand for healthcare across the EU.

In sum, judicial intervention in the field of free movement and healthcare is clearly more invasive than we have seen with regard to the application of the competition rules, but not necessarily in a way that undermines possibilities for policy coordination. Indeed as Hervey cogently notes (2006), the development of new forms of governance like the OMC can be seen as reactions to judicial intervention. Hervey describes the Court's healthcare rulings as a 'catalyst' producing a range of responses from the establishment of High-Level Groups, to the health and long-term care elements of the Social Protection and Social Inclusion OMC. Undoubtedly, there are political sensitivities around EU intervention in this field, highlighted not least by the removal of the provision of health services from the controversial Services Directive. Indeed, even intervention via the OMC has had to be presented as a 'light touch' process (Hervey, 2006: 192–3). But instead of seeing the issue in the rather stark terms of a zero-sum world of 'sovereignty' in which whatever the EU gains, the Member States must lose, it is better to view the influence of EU free movement law as an unsettling one, forcing political actors to reconfigure governance.

Freedom of Establishment and Freedom to Provide Services

If the freedom to receive services is, in practice, likely to have a limited effect on the powers of Member States to organize their social protection systems due to the small number of mobile citizens, the mobility of capital and labour has dramatized the apparent clash between EU economic law and institutions of national solidarity. The right of freedom of establishment (Article 49 TFEU) allows a company to decide which regulatory environment is most conducive to the operation of its business and to locate or de-locate accordingly. While it may be a different company law regime that is attractive,[55] it can also be the prospect of lower labour costs that drive delocalization. This is especially relevant in the context of asymmetries in wages in an enlarged EU (see Bercusson, 2007). Moreover, using the provisions of the Treaty relating to the provi-

[55] As the ECJ put it in its *Centros* ruling: 'the fact that a national of a Member State who wishes to set up a company chooses to form it in the Member State whose rules of company law seem to him the least restrictive and to set up branches in other Member States cannot, in itself, constitute an abuse of the right of establishment.' Case C-212/97, *Centros Ltd v Erhvervs- og Selskabsstyrelsen* [1999] ECR I-1459.

sion of services (Article 56 TFEU), a company established in one Member State can provide economic services in the territory of another Member State, including posting its own workers to that territory, raising crucial questions concerning the applicable labour law (particularly as regards relevant pay rates). It is the effect of these freedoms on processes of wage-setting that is of particular importance. Given the significance that the OMC attaches to low income as an indicator of the risk of poverty and given the stress that is placed on employment as a route out of poverty, the analysis of rulings of the ECJ on the exercise of these freedoms is relevant to determining the extent to which the OMC is constrained by economic constitutionalism.

Looking first at freedom of establishment, in its ruling in *Viking*,[56] the ECJ explicitly distinguished its earlier ruling in *Albany* in which it had created a limited zone of immunity from the reach of EU competition law for collective action via collective bargains. At issue was the collective action taken by trade unions against a ferry company that wished to avoid higher labour costs in Finland—wages being determined through collective agreements—by seeking to re-establish in Estonia. The ECJ rejected the applicability of its ruling in *Albany* outside the context of EU competition law. While in *Albany* the ECJ had accepted that a certain restriction on competition was inherent in collective agreements, the Court was not willing to concede that a certain restriction on economic freedoms was inherent in the right to take collective action even where that action was to defend wage levels set by collective agreements. Thus, whereas in the realm of competition law, any inherent restriction on freedom (to contract) resulting from collective bargains is in the public interest having regard to its limited effects on competition and its social aims, with regard to free movement law, restrictions on economic freedoms arising from collective action are regarded as not being in the public interest unless they can be justified. But even while allowing trade unions to invoke public interest justifications normally defended by states, in its strict application of the proportionality principle, the Court restricted the practical scope of attempts by trade unions to defend solidaristic action. The effect was that EU and national courts became the arbiters of whether strike action really was necessary to defend jobs and employment conditions or whether other action, less restrictive of the economic freedom, could be pursued: a much more activist approach than was taken in *Albany*.

[56] Above n. 6.

However, it has been in the area of the freedom to provide services that the fear of competitive deregulation through 'home country control' has been more acutely felt. This anxiety permeated the debate concerning the adoption of the 'Services Directive' (also know as the 'Bolkestein Directive').[57] Although references to the 'country of origin principle' were ultimately removed from the directive—and the directive clarified to remove certain areas from its scope including healthcare—Article 16 of the directive replicates the structure of court-driven free movement law by limiting the powers of the host state to defending non-discriminatory, necessary and proportionate rules with a defined public interest goal.[58] In this way, the 'fundamental' freedom to provide services on the basis of home country control—subject to recognized derogations—still frames the provision of services in the EU.

A key anxiety of opponents to the directive was the fear that cross-border service provision would particularly undermine the right of the host state to impose its own labour laws. As Article 16(3) of the directive identifies, local employment rules can, in accordance with EU law, be imposed by the host state. Of particular relevance here is the Posted Workers Directive (PWD)[59] which identifies the kinds of employment conditions that a host state can impose when a service provider posts its workers in the host state. Interestingly, Scharpf identified the directive as an example of the Council placing limits on negative integration by 'suspending some of the legal consequences of service liberalization' (1999: 164). However, the directive does not itself harmonize labour laws. Like other legislative examples identified in this chapter, its function is largely coordinative in terms of determining the relative application of home and host state labour laws.

Prior to the adoption of the PWD, when interpreting the Treaty directly, the approach of the ECJ, as Barnard notes (2007) was initially one of permitting the host state to extend the application of its labour laws—including

[57] Directive 2006/123/EC of the European Parliament and of the Council on services in the internal market: OJ [2006] L376/36.

[58] Not only must the Member States act in conformity with the Treaty, so too must the EU legislature, meaning that the directive will be interpreted consistently with the fundamental principles established by the ECJ, including the principle that derogations from a fundamental freedom will be narrowly construed. And of course, for those services excluded from the directive's scope—like healthcare—the provisions of the Treaty on service provision will apply to the extent that they applied anyway.

[59] Directive 96/71/EC of the European Parliament and of the Council concerning the posting of workers in the framework of the provision of services: [1997] OJ L18/1.

collective bargains—to workers posted to its territory.[60] From that position of relative deference to the host state, the ECJ moved in the direction of viewing the imposition of local labour laws as *prima facie* obstacles to free movement that required justification. As Kilpatrick identifies (2009) it is the ECJ's approach to the capacity of the host state to justify the imposition of its labour laws that lies at the heart of the controversies surrounding the effects of the PWD.

Article 3(1) of the PWD mandates the application of certain host state labour laws with which the service-provider must comply. This provision includes the imposition of statutory minimum wages, and minimum wages contained in collective agreements which have been made universal. In the *Laval* case,[61] the posting of Latvian workers to a construction project in Sweden raised the issue of whether it was permissible to demand the imposition of the collective bargain operating in the Swedish construction sector—including rates of pay—to the posted workers. Unlike other European countries, the approach in Sweden was neither for the legislature to lay down a minimum wage nor indeed for collective bargains generally to establish a minimum wage. Rather it was left to the social partners to negotiate wages in specific sectors (albeit that if negotiations reached a stalemate there was a 'fall-back' basic wage that could be enforced). The Court's view was that substantively, the rates of pay set by collective bargaining in the construction sector were not, then, minimum wages but rather were simply the going rate, and procedurally, the wage-setting mechanism was not one laid down by law or by a 'universal' collective bargain. Accordingly, the directive could not be relied upon to impose local wages on posted workers.

Article 3(7) of the directive does, however, provide that the directive shall not prevent the application of more favourable conditions for workers. Nonetheless, the ECJ did not interpret this as a means of allowing the host state to impose higher wages levels above the 'floor' level protected by Article 3(1). The conclusion, therefore, is that the host state does have a power to set minimum wages but that in order to rely on the directive it must either exercise that power directly through legislation or, if it allows it to be set by collective bargaining, the wage set must be explicitly a minimum wage and must be made universal. The Swedish model of wage regulation did not meet the conditions of the directive. In essence, the directive—while

[60] Case C-113/89, *Rush Portuguesa v Office national d'immigration* [1990] ECR I-1417.
[61] Above n. 7.

allowing host states to demand respect for minimum wages—does permit wage competition above that level.

The Court further confined the reach of the PWD some months later in its ruling in *Rüffert*.[62] This concerned the use of Polish subcontractors to carry out construction work on a prison. The law on the award of public contracts adopted by Land Niedersachsen was specifically intended to counteract distortions of competition resulting from the use of cheap labour by requiring service providers tendering for contracts to comply with local rules on wages laid down by collective agreements. As the law did not itself lay down a minimum wage, and because the collective agreement was only applicable to public contracts and was not one universally applicable, the Court again denied the ability of the state to rely on the PWD as a means to insist on the application of local wages.

A third case dealing with the interpretation of the PWD also sparked controversy. Unlike the others, it did not arise out of a specific dispute between private parties but rather was an infringement proceeding brought by the European Commission against Luxembourg.[63] It concerned, inter alia, rules on the indexation of wages to inflation. Consistent with its ruling in *Laval*, the ECJ took the view that this could not be given automatic protection by Article 3(1) PWD as it did not concern the setting of minimum wages. Nonetheless, the ECJ was asked to consider whether Article 3(10) of the PWD would permit the application of host state rules in the interest of 'public policy'.[64] In its ruling, the ECJ repeatedly noted that the matters definitively resolved in favour of the host state are exhaustively defined in Article 3(1) PWD, and therefore, Article 3(10) must be interpreted restrictively not only because of the structure of the PWD but also because it is a derogation from a fundamental freedom. So on the one hand, the ECJ holds open the possibility of allowing a Member State to argue that an apparent obstacle to free movement is justified in the public interest, but on the other hand, the ECJ made it clear that it would take some convincing on the public interest rationale put forward by the host state. As regards the indexation of wage

[62] Case C-346/06, *Rüffert v Land Niedersachsen* [2008] ECR I-1989.

[63] Case C-319/06, *Commission v Luxembourg* [2008] ECR I-4323.

[64] Article 3(10) provides:

> This Directive shall not preclude the application by Member States, in compliance with the Treaty, to national undertakings and to the undertakings of other States, on a basis of equality of treatment, of:
>
> —terms and conditions of employment on matters other than those referred to in the first subparagraph of paragraph 1 in the case of public policy provisions.

levels to cost-of-living increases, it did admit of the possibility of the host state justifying such rules under Article 3(10). However, it demanded that the Member State actually produce 'evidence to establish whether and to what extent the application to workers posted to Luxembourg of the rule concerning automatic adjustment of rates of pay to the cost of living is capable of contributing to the achievement [of the public policy objective]'.

Such has been the controversy surrounding the ECJ's rulings in this area that Scharpf himself floated the possibility that Member States might decide not to comply with a ruling of the ECJ unless the ruling was approved by the Council of Ministers (Scharpf, 2008). The European trade union movement reacted with some anger to ECJ rulings and attempted to link discontents with these rulings to the fate of the Lisbon Treaty in calling for a 'social progress' clause to be attached to the Lisbon Treaty.[65] Indeed, the Irish Technical, Engineering and Electrical Union highlighted the judgments in the cases discussed above to urge its members to vote 'No' in the Irish referendum on the ratification of the Lisbon Treaty.[66] The controversy surrounding this case law was also raised during the course of the 2010 parliamentary hearing for the nominee for the Social Affairs Commissioner.

At its bluntest, the discontent with the ECJ's judgment lies in an assertion that the cases are wrongly decided or wrongly reasoned. The argument goes that the Court allowed economic freedoms to trump domestic institutions of social solidarity and that it paid lip service to the recognition of collective bargaining and the right to strike while siding with the economic interests of service providers. The problem with this dramatization of these complex decisions is that it tends to lead to a type of arms race between economic and social values with calls for stronger constitutionalization of social values and more restrictions on economic values. It is far from clear that this will ever resolve the tensions between the competing interests at stake in these disputes.

More sophisticated analyses suggest that the ECJ should have allowed host state labour laws to apply as a buttress against wage competition driven in particular by service provision. There is an important point here. As Colin Hay has highlighted (2007), 'competiveness' in service provision is different from competitiveness in product markets not least because of the close relation between the cost of a service and the cost of labour. The promotion of

[65] Speech of Mr. John Monks, ETUC General Secretary to a hearing of the Employment and Social Affairs Committee of the EP, 26.02.08.

[66] Press Release, 4.05.08: <http://www.teeu.ie> (Accessed in March 2010).

competitiveness—not least as a key element of the Lisbon strategy—tends then to push in the direction of the lowering of wage costs and, as we have seen with regard to services, there is limited room for states to prevent wage competition. But as Hay highlights this not only rubs up against the social cohesion dimension of Lisbon, even on its own economic terms, it suppresses the potential for states to exploit their tax base to fund and sustain their social protection systems. As Hay puts it (2007: 41):

> If the ratio of net welfare recipients to net welfare contributors is rising, then the last thing Europe can afford is a set of public policy commitments that suppress the earnings—and hence the fiscal—potential of those in employment.

If Hay's analysis is right, then to the extent that the Court's approach is consistent with the Lisbon strategy's aim of enhancing competitiveness in service markets, the result may be one that undermines social cohesion and devalues the role of collective bargaining in the delivery of social protection in a way that not only diminishes the social side of Lisbon but also weakens the economic foundations of sustainable social protection systems.

Nonetheless, there is another side to this story. The economic and political context of the enlargement of the Union to central and eastern Europe cannot be ignored. These states were bound to seek to take competitive advantage of wage asymmetries in Europe and the Member States of the EU ought to have realized that. The situation in *Laval* is particularly pertinent. The Swedish unions sought to insist on the application of local wages to posted Latvian workers. The company posting those worker was willing to pay those workers a rate of €1,500 per month with additional meal and accommodation benefits on top. While less than the going rate under the Swedish collective bargain, it was a wage rate higher than even the highest minimum wage in the rest of the EU at the time, let alone what those workers would have received in Latvia. Therefore, the issue cannot simply be cast in terms of the potential diminution of wage levels in 'old' Europe (itself a complex question of arbitrage and competitive adjustment) but also the potential denial of increased levels of wages for workers from 'new' Europe.

Simply to demand that the coordination of applicable labour laws always be resolved in favour of the host state not only does not respect the legitimate economic interests of out-of-state service providers, it does not acknowledge the economic interests of the posted workers themselves. Instead, as Kilpatrick highlights (2009), there is a 'conundrum' with which the ECJ must wrestle. On the one hand collective bargaining legitimately seeks to reconcile the competing 'in-state' interests of workers and employers, including on matters of wage-setting. On the other hand this process is unlikely to take 'out-of-state' interests into account and in doing so is exclusionary to those interests. As with the approach of the ECJ to free movement in general, the ECJ will find it hard to accept such 'closed' processes of decision-making.

Therefore, the problem with these cases is far less that the ECJ got these rulings wrong—on which there can be legitimate debate and disagreement—and more that it is having to decide them at all. To that extent, there may be some common cause with those attacking the ECJ, but for entirely different reasons. Opponents of the ECJ's interventions in the social sphere often explicitly or implicitly attach motive to the Court as a willing driver of processes of marketization. Yet the ECJ is not in control of the litigation which comes before it. It cannot decline to hear cases. The ECJ, as Gerstenberg notes (2002), has been drawn increasingly into conflicts which it may not wish or be equipped to resolve. It is for this reason, that it might be better to look to alternative means to manage these conflicts. Already, if we look back to examples like the ECJ's decisions in *Watts* and *Altmark*, the ECJ can sometimes find mechanisms to proceduralize issues or set out substantive standards which allow parties to negotiate out solutions without continual resort to the courts. Indeed, it may be to new forms of governance that we can look to seek to try and resolve conflicts beyond the courts.

Conclusions

A number of conclusions can be drawn from the analysis presented in this chapter. The first is that the general thesis that EU economic law trumps domestic social sovereignty is simply far too blunt an analytical tool to make sense either of the general relationship between economic and social values in the EU or the more specific relationship between EU economic constitutionalism and social policy coordination. In particular, the thesis both overstates the coherence and 'tidiness' of EU law as a structuring medium and also fails to engage with the role of a principle of 'solidarity' in mitigating the influence of EU economic law. That is not to deny the influence or the effects of EU economic law on domestic social policy as the *Viking Line*, *Laval* and *Rüffert* cases illustrate. The point is rather that we need a means not only of making sense of these cases but also of relating them to other cases which are far less supportive of the thesis.

Secondly, and relatedly, one cannot treat EU 'economic law' as a monolith. The ECJ adopts rather different approaches to the interaction of competition law and social policy than it does in free movement areas (and even between the economic freedoms). If Boeger (2007) is right that the Court's competition law case law is deferential to 'solidarity' claims, what is it about the free movement cases that tilts the Court in a different direction? The answer seems to be that the Court has a rather narrow vision of how solidarity can be expressed. Because of their democratic legitimacy, the Court can more easily accept manifestations of solidarity when expressed in general laws imposing, for example, universal public service obligations than it can when those rules are either not publicly promulgated laws but collective bargains or, when those laws or agreements are not 'universal' but sectoral or particularistic. Boeger's analysis, therefore, requires modification to recognize that the Court's approach to the solidarity principle modulates depending on the ECJ's understanding of the relationship between solidarity and democratic legitimacy. Moreover, it may also modulate over time as new circumstances—such as the enlargement of the EU—arise. We need to avoid accounts of EU economic law that are simultaneously sweeping and yet static.

Thirdly, even if we accept that the 'Europeanizing' influence of EU economic law may have negative consequences for domestic social policy, that is not of itself evidence that OMC processes are necessarily shackled or undermined. The causal linkages between the constraint on domestic policy and the scope and ambitions of particular OMC processes need much further refinement than is offered by Scharpf's thesis. Moreover, as Hervey has suggested, the potentially constraining effect of EU economic law may in fact catalyse the use of new governance techniques like the OMC as she identifies in the sphere of healthcare. It is important to keep in mind that what the ECJ is often asked to do through judicial review is to give a rather narrow assessment of the legality/illegality of national measures. It will not necessarily enquire, therefore, into the best means of achieving a desired aim. Providing a course of action is legal, there is every scope to use OMC processes to consider whether the national policy context is effective. The point is a simple one: merely because EU economic law has an effect in a particular area does not lead to the conclusion that it undermines the rationale of OMC processes operating in the same domain.

Finally, nothing in the analysis above should be taken as suggesting that the ECJ is always right or that its role is always welcome. On the one hand, the scrutiny and supervision of the ECJ does open up the closed normative worlds of both public and private norm-making. On the other hand, it may simply unleash forces that it cannot easily control, or interests that it cannot reconcile. Therefore, a much more interesting question lies in where adjudication ought to fit alongside alternative forms of governance rather than setting up adjudication and new forms of governance as necessarily antithetical and oppositional to one another (see Dawson, 2009).

7

From Lisbon to Lisbon—Europeanization through Constitutionalism

Introduction

The first decade of the 21st century saw the Portuguese capital assume centre stage in the naming of two of the European Union's reform projects. The decade began with the launch of the Lisbon strategy to reform EU economic and social governance and ended with the entry into force of the Lisbon Treaty as the culmination of a troubled process of constitutional reform. Within the context of the Lisbon strategy, the Union's social identity was contested and its institutionalization unstable. The discussion in this chapter explores whether the Lisbon Treaty is capable of giving the Union a more stable social presence in a manner also capable of strengthening its governance interventions. In investigating the capacity of constitutional reform to provide a foundation for European social governance, the analysis once again explores issues of Europeanization. In his typology of meanings, Olsen identified 'Europeanization' as also referring to the 'political unification of Europe' and the development of Europe as 'a more distinct, coherent and strong political entity' (Olsen, 2002: 940). Here, that definition is explored in the context of the capacity of European constitutionalism to act as a mechanism of Europeanization.[1]

The deployment of 'constitutionalism' as an analytical device for exploring Europeanization may, at first blush, appear to hobble the enquiry at the outset with some unnecessary or even unwelcome baggage. After all, in the aftermath of the rejection of the Constitutional Treaty by voters in the Netherlands and France, EU political leaders declared their abandonment

[1] This connection between 'Europeanization' and 'constitutionalism' is also evident in Maduro, 2005.

of the 'constitutional concept' in favour of an apparent return to traditional diplomatic treaty negotiation. Even without such a rejection of the discourse of constitutionalism by political leaders, it might be thought that its use as an 'ideological resource' to bolster the 'symbolic authority' of the EU (Walker, 2002) had been exposed as lacking the level of popular legitimacy to sustain the artifice, thereby reducing constitutionalism in the EU context to a rather busted political flush. Moreover, it would always be open to contend that the discourse of constitutionalism had been stretched to the point of being an indeterminate concept with limited conceptual power even within the confines of certain state jurisdictions (Murkens, 2009) let alone when unleashed in the context of a non-state polity like the EU.

While the particular fate of the Constitutional Treaty does provide evidence from an important experiment in European constitutionalism, it does not mean that the turn to constitutionalism is itself a mistake. Nor is constitutionalism necessarily a wholly indeterminate concept if one is clear about its definitional and conceptual parameters. As a starting point the analysis adopts Walker's definition of constitutionalism as 'the normative discourse through which constitutions are justified, defended, contested, denounced or otherwise engaged with' (2002: 318). 'Constitutions' in this sense, can refer to the constitutional texts of Member States, but they can also refer to the treaties of the EU inasmuch as they imbue a system of political and legal authority with institutions, values and norms oriented towards collective self-government by a Union of states and peoples.[2] If constitutionalism is a reflexive discourse about what it does or can mean to talk in constitutional terms and in respect of what sort of polities, then it seems appropriate to keep entities like the EU within the conceptual ambit of the concept of constitutionalism even if its use is contestable and even if the capacity for constitutionalism to act as a unifying force beyond the nation state proves difficult. As is clear from Walker's definition, the contestation which surrounded the Constitutional and Lisbon Treaties is simply part and parcel of constitutionalism's nature as such: how could a project aimed at greater integration between nation states be anything other than a contested project? The more difficult questions relate to whether European constitutionalism is capable of articulating

[2] Of course, the Constitutional Treaty provoked numerous debates about whether the document was a 'constitution' or a 'treaty' or both: see Walker, 2006b; Weiler, 2005. For a wider discussion of the meanings of constitutions and constitutionalism see the helpful discussion in Craig, 2001.

a defensible social identity for the Union both as a means of legitimating the integration project and as a means of strengthening EU social governance.

The analysis is presented in three parts. The first part explores the capacities of constitutionalism to take on not just a procedural and institutional orientation—explored more fully in chapter four—but also a more substantive identity in advancing claims to promote and protect social solidarity in the EU. Three interpretations of the project of constitutionalism will be analysed, each of which offering different readings of the motivation to turn to constitutionalism in the name of social solidarity, and of the constitutional division of roles and capacities of the EU and its Member States in organizing solidarity. The second part of the chapter audits and analyses the manner in which the Constitutional Treaty and the subsequent Lisbon Treaty attempted to incorporate a social identity for the Union. It highlights the role played by social objectives and social values, and importantly, the role of social rights within the context of the EU Charter of Fundamental Rights. In light of the discussion in the first part of the chapter, the investigation reflects on how this most recent attempt to reboot the 'constitutional operating system' of the EU (Weiler, 1997) engaged with social issues and what sort of 'social self' emerged from the process.

The third part of the investigation considers the implications for EU social governance of any attempt to enhance the social character of the Union. While the chapter which follows pays particular attention to strengthening the OMC through reforms to its underlying governance architecture, the concern here is with whether the revised constitutional architecture of the Union provides resources and capacities upon which EU interventions to combat poverty and social exclusion might usefully draw. Building on work that suggests the possibility for new forms of governance to advance fundamental social values and social rights,[3] and that seeks to look beyond an oppositional relationship between 'constitutionalism' and 'new governance',[4] the possibilities for, and limits to, strengthening EU social governance through an enhanced recognition of fundamental social rights will be explored.

[3] See especially Armstrong, 2003, 2008; Bernard, 2003; de Búrca, 2005; de Schutter, 2005a.

[4] See de Búrca, 2003; Walker, 2006a; Walker and de Búrca, 2007 and more generally the essays in de Búrca and Scott, 2006.

Solidarity in EU Constitutionalism

With the exception of the tendency to use geometric metaphors relating to Europe's social 'dimension' or 'space', it is to more human metaphors that analysts often turn when referring to Europe's 'social self' (Maduro, 2000) or its 'social face' (Barnard, 2007). The 'personification' of the European polity (Gerstenberg and Sabel, 2002) might simply be a natural corollary of the attempt to think and speak 'constitutionally'. As Maduro notes (2003b: 81), we tend to think of constitutions as both presupposing and defining the polity, typically understood in terms of a 'people'. Yet, the idea that Europe's social self is to be found in the representation of a European *demos*, presupposed and defined by a European constitution would be to return to the debate initially sparked by the German Constitutional Court in its ruling on the Maastricht Treaty (Weiler, 1999),[5] and reignited by its subsequent 2009 judgment on the Lisbon Treaty,[6] concerning the absence of such a *demos* and of the need for the nation state to retain its normative authority. The question explored in the following sections is whether European constitutionalism can be imagined without the logical presupposition of a *demos* in a way that is capable of giving the EU the necessary social identity to sustain its integration efforts and to animate its social governance architecture.

Social Democracy: Solidarity and the Rescue of the Welfare State

The constitutional settlement of the EU has relied upon a division of responsibilities between the EU and the Member States. The original constitutional deal was premised upon a transfer of responsibilities for economic integration to EU institutions while domestic institutions retained their fundamental role in defending social solidarity. However, under pressures of free movement the domestic 'boundaries of welfare' (Ferrera, 2005) became more porous and the social 'sovereignty' (Leibfried, 2005) of nation states open to challenge. Spillover effects of market integration also drove the development of a further division of responsibilities with the EU taking on limited tasks of 'social regulation' (Majone, 1993). Redistributive 'social policy', however, remained within the competence and normative embrace of domestic institutions of social solidarity.

[5] Ruling of the German Constitutional Court on the ratification of the Maastrich Treaty (12 October 1993), BverfGE 89, 155.

[6] Ruling of the German Constitutional Court on the ratification of the Lisbon Treaty (30 June 2009), BverfG, 2 BvE 2/08.

In motivational terms, a demand for a new constitutional settlement that affords a heightened role for the EU in social solidarity rests in the diagnosis of a crisis in the capacity of contemporary European states to defend their social model against pressures from within the state (especially demographic change); from within the EU (reform and liberalization of public services and modernization of welfare provision); and from beyond the EU (the competitive globalized environment). European social democrats have, therefore, looked to the EU to preserve the European social model beyond the nation state. In a piece in the *New Left Review* coinciding with the beginning of the EU's self-conscious attempt to embrace an explicitly constitutionalist discourse, Jürgen Habermas sought to tackle head on the 'political unification of Europe' through the adoption of a 'Constitution'. For Habermas (2001), the constitutional project of the 21st century was not the same as that which might have inspired the architects of European unification in their more federalist moments, but rather its function was 'to *conserve* the great democratic achievements of the European nation-state, beyond its own limits'. (Habermas, 2001: 6). The development of the welfare state is one of those achievements and one viewed by scholars such as Habermas, Scharpf and Offe as under threat and in need of conservation. The inclusion of new social values and new social rights in a European constitution might then form the basis for a rescue mission for the embattled welfare state, intended to encode in European constitutionalism the same concerns and value-orientations of social democratic welfare systems.

Precisely where Habermas' conversion to the cause of European constitutionalism fits within his broader postnational theoretical architecture has been debated by scholars (see Murphy (2005); Grewal (2010)). There are self-evident tensions at play. The extent to which EU constitutionalism is given a stronger substantive identity opens the door to disagreements as to its substantive content. Social democrats may agree as to the problem but their solutions are likely to be contested by liberals. As Weiler correctly predicted and as will be illustrated in part two of the chapter, the Member States would seek to give expression to 'social solidarity' as a mechanism to 'give the European constitution political traction' and as a 'source of identity and identification' (2002: 570). Yet as he also identified this would provoke contestation. Attempts to reflect or mirror national social identities as a European consensus are likely simply to reproduce social conflicts and, ultimately to undermine the capacity of constitutionalism to drive European integration.

Habermas was not unaware of this problem. As the following passage makes clear, Habermas accepted that substantive contestation was likely to follow from a suggested turn to the EU, but that this was itself a necessary step in the process of endowing the EU with an institutional capacity to respond to the threat to the welfare state (Habermas, 2001: 12):

> This diagnosis suggests a normatively loaded, perhaps a 'social-democratic', reading of the economic justification for the European project. It might be objected that any such partisan view must divide the political spectrum along ideological lines. But in the absence of a stronger motivation, this may be necessary to mobilize public debate. As a strategy, it is innocent insofar as its success would at best be a procedural outcome—the creation of a more encompassing political framework.

In this way, Habermas falls back on proceduralism and a civic public sphere as supplying the necessary democratic foundations for managing substantive disagreement.[7] Yet it is the very weakness of these elements of the constitutional architecture of the EU that makes a turn to the EU as the defender of social solidarity particularly dilemmatic. On the one hand, the enhancement of its social identity is intended to galvanize the EU's capacity to attract legitimacy. On the other hand, there may be an unwillingness to view the EU as the defender of social values, without stronger democratic institutions at EU level or stronger transnational bonds of collective affinity.[8] In the end the EU may not be capable of generating the kind of popular legitimacy capable of making the defence of social values and rights credible even if the nation state is also losing its capacity to defend those values. Absent a resolution of this dilemma, the relationship between giving the EU a stronger social identity and giving the EU clearer social competences and increased capacity to draw in democratic legitimation becomes something of a 'chicken and egg' problem.

This is not the place for an extended discussion of Habermas' vision of European constitutionalism (but see also Gerstenberg and Sabel, 2002). What the analysis above is intended to demonstrate is that while European social democrats may well agree that the welfare state in Europe needs to be conserved, and while they may look to European constitutionalism as a vehicle for its rescue, there is, nonetheless, a dilemma as to the capacity of the EU to offer the necessary levels of democratic legitimation and

[7] For an extensive critique of this proceduralist paradigm, see Gerstenberg and Sabel, 2002.

[8] See Gerstenberg and Sabel's (2002) discussion of the role of a 'strong collective identity requirement' in Scharpf's work.

civic engagement necessary to get the project off the ground. Moreover, for authors like Scharpf, it is the EU—or rather the ECJ—which is part of the threat to the welfare state. There would be no guarantee that a stronger EU political apparatus would be capable either of reining in apparently court-driven processes of liberalization or, more importantly, of overcoming the substantially different social interests of 'old' and 'new' Member States as evidenced in the rulings of the ECJ to which Scharpf so vehemently objected (see chapter six for a discussion of Scharpf's position and a critique thereof).

Paradoxically, given the importance attached by social democrats to giving the EU a social identity, rescuing the welfare state through EU constitutionalism could turn out to be a potentially frustrating and disappointing venture.

Constitutional Pluralism: Solidarity in a Multi-Level System

In this section a rather different interpretation of postnationalism is explored which assumes a more ongoing role for nation states as sites of solidarity but subject to the motivating influence, and disciplining effects, of transnational sites of political and legal authority. Postnational constitutionalism takes as its starting point the idea that constitutionalism is not reducible to the institutions and patterns of constitutional authority found within nation states (Maduro, 2003b). There are indeed non-state polities and other sites of political and legal authority like the EU which trouble the traditional association between constitutionalism and 'the constitution' of a nation state. As Shaw highlights, the point is not that the features of national constitutionalism are now simply replicated in non-state contexts—although understandably some of the features of postnational constitutionalism will draw on the resources of constitutionalism as they have evolved in national contexts—but rather that postnational constitutionalism 'articulates an idea of change and transformation in relation to the nation state (changes *of* or *to* the nation state; change at the supra- or sub-state level *because* of change in the nation state)' (1999: 587). Postnationalism, therefore, recognizes the existence of sites of political and legal authority both above and below the level of the sovereign state but importantly insists on a 'constitutional pluralism' in which these boundaries are not closed but rather porous and 'at stake'. If, as Walker (2002) suggests, European constitutionalism ought to be conceptualized in more plural terms, can social values and objectives be realized within and across such plural sites in a way that avoids overloading normative expectations of the Union while at the same time addressing concerns as to the fate of the nation state as the repository of social solidarity?

The point of departure from the postnational vision articulated in the previous section is the idea of a constitutionalism that demarcates and negotiates the boundaries between the national and the supranational rather than a constitutionalism in which the boundaries of the nation state are in decline yet the boundaries of the supranational are still in the process of becoming. Instead of leaving social solidarity in a sort of constitutional limbo, one might look to the continuing realization of social solidarity within the boundaries of the nation state but buttressed and reinforced by the interaction between the domestic and European levels. While this would require the articulation of some kind of *ethos* of solidarity at EU level as an expression of a political community committed to certain social values and social rights, it would not necessarily depend on the legitimacy of the political institutions of the EU for their implementation and application. Rather, the nation state and its social and democratic institutions could continue to be the focal point for social solidarity albeit with obligations to ensure that the common ethos of solidarity is upheld and advanced.

This approach to European constitutionalism has resonances with Neil MacCormick's work on the EU as a 'civic political community' in which membership is voluntary and reflects a willingness to participate in and uphold common civic institutions. At the same time, there are 'contestable', 'overlapping but also diverging ideas' of what membership of this civic political community entails (MacCormick, 1996: 564). In this way, Member States can agree on solidarity and social justice as of common concern—and even articulate that concern in its constitutional texts—but without necessarily having to submit to, or seek to produce, a singular EU vision of how these values might be realized. Crucially, in the very act of consenting to cooperate, nation states also put themselves to the test. This point is developed by Weiler for whom the emergence of civic 'supranationalism'—political and legal authority above the nation state—is also a means to 'tame the national interest with a new discipline' (Weiler, 1999: 342).[9] It may well be that the nation state retains much of its responsibilities for social solidarity—and to return to MacCormick's work, it is here that the *institutions* of civic social

[9] Interestingly, as Murphy notes (2005), if one of Habermas' concerns was the threat to the nation state from globalization, his other was the threat of the nation state as evidenced by the more brutal episodes of European history. That inclination towards the need to 'tame' and 'discipline' the nation state is a theme which is also evident in Joseph Weiler's work.

solidarity are to be found—but supranationalism can also exert its influence. That need not be a wholly negative 'disciplining' influence but might also be a strengthening and animating social ethos oriented towards the encouragement of states to seek a continuing improvement in the social situation of those within its boundaries. The point is simply that social solidarity can form part of the civic ethos of a European polity while recognizing that it will be within the boundaries of nation states that this solidarity finds its more practical expression.

There is, nonetheless, the risk that statements and provisions in EU 'constitutional' texts end up being highly rhetorical or downright misleading if, in the end, it is to the nation state that we must continue to look for the practice of European social solidarity. Moreover, if the nation state is truly at risk as a guardian of that solidarity as feared by social democrats and if the EU is part of the cause of that threat, then this version of postnational constitutionalism may be simply an apology for Europe's incapacity to manage its own social decline. The strength of this critique is in large part an empirical question and as suggested in the previous chapter, there are reasons to suggest that nation states have perhaps lost less sovereignty than might be imagined—in terms of constraints on their authority to act—while recognizing that they, nonetheless, face significant social challenges. Moreover, from the perspective of constitutional pluralism, to the extent that the EU does constitute a limit on the social sovereignty of Member States, the extent to which such limits are to be viewed as acceptable or unacceptable does at least form part of the constitutional contestation between sites of political and legal authority. The tension between the EU and Member States is, therefore, to be understood as upping the ongoing demands of constitutional justification for both the EU and its Member States rather than as an external environmental motivation for grand new constitutional settlements.

A different critique suggests that this conceptualization of an ethos of solidarity between states is perhaps somewhat more intergovernmental than constitutional in the sense that it lacks a clear connection to the citizens for whose benefit this solidarity is sought. Legal scholars of the EU will recall the European Court of Justice's claim that the then European 'Community' was more than an agreement between states and that this process of constitutionalization conferred rights upon citizens which formed part of their legal heritage. The issue is whether postnational constitutionalism has a means of imagining the constitutional polity but without collapsing into an imagined *demos*. Drawing particularly on Shaw's work on postnational citizenship (eg Shaw, 1998; 2007), Weiler (1999: 324 *et seq.*) seeks to expand the membership of the European polity beyond its component Member States to include its citizens. The result is a postnational citizenship within a European polity that is something like Neil MacCormick's identification of the Union as a post-sovereign 'commonwealth'.[10] Without the EU itself becoming a replacement for the bonds of affinity which characterize national citizenship, EU citizenship opens up a range of political and legal resources for citizens both as against the EU and the Member States.

The turn to citizenship as a means of embedding an ethos of solidarity is paradoxical. On the one hand, it is a status that demands recognition beyond the boundaries of the state of which the individual is a national. In that sense, it can form a basis for claims to political and to social inclusion. On the other hand, insofar as those claims have real financial implications for states in terms of opening the boundaries of social welfare to meet claims of social solidarity, they are also likely to be met with resistance.[11] Indeed, it may be the political and social status of the individual as citizen that may be as disruptive to social welfare as the apparent threat from the exercise of market freedoms (see Barnard, 2007: 127–30).

EU citizenship—as currently legally conceived and practiced—also has other limits as a means of embedding an ethos of solidarity. It is a status that has had little direct leverage for nationals of a state who do not move, nor for EU-resident third country nationals who are not members of national political communities. In this way, while 'citizenship of the Union' draws the individual into the membership of the European polity and while postnational citizenship identifies the significant articulation of the relationship between supranationalism and nationalism, it is under-inclusive in its personal scope

[10] As MacCormick puts it (1997: 339):

> The particular point of what we can call a 'commonwealth' is that it should comprise a group of people to whom can reasonably be imputed some consciousness that they have a 'common weal', something which really is a common good, and who are able to envisage themselves or other political representatives and governing authorities realizing this or striving after it through some form of organized political structure, embodied in some common constitutional arrangement. In this sense, both member States and the Union are commonwealths, one more intensive and localised, more strongly rooted in a sense of tradition and of personal identity and loyalty, the other more extensive and broadly inclusive.

[11] In this regard it is to be noted that Article 7(1)b of the 'Citizenship Directive' makes the right of residency on the territory of another Member State for migrant EU nationals who have not acquired permanent residency in another Member State conditional upon possession of 'sufficient resources…not to become a burden on the social assistance systems of the host Member State…': Directive 2004/38 of the European Parliament and of the Council on the rights of citizens of the Union and their family members to move and reside freely in the territory of the Member States: [2004] OJ L229/35.

(migrant EU nationals) and its territorial influence (a state other than that of which the migrant citizen is a national).

One means of reorienting the practice of EU citizenship would be to look to an alternative—but related—means of bringing individuals within the scope of the European polity: the protection of fundamental rights. Contrasted with the two deficiencies of citizenship just identified, human rights law has the ambition to be universal in personal scope and exerts its authority within nation states even as regards the state's treatment of its own nationals. There has, of course, always been a vector of social policy—following the tradition of Marshall (1950)—that has viewed poverty and social exclusion as a denial of the fundamental rights of the members of the political community. Social NGOs in the EU have often fought to frame their claims for stronger social solidarity in the EU on the basis of fundamental rights arguments.

Nonetheless, we return to the dangers of an imbalance between a high constitutional rhetoric in which the EU is seen to be committed to the defence of fundamental rights yet it is to the nation state that we must look for such rights to be fulfilled. Moreover, the precise status of such rights—justiciable rights, normative principles, programmatic exhortations—remains to be clarified.

For the moment it is enough to recognize that an alternative vision of European constitutionalism looks less to a unifying constitutional settlement as a means of articulating social solidarity but instead seeks to promote a common ethos of solidarity as a common value of a postnational polity to be realized through an articulation of the relationship between the boundaries of the national and the supranational.

From Postnationalism to Polyarchy: Denationalizing Solidarity

Gerstenberg and Sabel (2002) suggest that the postnational position of Weiler and others does not go far enough in getting 'beyond the nation state'. Indeed, postnationalism may be better characterized as a concern with getting beyond the sovereign state while retaining a place for nationalism (see MacCormick 1993; 1996). For Sabel and his collaborators the task is more one of harnessing heterogeneity—the 'diverse solutions to the pressing problems of everyday life' (Gerstenberg and Sabel, 2002: 291)—towards the aim of learning from difference (Sabel and Zeitlin, 2008) through an experimentalist architecture dubbed 'directly deliberative polyarchy'. In this way, the social ethos that animates solidarity is neither to be found in the personification of the political community, nor in a supranational sphere of civic ethics and fundamental rights, but derives from the practice of concrete problem-solving which 'denationalizes' the search for solidarity. The vertical interplay between the national and supranational which is at the heart of Weiler's approach is transcended through a focus on the vertical coordination of a variety of horizontal processes that give specific expression to social values and indeed social rights through their realization in day-to-day practices of problem-solving. If boundaries of political and legal authority still matter to pluralists, for proponents of polyarchy, what counts is collaboration and the pooling of ideational and practical resources across boundaries whether they be vertical, horizontal, public or private in the building of a de facto solidarity.

Similarly, for Gerstenberg (2002), the realm of fundamental rights is not an abstract expression of an ethos of solidarity, nor merely the stuff of adjudication but rather as an 'enabling constraint' on processes of public deliberation with the objective being 'to move constitutional justification—the process of bringing social-citizenship related integrity-interests and economic-liberty interests into a coherent whole—away from the Court to new, politically accountable arenas of justification' (2002: 182). Whereas Weiler's postnational interpretation of fundamental rights views these rights as protected within 'fundamental boundaries' of vertically-distributed legal authority, for Gerstenberg the challenge is to bring fundamental rights into political and social discourse across horizontally-arranged *loci* of decision-making. In this way, fundamental but competing social and economic rights and values are simply put into play—the substance of which cannot be ignored—but without defining their meaning except in the actual process of applying them to concrete problems beyond the arena of courts.

Nonetheless, there is often a sense in the literature on directly deliberative polyarchy that while urging a radical rupture with prevailing forms of constitutionalism, much of the exhorted experimentalist architecture takes place against a background of the specific institutions and values of a polity that are simply taken for granted (Armstrong, 2006b). For example, the identification of different examples of an experimentalist governance architecture in the EU (Sabel and Zeitlin, 2008), has to accept that this governance architecture 'runs' off the constitutional and democratic resources of the EU and its Member States. Absent these resources, it is not clear how experimentalism would get off the ground in the first place. In other words, while there is a strongly articulated vision of the functional demands of experimentalist governance in building solidarity through concrete problem-solving within and across polities, the extent to which this governance architecture draws on pre-existing constitutional and democratic capacities or transforms them or dispenses with them entirely is, perhaps, more ambiguous.

In the second part of the chapter, the analysis turns from theoretical models of European constitutionalism to the practices of constitutional reform as evidenced first by the Constitutional Treaty and subsequently the Lisbon Treaty. Rather than seeking to show which model or interpretation has been followed, the aim is instead to highlight the complex and often contradictory forces at play in the politics of constitutional reform. Nonetheless, the discussion in this part does provide a set of tools through which to reflect on some of the dynamics at play.

Rebooting European Constitutionalism

The constitutional process which began in 2001 with the inauguration of the Convention on the Future of Europe and which ultimately ended with the Lisbon Treaty can be understood as an attempt to grapple with the EU's constitutional and social identity. With the launch of the Convention, proponents of a social Europe looked to the Convention and the constitutional process to institutionalize within the EU's constitutional architecture, a stronger commitment to social values and objectives as well as to the social rights contained in the EU Charter of Fundamental Rights. However, the prospects for a stronger social Europe initially appeared bleak. The working groups convened to assist the Convention's deliberations did not originally include a group devoted to social issues. Only after the other groups had finished their deliberations, and working to a very tight timetable with limited opportunities to meet or take evidence, was a working group on 'Social Europe' convened, and even then the draft of the first sixteen articles of the Constitution—including the articles setting out the values and objectives of the Union—was published without the report of the 'Social Europe Working Group' being taken into account (Shaw, 2003). In the two sections below, the institutionalization and constitutionalization of social values and objectives, and of social rights through the EU Charter are explored in turn.

Social Values and Objectives

The Social Europe Working Group of the Convention had requested that the Union's values include 'social justice, solidarity and equality, in particular, equality between men and women'. In the end Article I-2 of the

Constitutional Treaty (now replicated as Article 2 TEU post-Lisbon Treaty) stated that:

> The Union is founded on the values of respect for human dignity, freedom, democracy, equality, the rule of law and respect for human rights, including the rights of persons belonging to minorities.
>
> These values are common to the Member States in a society in which pluralism, non-discrimination, tolerance, justice, solidarity and equality between women and men prevail.

Significantly, while 'solidarity' was included,[12] the concept of 'social justice' was omitted from the list of values.

Interpreting the relationship between these two paragraphs is far from straightforward.[13] Inasmuch as the first paragraph states the values upon which the Union is founded, these seem to be strongly oriented towards democracy, human rights protection and the rule of law as expressions of the principles of democratic constitutionalism. The second paragraph associates solidarity with 'a society' but without the boundaries or identity of that society being clear. From a Habermasian perspective this society may refer to a civic European public sphere as the repository of these values. Or it may be that these values inhere more concretely in the individual societies of Member States yet also require to be respected by the Union in a more pluralist postnational interpretation.

Article I-3 of the Constitution (now Article 3 TEU post-Lisbon Treaty) identified the Union's 'objectives'. These are somewhat recast in the Lisbon Treaty version which provides in Article 3(3) TEU:

> The Union shall establish an internal market. It shall work for the sustainable development of Europe based on balanced economic growth and price stability, a highly competitive social market economy, aiming at full employment and social progress, and a high level of protection and improvement of the quality of the environment. It shall promote scientific and technological advance.
>
> It shall combat social exclusion and discrimination, and shall promote social justice and protection, equality between women and men, solidarity between generations and protection of the rights of the child.

The references to combating social exclusion and of promoting social justice and protection are limited elaborations of the existing treaty provisions,

[12] Although as Barnard notes (2006), this is a principle with a highly flexible meaning.

[13] In the Lisbon Treaty version of this article, the two paragraphs are combined into one paragraph but the two sentences are identical.

but significant, nonetheless, in committing the EU to broad social objectives. It is the concept of the 'social market economy' however, which is more question-begging.

For Azoulai (2008), the reference in the treaties to the concept of a social market economy is emblematic of a new type of pluralistic constitutionalization at work in the EU. If the constitutionalization of the past was about legal doctrine oriented towards achieving the hierarchical primacy of EU law over domestic law, this new constitutionalization is oriented to achieving a substantive balance in economic and social values. Yet, as Joerges and Rödl suggest (2004: 20), while the intention of the authors of the treaty might have been to use the concept of the social market economy 'to anchor the claim to develop and extend policies of social balance', they argue that it is an unlikely candidate concept through which to rebalance substantive European constitutionalism.

For Joerges and Rödl, the concept of a 'social market economy' is a policy model or strategy rather than a constitutional objective. Thus, while it might make sense for the Lisbon *strategy* to talk of developing a social market economy, it is a concept which makes less sense as a constitutional objective of the Lisbon Treaty. However, it is the historic origin of the concept that is more troubling for these authors. Indeed, the 'ordo-liberal' genesis of the concept might act as a limit on the EU's social ambitions rather than providing a new means through which to embed transnational market integration in social values. As Joerges and Rödl narrate, while the concept of the social market economy grew out of an attempt to give a social dimension to a legally protected market order—something to which the EU might also aspire—nonetheless, the extent of social intervention was limited by liberal concerns to limit discretionary political intervention and to seek social goals through market means. As the basis for giving the EU a social identity, the concept of a social market economy might then end up as more of a 'restriction for social objectives' (Joerges and Rödl, 2004: 20) than a basis for advancing social Europe.

We should, however, be cautious about attaching too much significance to the effects of including the concept of a 'social market economy' within the Union's constitutional aims and objectives. First, within the limits of competence—limits that existed even prior to the reference to the 'social market economy'—the clearer statement of social commitments within the Union's values and objectives establish a basis for debate about the constitutional and social identity of the EU. While that debate may elicit very different sorts of response, nonetheless, the significance is that it provides a starting point for that debate. Secondly, while the concept of a 'social market economy' may well have its roots in German ordoliberalism that does not mean that its meaning has for all time been fixed within those confines. It can simply be taken—albeit in a rather question-begging manner—to signify a need for a reconciliation of economic and social values and objectives. Without itself determining how that balance should be struck, the concept can be viewed as politically flexible rather than fixed. That is both its vice and its virtue. Thirdly, and perhaps surprisingly, the negotiation of the Lisbon Treaty marked a new departure for the balance of economic and social values. Up until that point, proponents of a more social Europe had sought to 'add in' more social provision to the mixture of values and competences rather than to 'take out' or constrain the economic vales that underpinned the internal market. However, the newly elected French President Sarkozy—perhaps mindful of the French rejection of the Constitutional Treaty amid concerns that it stood for an Anglo-Saxon model of economic liberalism—successfully removed a reference to 'undistorted competition' in the description of the internal market in Article 3 TEU.[14] This highlighted that even a core ordoliberal principle underpinning the social market economy concept could be tinkered with, not least as a means of trying to bolster the social policy credentials of the EU treaties in order to sell the Lisbon Treaty to a sceptical French electorate. In addition, new Treaty provisions, a Protocol and one of the articles of the EU Charter of Fundamental Rights were added to emphasize 'the place occupied by services of general economic interest in the *shared values* of the Union'.[15] In short, the presence of the language of the 'social market economy' and the absence of a direct reference to the 'European social model' cannot resolve the question of how to interpret the inclusion of new social values and objectives.

Of more immediate significance to this study is whether an enhanced recognition of social values and objectives strengthened the EU's capacity for intervention. Certainly the new social objectives in Article 2 TEU (post-Lisbon Treaty) would not found a basis for legislative harmonization in the sphere of action to combat social exclusion. Article 3(5) TEU makes clear that:

> The Union shall pursue its objectives by appropriate means commensurate with the competences which are conferred upon it in the Treaties.

[14] The removal of the reference to undistorted competition in the internal market is immediately counteracted by a 'Protocol on the Internal Market and Competition' attached to the treaties which states that 'that the internal market as set out in Article 3 of the Treaty on European Union includes a system ensuring that competition is not distorted'.

[15] See Article 14 TFEU, Protocol No. 26 and Article 36 EU Charter of Fundamental Rights.

Article 5 TEU further elaborates the principle of conferred powers and the mechanisms for implementation of the principles of subsidiarity and proportionality (including the new Protocol on the application of these principles and the powers of national parliaments under the 'early warning' system). Article 153 of the Treaty on the Functioning of the Union (TFEU—the renamed EC Treaty) maintains the position of the Nice Treaty in terms of only permitting 'measures designed to encourage cooperation between the Member States' in the areas of action to combat social exclusion and modernize social protection systems to the exclusion of any harmonization of the laws in these areas. Moreover, while prior to the treaty amendments of the 1990s and 2000s, creative use had been made of the 'residual' legal basis of Article 235 EEC (later 308 EC), the new 'flexibility clause' of the TFEU—as well as imposing new institutional constraints on the exercise of this legislative power[16]—also makes clear that '[M]easures based on this Article shall not entail harmonisation of Member States' laws or regulations in cases where the Treaties exclude such harmonisation.' (Article 352(3) TFEU).

For those looking not just for a constitutionalization of social values but also for an enhanced legislative competence for the EU in the social sphere, the Lisbon Treaty is likely to prove frustrating and disappointing. Policy coordination through the OMC remains the governance technique through which the newly articulated social values and objectives of the Union are to be pursued.

Fundamental Social Rights

Like social policy itself, fundamental rights were also a 'missing' dimension of the original EEC Treaty. The story of the Europeanization of fundamental rights is a well-known one.[17] However, this process of Europeanization of fundamental rights has been asymmetric in terms of the sorts of rights which have been given recognition within the EU legal order. The EU—not unlike other legal orders—has tended to prioritize the recognition of traditional civil and political rights over social and economic rights. In part this is because domestic constitutional traditions have adopted civil and political rights within their legal systems, while exhibiting variety as regards

[16] The German Constitutional Court, in its ruling on the legality of Germany's ratification of the Lisbon Treaty, also places certain demands and restrictions on the use of this power.

[17] See especially the collection of essays in Alston, 1999.

recognition of social and economic rights.[18] That variety relates both to whether or not certain social rights are recognized and as to the justiciability of such rights. But, it also reflects the dominant status of the European Convention on Human Rights as the privileged European human rights instrument. Article 6 TEU affords the Convention a special status in EU law as a foundation for fundamental rights protection. The Council of Europe's social and economic rights instrument—the European Social Charter—was denied privileged inclusion in Article 6 TEU and is instead referred to only in the substantive social policy title of the EC Treaty (and now TFEU). For de Witte (2005), this different handling of the two instruments was indicative of the higher status afforded to civil and political rights over social rights within the EU legal order. Moreover, while the new Lisbon Treaty makes provision for the EU to choose to become directly bound by the ECHR through accession (Article 6(2) TEU), no such provision is made in respect of the European Social Charter. This may be due to an inequality of status of the two instruments even within the Council of Europe itself; as Alston notes: 'the bottom line is that social rights remain the poor step-sister of civil and political rights and this is every bit as true within the Council of Europe as elsewhere.' (Alston: 2005: 47)

Therefore, the trajectory of *social* rights within the EU legal order has been distinctive with the ECJ playing a 'negligible' role and with limited political recognition of social rights compared to that afforded to civil and political rights (de Witte, 2005). Of course, the 1989 Charter of Fundamental Social Rights of Workers was a notable attempt to increase the visibility of the rights of workers and, while not legally binding or justiciable, the Social Charter was the basis for the Commission's development of an action programme to implement those rights—including formulation of the 1992 Recommendations on income adequacy—and for moves to increase EU social policy competence through the Maastricht 'social chapter'. Nonetheless, as Kenner highlights, the ambition had originally been to adopt an instrument that focused more generally on the social rights of citizens, and the shift of focus to workers, together with the legal constraints imposed on the rights so recognized, highlighted the unwillingness of Member States to develop a more ambitious social rights agenda at that time (Kenner, 2003). While the impact of the 1989 Social Charter is debateable (see de Witte, 2005), it has, in any event, been superseded by the agreement of a more encompassing EU

[18] See generally Fredman, 2006, and more particularly in the context of EU Member States, Fabre, 2005.

Charter of Fundamental Rights. The EU Charter of Fundamental Rights marks an important new chapter in EU fundamental rights protection. It is particularly significant because of its inclusion of a range of social rights alongside civil and political rights and its association of those rights not to the status of worker but to citizenship.

(a) *The Status of the EU Charter of Fundamental Rights*

The history of the drafting of the EU Charter of Fundamental Rights and its original 'solemn proclamation' by the EU's institutions will be familiar to many.[19] The failure to make the Charter legally binding as part of the general reform to the treaties undertaken at Nice, might have signalled a continuing gap between the rhetoric of fundamental rights and the mechanisms for their legal protection. Nonetheless, with the establishment of the Convention on the Future of Europe and a working group tasked to consider the future status of the Charter, a proposal emerged to incorporate the Charter as a legally binding element of a new Constitutional Treaty. Indeed, Part II of the 'Treaty establishing a Constitution for Europe' incorporated the Charter within the tripartite structure of the constitutional document and made its contents legally binding.

With the failure of the Constitutional Treaty and the abandonment of the 'constitutional concept' the future status of the Charter was once again at issue. In the constitutional origami of the EU, the tripartite structure of the singular text of the Constitutional Treaty was reformed and reshaped by the Lisbon Treaty to create three texts—the Treaty on European Union, the Treaty on the Functioning of the Union and the Charter of Fundamental Rights—all of the same legal value and acting as the normative and legal foundations of the Union. In this way, the Charter is to be made legally binding.

Just how transformative the Charter will be to the EU's legal order remains to be seen. As O'Leary has highlighted (2005), the European Court of Justice was noticeably initially reticent to make direct references to the Charter pending resolution of its legal status, although even without the Lisbon Treaty coming into force, the ECJ eventually broke its silence in that regard.[20] Nonetheless, the life of the Charter will be lived not only in

[19] Particularly useful discussions of the background debates as to the potential status of the Charter can be found in de Búrca, 2001b; Arnull, 2003; and Kenner, 2003.

[20] See in particular Joined Case C-402/05P and C-415/05P, *Yassin Abdullah Kadi and Al Barakaat International Foundation v Council of the European Union and Commission of the European Communities* [2008] ECR I-6351. As well as making direct reference to Article 47 of the Charter

the European courts and within legal discourse but more broadly, and in that regard, the Lisbon Treaty brings the Charter out of the twilight zone and creates new discursive opportunities for political as well as legal actors. Certainly, transnational social actors like EAPN and the Social Platform have always been keen to frame EU intervention to combat poverty and social exclusion within a fundamental rights discourse. In this way, the Charter adds to the possible range of discursive resources to which social and political actors look when framing their communicative strategies.

(b) Limiting the Effects of the Charter

As will be familiar to observers of these matters, social rights have often fallen foul of the rather dubious distinction between 'negative' rights—those rights that individuals claim against public authorities in order to prevent interference with individual autonomy and freedom—and 'positive' rights that place duties on public authorities to provide some form of public good. The distinction has been much critiqued (see especially Fredman, 2006). Nonetheless, it has played a powerful role in national constitutional traditions. Some states—including the UK—simply do not recognize social rights, viewing social entitlements as collective goods supplied at the discretion of the executive (albeit that the exercise of discretionary power is reviewable through mechanisms of judicial review of administrative action). Other states recognize social rights only as 'directive principles' which are to inform the policy-making choices of public authorities but which are not themselves justiciable. In other jurisdictions, without vesting as subjective rights, to varying degrees courts can take cognizance of the extent to which such rights are followed in executive and legislative acts. Although practices clearly vary (see Fabre, 2005; Fredman, 2006), the justiciability of social rights has often been denied in comparison to civil and political rights.

Viewed against this background, the approach of the EU Charter appeared promising. As commentators have highlighted, an important feature of the EU Charter of Fundamental Rights is that it contains within it, side-by-side, both civil and political rights and social and economic rights. Both are afforded an apparent equality of status within the single instrument of the Charter, reflecting an 'indivisibility' of rights protection. Nonetheless,

to support its judgment that there had been a denial of the fundamental right of effective judicial protection, the ECJ more generally gave a strong judgment on the responsibility of the EU courts to uphold the rule of law and to ensure protection of fundamental rights as a condition of the legality of the acts of the EU's institutions even where this might create conflict with other norms of international law, in this case, resolutions of the UN Security Council.

as Kenner argues (2003), the apparent indivisibility of rights and equality of status of social rights may be more of a mirage than a reality when it comes to the justiciability of those rights. Three barriers to justiciability can be discerned: the construction of social 'rights' as 'principles'; the protocol on the application of the Charter to the UK, Poland and latterly the Czech Republic; and the wording of particular 'solidarity' rights. Moreover, other more general limitations are placed on the scope of application of the Charter.

While avoiding a distinction between positive and negative rights, a different distinction—between 'rights' and 'principles'—found its way into the Charter. The relevant provision is found in Article 52(5) of the EU Charter:

> The provisions of this Charter which contain principles may be implemented by legislative and executive acts taken by institutions, bodies, offices and agencies of the Union, and by acts of Member States when they are implementing Union law, in the exercise of their respective powers. They shall be judicially cognisable only in the interpretation of such acts and in the ruling on their legality.

The distinction is odd and unhelpful. The Charter itself does not clearly identify which of its provisions are rights and which are principles and this may limit the effect of Article 52(5) if the EU courts tend to interpret the provisions of the Charter as 'rights'. However, some assistance might have been found in the 'explanations' which accompany the Charter.[21] The explanations illustrate the effect of Article 52(5) only in respect of three 'rights'—Article 25 (rights of the elderly), Article 26 (rights of the disabled) and Article 37 (environmental protection). Noticeably, the social rights contained in the 'Solidarity' section are not highlighted, but nor are they necessarily excluded from the category of 'principles'. In this way, the explanations are not particularly illuminating except in the sense that they did not go down the easy path of simply treating all social rights as principles.

In any event, few of the rights recognized in the Charter are likely to be invoked as immediately enforceable subjective rights. They will instead provide legal *standards* against which to test the legality of the acts of the EU's institutions. The distinction which Article 52(5) draws is the ability to use human rights standards as the basis for review of any act (rights), or review only of an act designed to implement that specific standard (principles).

[21] The 'explanations' were prepared by the Praesidium to the Convention which originally drafted the Charter. They were later updated during the course of the Convention preparing the draft Constitutional Treaty. Although not a legally binding text as such, Article 6(1) TEU requires that the Charter be interpreted 'with due regard' to these explanations.

The rationale for this distinction is simply not obvious let alone desirable. Moreover, as regards the history of fundamental rights protection, fundamental 'rights' developed in EU law as general 'principles'. It would be strange if the general constitutional upgrading of principles to rights left a category of newly recognized principles that were constitutionally downgraded in the sense that they could not act as free standing principles of legality against which to test the lawfulness of EU measures.

A more direct attempt to restrict justiciability can be found in the protocol originally agreed to clarify the effects of the Charter in the UK and Poland, but later extended to the Czech Republic as a concession for its ratification of the Lisbon Treaty. The protocol is not, however, an 'opt-out' from the Charter. The first article provides that the Charter does not 'extend' the ability of EU or national courts to find the laws of these Member States inconsistent with the rights, principles and freedoms contained in the Charter. Everything turns on the meaning of 'extend'. If it refers to a simple capacity of review then, even without the Charter, it has been possible to review the legality of national measures taken within the limits of discretion imposed by EU law. Therefore, this it is not a capacity that the Charter itself extends. However, 'extend' may have a more substantive meaning in the sense of referring to a post-Charter increase in the ability to find measures incompatible by reference to an enhanced range of rights. This leads to a rather arbitrary division between those rights which had hitherto already been recognized as general principles and those rights in the Charter which had not hitherto been so recognized; typically the social rights. However, Article 2 is even more explicit about the justiciability of social rights. It provides that:

> ...nothing in Title IV of the Charter creates justiciable rights applicable to Poland or the United Kingdom except in so far as Poland or the United Kingdom has provided for such rights in its national law.

This then attempts to render the social provisions of the chapter non-justiciable as far as these two jurisdictions are concerned.[22] Nonetheless, insofar as fundamental rights might influence or animate the design of EU policy interventions, then non-justiciability does not mean that the social rights contained in the Charter will have no bearing on the practices of these

[22] Nonetheless, Poland felt compelled to add the following Declaration (No. 62): 'Poland declares that, having regard to the tradition of social movement of "Solidarity" and its significant contribution to the struggle for social and labour rights, it fully respects social and labour rights, as established by European Union law, and in particular those reaffirmed in Title IV of the Charter of Fundamental Rights of the European Union.'

states. In other words, if alternative forms of governance utilize fundamental rights as an animating rationale, the protocol does not have the effect of insulating these Member States from Europeanizing influences in the social domain (further discussed below). Moreover, the protocol does not prevent other provisions not found in the 'Solidarity' section—eg the right to human dignity expressed in Article 1—from having a social meaning or effect.

Also of significance is the particular phrasing of some of the rights, by giving such rights a purely declaratory status in the sense that the Charter declares the Union's recognition of a right that is otherwise conferred, more typically through national laws and practices than through EU law itself. This is particularly important in respect of the one article of the Charter that deals explicitly with combating poverty and social exclusion. Article 34(3) provides that:

> In order to combat social exclusion and poverty, the Union recognises and respects the right to social and housing assistance so as to ensure a decent existence for all those who lack sufficient resources, in accordance with the rules laid down by Union law and national laws and practices.

This provision is clearly not intended to confer a right to social assistance, but rather simply recognizes the existence of such rights laid down principally in national law. Union law makes very limited provision for social assistance and while EU law has concerned itself with the right to equal treatment as regards access to a domestic right of social assistance, the issue of the adequacy of social protection has only been addressed through the means and mechanisms described elsewhere in this book.

Provisions were also written into the so-called 'horizontal clauses' of Articles 51 and 52 of the Charter to limit and qualify the field and scope of application of the Charter. Thus Article 51(2) of the Charter provides that:

> The Charter does not extend the field of application of Union law beyond the powers of the Union or establish any new power or task for the Union, or modify powers and tasks as defined in the Treaties.

As de Witte identifies (2005), while the Member States may legitimately have wished not to extend the formal legal competencies of the Union but rather to condition their legitimate exercise, the assertion that the Charter will not modify its powers and tasks is hard to reconcile with the very purpose of the Charter, namely to ensure that when exercising powers and tasks laid down in the Treaties that fundamental rights are not only respected but also, 'promoted' in terms of Article 51(1) of the Charter.

(c) *The Identity of Social Rights*

If we are to assess the contribution of the EU Charter to the realization of fundamental social rights, it is important to identify and consider the substantive social rights at issue. The Charter is divided into six 'titles' of substantive rights covering 'dignity', 'freedoms', 'equality', 'solidarity', 'citizens' rights', and 'justice'. Not surprisingly, attention has focused on the solidarity title (Articles 27–38) as an expression of social rights. Articles 27–33 are primarily concerned with matters of labour law and health and safety of workers; Articles 34 and 35 with social security and social assistance and health care, respectively; Article 36 with services of general economic interest; Articles 37 and 38 with environmental and consumer protection respectively.

The mix of rights contained in this title is eclectic: it is not obvious that consumer protection is either a fundamental right or if it is, that it reflects the value of solidarity. If the title includes certain rights that might appear curious it also omits rights that are found in other European social rights instruments, including the European Social Charter and the Revised European Social Charter (see below). Moreover, this title is not exhaustive of the social rights recognized in the Charter. Indeed, there is an interesting division of labour between the 'equality' and 'solidarity' titles. Perhaps reflecting the way in which these issues are handled in EU law more generally, the rights of the disabled and elderly—rights which would happily be considered as 'social'—are conceptualized as equality rights: the right to social assistance is not, however, viewed as a matter of equality but of solidarity. Moreover, the right to human dignity in Article 1 and the rights of the child in Article 24 can be important foundations for EU intervention to combat poverty and social exclusion given both that poverty is incompatible with the right to human dignity and that child poverty is a particular problem in many European states.

The rights contained in the solidarity title derive from a plurality of sources as is revealed by the 'explanations' accompanying the Charter. Thus, the rights contained in Articles 27–33 draw extensively on the 1961 European Social Charter and the 1989 Community Charter, but with references also to provisions of the Treaty on the Functioning of the Union as well as EU legislation. Significantly, not all of the sources are of relevance to all states. The 1989 Community Charter was famously not signed by the UK. But more significant are the references to rights deriving from the Revised Social Charter that entered into force in 1999. While all EU states are signatories, ten Member States have not ratified the revised Charter, and of those states that have ratified, there is variation in the Articles to which the states have agreed to be bound. Thus, while it is one thing to view the social rights contained in this title as drawing normative strength from the plurality of European and EU instruments to which all states bound, there is a danger that rights which draw from an instrument to which states are not signatories will conversely be weakened.

Given the 'pick and mix' approach to what rights to recognize and from what source, the treatment of poverty and social exclusion in the Charter is of interest. The only direct reference to poverty and social exclusion is found in Article 34(3) of the Charter (quoted above). That provision is one of the rights that the Union 'recognises and respects' and as the explanations accompanying the provision identify, Article 34(3) derives from Article 13 of the 1961 Social Charter and Articles 30 and 31 of the Revised Social Charter. Yet Article 34 is a significantly more limited right than that contained in Article 30 of the Revised Social Charter which is a much fuller and positive provision. It provides that:

> With a view to ensuring the effective exercise of the right to protection against poverty and social exclusion, the Parties undertake:
>
> (a) to take measures within the framework of an overall and co-ordinated approach to promote the effective access of persons who live or risk living in a situation of social exclusion or poverty, as well as their families, to, in particular, employment, housing, training, education, culture and social and medical assistance;
>
> (b) to review these measures with a view to their adaptation if necessary.

Without conferring a subjective right as such, this provision requires the parties to the Revised Social Charter to engage in coordinated action across a range of areas in order to ensure protection against poverty and social exclusion, and to review and adapt measures over time. Paragraph (a) is not unlike the first of the Nice common objectives underpinning the early cycles of the OMC. Indeed, Article 30 would have provided a clear foundation for the OMC to combat social exclusion, embedded and institutionalized in a fundamental rights framework. This would then have been a particularly obvious candidate to see more directly replicated in the EU Charter. To be sure, not all Member States have ratified the Revised Social Charter. Yet that does not appear to have been a barrier either to the sources to which the authors of the Charter looked, or to their willingness to refer directly to this provision in the accompanying explanations.

It seems evident that despite the enhanced references to social values and objectives, and notwithstanding the recognition of social rights as fundamental rights alongside traditional civil and political rights, the EU is not set to take on the primary role in promoting and protecting social solidarity in the EU. Indeed, the end result of the process of constitutional reform may be something which is not satisfactory whatever one's preferred approach to constitutionalism. While the social democrat may bemoan that what is lost on the national swings is not made up on the supranational roundabouts, the pluralist may object to the rigidity of the constitutional division of powers which limits the capacity for mutual adjustment between the roles of the EU and its Member States. For proponents of experimentalist governance, this sort of constraining constitutionalism can be precisely the fertile ground from which experimentalism might grow. The very limits of the justiciability of social rights, for example, may be exactly the impetus to move fundamental rights out of a privileged legal discourse and into the practices of collective decision-making. Yet, the danger is that it casts constitutionalism and new forms of governance as being on a collision course with experimentalist governance pathologized as the unruly beast in need of the disciplining and taming effects of constitutional law.

The difficulty seems to be that while substantively seeking to embed a common ethos of social solidarity within its constitutional architecture, the impulse to constitutionalize has been overshadowed by a desire to treat constitutionalism as virtually synonymous with 'limited government' (on which see Walker, 1996). While Azoulai (2008) may be correct in noting the shift from a hierarchical constitutionalism—what Weiler once referred to as 'normative supranationalism' (Weiler, 1991)—to the constitutionalization of the values and processes of EU governance itself—'decisional supranationalism' in Weiler's terms—the result is a constraining rather than an animating constitutionalism. Indeed, much of the constitutional project can be read as preoccupied with the placing of politics and the exercise of public power under law. In this way, the almost hyper presence of law—not just the drafting of treaties but also the proliferation of protocols and declarations as well as the adoption of the EU Charter of Fundamental Rights as a legally binding text—and the desire to categorize and catalogue EU competences together with new mechanisms for implementing the subsidiarity principle, all suggest a manifestation of the ideal of limited government as an abiding preoccupation of EU constitutionalism.

In this way, the task here is not to review the resulting treaty texts and declare one or other interpretation of constitutionalism as the best fit with the treaties, but rather to suggest that from the perspective of all three interpretations of constitutionalism there is cause for dissatisfaction with the manner in which the common concern to realize social solidarity has been rendered in the post-Lisbon constitutional settlement. In the final part of this chapter, attention turns to what may usefully be salvaged from these constitutional resources in the name of promoting social solidarity and in combating poverty and social exclusion.

Constitutionalism and the OMC

For some, the enduring centrality of non-legislative or non-justiciable governance tools as the means through which to advance social aims is emblematic of a disjuncture between, on the one hand, the high rhetoric and symbolism of the new social provisions of the treaties, and on the other hand, the constraints on EU social policy competence that leave Europe's social self—as Fredman suggests (2006:43)—tethered like a modern Gulliver, in a Europe that is unwilling to allow its social self to flex its muscles. It is this apparent disjuncture which saps the credibility of the Union's social aspirations and, for some, explains the seemingly paradoxical unwillingness of citizens to support contemporary EU constitutional reforms, even when they do advance social objectives (Hatzopoulos, 2007). It is easy then to view the OMC as the unwanted child of a marriage of convenience between social democratic aspirations for European constitutionalism and a liberal constitutionalist concern with limited government.

The objective of the discussion in this final part is to seek to move beyond the potential paralysis of constitutional disappointment and dismissive depictions of the role of new forms of governance. Instead, the concern is to seek to harness what has been achieved by way of treaty reforms to the cause of strengthening commitments to combat poverty and social exclusion through the OMC. In one sense the OMC ought to be the beneficiary of the enhanced commitments to social values and objectives if for no other reason than, in the absence of other governance tools and instruments, then how else are these values and objectives to be pursued? Yet as we have witnessed with regard to the Lisbon strategy, general commitments to social objectives are apt to fall victim to shifts in political winds. In part this institutional instability arises from the relative role of social policy in the overarching policy matrix of the Lisbon strategy. But even if the Lisbon strategy had never existed, the more relevant issue is whether EU social policy itself lacks a clear motivating set of rationales which the new treaty provisions might help articulate.

Historically, EU social policy interventions have developed, as Barnard describes them (1999), as a 'patchwork' of different activities in different fields in a rather 'spasmodic' manner. Different rationales have been advanced to support these interventions ranging from functionalist connections between EU social policy and market integration to attempts to build a stronger EU polity through social rights.

However, notwithstanding the solemn proclamation of the EU Charter of Fundamental Rights at the same time as the adoption of the original Nice objectives for the social OMC, the potential connection between developing social policy through the OMC and the protection of fundamental rights has been largely limited to the communicative discourses of social NGOs. While certain social areas like non-discrimination have been more clearly rationalized within a rights and equality framework, as Mabbett has noted (2005: 109), notwithstanding attempts in the 1990s to conceptualize social exclusion as a denial of fundamental rights, Member States have resisted linkages between the development at EU-level of a corpus of non-discrimination rights and their coordination of policies to combat social exclusion via the OMC. Could the protection of fundamental rights—particularly with the EU Charter becoming a legally binding text—form the basis for articulating EU social policy interventions?

As both de Búrca (1999) and Mabbett (2005) note, rights discourse operates at two different levels. It operates at the level of 'legitimation' and 'integration' (de Búrca, 1999) in the sense of connecting a vision of society to the impetus for further European integration. It is in this sense that we might speak of a Europeanization through constitutionalism. However, rights discourse also operates more directly at the policy level in framing policy initiatives and programmes. Indeed, the protection of fundamental rights is capable of being the subject of a policy in its own right (see Alston and Weiler, 1999). The desirability or otherwise of a specific human rights policy for the EU and of the use of an OMC-type process to advance such a policy for the Union lies beyond the scope of this work (see de Búrca 2005; de Schutter 2005a). Moreover, the limitation in the field of application of the EU Charter contained in Article 51(2) suggests an unwillingness on the part of the Member States to allow the Charter to found the basis of new human rights powers or competences. Rather, the interest lies more in the influence of fundamental rights within social policy itself and in shaping EU social governance.

For some, the primary function of fundamental social rights ought to be to preserve a realm of domestic social policy autonomy and to buttress that autonomy against the deregulatory effects of the application of EU economic law. However, as was noted in chapter six, the recognition of fundamental social rights simply demands that such rights are balanced against economic freedoms rather than operating as a constitutional trump card. In that regard it is not necessarily the case that a constitutional upgrade of the recognition of social rights will serve to defend the powers of Member States to apply unaltered their local social laws and practices.

For authors such as Offe, the deregulatory thrust of EU intervention comes not only directly from 'hard' economic law of the EU but also from the 'soft' coordination of OMC processes themselves. Therefore, one vision of the role of fundamental social rights would be to act as a backstop or limit to any deregulatory tendencies of 'soft' coordination (Smismans, 2005; Fredman, 2006). As Smismans elaborates, '[F]undamental rights could then appear as a threshold below which the OMC should not go.' (2005: 237). In this way, the framing function of fundamental rights would be to confine and constrain an OMC process rather than providing it with an operational rationale.

Already in its ruling in *Mangold*,[23] the ECJ required that when implementing employment policy changes designed to keep older workers in employment—an objective of EU employment policy coordination—the Member States, nonetheless, had to conform to the fundamental principle of equality and avoid age-discrimination (in this case by requiring older workers to accept fixed-term contracts). One can conceive of possibilities for making similar arguments about whether aspects of domestic welfare reform undertaken in consequence of EU policy coordination are consistent with fundamental rights guaranteed by the Charter, for example, the rights of the child or the protection of human dignity. Nonetheless, there are causal and jurisdictional limitations which might make this kind of litigation generally unlikely to arise.[24] If we look 'upstream' to the setting of objectives

[23] Case C-144/04, *Werner Mangold v Rüdiger Helm* [2005] ECR I-9981.

[24] In its protection of fundamental rights as 'general principles' of Union law, the ECJ considers that Member States are bound when they act within the 'scope' of Union law. The EU

and guidelines for EU policy coordination, as both Bernard (2003) and Smismans (2005) highlight, the non-binding nature of OMC guidelines and recommendations make any direct judicial review of these in light of fundamental rights highly unlikely. In short, the idea of fundamental rights as a constraining backstop to the OMC would seem to have limited application let alone normative purchase.

There may instead be more scope for thinking about the role of fundamental social rights and social values as a positive *ex ante* means of shaping EU policy coordination (Smismans, 2005). Consistent with the approach adopted elsewhere in this book, we can think of this influence at three substantive levels: policy framing, policy paradigms and specific policy discourses around particular issues.

As was noted in earlier chapters, EU interventions to combat poverty and social exclusion have been framed by reference to a range of policy fields—economic, employment and social policy within the context of the Lisbon strategy, and by reference to various sub-fields within social policy—social protection and social inclusion. These different frames are reflected in the overarching and common objectives of the OMC. Their function is less to give specific and direct steering to the OMC but instead to normatively frame the process and to position it within a policy matrix. A more explicit recognition of fundamental rights within these objectives might serve to strengthen the normative foundations of social policy coordination.

A second level of analysis relates to the relative influence of different social policy paradigms. In this study we have identified the important role played by the 'activation' paradigm in connecting the modernization of social protection systems to increasing inclusion via the labour market. While this supports a rationale for EU social policy as a 'productive factor', it is a paradigm that is both contestable in terms of the primacy it attaches to the labour market as a mechanism of inclusion and insufficient to grasp the 'multidimensionality' of social exclusion beyond the labour market. Framing EU intervention in terms of the realization of fundamental rights could instead give added significance to a social 'citizenship' paradigm as a

Charter of Fundamental Rights more narrowly defines its field of application to the Member States as being when they 'implement' EU law. It is open to argument whether action taken by Member States within the framework of an OMC process would constitute action in implementation of EU law. Moreover, as the analysis in chapter five demonstrates, there are significant problems of causation in tracing domestic change to OMC processes. It is much more likely that the constitutionality of domestic changes to welfare law will be litigated in the light of domestic constitutional guarantees than via the medium of EU fundamental rights protection.

basis for combating social exclusion.[25] Whereas Marshall (1950) developed his approach to poverty as a denial of the rights of citizenship within the confines of the nation state, it would be a more 'postnational' concept of citizenship to which one might turn. In other words, a rationale for the OMC may be that it advances fundamental rights as both the expression of a common ethos of solidarity and of the rights of citizens to be protected against poverty and social exclusion, but does so in a manner that recognizes that this ethos and its mechanism of protection are not singular but plural.

The third level of analysis concerns the capacity of fundamental rights to inform more specific social policy discourses in the course of articulating particular priorities or policy issues which ought to be reflected in domestic strategies. A prime example would be in the area of child poverty which, as we saw in chapter four, became an issue of particular focus for the OMC. Article 3(3) TEU makes protection of the rights of the child an objective of the EU alongside combating social exclusion. While protecting the rights of the child has been more evident in the context of the EU's external relations policy, Article 24 of the EU Charter of Fundamental Rights upholds the rights of the child to 'such protection and care as is necessary for their well-being' and has clear application within the EU itself. As the 'Explanations' attached to the Charter make clear, this right is based on the UN Convention on the Rights of the Child. This Convention is a highly visible human rights instrument with a mechanism for state parties to report on their implementation of the Convention and for a UN Committee to adopt Concluding Observations addressed to state parties. Action to combat child poverty has formed part of those observations. There is, thus, an increasing linkage between drawn between the fundamental rights of the child and action taken to combat child poverty. Importantly, in its 2006 Communication *Towards an EU Strategy on the Rights of the Child* (European Commission, 2006e), in the context of giving effect both to EU and international human rights instruments, action to combat child poverty through the OMC is highlighted as a vehicle for implementing the strategy. Again we see the developing interconnection not only between action to combat child poverty and the protection of fundamental rights but also between protecting fundamental rights and the OMC. Although discourses surrounding child poverty are, perhaps the most prominent example of the connection between fundamental rights and particularistic policy discourses, as will be noted in chapter eight, EU strategies on minimum income guarantees and

[25] See also in this regard, Bercusson et al, 1997.

activities within the framework of the European Year against Poverty and Social Exclusion have also been framed in terms of a fundamental right to human dignity as expressed in Article 1 of the EU Charter.

If the discussion above suggests a certain slippage between an ideational and symbolic register of fundamental rights within European constitutionalism and a more policy-oriented role, then the very idea of policy coordination as a mechanism of fundamental rights protection may ultimately collapse the distinction between the 'constitutional' status of fundamental rights and their 'policy' framing role in ways anticipated by an 'experimentalist' interpretation of fundamental social rights. For example, as noted above, in terms of Article 30 of the Revised European Social Charter, the development of coherent integrated strategies is the essence of the right to protection again poverty. Had the EU Charter of Fundamental Rights adopted this provision directly, a process of EU-wide coordination would be the vehicle through which states would enhance their policy efforts to produce coherent and integrated strategies and from which they could learn about the effectiveness of different policy options. In this way, the OMC would serve as a mechanism for the concrete realization of fundamental rights within a framework of problem-solving in ways anticipated in Gerstenberg's (2002) discussion of constitutionalism 'beyond the court' and in ways that go beyond Weiler's postnational conceptualization of fundamental rights within 'fundamental boundaries' (Weiler, 1999). The EU Charter of Fundamental Rights did not, of course, adopt this specific provision but this does not negate the general argument that fundamental social rights can form the basis for the elaboration of both policies and processes to combat poverty and social exclusion. Policy-making within the context of EU policy coordination could indeed serve as an experimental laboratory for puzzling through reform strategies which seek to ensure that fundamental social rights and social values are not only respected, but are actively protected and promoted in the course of reforms.

All of this suggests that even within the clumsy constitutional architecture of the EU, spaces exist through which to animate and orient existing social policy coordination processes in novel ways. In different ways, the enhanced recognition of fundamental rights within the EU Charter might be incorporated within the coordinative discourses and practices of the OMC. There is, nonetheless, a fear that in dislocating fundamental rights from the official circles of lawyerly and judicial discourse that they become somewhat less like 'rights' and less 'fundamental' (see de Búrca, 2005). Yet there is equally a fear among Member States, that the more justiciable social rights become, the more that difficult political choices end up being made by unelected judges. The approach outlined above, attempts to chart a middle path: something more normatively robust than the existing policy framework animating the social OMC while something less than a court-driven process of social rights protection. Moreover, it bears repeating that the suggestion is not to turn the social OMC into a human rights monitoring mechanism. Rather, the concern is to seek to strengthen the capacity of the social OMC to render Member States accountable for the quality of their anti-poverty strategies by conceptualizing these strategies as a means of realizing the fundamental social rights of citizens.

Conclusions

Constitutionalism is a difficult vehicle for Europeanization. It is as apt to make European integration stall as it is to proceed. It is likely to provoke debate as to the direction in which it proceeds and who is to drive the process. Returning to the different interpretations of constitutionalism offered in the first part of this chapter, the approach adopted here is one that accepts that some sort of substantive social identity is a necessary part of the dynamics of constitutionalism and integration for which governance alone does not substitute. Yet at the same time, it equally accepts that this cannot be a singular European social self as the successor to the nation state but rather a commitment to a shared ethos of solidarity within which different social identities are formed and contested. It is an approach that both accepts the inclination of proponents of experimentalist governance to look across the boundaries of nation states in building collective solidarity horizontally, yet at the same time, is more inclined to the postnational pluralist position which might identify nation states as still the primary locus for social identity and social solidarity formation. Nonetheless, experimentalist governance approaches do offer postnational pluralists something by suggesting forms of governance like the OMC that may avoid the sort of normative clashes and tendencies towards constitutional irresolution that are the vice of constitutional pluralism. While scholars like Kumm have sought to elaborate rules to guide conflicts between plural sites of authority (Kumm, 2005), these problems are simply far less evident when EU states simply agree to engage in policy coordination.

If the function of court-led economic constitutionalism is often to prise open the nation state and require Member States to demonstrate how national policies are to be reconciled with EU economic objectives, then the function of OMC-driven social constitutionalism may equally be to put EU Member States to the test and to demand explanations of how exercises of domestic social sovereignty attain the social policy objectives and values of the Union while protecting fundamental rights. In this way, social solidarity in the name of combating poverty and social exclusion is a substantive jumping-off point to be articulated through practices of governance, but it is also an irreducible point in the sense that it cannot be avoided.

8

Strengthening the Governance of Social Inclusion

Introduction

In 2007, 17 per cent of the population of the enlarged European Union lived in a household below the relative income poverty threshold, representing some 84 million people (EUROSTAT, 2010). Ten years on from the Amsterdam Treaty's commitment to 'combat social exclusion' and after a decade of governance through EU policy coordination, nothing like a 'decisive impact' on the eradication of poverty had been achieved. Moreover, whatever gains there had been by way of economic growth and increasing employment risked being lost in the aftermath of a global financial crisis and ensuing recession. Neither the pursuit of 'growth and jobs' nor an elaborate structure of social governance had fundamentally altered the prevalence of poverty. On the basis of this evidence alone, there would seem to be every good reason to be pessimistic about the capacity of EU policy coordination to influence domestic strategies and policies to combat poverty and social exclusion.

Whatever the theoretical and conceptual novelty of policy coordination through the OMC, and whatever its experimental virtues, the evidence of persistent and prevalent poverty in the EU is itself illustrative of weaknesses in the governance architecture. Indeed, while it is appropriate to note that there are multiple and variegated examples of a new experimentalism in the governance architecture of the EU (Sabel and Zeitlin, 2008), it is equally apparent that institutional design does still matter in building architectural forms that are more or less effective in achieving their aims. The preoccupation of this final chapter, therefore, lies with attempts to strengthen the governance of social inclusion.

The designation of 2010 as the European Year against Poverty and Social Exclusion could hardly be more timely as a point to reflect on how best to strengthen EU interventions in the social sphere. Against the backdrop of a financial crisis, it would be the year that the EU and Member States would seek to adopt a strategy to replace the Lisbon strategy. As one Lisbon (strategy) ended, another Lisbon (Treaty) sprang into life introducing new substantive and institutional provisions. Meanwhile new terms of office for the European Commission and the European Parliament began and a new President of the European Council took up office. Therefore, the first part of the chapter looks to the patterns of continuity and change in the political context and the policy environment surrounding EU social policy coordination.

The second part of the chapter focuses more specifically on the governance dimension of the OMC and considers two new 'hybrid' mechanisms for strengthening EU social policy coordination. These are the designation of 2010 as the European Year against Poverty and Social Exclusion and the adoption of a Commission Recommendation on 'Active Inclusion'.

The third part of the chapter looks to candidate institutional models for strengthening the social OMC. It highlights the limitations of an understanding of the OMC as a form of soft law or soft governance if that means that the archetypal means of strengthening the OMC is to make it more like 'hard' law or to bring it closer to the institutional design model of apparently 'harder' coordination process like the treaty-based economic and employment processes. Instead, the analysis demands that we take seriously the weaknesses of the OMC as identified by a decade of its practice. Drawing on issues identified in the empirical chapters and elsewhere, it is contended that at least part of the weakness of the OMC is, paradoxically, the lack of coordination within its internal methodologies and the lack of clarity as to the purposes of its architectural features.

After Lisbon

As a reform programme, the Lisbon strategy was premised on developing a consensus around prudent macroeconomic management, increasing employment—through labour reform and initiatives to promote skills and innovation—and modernizing social welfare systems to make them adequate, sustainable and 'activating'. The rationale and purpose of EU social coordination was framed by that policy context, although it was also framed by older legacies and concerns with poverty and inequality. The aim of the discussion below is to reflect on two developments that would have a bearing on discussions concerning the role of EU social policy coordination. The first issue concerns the changed economic and political environment in which a post-Lisbon strategy would emerge. The second issue is the nature of that post-Lisbon strategy itself: 'Europe 2020'.

A Changed Economic and Political Context

The near-collapse of global financial markets and the ensuing global recession in the latter years of the first decade of the new millennium created a very different economic context and environment from that which formed the background to the launch of the Lisbon strategy and the initiation of EU social policy coordination in 2000. Rather than a rising economic tide lifting all boats, the spreading tsunami of recession wiped out many of the decade's gains in growth and jobs and—like the natural disasters which engulfed the citizens of New Orleans and South East Asia—threatened to reveal who gets left behind when the waters recede: the poor and socially excluded. The Lisbon strategy's policy coordination architecture risked being swept away as economies contracted, fiscal discipline was abandoned and unemployment rose. However, the lessons to be learned from the financial crisis drew sharply contrasting political interpretations of whether what was needed was a radical reappraisal of the philosophy and direction of the Lisbon strategy or instead a reinforcement and greater commitment to its underlying message and methods.

Building on work developed originally between the Social Platform, the European Environment Bureau and the European Trade Union Confederation, a new European-level NGO network—the Spring Alliance—published a 'manifesto' critiquing the Lisbon strategy's focus on competitiveness and demanding a reversal of economic strategy to put the environment and people at the centre of policymaking.[1] The aim of the manifesto was to self-consciously take advantage of the timing of the review of the Lisbon strategy—also coinciding with the new Commission and new Parliament—and to use this 'unique opportunity' to influence the strategic direction of the EU. Along the same lines, EAPN's position paper on the post-2010 strategy called for a four-pillared policy strategy giving equal prominence to social and environmental objectives alongside economic and employment policy goals (EAPN, 2009a). However, if the communicative

[1] <http://www.springalliance.eu/images/manfinal.pdf> (Accessed in March 2010).

discourses of social actors were urging a redirection and reframing of the EU policy matrix, the political winds were not wholly in their favour.

While the economic crisis might have been thought to play into the hands of the Left in Europe, parties on the Left found themselves incapable of capitalizing on the crisis. In domestic politics, leaders on the Right retained office—eg Chancellor Merkel in Germany, while those on the Left struggled to retain power—eg Prime Minister Brown in Britain losing the May 2010 election. In elections to the European Parliament, the Socialists lost ground to parties of the Right. Yet at the same time, the Left could still exert a certain force on EU politics by pointing to popular discontents with market liberalism expressed by voters in France, the Netherlands and Ireland during the protracted process of treaty revision and ratification which had dominated EU political life for far more time than EU leaders could ever have imagined. In this way, even apparently Right-leaning leaders like President Sarkozy of France appeared to support a more strongly regulated market in Europe.

Against this somewhat difficult economic and political backdrop we need to consider in particular the appointment of a new European Commission. It would be the Commission that would be required to read the political tea leaves and to come up with an approach to the revision of the Lisbon strategy that would be politically acceptable. Once again, issues of timing were significant. The term of office of the European Commission expired in the autumn of 2009, at the very time when the fate of the Lisbon Treaty was in the balance awaiting the outcome of the second Irish vote on the Treaty and on Polish and Czech ratification. With the Lisbon Treaty creating new rules on the nomination of the Commission President and members of the College of Commissioners, it was not clear which rules would ultimately apply. In terms of the Lisbon Treaty, the European Council would be required to nominate their candidate for Commission President, having regard to the outcome of the European elections.[2] With those elections indicating a move to the Right, the nomination of the centre-right José Manuel Barroso for a second term as Commission President would not be inappropriate. Operating

[2] Article 17(7) TEU: 'Taking into account the elections to the European Parliament and after having held the appropriate consultations, the European Council, acting by a qualified majority, shall propose to the European Parliament a candidate for President of the Commission. This candidate shall be elected by the European Parliament by a majority of its component members. If he does not obtain the required majority, the European Council, acting by a qualified majority, shall within one month propose a new candidate who shall be elected by the European Parliament following the same procedure.'

under the Nice Treaty rules, it would be enough for the nominee to secure a simple majority. Had the Lisbon Treaty been in force, an absolute majority would have been required and the Socialist Group in the Parliament sought to use this as leverage to gain political concessions from the nominee by suggesting that without an absolute majority vote in his favour, Barroso would lack the necessary authority to lead a Commission implementing the Lisbon Treaty.[3] However, the Socialist Group could not agree an alternative acceptable nominee and in the end, Barroso obtained a clear majority with votes by MEPs in the Socialist Group split (MEPs in the UK, Spain and Portugal were reported to have backed the reappointment of President Barroso).

The reappointment of Barroso is significant for two reasons. First, he was personally associated with the relaunch of the Lisbon strategy in 2005 and its refocusing on 'growth and jobs' at the apparent expense of Lisbon's 'social dimension'. Secondly, given the political manoeuvrings surrounding his renomination, the political positioning of the Presidential nominee—particularly the 'Political Guidelines' for the new Commission presented to the EP in advance of the vote on his nomination—is of interest. To be sure, we need to be careful in the weight we attach to the discourse and rhetoric surrounding Barroso's political lobbying for renomination, but at the same time, the content of those Guidelines could be used to hold the new Commission to account.

For Barroso, this was 'not the time for business as usual or for routine'.[4] Indeed, he indicated the need for a 'new, much stronger focus on the social dimension in Europe' with repeated references to the need to fight poverty both in the EU and globally. In a meeting with the Spring Alliance following his renomination, President Barroso was keen to suggest that the political guidelines he had set for the Commission were consistent with the themes of the manifesto adopted by the Spring Alliance.[5] Yet, if there are elements suggestive of a renewed commitment to the EU's role in tackling poverty and social exclusion within a revised Lisbon strategy, there was also a fair measure of 'business as usual' and a sense that the response to the financial crisis was not less Lisbon but rather more. In part, this was a function of a more general construction of the economic crisis as signifying a need for more rather than less European cooperation and coordination: in an interesting

[3] 'Vote gives Commission more "authority", says Barroso': *EU Observer* (16.9.2009) <http://euobserver.com/9/28674> (Accessed in April 2010).

[4] J. Manuel Barroso, 'Political guidelines for the next Commission': <http://ec.europa.eu/commission_2010-2014/president/pdf/press_20090903_en.pdf> (Accessed in April 2010).

[5] Speech 09/419, J. Manuel Barroso: <http://europa.eu/rapid/> (Accessed in March 2010).

switch of metaphors, the European Commission's communication on an EU recovery plan suggested that '[W]e sink or swim together.' (European Commission, 2008a). More specifically, the recovery plan put the Lisbon strategy at the very heart of the process of responding to the economic crisis. While claiming that 'the fundamental principle' of the plan was 'solidarity and social justice', substantively the plan proposed by the Commission was one in which: fiscal stimulus would be coordinated but short term and conducted within the framework of the Stability and Growth Pact; the micro-economic structural reforms of the Lisbon strategy would be supported; and activation and flexicurity policies to tackle rising unemployment reinforced. In this way, key themes of the Lisbon strategy were identified as a means of encouraging recovery (see also European Commission, 2009a; 2009b).

The point is simply to highlight that the direction of the post-Lisbon strategy would be shaped not only by the economic context of the recession but also by the political context of a new European Parliament and a new European Commission whose President would have to navigate political waters that on the one hand would see the Commission urged to head off in a direction of a stronger social Europe but on the other would equally see the Commission tempted to move full steam ahead in its existing direction of travel.

Looking beyond the nomination of the Commission President, in November 2009, the nominees for the College of Commissioners were revealed, with a left-leaning Hungarian economist—László Andor—the surprise nominee for the renamed 'Employment, Social Affairs and Inclusion' portfolio. With hearings before the European Parliament in January 2010, the new Commissioners would not formally take office until February 2010,[6] with the existing College of Commissioners carrying on in a caretaker capacity. During this political hiatus, the caretaker Commission was not supposed to take any policy decisions. Nonetheless, in November 2009, the Commission launched its consultation on the post-Lisbon strategy (European Commission, 2009c) with a view to having a communication to present to the European Council's spring summit in March 2010. The sense that this important decision concerning the future direction of the Lisbon strategy was being taken in a hurry and without adequate consultation and participation of relevant stakeholders motivated the Platform of European Social NGOs to write to the Presidents of the EU institutions urging the

[6] The vote approving the new Commission was delayed due to the withdrawal of the original Bulgarian Commission nominee.

decision on the post-2010 strategy to be pushed back to the second half of 2010.[7] In terms of timing, there might be good reason for a European social NGO like the Social Platform to seek to have decisions about the future strategy delayed. Notwithstanding the creation of the post of President of the European Council under the Lisbon Treaty, there is still a rotating Presidency of the Council, with Belgium holding the Presidency in the latter half of 2010. With Belgium viewed as a state normally sympathetic to the development of the EU's social dimension, the combination of a Belgian European Council President and a Belgian Council Presidency might have been considered to be a particularly amenable environment within which to seek to strengthen EU social policy intervention. However, even business groups in Europe were critical of the timing and handling of the Commission's consultation process.[8]

Nonetheless, and mindful of the need to be seen—not least by the financial markets—to be taking action to get a grip on the EU's economic governance, the Commission stuck to its short consultation timetable and on 3 March 2010 published its communication on the post-Lisbon strategy: 'Europe 2020'.

'Europe 2020'

A number of important issues are at stake in the Europe 2020 debate that are relevant to this study. First, there is the issue of the balance of the policy matrix. If Lisbon II was widely criticized for having sidelined the social dimension, proponents of a stronger social dimension looked to the Europe 2020 agenda as a means of delivering on the promise of a balanced and integrated policy matrix. Second, there is the related question of the governance architecture. Much of the debate surrounding the Europe 2020 agenda was preoccupied with strengthening EU economic governance, with the Spanish Presidency initially appearing to throw its weight behind more EU targets and more sanctioning mechanisms. The high budgetary deficits of many Eurozone members—not least Greece—were also causing concern and unsurprisingly raised the issue of whether the Commission needed stronger powers of monitoring and enforcement. Of more direct interest for present purposes are the implications of the governance architecture of Europe 2020 for the social OMC, particularly if this entailed the adoption

[7] Social Platform letter, 19 November 2009.

[8] 'EU business leaders criticise EU 2020 consultation procedure': *EU Observer* (25.1.2010) <http://euobserver.com/9/29327> (Accessed in April 2010).

of EU targets on poverty reduction. Finally, there is the question of where institutional leadership might lie in this new strategy.

Perhaps unsurprisingly, the different policy coordination committees and different Council configurations placed rather different emphases on the mix and balance of policies they wished to see pursued in the post-Lisbon strategy. The approach of the Social Protection Committee was to make the case for the inseparability and interrelationship of economic, employment and social policies. In November 2008 the Social Protection Committee established the Indicators Sub-Group 'Task Force' to report on the evidence concerning the impact of growth and employment policies on social outcomes, as well as the contribution of social policies to economic and employment goals. A number of key messages were conveyed in the Task Force report (Social Protection Committee, 2009) which the SPC later picked up in its opinion on the post-Lisbon strategy. The first related to the impact of economic growth on social inclusion and social protection outcomes. The Task Force concluded that while growth was clearly necessary to fund social expenditures, inequalities often remained or grew. While very high levels of growth did 'erode' deprivation, relative poverty persisted and had even increased in states that were traditionally good performers. Child poverty remained a persistent problem in Europe. As regards employment, the second key message repeated the key tenet of the social dimension of the Lisbon strategy, namely that having a job is the best safeguard against the risk of poverty. However, and echoing earlier joint reports generated by the OMC, increasing employment rates in Europe were identified as not reaching those furthest from the labour market, with in-work poverty accompanying the creation of insecure and temporary employment. While activation policies have long been viewed as central to balancing social protection with labour market inclusion, the Task Force report placed particular emphasis on these policies to prevent the recession resulting in long-term unemployment. At the same time, the report highlighted the need to ensure the adequacy of social protection systems as well as their activating capacity: in essence, the more social protection systems promote labour market inclusion the better funded they can be for those who cannot work. Modernization of social protection, particularly in respect of pensions and long-term care underpinned the third key message. However, it is the fourth key message which is noteworthy as it identified that the economic crisis had revealed that the capacity of states to manage the crisis—with social expenditure acting as an automatic stabilizer—varied widely across states. Thus good economic performance—particularly sound public finances—was identified as a precondition for well-functioning social protection systems. The report stressed the need for increased social expenditure as part of short-term stimulus packages but with the need to avoid 'ballooning deficits'. Overall, the Task Force report reinforced the interrelated nature of the economic, employment and social objectives of the Lisbon strategy.

Building on the Task Force report and its key messages, the SPC Opinion on the post-Lisbon strategy suggested that:[9]

> the post-2010 agenda needs to foster at the same time and in an integrated approach sustainable growth, job creation and social cohesion and environmental protection. . . . Reinforced interaction between economic, employment and social policies is thus essential when designing the future strategy.

The other coordination committees and the relevant Council configurations began publishing their inputs into the process to define the post-2010 strategy in late autumn of 2009. In its Opinion,[10] the Employment Committee reiterated the need for a mutually reinforcing policy matrix and a strong social dimension, but not surprisingly—and especially as a consequence of the economic crisis—emphasized that '[M]ore than ever, Europe needs more and better jobs'. In Conclusions adopted by the Employment, Social Affairs, Health and Consumer Affairs Council,[11] the Council stressed the need to reinforce the employment strategy and the principles of flexicurity and 'active inclusion' in order to face the long-term challenges of labour market reform, and not just as a response to short-term concerns with recessionary rises in unemployment.

If the SPC, EMCO and ESPHCA Council coordinative discourses suggested a stronger social dimension for the Europe 2020 strategy with social protection and employment policies playing an active role, the discourse of the Economic and Monetary Affairs Council struck a rather different note.[12] In stressing the need for the EU to return to a trajectory of economic growth, the Council also:

> . . . [E]xpresses its conviction that better integrating the social dimension and climate change policies into a new strategy should be done in a manner that maintains and

[9] SPC Opinion on the post-2010 strategy: Doc. 15850/09.

[10] EMCO Opinion, 'The European Employment Strategy within the post-2010 Lisbon agenda': Doc. 15529/09.

[11] Council Conclusions on 'Promoting labour market inclusion—Recovering from the crisis and preparing for the post-2010 Lisbon Agenda', 2980th meeting of the Council (Employment, Social Policy, Health and Consumer Affairs), 30 November 2009.

[12] Council Conclusions on the Lisbon Strategy post-2010, 2981st meeting of the Council (Economic and Financial Affairs), 2 December 2009.

reinforces the clear focus on growth and jobs. New elements should be integrated in an economically sound manner, i.e. new policies should be designed cost-effectively and assessed according to their implications for growth and jobs.

In this way we can see tensions in the discourses surrounding the Europe 2020 strategy emerging between, on the one hand, the employment and social affairs ministers and officials embracing a philosophy of policy integration and mutual interaction of policies and, on the other, the view expressed by the economic and financial affairs ministers that were more consistent with the agenda of the 2005 relaunched Lisbon strategy in which social outcomes were viewed as the product of growth and jobs.

Yet even among proponents of a stronger EU social dimension there is a tension between the coordinative discourses of governmental actors—where strengthening the social dimension is constructed as a continuation of the original philosophy of the Lisbon strategy—and the communicative discourses of groups like EAPN, the Social Platform and the Spring Alliance, for whom a commitment to a strengthened social dimension entails an apparent break with the past and a paradigm shift. In its reaction to the European Commission's consultation document on Europe 2020, the EAPN commented that it represented a 'greener Growth and Jobs strategy' with a relatively impoverished social vision (EAPN, 2009b). Importantly, for EAPN, the Commission consultation document fell short of the promise of a strong social vision as articulated by President Barroso when seeking renomination as Commission President.

In March 2010, the European Commission published its Communication on the Europe 2020 strategy (European Commission, 2010). In it, the Commission proposed 'three mutually reinforcing priorities' rather than the 'four pillared' strategy proposed by the Spring Alliance. These priorities were:

- smart growth: developing an economy based on knowledge and innovation;
- sustainable growth: promoting a more resource efficient, greener and more competitive economy; and
- inclusive growth: fostering a high employment economy delivering social and territorial cohesion.

While presented as the modern 'green' manifestation of Europe's 'social market economy', it was also reminiscent of the policy matrix of the original Lisbon strategy after its infusion of environmental policy following the Göteborg 2001 European Council. Five headline EU targets were proposed including reducing the number of people at risk of poverty by 20 million people (a 25 per cent cut). The Commission also announced 'seven flagship initiatives' to pursue each priority. For social inclusion, the Commission proclaimed that it would:

> ...transform the open method of coordination on social exclusion and social protection into a platform for cooperation, peer-review and exchange of good practice, and into an instrument to foster commitment by public and private players to reduce social exclusion, and take concrete action, including through targeted support from the structural funds, notably the ESF.

While the setting of a poverty target was no doubt intended to bolster the Commission's social policy credentials, and while there was a superficial nod to a balanced policy agenda, there can be little doubt that the centre of gravity in policy terms remains on growth and jobs: understandable in the economic context in which the Communication was published. The future governance of the social OMC will be discussed in detail below but what is of concern here is whether the proposed governance architecture of the Europe 2020 strategy would have specific implications for the OMC.

The difficulty is that the governance architecture outlined in the Commission's Communication was unclear and, in any event, would need to be agreed by European leaders. The Communication referred obliquely to a 'thematic approach' based on the three priorities, the five targets (including the poverty target), and the seven 'flagship' initiatives within the strategy. What was not clear was whether separate extant governance architectures would be harnessed towards these goals or whether a new overarching and integrated architecture would replace the existing processes. The Communication referred to the adoption of a smaller set of integrated 'Europe 2020' guidelines to replace the twenty-four growth and jobs guidelines with the new guidelines reflecting the agreed targets. Given the poverty target, it might then follow that these guidelines would include poverty reduction objectives. Yet it seems evident that these integrated guidelines would remain focused on economic and employment issues, not least because the treaty lays down mechanisms for the adoption of guidelines in these fields.[13] That a reformed growth and jobs policy coordination architecture would include guidelines with a poverty reduction target—important in

[13] As noted in chapter four, Article 156 TFEU does envisage the possibility of a social OMC with guidelines. The problem, however, is that it is not clear whether this article has direct application to action to combat poverty and social exclusion.

measuring the social impact of economic and employment policies—would not itself dispense with the need for a social OMC—important as a means of pursuing the broader objectives of the social OMC as well as supporting employment activation.

A headline poverty target itself is not uncontroversial. The Council did not endorse EU level targets when the OMC was initiated and some states—including the UK—consistently opposed EU level targets preferring instead national targets. One approach would be to aggregate national targets into a descriptive EU target. However, what the Commission proposed was a prescriptive EU target that would then be disaggregated into national targets negotiated with Member States. The meeting of the Employment, Social Policy, Health and Consumer Affairs Council held the week after the launch of the Commission Communication produced a range of national responses.[14] When the Commission's proposals for Europe 2020 were presented to the Spring European Council meeting in March 2010, European leaders failed to agree on a specific poverty target and left this for further discussion and agreement at the June European Council meeting.

If the intention of the Commission was to depart from 'business as usual' and to herald a new strategy and new governance architecture it was not wholly apparent from its Europe 2020 strategy that this would turn out to be true. In any event it would be for European leaders to decide whether to endorse this replacement to the Lisbon strategy and to elaborate the details of its governance architecture. In that respect, what was also noteworthy about the Commission's Communication was that it placed responsibility for ownership of the strategy squarely within the strategic leadership of the European Council. While for some, it was to the European Commission that one ought to look for independent leadership, the Commission seemed content to pass the responsibility—and the accountability—over to the European Council. The effect of this might then have been to reinforce the

[14] 3000th meeting of the Council (8.3.10). The minutes of the meeting (Doc. 7033/10) noted that:

> The need to strengthen efforts in the fight against poverty was also stressed. In this context, some ministers welcomed the proposed EU-level target (20 million fewer people should be at risk of poverty by 2020) as a strong signal of the EU commitment in the framework of the 2010 European year against poverty and social exclusion. Other ministers wondered if the EU target would be appropriate as it referred to relative, and not absolute, poverty. Several ministers warned that such a target could create disincentives to take up work if it was to be reached through redistributive policies.

domestic rather than the foreign policy role of the new European Council President.

At the time of writing, the precise shape and structure of the Europe 2020 strategy was not fixed. While it was predictable that as regards the policy matrix, the new strategy would reflect social and environmental concerns, the detail of the underpinning governance arrangements was not known. However, the forces acting on the future governance of the social OMC were not solely those of the Europe 2020 agenda but also more focused debates on how to strengthen the social OMC. It is to these issues that the analysis now turns.

Strengthening the Governance Architecture: 'Hybrid' Solutions

This study has focused on policy coordination as a technique of EU intervention to combat poverty and social exclusion. This is not, of course, the only instrument through which the EU seeks to promote social inclusion, and the use of other instruments such as the European Social Fund (ESF), for example, is clearly of relevance.[15] The challenge for the EU—as its own 'renewed' social agenda highlighted (European Commission, 2008b)—is to develop a 'smarter mix' of instruments to achieve its social goals. In the context of the reinvention of the Lisbon strategy as 'Europe 2020', the Commission once again proposed a 'better use of the instruments at hand'. (European Commission, 2009c: 2).

The discussion in this part of the chapter focuses on the addition of two new instruments to the governance mix: the funding of a 'European Year against Poverty and Social Exclusion' in 2010 and the adoption of a Commission Recommendation on 'active inclusion'. Recalling the discussion in chapter two, the addition of these instruments and their interconnection with the OMC can be viewed as examples of 'hybrid' governance. In particular, by yoking different instruments to the OMC, the intention is to seek to strengthen EU interventions. Nonetheless, it will be suggested that the emergence of new instruments can also exacerbate or highlight underlying tensions within the overall governance architecture.

[15] Indeed, anti-poverty groups like EAPN and the Social Platform have long argued for a closer connection between the ESF and EU policy coordination (EAPN, 2008b; Social Platform, 2009).

European Year against Poverty and Social Exclusion

It will be recalled that the 'Poverty Programmes' of the 1970s and 1980s eventually stalled over the question of the legal basis for funding the activities of these programmes. With the Amsterdam Treaty, Article 137 EC (now Article 153 TFEU) created a basis for the EP and Council to adopt instruments that would allow expenditure to continue to support EU interventions to combat poverty and social exclusion. As highlighted in chapters three and four, that legal basis supported an 'action programme' with core funding to social NGOs and the support of peer reviews, with the programme subsequently rolled into the broader PROGRESS framework. This legal basis was also used to designate 2010 the European Year against Poverty and Social Exclusion.[16]

As the recitals to the Decision establishing 2010 as the European Year against Poverty and Social Exclusion made clear, the programme of events surrounding this year were intended to 'strengthen' the OMC by acting as 'a catalyst for raising awareness, for building momentum and for exchanging best practices between the Member States, local and regional authorities and international organizations involved in the fight against poverty.' Article 2 of the Decision identified four priorities for the activities to be conducted within the framework of the €17 million budget:[17]

- Recognition of rights
- Shared responsibility and participation
- Cohesion
- Commitment and concrete action.

[16] Decision 1098/2008/EC of the European Parliament and of the Council of 22 October 2008 on the European Year for Combating Poverty and Social Exclusion (2010): [2008] OJ L 298/20.

[17] These priorities are to be read in conjunction with the Annex to the Decision which sets out a list of more specific themes:

— promoting multidimensional integrated strategies;
— fighting child poverty;
— promoting inclusive labour markets;
— tackling disadvantages in education and training, promoting e-inclusion;
— gender and age dimensions of poverty;
— equal access to adequate resources and services;
— access to culture and leisure;
— inclusion of immigrants and ethnic minorities;
— active inclusion;
— addressing needs of vulnerable groups.

The second and the last of these priorities were aimed at strengthening political commitment and awareness—not least of the OMC—as well as promoting participation of a range of actors in the funded events. The more substantive orientation is found in the 'rights' and 'cohesion' priorities. The former refers to 'recognising the fundamental rights of people in a situation of poverty and social exclusion to live in dignity and play a full part in society.' The latter is stated to include 'the benefits for all of a society where poverty is eradicated, fair distribution is enabled and no one is marginalised'. Taken with the numerous references to the need for a 'multidimensional' approach, the priorities are consistent with a 'citizenship' paradigm—focusing on social exclusion as a fundamental right—but also with the concerns of a 'redistribution' paradigm—the stronger egalitarian emphasis placed on enabling a 'fair distribution' of resources. Recalling the discussion in chapter seven, this usefully illustrates that fundamental rights discourse appears to be an ascendant political discourse in initiatives to combat poverty and social exclusion. Moreover, it is interesting that it is the fundamental right to human dignity—the first fundamental right recognized in the EU Charter—which is referred to. It may well be that a heightened fundamental rights discourse in the social sphere will draw on this general articulation of a fundamental right more than the eclectic mix of 'Solidarity' rights contained in the EU Charter of Fundamental Rights.

In operational terms, the activities of the European Year were essentially decentralized with 'National Implementing Bodies' ('NIBs') responsible for drawing up 'National Programmes' and for tendering and awarding contracts. In terms of Article 6 of the Decision establishing the European Year, the NIBs were obliged to 'closely consult and cooperate' with a broad range of stakeholders including civil society, social partners, local and regional authorities. The original proposal had required the NIBs to consult a 'National Advisory Group' which would also have included representatives from the national parliament. However, the UK House of Commons European Scrutiny Committee[18] took the view that the arrangements laid down in Article 6 were too prescriptive and 'clearly inconsistent both with the principle of subsidiarity and the right of parliaments (in particular the Westminster Parliament) to regulate their own affairs.' The Decision

[18] HC 16–ix (2007–8), chapter 3 (23 January 2008). Clearly the Scrutiny Committee felt that this experience was a good example of the potential overreach of certain provisions of EU proposals and thus included the example in its report on the application of the subsidiarity principle under the Lisbon Treaty: see HC 563 (2007–8) (8 October 2008), paras 29–31.

adopted did not include the establishment of the National Advisory Group and, in doing so, left mandatory cooperation with national parliaments out of the domestic implementation process. In fact, the UK did establish an 'EY2010 Stakeholder Group' of representatives of national and devolved governments and social NGOs, but without parliamentary representation. Anticipating the discussion below on the role of national parliaments, if one of the weaknesses of EU governance—including the OMC—is an apparent tendency towards 'deparliamentarization' (but see Duina and Raunio, 2007), then the evidence of this example may be that this may be as much a result of self-defeating parliamentary strategies as it is conscious efforts to exclude parliaments. Strengthening EU interventions by strengthening national parliamentary involvement rather depends on the willingness of national parliaments to take the opportunities for engagement that national social NGOs have seized upon.

The NIBs were accountable to the Commission for the management of their programmes. The programmes, however, had to be consistent not only with the objectives of the Decision but also the Strategic Framework Document drawn up by the Commission. This document emphasized the need for consistency between the domestic programmes and the NSRs adopted by the Member States under the OMC. Centralized coordination was undertaken through a comitology process with an 'advisory committee' established under the Decision. This was a different committee from the PROGRESS management committee albeit that there was a limited overlap of personnel. This proliferation of committees highlights important issues of coordination among the different aspects of EU interventions to combat poverty and social exclusion; an issue that is explored further below.

In sum, the aim of establishing 2010 as the European Year against Poverty and Social Exclusion was to strengthen EU governance by giving greater visibility to EU interventions within the Member States and in that way, also to focus attention on the NSRs prepared by Member States within the context of the OMC. Nonetheless, there is an apparent tension between the discourse underpinning the objectives of the European Year—preoccupied with framing activities within a 'citizenship' paradigm and the protection of fundamental rights—and that of the objectives underpinning the OMC with their emphasis upon the centrality of the 'activation' paradigm. There is also a sense in which the less directly politicized activities funded through the action programme may have been freer to develop within a social citizenship paradigm—in a way that reminds us of the early work on social exclusion carried out by the European Observatory on Policies to Combat

Social Exclusion set up under the old 'Poverty Programmes' (see Room, 1995)—whereas political policy coordination focused its efforts more narrowly within an activation paradigm. In this way, not only is there a potential problem of coordination between the activities of the action programme and the cyclical reporting under the OMC, there may be a more significant normative distance between these two instruments. The result may be less of a mutually transformative hybrid governance and more of normative rivalry or incoherence.[19]

'Active Inclusion'

As intimated in chapter four, the concept of 'active inclusion' developed within EU discourse in the second generation of the OMC. It appeared to be a term around which social NGOs and Member States could coalesce. On the one hand, it self-evidently echoed the concept of 'activation' associated particularly with inclusion through employment. On the other hand, it became a vehicle for identifying non-labour market inclusion and income adequacy as issues of EU concern. Moreira (2008) has identified an 'activation dilemma'. The dilemma is not just whether inclusion ought to refer to social rather than economic inclusion (see Levitas, 1998), but also whether the objective of activation policies is to place obligations on individuals to take up paid work (albeit with support and incentives) or whether it refers to a right of individuals to adequate minimum resources and the removal of obstacles to participation (economic and societal). The concept of 'active inclusion' appeared to reproduce these dilemmas. In this section, the analysis explores the attempt by the European Commission to institutionalize the concept in a new instrument and to harness the OMC towards its ends.

The story of EU interventions in the social sphere has often been one of the European Commission opportunistically and creatively using provisions and powers to fashion instruments towards the social goals contained in the treaties (Cram, 1993). The history of what became a Commission Recommendation on Active Inclusion is a further instance of such creativity.[20] It will be recalled that in the 1990s the Council had adopted two recommendations—the '1992 Recommendations'—oriented towards a 'convergence' of national social assistance measures. The European Commission looked to update these recommendations but in the context of

[19] See Trubek and Trubek (2007) for further discussion of hybridity.

[20] Commission Recommendation 2008/867/EC on the active inclusion of people excluded from the labour market: [2008] OJ L307/11.

new treaty provisions and new policy instruments including the OMC. The first part of the analysis explores the attempt by the Commission to fashion an instrument that would develop its strategy on activation policies. The second part analyses the substance of the measure adopted and its means of implementation.

In its 2000 Communication on *Building an Inclusive Europe* (European Commission, 2000b), the European Commission had looked to Article 137 EC (now Article 153 TFEU) as a basis for developing interventions to combat social exclusion. This included action to promote the integration of persons excluded from the labour market and the power to adopt—by means of directives—'minimum requirements for gradual implementation' (post-Nice Article 137(2)(b) EC). A pledge to launch a consultation on the 'best ways and means to promote the integration of people excluded from the labour market' was made in the Commission's 2000 *Social Policy Agenda* (European Commission, 2000a). With no action taken, the 2005 *Social Policy Agenda* committed the Commission to launching an initiative on minimum income schemes and the integration of people excluded from the labour market (European Commission, 2005c: 9). In 2006, the Commission adopted a Communication (European Commission, 2006b) launching a consultation using the mechanism under Article 138 EC (now 154 TFEU) for consultation of the social partners. This was a rather odd mechanism for consultation given that the design and delivery of minimum income schemes does not fall to the social partners. In reality, the consultation was widened out to all relevant actors and the use of Article 138 EC was simply a device through which to launch the consultation.

If the initiative on 'active inclusion' exposed an innovative use of consultation processes, the responses to the consultation were also significant in highlighting the range of tools and mechanisms through which the EU might potentially intervene. In addition to the role of European Social Funds to support labour market integration, the governance debate revolved largely around three main models: (1) the use of the OMC; (2) a possible directive; and (3) whether to revise or replace the 1992 Recommendations with a new recommendation or set of guiding principles. For a Member State like the UK, the message was that no new processes were required and that any EU action ought to be undertaken within the confines of the OMC. For a social NGO like EAPN, the answer was to work on all three main options (EAPN 2006b). Overall, there was broad support for the Commission's initiative, underlined by the importance attached to 'active inclusion' in the 2007 joint report (European Commission and Council, 2007).

The Commission's proposal (European Commission, 2007f) was to embrace hybridity by seeking to 'deepen' the OMC through the adoption of a recommendation building on and developing the principles laid down in the 1992 Recommendations. The substance of the measure and its interaction with the OMC will be discussed below. For the moment, the analysis develops the argument that the Commission sought to strengthen EU interventions through a creative use of legal processes and instruments.

It will be recalled that unlike the treaty-based coordination processes which make specific provision for collective or individual recommendations to be addressed to Member States, no such treaty basis exists for the social OMC. While the 1992 Council Recommendations adopted Article 235 EEC (Article 308 EC, now 352 TFEU) as a legal basis, the Commission's Legal Service was of the view that in light of changes to the treaties since 1992, resort could no longer be had to this 'residual' legal basis and one had, instead to look to the more specific social policy provisions under Article 137 EC.[21] However, the Legal Service also noted that Article 137 EC could not provide a legal basis for the Council alone to adopt a recommendation given that this provision specifically envisaged action by means of directives adopted *jointly* by the EP and Council under the co-decision procedure. With these institutional constraints in place, the Commission Legal Service proposed an innovative solution: a *Commission* recommendation with the EU legislative institutions associated with the measure by the Council adopting 'conclusions' and the EP adopting a 'resolution' in a way that would mimic co-decision's tripartite institutional arrangements. Using Article 211 EC as a legal basis, a Commission Recommendation on 'active inclusion' was duly adopted in 2008.

This use of Article 211 EC was unusual. The treaty article provided that:

> [I]n order to ensure the proper functioning and development of the common market, the Commission shall...formulate recommendations or deliver opinions on matters dealt with in this Treaty, if it expressly so provides or if the Commission considers it necessary.

Although use of this legal basis has been very widespread in relation to technical matters relating to the internal market, its use as a basis for

[21] The *lex specialis* rule demands that where a more specific basis exists within the treaties then resort may no longer be had to a general legal basis like Article 308 EC (now 352 TFEU) and any limitations on the instrument or form of action laid down by that specific legal basis cannot be circumvented through resort to this type of residual legal basis. In this case, action in respect of persons excluded from the labour market was governed specifically by Article 137 EC (now 153 TFEU).

intervention in the realm of social policy is—to this author's knowledge—highly unusual. Moreover, it is a legal basis which has been repealed by the Lisbon Treaty. Article 17 TFEU now simply states that: '[T]he Commission shall promote the general interest of the Union and take appropriate initiatives to that end ...' without making explicit its capacity to adopt recommendations. While, of course, that need not prevent this provision acting as a legal basis for such interventions, we simply need to look to the way in which the treaties do make explicit the power to adopt recommendations in other policy areas. For example, there is a clearer competence to adopt recommendations in the areas of education and sport (Article 165 TFEU) than there is in support of EU initiatives to combat poverty and social exclusion. On the one hand, this highlights the constrained constitutional and institutional context in which EU social policy continues to develop. On the other hand, it also indicates the possibilities for institutional change in EU social policy that can occur by the actions of a 'purposeful opportunist' (Cram, 1997).

In substantive terms, the Commission Recommendation focuses on three areas: (1) the adequacy of income support; (2) inclusive labour markets; and (3) access to quality services. Thus, while building on the 1992 Recommendations—which are not replaced but remain as 'reference points'—the 2008 Recommendation is somewhat more encompassing not least in respect of its treatment of access to services. Nonetheless, the measure remains largely concerned with issues of domestic process and institutional design rather than with an attempt to be more prescriptive and certainly avoids any attempt to define or impose common minimum income guarantees. In this way, the Recommendation lays down a set of principles under each of the three strands with it being left to Member States to adopt these principles into their national systems. Monitoring and evaluation of implementation is to be conducted within the context of the OMC.

What is striking and significant about the Recommendation is that the very first recital frames the intervention in terms of respect for human dignity and the right to social and housing assistance recognized in Article 34 of the EU Charter of Fundamental Rights. Moreover, Member States are requested to ensure inter alia that activation policies 'respect the implementation of fundamental rights'.[22] Again, this framing of the intervention

[22] Article 3 of the Recommendation sets out certain overarching principles to be incorporated into the design of domestic activation policies:

(a) support the implementation of fundamental rights;
(b) promote gender equality and equal opportunities for all;

is consistent with a social citizenship paradigm and is one reason why—together with its attempt to fashion a 'holistic' approach and its extension to quality social services—social NGOs in the EU have broadly been supportive of the measure. In terms of the substantive principles, as regards income support, the emphasis on the *adequacy* of social assistance measures is significant in framing the debate in terms other than the *sustainability* of social welfare as a facet of fiscal discipline. In other words, the intervention is framed more in terms of social than economic policy, albeit that the Commission was keen to stress the compatibility of the measure with the Lisbon growth and jobs strategy. Nonetheless, the Recommendation seeks to strike a balance between the stress, on the one hand, on the adequacy of income support and access to services, and on the other hand, the emphasis on inclusive labour markets. Moreover, there is reference to both the 'right' to resources but also the conditional 'obligations' to be actively available for employment or to be subject to other economic or social integration measures and reminds us of the activation 'dilemma' discussed above.

In the context of a non-binding instrument like a recommendation, it is possible that the activation dilemma is more pronounced. That is to say, where the outcome will be a non-binding instrument, it may be attractive simply to include language which will appeal to a wide range of actors by combining different social policy paradigms and discourses. In this way, far from the presence of multiple paradigms and discourses being a virtue, it ends up being a rather meaningless menu of policy ideas. As we have already seen with regard to negotiations over the common objectives of the OMC, these negotiations can become language games which create interpretative rivalry. That said, it is equally evident that had the negotiations been conducted in the context of a binding instrument then the reality may have been either some kind of stalemate[23] or the dominance of one social vision over another. The very fact that the instrument was non-binding at least opened the door to the inclusion of the sort of rights discourse that has sometimes been absent from EU social policy precisely because of the fear among some states that it would result in legalization and judicialization Thus, thinking

(c) take careful consideration of the complexities of multiple disadvantages and the specific situations and needs of the various vulnerable groups;
(d) take due account of local and regional circumstances and improve territorial cohesions; be consistent with a lifecycle approach to social and employment policies so they can support intergenerational solidarity and break the intergenerational transmission of poverty.

[23] One can think of the protracted and stalled negotiations over revisions to the Working Time Directive.

back to chapter one, far from alternative forms of governance being a distracting side-show from the analysis of 'hard' law and processes of legalization, they may be reactions to such processes which in turn create opportunities for institutional change through more flexible forms of influence.

The Recommendation envisages implementation and monitoring through the OMC. As noted in chapter four, already the common objectives of the OMC refer to promoting access to services and the promotion of active inclusion and it will need to be seen whether future National Strategy Reports show any domestic response to this new source of EU influence. What might be more significant is the effect of the Recommendation on the monitoring and evaluation of the NSRs. If we look specifically at the issue of adequacy of resources, while the Recommendation does not attempt a substantive harmonization of this by setting down a common minimum requirement, the joint reports could, nonetheless, evaluate the adequacy of national social protection systems in providing resources that bring households above the at-risk-of-poverty threshold of 60 per cent of median equivalized income. Although not one of the primary or secondary indicators used in the OMC, in collaboration with the OECD, a 'context indicator' was developed to measure the net income of social assistance recipients as a percentage of the at-risk-of-poverty threshold across three different household types (single person, lone parent with two children, and couple with two children). In 2006, in fourteen Member States, social assistance was not adequate to raise household income above the poverty threshold for all three household types. Only in the UK were all three households lifted above the threshold (European Commission, 2008c: Figure 3). The extent to which this indicator gains prominence within the review of Member States' NSRs will be one means of evaluating the influence of the active inclusion Recommendation in strengthening the OMC.

Reinforcing Social Policy Coordination: Institutional Change, Institutional Models and Institutional Design

In this third and final section, the analysis returns to the specific features of the OMC on Social Protection and Social Inclusion. Short of the Europe 2020 debate resulting in a complete abandonment of the OMC, it seemed likely that policy coordination would continue in some form. While new instruments emerged as discussed in the previous section, it was to the OMC that these instruments also looked. In putting the future of EU social policy coordination at the centre of the remaining discussion, the analysis below explores possible ways of strengthening EU social policy coordination. That analysis is undertaken in three stages. The first stage is a reflection on what it is we might mean by 'strengthening' with a particular emphasis on the questionable utility of the hard law/soft law distinction as a conceptual model to guide institutional change. The second stage looks to other examples of policy coordination—in particular, the treaty-based coordination processes—as institutional models to which the future design of the social OMC might aspire. The third stage draws on the direct experience of social policy coordination in confronting more directly the weaknesses in its institutional design.

Beyond Hard and Soft Law

If one were to take the view that the OMC constitutes a form of 'soft' law, then it would seem to follow naturally that to strengthen intervention would be to look towards 'hard' law and processes of 'legalization'. To use the typology of Abbott and his collaborators (Abbott and Snidal, 2000; Abbott et al, 2000) this would involve a strengthening across the three dimensions of 'obligation, 'delegation' and 'precision'. While this strategy might resonate in the context of an instrument which in many ways look like a potential 'hard' law candidate—albeit currently 'deficient' across one or more of the three dimensions—its conceptual purchase when applied to instruments like the OMC is at best more nuanced and, at worst, highly attenuated (Armstrong and Kilpatrick, 2007).[24] As will become apparent, the nature of EU social policy coordination as an assemblage of methodologies militates against simplistic assumptions that the paradigmatic normative template for strengthening the OMC lies in increasing the levels of obligation, delegation and precision.

As regards the dimension of 'obligation' as we have seen with regards to the social OMC process, there has been a strong resistance to transforming voluntary coordination into a treaty-mandated process, with the social OMC process remaining a discretionary process in terms of Article 5(3) TFEU. Authors like Scharpf have, nonetheless, counselled for the use of directives as a means of embedding the OMC (Scharpf, 2002). As a strategy for underscoring political commitments, there may be something to be said for this

[24] However, Schelkle (2007) has developed the Abbott et al framework in her analysis of changes in EU fiscal governance.

approach, but one should be cautious about assuming that such an approach on its own would enhance the quality of policy coordination. A potentially more fruitful approach would be to look to 'hybrid' governance arrangements that would yoke the OMC to basic norms set out in directives (see Hervey and Trubek, 2007). Certainly, if the principles set out in the 2008 Recommendation on 'active inclusion' were to form the subject of a directive, but with the OMC used to monitor and evaluate its implementation, then this would indeed create exactly this sort of hybridity. Yet legalization in the sense of the increased use of binding instruments runs the risk of denying governance a certain flexibility in how it evolves. Moreover, it creates the possibilities for 'joint decision traps' (Scharpf, 2006) which can be avoided by keeping more elements of cooperation voluntary. In this way, we need to recognize that the nature and status of the OMC is not the result of a pathological failure to achieve legalization—it is not a 'second best'—but is a strategic choice and changes in the legal context imply changes to that choice.

Enhancing delegation as an aspect of legalization typically implies an increased role for enforcement agencies like courts. As is evident from this study, national and EU courts have played little or no role in the OMC. That is hardly surprising given that the function of the OMC is one of seeking to influence *ex ante* the domestic strategic and policy environment: not a role typically played by courts. There is, nonetheless, an accountability dimension to the OMC in terms of the reporting obligations on Member States, and the monitoring and evaluation undertaken at EU level. As will be suggested below, there is scope for enhancing the delegation of authority of non-judicial institutions to evaluate policy performance, and changes in the institutional design of delegated authority will be explored.

The dimension of precision is key to Lodge's critique of the OMC (Lodge, 2007) in that, for him, OMC processes often fail precisely to define the standards that could form the normative basis for domestic policy influence and against which the extent of influence might be judged. Yet that sort of critique is difficult to operationalize in terms of a consequential demand for greater precision. As has been suggested throughout this study there is an important methodological difficulty in locating the textual source of the norms whose precision ought to be enhanced. There is no singular text to which one can look to enhance precision. Moreover, there is a multiplicity of sources of normative and cognitive discourse. The problem of standards in the OMC is often more about normative rivalry, with discursive and paradigmatic divergences across and within methodological elements of the coordination process, and of tensions as to the philosophy of coordination, whether the objective of coordination is to seek convergence around a singular normative vision in a 'top-down' fashion or to permit forms of contextualized 'bottom-up' learning in which what is learned is more elective and selective. These are more wide-ranging issues than can be captured by a simple focus on questions of normative precision.

The argument presented here, therefore, is one which—consistent with the study throughout—avoids conceptualizing the OMC on a hard law/soft law continuum that assumes that the imperative ought to be to move it from one end to the other. Rather the issues facing the OMC are more complex ones of institutional coherence and institutional design. That is to say, the concern is less with strengthening the OMC—conceptualized as a singular 'mode of governance'—and more with making an assemblage of methodologies function as an effective governance architecture.

Treaty-based Coordination as an Institutional Model for the Social OMC

The lesson that one might learn from the preceding section could be that instead of looking to hard law models of governance as a means of strengthening the OMC, a more appropriate approach would be to consider 'harder' EU policy coordination models. With that possibility in mind, the analysis presented below explores the manner in which a debate about how to 'reinforce' the OMC unfolded. Even in advance of the 'Europe 2020' initiative, the European Commission had in 2008 produced a Communication on *A Renewed Commitment to Social Europe* and conducted an impact assessment of possible approaches to 'reinforcing' the OMC (European Commission, 2008d; 2008e). An important aspect of the analysis of these and other contributions to the debate lies in highlighting tendencies to look towards institutional isomorphism as a mean of strengthening the OMC, sometimes at the expense of learning more directly from the experiences and practices of two generations of social policy coordination.

Although different from the evaluation conducted in 2005 (European Commission, 2006c), the impact assessment accompanying the Commission's communication on reinforcing the OMC performed much the same function in terms of identifying perceived weaknesses and strengths of the OMC. Key weaknesses of the OMC were identified:

- a lack of political commitment to, and visibility, of the process;
- the need for stronger EU and national horizontal coordination and mainstreaming of social protection and social inclusion policies across all policy areas;

- the need for stronger analytical underpinning of policy;
- the need to better involve the regional and local levels in the OMC;
- lack of participation of stakeholders; and
- the need to strengthen mutual learning.

On the basis of the identification of these weaknesses, the impact assessment identified four objectives against which options for the future of the OMC might be assessed:

1. increase political commitment and visibility;
2. strengthen positive interaction with other EU policies;
3. reinforce the analytical underpinnings of the process;
4. increase ownership in Member States, boost implementation and enhance mutual learning.

The impact assessment then laid out three main options for the 'social OMC':

- the *status quo* with the OMC continuing to make incremental changes;
- fundamental overhaul: making the OMC embrace all dimensions of EU social policies to become a 'social Lisbon';
- comprehensive change representing substantial improvements to be phased in.

The assessment referred *en passant* to two other options: complete abandonment of the OMC—which it rejected—and absorption of the social OMC into the broader Lisbon strategy, consideration of which it left to the debate about the post-2010 Lisbon strategy (see above). Its conclusion was that the third option of comprehensive but phased change was desirable.

The approach adopted by the impact assessment is not entirely satisfactory. The weaknesses identified struggle to get beyond rather superficial assessments of the OMC. This is not to say that there is not validity to these assessments but rather that policy coordination as 'the OMC' tends to be treated as a coherent entity with little attempt made to judge whether the different elements of the policy coordination architecture are fit for purpose; how well the elements interact; or what the relationship might be between seeking to strengthen 'top-down' substantive influences on the domestic strategic and policy environment, and seeking to enhance 'bottom-up' or 'horizontal' mechanisms of accountability for the strategies states choose to follow. Detailed analysis of the intricacies, ambiguities and tensions within the policy coordination governance architecture was absent.

Moreover, in asking how well each of the possible reform initiatives might meet the four objectives, the answers for each option were simply different points on the same scale: from a relatively unambitious status quo through to radical reform. Hardly surprising then that the impact assessment charted a pragmatic middle ground with a strong emphasis on the 'feasibility' of change. In this way, the parameters of the reform debate were set in such a way as to confine the potential for institutional change.[25]

The Communication on reinforcing the social OMC followed the approach of proposing significant rather than radical reforms. It proposed to strengthen social policy coordination along four dimensions:

- increasing political visibility and commitment;
- strengthening interaction with other EU policies;
- reinforcing analytical tools; and
- better ownership through peer reviews, mutual learning and involvement of relevant actors.

What was especially striking was the explicit depiction of the Lisbon strategy for 'growth and jobs' as an institutional model to which the social OMC might aspire. More concretely, it was to the setting of targets and the use of recommendations that particular attention was drawn.

The idea of a headline EU poverty target like that subsequently proposed by the European Commission in its 'Europe 2020' Communication would indeed be a significant institutional innovation and departure from the practices of the social OMC, although it was something that EU-level social NGOs tended to support (EAPN, 2008c; Social Platform, 2009).[26] It will be recalled that in 2000 the Commission had floated some high level European targets for poverty reduction but these were never incorporated into the OMC process. The mid-term evaluation of the OMC also saw Member States generally resistant to the idea of EU targets (European Commission, 2006c: 16). Instead, encouragement has been given to Member States to

[25] There is an inherent limitation to the capacity of impact assessments to engage with new forms of governance like the OMC. Indeed, Baldwin (2005) highlights the paradox that the same impulse towards 'better regulation' which leads to impact assessments is the same force pushing for the sorts of less hierarchical forms of governance which impact assessments might struggle to evaluate.

[26] Headline EU-level targets suggested by EAPN included:

1. Reduction in at-risk of poverty levels to 14% by 2010 and 10% by 2013, and eradication by 2020;
2. Child poverty reduction to 15% by 2010, 10% by 2013 and eradication by 2020;
3. Working poverty reduction to 15% by 2010, 4% by 2013 and eradication by 2020.

develop national targets. Indeed, the second generation of the OMC reinforced a model in which Member States would select which substantive policy priorities to feature in its NAPincls and where possible to develop national targets around these priorities.

While it is appealing to think of EU-level targets as injecting energy and momentum into EU interventions to combat poverty and social exclusion, the danger is that simply borrowing from the Lisbon strategy model may crowd out some of the more interesting suggestions about targets. For example, among the dozen recommendations proposed by the EU's Network of Independent Experts (Frazer and Marlier, 2008a), there was the suggestion that national targets would not simply be selected by the Member States themselves but agreed in the context of a bilateral dialogue between the Commission and each Member State. Moreover, the Commission's communication on reinforcing the social OMC highlighted the possibility that similarly-situated groups of states could work within 'differentiated pathways' towards common goals and targets. Whatever the individual merits or limitations of these proposals, the very simple point is that there is more to strengthening EU policy coordination than a simple reflex of centralizing authority for target-setting and mimicking aspects of the treaty-based coordination models. As the discussions around targets in the 'Europe 2020' programme illustrated, there is not even agreement that EU level targets for economic and employment policy coordination are a good thing.[27]

As regards the role of 'recommendations', it was noted in earlier chapters that a key point of departure for the social OMC from the treaty-based coordination processes was the absence of a power to make either collective or individual Member State recommendations. Instead, it has been left to a range of resources to identify issues common to the Member States and to the country fiches of the joint reports to highlight issues particular to Member States. Much like the discussion around targets, it would be understandable to look to enhanced possibilities for the adoption of recommendations to strengthen the social OMC. Indeed, recommendations had already emerged in different ways. In the area of child poverty, a report on *Child Poverty and Well-Being in the EU* endorsed by the SPC (European Commission, 2008f) contained fifteen recommendations addressed to the Member States.

[27] The Spanish Presidency of the Council had initially floated the idea of binding economic targets and enhanced 'corrective measures: 'Spain to push for binding EU economic goals', EUObserver.com (8.1.10). Nonetheless, one Europe-based think-tank suggested that the greater incentive for economic reforms was failure to reform and noted that the Commission's record on enforcement was 'abysmal': Lisbon Council, 'Comment', European Voice (14.1.10).

Nonetheless, even if the nomenclature is the same, we need to be cautious about assuming that recommendations under the social OMC ought to or would play the same role as under the Lisbon process. The Commission's Communication on reinforcing the social OMC looked to the Commission Recommendation on 'active inclusion' as an example of the use of recommendations. Yet this quasi-legislative approach—the setting out of a set of principles which would not look odd in a directive—is different from a more executive style of act laying down short-term priorities for states either collectively or individually.

Indeed, diversity in the style and nature of recommendations may reflect important differences in the underlying rationale and philosophy of different coordination processes. In chapter two, competing rationales for coordination—from the management of the externalities of autonomous policy choices to enhancing problem-solving capacity—were noted. Different philosophies of 'convergence' and 'cooperation' with their diverging orientations towards policy autonomy, policy diversity, and centralization/decentralization of policymaking were highlighted. Across and within economic, employment and social policy coordination we find different rationales and philosophies at play. It is evident from this study that social policy coordination has tended to be accepting of the policy autonomy and policy diversity of Member States while simultaneously seeking to influence the domestic strategic environment and to develop tools of policy analysis through the use of indicators and data. A greater level of centralization through the adoption of EU targets and recommendations has largely been resisted because of this philosophical understanding of EU social policy coordination as a species of decentralized policy-making within an EU context. Institutional change has occurred, but within a process that has largely sought to emphasize a 'bottom-up' learning process. The adoption of EU level targets and formal EU recommendations could result in a move towards a more 'top-down' approach to the OMC which may not necessarily reinforce EU interventions but could in fact weaken them. Indeed, the more expectations shift towards EU institutions in the governance of social inclusion, the more scope there might be for blame shifting to the EU level, for example, if national policies track EU targets or follow EU recommendations that have unintended or negative domestic consequences. Of course, it is possible to develop national targets and recommendations in the style of the active inclusion recommendation that would be consistent with the manner in which the social OMC has evolved. The more general point, however, is the need to avoid the temptation to conclude that because the political energy shifted to the Lisbon growth and jobs strategy with an apparent sidelining of the social dimension that the way to strengthen the social OMC is to make it look more like, or bring it closer to, the Lisbon treaty-based processes.

Importantly, an assumption that the integrated Lisbon process ought to be the way forward for the social OMC negates the recognition that the governance process of the latter has been much more successful than the former in engaging and mobilizing stakeholders. It can be argued that the social OMC process pursued a credible—if not always effective—counter strategy that sought to foster a variety of vertical and horizontal linkages between governmental and non-governmental actors and between social science expertise and policymakers. In this way, simply emulating elements of the Lisbon strategy is neither the only viable strategy nor necessarily the most effective.

Coordinating Coordination: Learning from Experience

There are weaknesses in the OMC architecture that do require to be addressed. In its response to the Commission's communication on reinforcing the social OMC, while the SPC was silent on the idea of following the model of the Lisbon growth and jobs governance architecture, perhaps tellingly, it stated that it 'expects the Commission to make extensive use of the experience accumulated by the SPC and by its Indicators Sub-Group with a view to improving working methods and to fully exploiting the potential of the Social OMC'. In this way, the SPC sought reforms based not on the experience of a different coordination process but rather to learn the lessons of its own experience. One of Zeitlin's critiques of the relaunch of the Lisbon strategy was that changes were made that did not draw on the past practical experience of policy coordination, for example, the loss of the distinct NAP on employment (Zeitlin, 2005a). This statement from the SPC was suggestive of a wish not to ignore the specific experience of EU social policy coordination but rather to draw on it as a means to strengthen the OMC.

It may be the paradox of governance by policy coordination that its weakness lies as much in the lack of coordination between its different methodological elements as with deficiencies with individual elements. In this final part of the chapter, the analysis looks to possibilities for strengthening the social OMC both by reflecting back on the experience of a decade of policy coordination in the social sphere and by looking forward to alternative institutional design models for policy coordination.

Looking at the evaluations contained in the impact assessment (European Commission, 2008e) and in the Network of Independent Experts report (Frazer and Marlier, 2008a), there is a high level of consensus as to the *general* weaknesses of the OMC process. Typically, these relate to issues of: political commitment to, and visibility of, the OMC; the participation of relevant actors; monitoring and evaluation including the analytical capacity of the process; and lesson-drawing and mutual learning. These weaknesses are a function both of problems with individual aspects of the OMC and with overarching issues of institutional design.

Following the SPC's inclination to look to the past experience of the OMC as a means of strengthening working methods, what lessons might we draw? Perhaps the first lesson is that notwithstanding the streamlining of the different social coordination processes, the strand of activity on social exclusion has more or less continued to be viewed as a distinct process. Even the very nomenclature of the 'NAPincl' was retained. It is not apparent that the combination of the social inclusion, pensions and healthcare processes has produced any added-value and it would probably be better if they were each conducted as distinct processes (if indeed, there is a continuing justification and value to be ascribed to each process). The alternative approach of merging the social OMC into an overarching 'Europe 2020' coordination process would be a mistake. Notwithstanding the buffeting the social OMC took as a result of the 2005 relaunch of the Lisbon strategy, the evolution of the process probably benefited by not being too close to the Lisbon strategy. It is understandable to think that if one of the deficiencies of the social OMC is lack of political commitment and visibility, then the solution might be to associate it more strongly with the politically more visible replacement to the Lisbon strategy. Yet this would be to underestimate the different path the social OMC has followed in trying to build political commitment from the bottom-up. Moreover, there would be every danger of the social process being sidelined as the EU faced up to its problems of economic and fiscal governance—particularly within the Eurozone—in the wake of the financial crisis. The arguments for a singular and focused process to combat poverty and social exclusion in order to achieve the poverty reduction seem to be the more compelling.

The second lesson is that the common objectives of the social OMC ought not to be viewed as directive norms in the sense of forming the basis for driving 'first order' change in domestic policy. At best, the objectives are contextualizing 'second order' paradigmatic or framing norms that explain and justify why the EU has any role to play in combating poverty and social exclusion. In that way, the goal of reform ought not to be to make these objectives more detailed or more prescriptive: indeed, the opposite. Consistent with the argument presented in the previous chapter, revised objectives for a distinct OMC to combat poverty and social exclusion might usefully adopt an overarching objective which justifies EU intervention in terms of the realization of shared social values, common social objectives and the protection of fundamental social rights as articulated in the Lisbon Treaty. The contributions of economic, employment and social policies to achieving this overarching objective might then form the basis for recasting the existing objectives. In many ways this does not resolve the tension between the different paradigmatic representation of poverty and social exclusion highlighted in this study. However, it would be demanding that whether narrowly focused on activation policies or concerned principally with income poverty or widening out to a more multidimensional approach to social exclusion, the rationale for coordination is as strongly rooted in the realization of fundamental rights of citizens as it is in the interaction of economic, employment and social policies.

The third lesson is that some level of stability and continuity is required if common EU indicators are to form a useful basis for policy analysis and comparison. The transition from ECHP to EU-SILC as a data source overshadowed the early life of the OMC. While it was inevitable that there would be difficulties as the process of indicator-setting and data collection was itself 'Europeanized', problems of lack of data or lack of comparability simply undermine claims that the OMC can develop capacities for problem-identification and cross-national policy learning.

Clarification of the role and identity of the NAPincl is the fourth lesson to learn. The debate has largely revolved around a tension between the descriptive orientation of the NAPincl—the extent to which it is about reporting and information-sharing—and a more prescriptive role—variously that the NAPincls constitute a 'strategy' or more directly shape domestic policy. Indeed, there is detectable frustration between social NGOs and national governments as to the call from the former that the Member States produce something more than a report and the typical compliance response of the latter which is to produce a NAPincl that conforms to a reporting template. The tension is compounded by the cyclical nature of the process. Strategies are put in place with a view to medium to long-term planning. Reports are more short-term periodic accounts of developments, including progress in delivering on a strategy. The cyclical nature of the OMC encourages Member States to produce reports rather than strategies.

The better approach would be to view the NAPincl as a report both of the Member States' strategic policy environment and of the policies and practices developed in the context of that strategic environment. While the OMC might stimulate a Member State to adopt a strategy that it did not previously have—and even to use the NAPincl as its strategic document—there is no good reason why the domestic strategy ought not to be found in different domestic sources. By analogy with the implementation of directives where Member States have the choice of means of implementation, provided the basic objective is met—to have a strategic environment for combating poverty and social exclusion—there is no reason why the NAPincl has to be the basis of the strategy rather than the mechanism for reporting on what strategies exist. Again, the point is that the OMC is not about first order governing by other means, ie it is not about the transmission of an EU anti-poverty strategy to the Member States, but is instead the governance of governance—monitoring and evaluating the extent to which Member States have themselves adopted a strategic approach and analysing the performance of the resulting policies. This identifies the NAPincls as part of a process of 'dynamic accountability' (Sabel and Zeitlin, 2008).

The quality of monitoring and evaluating as evidenced by the joint reports takes us to the fifth lesson. The joint reports have attempted to ride two different horses. On the one hand, they aim to be a source of expert-led policy analysis and evaluation, drawing particularly on the information provided via the cyclical reporting mechanism. On the other hand, they also aspire to political lesson-drawing and priority-setting. While lesson-drawing self-evidently follows from problem-identification, attempting to combine the two aspects and to combine expert policy analysis with political lesson-drawing may make the joint report a rather unruly beast.

Looking first to policy analysis and evaluation, as the experience of the UK's *Opportunity for All* report demonstrated, it is very difficult to maintain political interest in these sorts of analytical reports over time. There is often a tension between maintaining a consistency in the style of the report—particularly in terms of showing progress against core indicators—and introducing novel and thematic elements. This tension is apparent in the joint reports. The general presentation of data using the common indicators ends up competing with the more thematic analysis which developed in the years between national reports. The result has been reports that are simply too long, too burdened with detail and which ultimately lack political visibility not least when compared to the rival sources of national data analysis and communication. One response would be for EUROSTAT to produce a concise periodic report (or series of reports as data becomes available) on the commonly agreed indicators highlighting key trends and development.

As for the more thematic policy analysis and evaluation, it is noteworthy that this work drew increasingly on sources beyond those of the cyclical reports prepared by Member States, including work developed by the SPC and its Indicators Sub-Group, supported by the European Commission. The difficulty is that this thematic analytical work is also undertaken under the auspices of the PROGRESS action programme—with its own comitology committee and Network of Independent Experts—and reveals a problematic lack of organizational coordination and institutional ownership of policy analysis and evaluation. In many ways, there was a lot to be said for the old 'European Observatory on Policies to Combat Social Exclusion' established under the 'Poverty Programmes' as a hub for coordinating thematic research and analysis.

If some greater centralized coordination of policy analysis is required, then the question arises as to whether the SPC ought to be the focal point for this role. While there may be merit in associating the SPC with this type of analysis in promoting evidence-led policy-making, following trends in EU risk regulation, it might be preferable to distinguish between coordinated centralized 'risk assessment'—the independent, expert analysis of the risks of poverty—from coordinated decentralized 'risk management'—the political lessons that states might collectively and individually choose to learn from such assessments. With the agenda of the SPC already overcrowded, it might make sense for an alternative structure to emerge to provide independent coordinating oversight of policy analysis and evaluation. The SPC could then focus more on political lesson-drawing and priority-setting while providing an overarching coordinating role for the OMC as a whole.

As for lesson-drawing, if one of the weaknesses of the NAPincls was that they each tended to report a wide array of strategies and initiatives, then the joint reports amplified the problem by frequently re-reporting what all twenty-seven Member States had presented. To be sure, the short key messages elements of the joint reports did identify some common challenges and thematic priorities. Yet with the attempt to cover three processes, even that aspect was somewhat compromised. The very idea of a 'joint' report of the Commission and Council may be viewed as problematic insofar as the Member States are both the individual account-giver and collectively one of the account-holders. The argument might be that the European Commission should have a more prominent independent role in drawing out policy lessons and adopting more critical political messages.

There is an evident problem with the European Commission adopting a heightened role in the OMC. As was noted in chapter five, there may be a reluctance to give the Commission a more independent role if it means that the OMC is viewed as a vehicle for the supranational level to acquire more power. Moreover, it is interesting that in its Europe 2020 Communication, it was to the European Council that the Commission itself looked to take the institutional responsibility for driving the process forward. How then should the roles of the European Commission and the representatives of the Member States be reconciled in a manner that allows political priorities to be set and political lessons drawn? The answer might simply be for the Commission—drawing on expert policy assessments—to produce a concise Communication focusing on key collective political messages and country-specific issues (currently produced in the country fiches) and for the SPC to adopt an Opinion both of which are then transmitted to the Spring European Council for political leaders to endorse, amend or revise according to working procedures to be developed by the new European Council President and the Member States' permanent representations.

Enhancing mechanisms for expert-driven problem identification and for drawing out consequential collective political priorities and individual political messages ought also to be capable of addressing another weakness of the OMC, namely the role of thematic peer review conducted within the PROGRESS programme. While useful processes in their own terms, they have suffered from a lack of coordination with other elements of the OMC and from an incapacity to resonate with the wider political environment. If the practices selected owed less to the random selections of Member States and more from issues identified within the OMC process, responsiveness of states to the experiences of these peer reviews is something that the OMC might itself monitor.

The final lesson to consider is the role of other actors outside of the immediate circle of the European Commission and representatives of the Member States. In particular, the relative roles of NGOs and of parliamentarians need to be considered. One of the apparent strengths of the social OMC has been its capacity to reach out to a range of civil society actors at transnational, national and subnational levels. At the same time, one of its alleged weaknesses has been its limited engagement of parliamentary structures. This has often resulted in an apparent clash of legitimacy with the OMC variously—but not very convincingly—justified as an example of participatory democracy, with the traditional institutions of representative democracy conceptualized as largely incompatible with the experimentalism of the OMC (see Dawson, 2009: 285 *et seq.*). However, much of the sting of the participatory versus representative democracy argument is drawn inasmuch as the OMC is not itself a mechanism for direct first order governing which remains within the legitimating structures of domestic collective will-formation. Again, this evidences why the discursive treatment of the OMC as 'soft law' tends to confuse more than it reveals inasmuch as it tends to treat the OMC as like first order governing through hard law but only by other means. Indeed, if greater emphasis is placed on the role of the OMC as a mechanism of accountability (albeit one with feedback loops which would be strengthened if the analysis above were to be followed), then a supervisory role for parliaments becomes quite obvious. Like civil society actors, parliamentary structures act as accountability forums (see chapter two and Bovens, 2007). The task is to think of ways of opening up channels to ensure that the coordinative discourses of national and EU officials are exposed to the communicative discourses of civil society and of parliamentarians without blurring the boundaries of political responsibility and accountability. For the European Parliament this may require it to find ways both of becoming more familiar with the sources of information, data and analysis utilized in the OMC, and of feeding views into the European Council alongside those of the European Commission and the SPC. For civil society, while the informalism of their engagement with EU and national officials may have helped drive the process at national and EU levels, it may be to more formalized civic forums that the OMC may ultimately turn. As was noted in chapter five, the UK has moved to adopt a more formalized structure for engaging with stakeholders in respect of its NAPincls. At EU-level there are also examples of more formalized civic forums as advisory bodies.[28]

Conclusions

In writing about a governance process that has been in flux since the moment it was initiated, there has always been a lurking danger that any conclusions

[28] Article 10 of the Regulation establishing the Fundamental Rights Agency requires the Agency to cooperate with NGOs and civil society actors. To facilitate that cooperation a 'Fundamental Rights Platform' is established as a 'mechanism for the exchange of information and pooling of knowledge'. In this way, non-governmental actors are recognized as a source of expertise that is to be associated with the work of the FRA. See Council Regulation 168/2007/EC establishing a European Union Agency for Fundamental Rights: [2007] OJ L53/1.

to be drawn might at best be provisional or at worst redundant; no more so than in the context of this final chapter when both the outcome of the Europe 2020 debate and of proposals to reinforce the social OMC would be decided after publication. Therefore, the objective of this chapter has been as much about how to position how we might think about strengthening the OMC—its role in different policy environments, its relationship to ideas of 'hybridity', the kinds of institutional model that might or might not be appropriate—as it has been about drawing clear conclusions. Nonetheless, and consistent with the approach adopted throughout this study, it has sought to delve beneath the superficial identification of the OMC as a 'mode of governance' to explore the manner in which different methodological elements that combine to form 'the OMC' might be strengthened.

Whatever might be done to reinforce the capacity of the OMC to assess risks of poverty, to evaluate policy performance, and to draw out priorities and lessons for Member States, it is the Member States themselves who hold the key levers by which a decisive impact on poverty might be made. It is the function of the OMC to help Member States develop their capacities to identify policy problems and seek appropriate solutions within a framework where ultimate responsibility for levels of poverty and social exclusion lies with the Member States themselves. Although it may be tempting to think that the way to strengthen the governance of social inclusion is simply to transfer more responsibilities for governance to the EU-level, like many temptations, it is an impulse best resisted.

BIBLIOGRAPHY

Abbott, Kenneth W. et al (2000), 'The Concept of Legalization', *International Organization*, 54 (3), 401–19.

Abbott, Kenneth W. and Snidal, Duncan (2000), 'Hard and Soft Law in International Governance', *International Organization*, 54 (3), 421–56.

Alston, Philip (ed.) (with Mara R. Bustelo and James Heenan) (1999), *The EU and Human Rights* (Oxford: Oxford University Press).

— (2005), 'Assessing the Strengths and Weaknesses of the European Social Charter's Supervisory Mechanism', in Gráinne de Búrca and Bruno de Witte, (eds.) (with Larissa Ogertschnig), *Social Rights in Europe* (Oxford: Oxford University Press), 45–67.

Alston, Philip and Weiler, Joseph H. H. (1999), 'An "Ever Closer Union" in Need of a Human Rights Policy: The European Union and Human Rights', in Philip Alston (ed.) (with Mara R. Bustelo and James Heenan), *The EU and Human Rights* (Oxford: Oxford University Press), 3–66.

Annesley, Claire (2003), 'Americanised and Europeanised: UK social policy since 1997', *The British Journal of Politics & International Relations*, 5 (2), 143–65.

— (2007), 'Lisbon and social Europe: towards a European "adult worker model" welfare system', *Journal of European Social Policy*, 17 (3), 195–205.

Armstrong, Kenneth A. (1998a), 'Legal Integration: Theorizing the Legal Dimension of European Integration', *Journal of Common Market Studies*, 36 (2), 155–74.

— (1998b), 'New Institutionalism and European Union Legal Studies', in Paul Craig and Carol Harlow (eds.), *Lawmaking in the European Union* (London: Kluwer Law International), 89–110.

— (2003), 'Tackling Social Exclusion Through OMC: Reshaping the Boundaries of European Governance', in Tanja Börzel and Rachael Cichowski (eds.), *The State of the European Union: law, politics, and society* (Vol. 6) (Oxford: Oxford University Press), 170–94.

— (2005), 'How Open is the United Kingdom to the OMC Process on Social Inclusion' in Jonathan Zeitlin and Philippe Pochet (eds.), *The Open Method of Co-ordination in Action: The European Employment and Social Inclusion Strategies* (Brussels: P.I.E. Peter Lang), 287–310.

— (2006a), 'The "Europeanisation" of Social Exclusion: British Adaptation to EU Co-ordination', *The British Journal of Politics and International Relations*, 8 (1), 79–100.

— (2006b), 'Inclusive Governance? Civil society and the open method of co-ordination', in Stijn Smismans (ed.), *Civil Society and Legitimate European Governance* (Cheltenham: Edward Elgar), 40–67.

— (2008), 'Governance and Constitutionalism After Lisbon', *Journal of Common Market Studies*, 46 (2), 415–26.

Armstrong, Kenneth A. and Bulmer, Simon (1998), *The Governance of the Single European Market* (Manchester: Manchester University Press).

Armstrong, Kenneth A. and Kilpatrick, Claire (2007), 'Law, Governance or New Governance? The Changing Open Method of Coordination', *Columbia Journal of European Law*, 13 (3), 649–77.

Arnull, Anthony (2003), 'From Charter to Constitution and Beyond: Fundamental Rights in the New European Union', *Public Law*, 774–93.

Arrowsmith, James, Sisson, Keith and Marginson, Paul (2004), 'What can "benchmarking" offer the open method of co-ordination?', *Journal of European Public Policy*, 11 (2), 311–28.

Ashiagbor, Diamond (2005), *The European Employment Strategy: Labour Market Regulation and New Governance* (Oxford: Oxford University Press).

Atkinson, Anthony B. (2003), 'Social Europe and Social Science', *Social Policy and Society*, 2 (4), 261–72.

Atkinson, Anthony B., Cantillon, Bea, Marlier, Eric and Nolan, Brian (2002), *Social Indicators: the EU and social inclusion* (Oxford: Oxford University Press).

— (2005), 'Taking Forward the EU Social Inclusion Process', (Luxembourg: Luxembourg Presidency of the Council).

Atkinson, Anthony B., Marlier, Eric and Nolan, Brian (2004), 'Indicators and Targets for Social Inclusion in the European Union', *Journal of Common Market Studies*, 42 (1), 47–75.

Azoulai, Loïc (2008), 'The Court of Justice and the Social Market Economy: The emergence of an ideal and the conditions for its realization', *Common Market Law Review*, 45 (5), 1335–56.

Baldwin, Robert (2005), 'Is Better Regulation Smarter Regulation?', *Public Law*, 485–511.

Baquero Cruz, Julio (2002), *Between Competition and Free Movement: the economic constitutional law of the European Community* (Oxford and Portland: Hart Publishing).

— (2005), 'Beyond Competition: Services of General Interest and European Community Law', in Graínne de Búrca (ed.), *EU law and the Welfare State: in search of solidarity* (Oxford: Oxford University Press), 169–212.

Barnard, Catherine (1999), 'EC "Social" Policy', in Paul Craig and Gráinne de Búrca (eds.), *The Evolution of EU Law* (Oxford, Oxford University Press), 479–516.

— (2006), 'Solidarity and New Governance in Social Policy', in Gráinne de Búrca and Joanne Scott (eds.), *Law and New Governance in the EU and the US* (Oxford: Hart Publishing), 153–77.

— (2007), 'Social Policy Revisited in the light of the Constitutional Debate', in Catherine Barnard (ed.), *The Fundamentals of EU Law Revisited: Assessing the Impact of the Constitutional Debate* (Oxford: Oxford University Press), 109–51.

Bauer, Michael M. (2002), 'The Commission and the Poverty Programmes', *Journal of Common Market Studies*, 40 (3), 381–400.

Begg, Iain (2008), 'Is There a Convincing Rationale for the Lisbon Strategy?', *Journal of Common Market Studies*, 46 (2), 427–35.

Begg, Iain and Berghman, Jos (2002), 'Introduction: EU social (exclusion) policy revisited?' *Journal of European Social Policy*, 12 (3), 179–94.

Belsky, Jay et al. (2006), 'Effects of Sure Start local programmes on children and families: early findings from a quasi-experimental, cross sectional study', *British Medical Journal*, 332 (7556), 1476.

Bennett, Fran and Bradshaw, Jonathan (2008), *Assessment of the 2008–10 National Reform Programmes From a Social Inclusion Perspective: The extent of synergies between growth and jobs policies and social inclusion policies*, <http://www.peer-review-social-inclusion.eu/network-of-independent-experts/2008/second-semester-2008> (Accessed in March 2010).

Benz, Arthur (2007), 'Accountable Multilevel Governance by the Open Method of Coordination?' *European Law Journal*, 13 (4), 505–22.

Bercusson, Brian (2007), 'The Trade Union Movement and the European Union: Judgment Day', *European Law Journal*, 13 (3), 279–308.

Bercusson, Brian, Deakin, Simon, Koistinen, Pertti, Kravaritou, Yota, Muckeberer, Ulrich, Supiot, Alain and Veneziana, Bruno (1997), 'A Manifesto for Social Europe', *European Law Journal*, 3 (2), 189–205.

Berghman, Jos (1995), 'Social Exclusion in Europe: Policy Context and Analytical Framework', in Graham Room (ed.), *Beyond the Threshold: the measurement and analysis of social exclusion* (Bristol: Policy Press), 10–28.

Bernard, Nick (2003), 'Economic, Social and Cultural Rights in a Multi-Level Legal Order', in Tamara Hervey and Jeff Kenner (eds.), *Economic and Social Rights under the EU Charter of Fundamental Rights* (Oxford: Hart Publishing), 247–68.

— (2005), 'Between a Rock and a Soft Place: Internal Market versus Open Coordination in EU Social Welfare Law', in Eleanor Spaventa and Michael Dougan (eds.), *Social Welfare and EU Law* (Oxford: Hart Publishing), 261–86.

Biagi, Marco (1998), 'The Implementation of the Amsterdam Treaty with Regard to Employment: Co-ordination or Convergence?', *International Journal of Comparative Labour Law and Industrial Relations* 14 (4), 325–36.

Biondi, Andrea and Rubini, L. (2005), 'Aims, Effects and Justifications: EC State Aid Law and Its Impact on National Social Policies', in Michael Dougan and Eleanor Spaventa (eds.), *Social Welfare and EU Law* (Oxford: Hart Publishing), 79–103.

Boeger, Nina (2007), 'Solidarity and EC Competition Law', *European Law Review*, 32 (3), 319–40.

Borrás, Susana and Jacobsson, Kerstin (2004), 'The open method of co-ordination and new governance patterns in the EU', *Journal of European Public Policy*, 11 (2), 185–208.

Börzel, Tanja (2002), 'Pace-Setting, Foot-Dragging and Fence-Sitting: Member State Responses to Europeanization', *Journal of Common Market Studies*, 40(2), 193–214.

— (2005), 'Europeanization: How the European Union Interacts with its Member States' in Simon Bulmer and Christian Lequesne (eds.), *The Member States of the European Union* (Oxford: Oxford University Press), 45–69.

Börzel, Tanja A. and Risse, Thomas (2003), 'Conceptualising the Domestic Impact of Europe' in Kevin Featherstone and Claudio Radaelli (eds.), *The Politics of Europeanization* (Oxford: Oxford University Press), 57–80.

Börzel, Tanja A. and Cichowski, Rachel A. (eds.) (2003), *The State of the European Union: law, politics, and society* (Vol. 6) (Oxford: Oxford University Press).

Bovens, Mark (2007), 'Analysing and Assessing Accountability: A Conceptual Framework', *European Law Journal*, 13 (4), 447–68.

Bowring, Finn (2000), 'Social exclusion: limitations of the debate', *Critical Social Policy*, 20 (3), 307–30.

Bradshaw, Jonathan and Bennett, Fran (2003), *Report on United Kingdom National Action Plan on Social Inclusion* (York: Social Policy Research Unit).

Brewer, Mike, Goodman, Alissa, Muriel, Alistair and Sibieta, Luke (2007), *Poverty and Inequality in the UK: 2007* (London: Institute for Fiscal Studies).

Büchs, Milena (2007), *New Governance in European Social Policy: the open method of coordination* (Basingstoke: Palgrave Macmillan).

Bulmer, Simon (2007), 'Theorizing Europeanization', in Paolo Graziano and Maarten P. Vink (eds.), *Europeanization: New Research Agendas* (Basingstoke: Palgrave Macmillan), 46–58.

— (2009), '*Politics in Time* meets the politics of time: historical institutionalism and the EU timescape', *Journal of European Public Policy*, 16 (2), 307–24.

Bulmer, Simon and Burch, Martin (2005), 'The Europeanization of UK Government: From Quiet Revolution to Explicit Step-Change?', *Public Administration*, 83 (4), 861–90.

Bulmer, Simon and Padgett, Stephen (2005), 'Policy Transfer in the European Union: An Institutionalist Perspective', *British Journal of Political Science*, 35 (1), 103–26.

Caporaso, James A. (1996), 'The European Union and Forms of State: Westphalian, Regulatory or Post-Modern?', *Journal of Common Market Studies*, 34 (1), 29–52.

— (2007), 'The Three Worlds of Regional Integration Theory' in Paolo Graziano and Maarten P. Vink (eds.), *Europeanization: New Research Agendas* (Basingstoke: Palgrave Macmillan), 23–45.

Chalmers, Damian and Lodge, Martin (2003), 'The Open Method of Co-ordination and the European Welfare State', *Discussion Paper No. 11* (London: ESRC Centre for the Analysis of Risk and Regulation).

Cichowski, Rachel A. and Börzel, Tanja A. (2003), 'Law, Politics and Society in Europe' in Tanja A. Börzel and Rachel A. Cichowski (eds.), *The State of the European Union: law, politics, and society* (Vol. 6) (Oxford: Oxford University Press), 3–17.

Citi, Manuele and Rhodes, Martin (2007), 'New Modes of Governance in the EU: Common Objectives versus National Preferences', *European Governance Papers (EUROGOV)*, N-07–01. <http://www.connex-network.org/eurogov/pdf/egp-newgov-N-07–01.pdf> (Accessed in March 2010).

Cohen, Joshua and Sabel, Charles F. (2003), 'Sovereignty and Solidarity: EU and US' in Jonathan Zeitlin and David M Trubek (eds.), *Governing Work and Welfare in a New Economy: European and American experiments* (Oxford: Oxford University Press), 345–75.

Collignon, Stefan C., Dehousse, Renaud, Gabolde, Jean, Jouen, Marjorie, Pochet, Philippe, Salais, Robert, Sprenger, Rolf-Ulrich and Zsolt de Sousa, Hugo (2005). The Lisbon strategy and the open method of coordination, *Notre Europe*, Paper No. 12.

Craig, Paul (2001), 'Constitutions, Constitutionalism, and the European Union', *European Law Journal*, 7 (2), 125–50.

Cram, Laura (1993), 'Calling the Tune without Paying the Piper? Social policy regulation: the role of the Commission in European Community social policy', *Policy & Politics*, 21 (2), 135–46.

— (1997), *Policy-making in the European Union: conceptual lenses and the integration process* (London: Routledge).

Daly, Mary (2003), 'Governance and Social Policy', *Journal of Social Policy*, 32 (1), 113–28.

— (2006), 'EU Social Policy after Lisbon', *Journal of Common Market Studies*, 44 (3), 461–81.

— (2008), 'Whither EU Social Policy? An Account and Assessment of Developments in the Lisbon Social Inclusion Process', *Journal of Social Policy*, 37 (1), 1–19.

Dawson, Mark (2009), 'New Governance and the Proceduralisation of European law : the case of the open method of coordination', PhD dissertation (Florence: European University Institute).

de Búrca, Gráinne (1999), 'The Language of Rights and European Integration' in Jo Shaw and Gillian More (eds.) *New Legal Dynamics of European Union* (Oxford: Oxford University Press), 29–54.

— (2001a), 'Human Rights: the Charter and Beyond', *Jean Monnet Working Paper*, 10/01.

— (2001b), 'The Drafting of the European Union Charter of Fundamental Rights', *European Law Review*, 26 (2), 126–38.

— (2003), 'The Constitutional Challenge of New Governance in the European Union', *European Law Review*, 28 (6), 814–39.

— (2005), 'New Modes of Governance and the Protection of Human Rights', in Philip Alston and Olivier de Schutter (eds.), *Monitoring Fundamental Rights in the EU: the Contribution of the Fundamental Rights Agency* (Oxford: Hart Publishing), 25–36.

— (2006a), 'EU Race Discrimination Law: A Hybrid Model?' in Gráinne de Búrca and Joanne Scott (eds.), *Law and New Governance in the EU and the US* (Oxford: Hart Publishing), 97–120.

de Búrca, Gráinne and Aschenbrenner, Jo Beatrix (2004), 'European Constitutionalism and the Charter' in Steve Peers and Angela Ward (eds.), *The European Union Charter of Fundamental Rights* (Oxford: Hart Publishing), 3–34.

de Búrca, Gráinne and Scott, Joanne (eds.) (2006), *Law and New Governance in the EU and the US* (Oxford: Hart Publishing).

de Búrca, Gráinne and Zeitlin, Jonathan (2003), 'Constitutionalising the Open Method of Coordination: What Should the Convention Propose?' *CEPS Policy Brief*, No. 31, 1–9.

de la Porte, Caroline (2002), 'Is the Open Method of Coordination Appropriate for Organising Activities at European Level in Sensitive Policy Areas?', *European Law Journal*, 8 (1), 38–58.

— (2008), 'The European Union Development and National Level Influence of the Open Method of Coordination: The Cases of Employment and Social Inclusion', PhD Dissertation, (Florence: European University Institute).

de la Porte, Caroline and Pochet, Philippe (2002), 'Supple Co-ordination at EU Level and the Key Actors' Involvement', in Caroline de la Porte and Philippe Pochet (eds.), *Building Social Europe through the Open Method of Co-ordination* (Brussels: P.I.E. Peter Lang), 27–68.

de Schutter, Olivier (2005a), 'The Implementation of Fundamental Rights Through the Open Method of Co-ordination' in Olivier de Schutter and Simon Deakin (eds.). *Social Rights and Market Forces: Is the Open Coordination of Employment and Social Policies the Future of Social Europe?* (Brussels: Bruylant), 279–434.

— (2005b), 'Mainstreaming Human Rights in the European Union' in. Philip Alston and Olivier de Schutter (eds.), *Monitoring Fundamental rights in the EU* (Oxford: Hart Publishing), 37–72.

De Witte, Bruno (2005), 'The Trajectory of Fundamental Social Rights in the European Union' in Gráinne de Búrca and Bruno de Witte (eds.) (with Larissa Ogertschnig), *Social Rights in Europe* (Oxford: Oxford University Press), 153–68.

Del Mar, Maksymilian and Bankowski, Zenon (2009), *Law as Institutional Normative Order* (Farnham: Ashgate).

Deroose, Servaas, Hodson, Dermot and Kuhlmann, Joost (2008), 'The Broad Economic Policy Guidelines: Before and After the Re-launch of the Lisbon Strategy', *Journal of Common Market Studies*, 46 (4), 827–48.

Duina, Francesco and Raunio, Tapio (2007), 'The open method of co-ordination and national parliaments: further marginalization or new opportunities?', *Journal of European Public Policy*, 14 (4), 489–506.

DWP (2008), *No one written off: reforming welfare to reward responsibility* (Norwich: The Stationery Office).

EAPN (1999), 'A Europe for All: a European Strategy to Combat Social Exclusion' (Brussels: EAPN).

— (2000), 'EAPN Proposals for adequate objectives for a European strategy against poverty and social exclusion' (Brussels: EAPN). <http://www.eapn.eu/images/docs/objectives2000-en.doc> (Accessed in April 2010).
— (2003), 'Maintaining a Visible European Social Inclusion Strategy' (Brussels, EAPN).
— (2005), 'Analysis of the Strengths and Weaknesses of the EU Constitutional Treaty', (Brussels: EAPN).
— (2005a) Response to the Commission's Communication *Working together for growth and jobs: A new start for the Lisbon Strategy*, (Brussels, EAPN).
— (2005b), 'The Open Method of Coordination on social protection and social inclusion: streamlined objectives', (Brussels, EAPN).
— (2006), 'Combating growing levels of poverty and inequality is essential for the future of the EU', (Brussels: EAPN).
— (2006a), 'Combating growing levels of Poverty and Inequality is essential for the future of the EU', (Brussels, EAPN).
— (2006b), 'Ensuring a Decent Income and a Better Life for All', (Brussels: EAPN).
— (2008a), 'Building Security, Giving Hope. EAPN Assessment of the National Strategic Reports on Social Protection and Social Inclusion 2008–10, (Brussels: EAPN).
— (2008b), 'Developing social inclusion indicators for the structural funds', (Brussels: EAPN).
— (2008c), 'EAPN Proposals for Strengthening the OMC', (Brussels: EAPN).
— (2008d), 'A stronger OMC, but not enough to make the difference!', (Brussels: EAPN).
— (2009a), '"An EU we can trust". EAPN Proposals on a new EU post-2010 Strategy', (Brussels: EAPN).
— (2009b), 'EAPN Response to the Consultation on the Future "EU2020" Strategy', (Brussels, EAPN).
European Commission (1989), *Communication Relating to the Implementation of the Community Charter of Basic Social Rights for Workers*, COM (89) 568.
— (1991), *Proposal for a Council Recommendation on the Convergence of Social Protection Objectives and Policies*, COM (1991) 228.
— (1995), *The Future of Social Protection: Framework for a European Debate*, COM (1995) 466.
— (1996), *Reinforcing Political Union and Preparing for Enlargement*, COM (1996) 90.

— (1997), *Modernising and Improving Social Protection in the European Union*, COM (1997) 102.
— (1999), *A Concerted Strategy for Modernising Social Protection*, COM (1999) 347.
— (2000a), *Social Policy Agenda*, COM (2000) 379.
— (2000b), *Building an Inclusive Europe*, COM (2000) 79.
— (2000c), *Structural Indicators*, COM (2000) 594.
— (2000d), *The Future Evolution of Social Protection from a Long-Term Point of View: Safe and Sustainable Pensions*, COM (2000) 622.
— (2001a), *Draft Joint Report on Social Inclusion*, COM (2001) 565.
— (2001b), *Supporting national strategies for safe and sustainable pensions through an integrated approach*, COM (2001) 362.
— (2001c), *European Governance—A White Paper*, COM (2001) 428.
— (2002a), *The Lisbon Strategy—Making Change Happen*, COM (2002) 14.
— (2002b), *Streamlining the Annual Economic and Employment Policy Coordination Cycles*, COM (2002) 487.
— (2003a), *Structural Indicators*, COM (2003) 585.
— (2003b), *Strengthening the Social Dimension of the Lisbon Strategy: streamlining open coordination in the field of social protection*, COM (2003) 261 final.
— (2003c), *Modernising Social Protection for More and Better Jobs—a comprehensive approach contributing to making work pay*, COM (2003) 842.
— (2004), *Modernising social protection for the development of high-quality, accessible and sustainable health care and long-term care: support for the national strategies using the 'open method of coordination'*, COM (2004) 304.
— (2005a), *Working together, working better: A new framework for the open coordination of social protection and inclusion policies in the European Union*, COM (2005) 706.
— (2005b), *Working together for growth and jobs: a new start for the Lisbon Strategy*, COM (2005) 24.
— (2005c), *Communication on the Social Agenda*, COM (2005) 33.
— (2005d), *Common Actions for Growth and Employment: the Community Lisbon Programme*, COM (2005) 330.
— (2005e), *Report on Social Inclusion 2004: An analysis of the National Action Plans on Social Inclusion (2004–2006) submitted by the 10 new Member States*, SEC (2005) 256.
— (2005f), *Joint Report on Social Protection and Social Inclusion*, COM (2005) 14.
— (2005g), *Joint Report on Social Protection and Social Inclusion—Technical Annex*, SEC (2005) 69.

— (2005h), *Compliance with the Charter of Fundamental Rights in Commission legislative proposals*, COM (2005) 172.
— (2006a), *Evaluation of the EU Programme to promote Member State co-operation to combat social exclusion and poverty: Executive Summary* (Brussels).
— (2006b), *Communication from the Commission concerning a consultation on action at EU level to promote the active inclusion of the people furthest from the labour market*, COM (2006) 44.
— (2006c), *Evaluation of the Open Method of Coordination For Social Protection and Social Inclusion*, SEC (2006) 345.
— (2006d), *Implementation and Update Reports On 2003–2005 Naps/Inclusion and Update Reports On 2004–2006 Naps/Inclusion*, SEC (2006) 410.
— (2006e), *Towards an EU Strategy on the Rights of the Child*, COM (2006) 367.
— (2007a), *Member States and Regions delivering the Lisbon strategy for growth and jobs through EU cohesion policy, 2007–2013*, COM (2007) 798.
— (2007b), *Strategic report on the renewed Lisbon strategy for growth and jobs: launching the new cycle (2008–2010)*, COM (2007) 803.
— (2007c), *Joint Report on Social Protection and Social Inclusion*, COM (2007) 13.
— (2007d), *Joint Report on Social Protection and Social Inclusion: Supporting Document*, SEC (2007) 329.
— (2007e), *Joint Report on Social Protection and Social Inclusion: Country Profiles*, SEC (2007) 272.
— (2007f), *Modernising social protection for greater social justice and economic cohesion: taking forward the active inclusion of people furthest from the labour market*, COM (2007) 620.
— (2008a), *A European Economic Recovery Plan*, COM (2008) 800.
— (2008b), *Renewed social agenda: Opportunities, access and solidarity in 21st century Europe*, COM (2008) 412.
— (2008c), *Communication on a Commission Recommendation on the active inclusion of people excluded from the labour market*, COM (2008) 639.
— (2008d), *A renewed commitment to social Europe: Reinforcing the Open Method of Coordination for Social Protection and Social Inclusion*, COM (2008) 418.
— (2008e), *A renewed commitment to social Europe: Reinforcing the Open Method of Coordination for Social Protection and Social Inclusion—Impact Assessment*, SEC (2008) 2170.
— (2008f), *Child Poverty and Well-Being in the EU: current status and way forward* (Luxembourg: Office for Official Publications of the European Communities).
— (2009a), *A shared commitment for employment*, COM (2009) 257.

— (2009b), *Driving European recovery*, COM (2009) 114.

— (2009c), *Consultation on the Future "EU2020" Strategy*, COM (2009) 647.

— (2009d), *Mainstreaming sustainable development into EU policies: 2009 Review of the European Union Strategy for Sustainable Development*, COM (2009) 400.

— (2009e), *Joint Report on Social Protection and Social Inclusion: Supporting Document*, SEC (2009) 141.

— (2010), *Europe 2020. A strategy for smart, sustainable and inclusive growth*, COM (2010) 2020.

European Commission and Council (2002), *Joint Report on Social Inclusion* (Luxembourg: Office for Official Publications of the European Communities).

— (2004), *Joint Report on Social Inclusion* (Luxembourg: Office for Official Publications of the European Communities).

— (2005), *Joint Report on Social Inclusion* (Luxembourg: Office for Official Publications of the European Communities).

— (2006), *Joint Report on Social Inclusion* (Luxembourg: Office for Official Publications of the European Communities).

— (2007), *Joint Report on Social Inclusion* (Luxembourg: Office for Official Publications of the European Communities).

— (2008), *Joint Report on Social Inclusion* (Luxembourg: Office for Official Publications of the European Communities).

— (2009), *Joint Report on Social Inclusion* (Luxembourg: Office for Official Publications of the European Communities).

EUROSTAT (2010), *Combating Poverty and Social Exclusion: A statistical portrait of the European Union 2010* (Luxembourg: Publications Office of the European Union).

Exadaktylos, Theofanis and Radaelli, Claudio M. (2009), 'Research Design in European Studies: The Case of Europeanization', *Journal of Common Market Studies*, 47 (3), 507–30.

Fabre, Cécile (2005), 'Social Rights in European Constitutions' in Gráinne de Búrca and Bruno de Witte (eds.), *Social Rights in Europe* (Oxford: Oxford University Press), 15–28.

Falkner, Gerda (1998), *EU Social Policy in the 1990's : towards a corporatist policy community* (London: Routledge).

Ferrera, Maurizio (2005), *The Boundaries of Welfare: European integration and the new spatial politics of social protection* (Oxford: Oxford University Press).

Ferrera, Maurizio, Matsaganis, Manos, and Sacchi, Stefano (2002), 'Open co-ordination against poverty: the new EU "Social Inclusion Process"', *Journal of European Social Policy*, 12 (3), 107–21.

Fligstein, Neil and Stone Sweet, Alec (2001), 'Institutionalizing the Treaty of Rome' in Alec Stone Sweet, Wayne Sandholtz and Neil Fligstein (eds.), *The institutionalization of Europe* (Oxford: Oxford University Press), 29–55.

Follesdal, Andreas and Hix, Simon (2006), 'Why There is a Democratic Deficit in the EU: A Response to Majone and Moravcsik', *JCMS: Journal of Common Market Studies*, 44 (3), 533–62.

Foucault, Michel and Magritte, Rene (1983), *This is Not a Pipe* (Berkeley; London: University of California Press).

Frazer, Hugh and Marlier, Eric (2008a), 'Building a stronger EU Social Inclusion Process: Analysis and Recommendations of the EU network of independent national experts on social inclusion', (Social Inclusion Policy and Practice, CEPS/INSTEAD).

— (2008b), '"Feeding in" and "Feeding out": The extent of synergies between growth and jobs policies and social inclusion policies across the EU', (Social Inclusion Policy and Practice, CEPS/INSTEAD).

Fredman, Sandra (2006), 'Human Rights Transformed: Positive Duties and Positive Rights', *Public Law*, 498–520.

Freud, David (2007), *Reducing dependency, increasing opportunity: options for the future of welfare to work* (London: HMSO).

Gardner, A (1995), 'The Velvet Revolution: Article 90 and the Triumph of the Free Market in Europe's Regulated Sectors', *European Competition Law Review*, 16 (2), 78–86.

Gerstenberg, Oliver (2002), 'Expanding the Constitution Beyond the Court: The Case of Euro-Constitutionalism', *European Law Journal*, 8 (1), 172–92.

Gerstenberg, Oliver and Sabel, Charles F. (2002), 'Directly-Deliberative Polyarchy: An Institutional Ideal for Europe?' in Christian Joerges and Renaud Dehousse (eds.), *Good Governance in Europe's Integrated Market* (Oxford: Oxford University Press), 289–341.

Giubboni, Stefano (2001), 'Social Insurance Monopolies in Community Competition Law and the Italian Constitution: "Practical" Convergences and "Theoretical" Conflicts', *European Law Journal*, 7 (1), 69–94.

— (2006), *Social Rights and Market Freedom in the European Constitution: a labour law perspective* (Cambridge: Cambridge University Press).

— (2007), 'Free Movement of Persons and European Solidarity', *European Law Journal*, 13 (3), 360–7.

Graziano, Paolo and Vink, Maarten P. (eds.) (2007), *Europeanization: New Research Agendas* (Basingstoke: Palgrave Macmillan).

Gregg, Paul (2008), *Realising Potential: A Vision for Personalised Conditionality and Support* (London: The Stationery Office).

Grewal, Shivdeep Singh (2010), 'Habermas, Law and European Social Policy: a rejoinder to Murphy', *Journal of European Public Policy*, 17 (2), 282–98.

Griffiths, J.A.G. (1979), 'The Political Constitution', *Modern Law Review*, 42 (1), 1–21.

Habermas, Jürgen (2001), 'Why Europe Needs a Constitution', *New Left Review*, 11, 5–26.

Hajer, Maarten and Laws, David (2006), 'Ordering through Discourse' in Michael Moran, Martin Rein, and Robert E. Goodin, (eds.), *The Oxford Handbook of Public Policy* (Oxford: Oxford University Press), 251–68.

Hall, Peter A. (1993), 'Policy Paradigms, Social Learning and the State: The Case of Economic Policymaking in Britain', *Comparative Politics*, 25 (3), 275–96.

Hall, Peter A. and Taylor, Rosemary C. R. (1996), 'Political Science and the Three New Institutionalisms', *Political Studies*, 44 (5), 936–57.

Harding, Christopher (2000), 'The Identity of European Law: Mapping Out the European Legal Space', *European Law Journal*, 6 (2), 128–47.

Harker, Lisa (2006), *Delivering on child poverty: what would it take?: a report for the Department for Work and Pensions* (Norwich: The Stationery Office).

Hatzopoulous, Vassilis (2002), 'Killing National Health and Insurance Systems but Healing Patients? The European Market for Healthcare Services after the Judgments of the ECJ in *Vanbraekel* and *Peerbooms*', *Common Market Law Review*, 39 (4), 683–729.

— (2005), 'Health Law and Policy: The Impact of the EU', in Graìnne de Bùrca (ed.), *EU Law and the Welfare State* (Oxford: Oxford University Press), 111–68.

— (2007), 'Why the Open Method of Coordination Is Bad For You: A Letter to the EU', *European Law Journal*, 13 (3), 309–42.

Haverland, Markus (2007), 'Methodology', in Paolo Graziano and Maarten P. Vink (eds.), *Europeanization: New Research Agendas* (Basingstoke: Palgrave Macmillan), 59–70.

Hay, Colin (2007), 'What Doesn't Kill You Can Only Make You Stronger: The Doha Development Round, the Services Directive and the EU's Conception of Competitiveness', *JCMS: Journal of Common Market Studies (Annual Review)*, 45, 25–43.

Heidenreich, Martin and Bischoff, Gabriele (2008), 'The Open Method of Co-ordination: A Way to the Europeanization of Social and Employment Policies?', *Journal of Common Market Studies*, 46 (3), 497–532.

Heidenreich, Martin and Zeitlin, Jonathan (eds.) (2009), *Changing European Employment and Welfare regimes: the influence of the open method of coordination on national labour market and social welfare reforms* (London: Routledge).

Hervey, Tamara K. (2000), 'Social Solidarity: A Buttress Against Internal Market Law?' in Jo Shaw (ed.), *Social Law and Policy in an evolving European Union* (Oxford: Hart Publishing), 31–47.

— (2006), 'The European Union and the Governance of Health Care', in Graínne de Búrca and Joanne Scott (eds.), *Law and New Governance in the EU and the US* (Oxford: Hart Publishing), 179–210.

Hervey, Tamara K. and Kenner, Jeff (eds.) (2003), *Economic and Social Rights under the EU Charter of Fundamental Rights: a legal perspective* (Oxford: Hart Publishing).

Hervey, Tamara K. and McHale, Jean V. (2005), 'Law, health and the European Union', *Legal Studies*, 25 (2), 228–59.

Hervey, Tamara K. and Trubek, Louise (2007), 'Freedom to Provide Healthcare Services within the EU: An Opportunity for a Transformative Directive', *Columbia Journal of European Law*, 13 (3), 623–47.

Hillyard, Paddy, Rolston, Bill, and Tomlinson, Mike (2005), *Poverty and Conflict in Ireland: an international perspective* (Dublin: IPA and Combat Poverty Agency).

HM Treasury (2004), *Child Poverty Review*, (Norwich: HMSO).

Hodson, Dermot and Maher, Imelda (2001), 'The Open Method as a New Mode of Governance: The Case of Soft Economic Policy Co-ordination', *Journal of Common Market Studies*, 39 (4), 719–46.

— (2004), 'Soft law and sanctions: economic policy co-ordination and reform of the Stability and Growth Pact', *Journal of European Public Policy*, 11 (5), 798–813.

Horvath, Anna (2008), 'From Policy to Politics? Informal Practices within the Social Protection Committee after the Enlargement', *Journal of European Integration*, 30 (4), 545–61.

Howarth, David (2007), 'Internal Policies: Reinforcing the New Lisbon Message of Competitiveness and Innovation', *JCMS: Journal of Common Market Studies (Annual Review)*, 45, 89–106.

Idema, Timo and Keleman, Daniel R. (2006), 'New modes of governance, the Open Method of Co-ordination and other fashionable red herring', *Perspectives on European Politics and Society*, 7 (1), 108–23.

Immervol, Herwig (2009), *Minimum-Income Benefits in OECD Countries: Policy Design, Effectiveness and Challenges, IZA Discussion Papers No. 4627* (Bonn: Forschungsinstitut zur Zukunft der Arbeit).

ippr (2004), 'The State of the Nation: An Audit of Injustice in the UK', (London: Institute for Public Policy Research).

Jacobsson, Kerstin (2005), 'Trying to Reform the "Best Pupils in the Class"? The Open Method of Co-ordination in Sweden and Denmark', in Jonathan Zeitlin and Philippe Pochet (eds.), *The Open Method of Co-ordination in Action: The European Employment and Social Inclusion Strategies* (Brussels: P.I.E. Peter Lang), 107–36.

Joerges, Christian and Rödl, Florian (2004), '"Social Market Economy" as Europe's Social Model', *EUI Working Paper*, 2004/8.

— (2009), 'Informal Politics, Formalised Law and the 'Social Deficit' of European Integration: Reflections after the Judgments of the ECJ in *Viking* and *Laval*', *European Law Journal*, 15 (1), 1–19.

Kenner, Jeff (2003), 'Economic and Social Rights in the EU Legal Order: the Mirage of Indivisibility' in Tamara K. Hervey and Jeff Kenner (eds.), *Economic and Social Rights under the EU Charter of Fundamental Rights: a legal perspective* (Oxford: Hart Publishing), 1–25.

Kerber, Wolfgang and Eckardt, Martina (2007), 'Policy learning in Europe: the open method of co-ordination and laboratory federalism', *Journal of European Public Policy*, 14 (2), 227–47.

Kilpatrick, Claire (2006), 'New EU Employment Governance and Constitutionalism', in Joanne Scott and Gráinne de Búrca (eds.), *Law and New Governance in the EU and the US* (Oxford: Hart Publishing), 121–51.

— (2009), 'Laval's Regulatory Conundrum: collective standard-setting and the Court's new approach to posted workers', *European Law Review*, 34 (6), 844–65.

Kohler-Koch, Beate and Rittberger, Berthold (2006), 'Review Article: The "Governance Turn" in EU Studies', *Journal of Common Market Studies*, 44 (Annual Review), 27–49.

Kok, Wim et al. (2004), *Facing the Challenge: The Lisbon Strategy for Growth and Employment. Report from the High-Level Group.* (Brussels: European Commission).

Kooiman, Jan (2002), *Governing as Governance* (London: Sage).

Kröger, Sandra (2008), *Soft Governance in Hard Politics: European coordination of anti-poverty policies in France and Germany* (Wiesbaden: VS Verlag für Sozialwissenschaften).

Kumm, Mattias (2005), 'The Jurisprudence of Constitutional Conflict: Constitutional Supremacy in Europe before and after the Constitutional Treaty', *European Law Journal*, 11 (3), 262–307.

Laffan, Brigid and Shaw, Colin (2005), 'Classifying and Mapping OMC in Different Policy Areas', *NewGov—New Modes of Governance* <http://www.eu-newgov.org/database/DELIV/D02D09_Classifying_and_Mapping_OMC.pdf>.

Leibfried, Stephan (2005), 'Social Policy: Left to the judges and the markets?', in Helen Wallace, William Wallace, and Mark Pollack (eds.), *Policy-making in the European Union* (5th edn) (Oxford: Oxford University Press), 243–78.

Leibfried, Stephan and Pierson, Paul (1995), 'Semisovereign Welfare States: Social Policy in a Multitiered Europe', in Stephan Leibfried and Paul Pierson (eds.), *European Social Policy: Between Fragmentation and Integration* (Washington D.C.: The Brookings Institution), 43–77.

Lenschow, Andrea (2005), 'Environmental Policy: Contending Dynamics of Policy Change', in Helen Wallace, William Wallace, and Mark A. Pollack (eds.), *Policy-making in the European Union* (5th edn) (Oxford: Oxford University Press), 305–27.

Levitas, Ruth (1998), *The Inclusive Society?: Social Exclusion and New Labour* (Basingstoke: Macmillan).

Lister, Ruth (2004), *Poverty* (Cambridge: Polity).

Lodge, Juliet (1998), 'Negotiations in the European Union: The 1996 Intergovernmental Conference', *International Negotiation*, 3 (3), 481–505.

Lodge, Martin (2007), 'Comparing Non-Hierarchical Governance in Action: the Open Method of Co-ordination in Pensions and Information Society', *Journal of Common Market Studies*, 45 (2), 343–65.

Mabbett, Deborah (2005), 'The Development of Rights-based Social Policy in the European Union: The Example of Disability Rights', *Journal of Common Market Studies*, 43 (1), 97–120.

— (2007), 'Learning by numbers? The use of indicators in the co-ordination of social inclusion policies in Europe', *Journal of European Public Policy*, 14 (1), 78–95.

MacCormick, Neil (1993), 'Beyond the Sovereign State', *Modern Law Review*, 56 (1), 1–18.

— (1996), 'Liberalism, Nationalism and the Post-sovereign State', *Political Studies*, 44 (3), 553–67.

— (1997), 'Democracy, Subsidiarity and Citizenship in the "European Commonwealth"', *Law and Philosophy*, 16 (4), 331–56.

Maduro, Miguel Poiares (2000), 'Europe's Social Self: "The Sickness Unto Death"', in Jo Shaw (ed.), *Social Law and Policy in an Evolving European Union* (Oxford: Hart Publishing), 325–49.

— (2003a), 'The Double Constitutional Life of the Charter of Fundamental Rights of the European Union', in Tamara K. Hervey and Jeff Kenner (eds.), *Economic and Social Rights under the EU Charter of Fundamental Rights: a legal perspective* (Oxford: Hart Publishing), 269–99.

— (2003b), 'Europe and the Constitution: what if this is as good as it gets?', in Joseph Weiler and Marlene Wind (eds.), *European Constitutionalism Beyond the State* (Cambridge: Cambridge University Press), 74–102.

— (2005), 'The importance of being called a constitution: Constitutional authority and the authority of constitutionalism', *International Journal of Constitutional Law*, 3 (2–3), 332–56.

Majone, Giandomenico (1993), 'The European Community between Social Policy and Social Regulation', *Journal of Common Market Studies*, 31 (2), 153–70.

— (1996), *Regulating Europe* (London: Routledge).

— (1998) 'Europe's Democratic Deficit', *European Law Journal*, 4 (1), 5–28.

Marlier, Eric (2003), 'The EU Social Inclusion Process: Where we were, Where We are and What we should aim at', in Michael F. Förster, Flip Maas, Bernd Marin (eds.), *Understanding Social Inclusion in a Larger Europe. An Open Debate*, Eurosocial Reports Vol 71, 55–68.

Marshall, T. (1950) *Citizenship and Social Class* (Cambridge: Cambridge University Press).

Martinsen, Dorte Sindbjerg (2005a), 'The Europeanization of Welfare—The Domestic Impact of Intra-European Social Security', *JCMS: Journal of Common Market Studies*, 43 (5), 1027–54.

— (2005b), 'Social Security Regulation in the EU: The De-Territorialization of Welfare?', in Gráinne de Búrca (ed.), *EU Law and the Welfare State* (Oxford: Oxford University Press), 89–110.

Mastenbroek, Ellen and Kaeding, Michael (2006), 'Europeanization Beyond the Goodness of Fit: Domestic Politics in the Forefront', *Comparative European Politics*, 4 (4), 331–54.

McKnight, Abigail (2005), 'Employment: tackling poverty through "work for those that can"', in John Hills and Kitty Stewart (eds.), *A More Equal Society? New Labour: poverty, inequality and exclusion* (Bristol: The Policy Press), 23–46.

Moravcsik, Andrew (2002), 'In Defence of the "Democratic Deficit": Reassessing Legitimacy in the European Union', *Journal of Common Market Studies*, 40 (4), 603–24.

Moreira, Amilcar (2008), *The Activation Dilemma: reconciling the fairness and effectiveness of minimum income schemes in Europe* (Bristol: Policy Press).

Mosher, James S. and Trubek, David M. (2003), 'Alternative Approaches to Governance in the EU: EU Social Policy and the European Employment Strategy', *Journal of Common Market Studies*, 41 (1), 63–88.

Murkens, Jo (2009), 'The Quest for Constitutionalism in Public Law Discourse' *Oxford Journal of Legal Studies*, 29 (3), 1–29.

Murphy, Mark (2005), 'Between Facts, Norms and a Post-national Constellation: Habermas, Law and European Social Policy', *Journal of European Public Policy*, 12 (1), 143–56.

Newman, Janet (2001), *Modernising Governance: New Labour, Policy and Society* (London: Sage).

O'Brien, Martin and Penna, Sue (2008), 'Social exclusion in Europe: some conceptual issues', *International Journal of Social Welfare*, 17 (1), 84–92.

O'Leary, Siofra (1995), 'The Relationship between Community Citizenship and the Protection of Fundamental Rights in Community Law', *Common Market Law Review*, 32, 519–54.

— (2005), 'Solidarity and Citizenship Rights in the Charter of Fundamental Rights of the European Union', in Gráinne de Burca (ed.), *EU Law and the Welfare State* (Oxford: Oxford University Press), 39–87.

Odudu, Okeoghene (2004–5), 'The Meaning of Undertaking within 81 EC', *Cambridge Yearbook of European Law* 7, 211–41.

Offe, Claus (2003), 'The European Model of "Social" Capitalism: Can It Survive European Integration?', *Journal of Political Philosophy*, 11 (4), 437–69.

Office for National Statistics (2009), *Work and worklessness among households 2009*, (Newport: ONS).

OFMDPM (2004), *New TSN—the way forward* (Belfast, Office of the First Minister and Deputy First Minister).

— (2006), *Lifetime Opportunities* (Belfast, Office of the First Minister and Deputy First Minister).

Olsen, Johan P. (2002), 'The Many Faces of Europeanization', *Journal of Common Market Studies*, 40 (5), 921–52.

Peers, Steve and Ward, Angela (eds.) (2004), *The European Union Charter of Fundamental Rights* (Oxford: Hart Publishing).

Pemberton, Simon (2008), 'Social Inclusion and the "Get Heard" Process: Implications for the Horizontal and Vertical Integration of

Governance and Policy in the UK', *Public Policy and Administration*, 23 (2), 127–43.

Pemberton, Simon and Mason, Jennifer (2009), 'Co-production and Sure Start Children's Centres: Reflecting upon Users', Perspectives and Implications for Service Delivery, Planning and Evaluation', *Social Policy and Society*, 8 (1), 13–24.

Peters, B. Guy (1999), *Institutional Theory in Political Science : the 'new institutionalism'* (London: Pinter).

Pierre, Jon (ed.), (2000), *Debating Governance: authority, steering, and democracy* (Oxford: Oxford University Press).

Pierson, Paul (1996), 'The Path to European Integration: A Historical Institutionalist Analysis', *Comparative Political Studies*, 29 (2), 123–63.

Pollack, Mark (2005), 'Theorizing EU Policy-Making' in Wallace, Helen, Wallace, William, and Pollack, Mark A. (eds.) (2005), *Policy-making in the European Union* (5th edn) (Oxford: Oxford University Press), 13–48.

Pollitt, Christopher (2001), 'Convergence: The Useful Myth?', *Public Administration*, 79 (4), 933–47.

Radaelli, Claudio M. (2003a), 'The Europeanization of Public Policy' in Kevin Featherstone and Claudio M. Radaelli (eds.), *The Politics of Europeanization* (Oxford: Oxford University Press), 27–56.

— (2003b), *The Open Method of Coordination: A new governance architecture for the European Union?* (Stockholm: Swedish Institute for European Policy Studies).

— (2008), 'Europeanization, Policy Learning, and New Modes of Governance', *Journal of Comparative Policy Analysis: Research and Practice*, 10 (3), 239–54.

Radaelli, Claudio M. and Pasquier, Romain (2007), 'Conceptual Issues' in Paolo Graziano and Maarten P. Vink (eds.), *Europeanization: New Research Agendas* (Basingstoke: Palgrave Macmillan), 35–45.

Regent, Sabrina (2003), 'The Open Method of Coordination: A New Supranational Form of Governance?', *European Law Journal*, 9 (2), 190–214.

Rhodes, Martin (1991), 'The Social Dimension of the Single European Market: National Versus Transnational Regulation', *European Journal of Political Research*, 19 (2–3), 245–80.

Rodrigues, Maria João (2001), 'The Open Method of Coordination as a New Governance Tool', *Europa/Europe*, 2 (3), 96–107.

Room, Graham (1991), 'European Community observatory on national policies to combat social exclusion: first annual report', (Bath: Centre for Research in European Social and Employment Policy).

— (1995), 'Poverty and Social Exclusion: The New European Agenda for Policy and Research' in Graham Room (ed.), *Beyond the Threshold: the measurement and analysis of social exclusion* (Bristol: Policy Press), 1–9.

— (2005), 'Policy Benchmarking in the European Union: Indicators and Ambiguities', *Policy Studies*, 26 (2), 117–32.

Ross, Malcolm (2000). 'Article 16 EC and Services of General Interest: From Derogation to Obligation', *European Law Review*, 25(1), 22–38.

Rubio, Eulàlia (2009), 'The EU Renewed Social Agenda: the right way forward?', in Robert Taylor (ed.), *Social Europe and the Single Market: where next?* (London: The Smith Institute).

Sabel, Charles F. and Simon, William J. (2004), 'Destabilization Rights: How Public Law Litigation Succeeds', *Harvard Law Review*, 117, 1015–101.

Sabel, Charles F. and Zeitlin, Jonathan (2008), 'Learning from Difference: The New Architecture of Experimentalist Governance in the EU', *European Law Journal*, 14 (3), 271–327.

Sapir, André et al (2004), *An Agenda for a Growing Europe: the Sapir report* (Oxford: Oxford University Press).

Sapir, André (2006), 'Globalization and the Reform of European Social Models', *JCMS: Journal of Common Market Studies*, 44 (2), 369–90.

Scharpf, Fritz (1999), *Governing in Europe: effective and democratic?* (Oxford: Oxford University Press).

— (2002), 'The European Social Model: Coping With Diversity', *Journal of Common Market Studies*, 40 (4), 645–70.

— (2006), 'The Joint-Decision Trap Revisited', *Journal of Common Market Studies*, 44 (4), 845–64.

(2008), '"The only solution is to refuse to comply with ECJ rulings"', *Social Europe Journal*, 4 (1), 16–21.

Scheinin, Martin (2005), 'The Relationship between the Agency and the Network of Independent Experts', in Philip Alston and Olivier de Schutter (eds.), *Monitoring Fundamental Rights in the EU* (Oxford: Hart Publishing), 73–90.

Schelkle, Waltraud (2007), 'EU Fiscal Governance: Hard Law in the Shadow of Soft Law', *Columbia Journal of European Law*, 13 (3), 705–31.

Schmidt, Vivien A. (2008), 'Discursive Institutionalism: The Explanatory Power of Ideas and Discourse', *Annual Review of Political Science*, 11 (1), 303–26.

Schmidt, Vivien A. and Radaelli, Claudio M. (2004), 'Policy Change and Discourse in Europe: Conceptual and Methodological Issues', *West European Politics*, 27 (2), 183–210.

Schneider, Gerald and Aspinwall, Mark (eds.) (2001), *The Rules of Integration: institutionalist approaches to the study of Europe* (Manchester: Manchester University Press).

Scott, Colin (2002), 'The Governance of the European Union: The Potential for Multi-Level Control', *European Law Journal*, 8 (1), 59–79.

Shaw, Jo (1996), 'European Union Legal Studies in Crisis? : Towards a New Dynamic', *Oxford Journal of Legal Studies*, 16 (2), 231–53.

— (1998), 'The Interpretation of European Union Citizenship', *Modern Law Review*, 61 (3), 293–317.

— (1999), 'Postnational constitutionalism in the European Union', *Journal of European Public Policy*, 6 (4), 579–97.

— (2003), 'A Strong Europe is a Social Europe', *The Federal Trust Online Papers*, 05/03, 1–5.

— (2007), *The Transformation of Citizenship in the European Union: electoral rights and the restructuring of political space* (Cambridge: Cambridge University Press).

Silver, Hilary (1994), *Social exclusion and social solidarity: three paradigms* (Geneva: International Institute for Labour Studies).

Silver, Hilary and Wilkinson, Frank (1995), *Policies to Combat Social Exclusion : a French-British comparison* (Geneva: International Institute for Labour Studies).

Slaughter, Anne-Marie, Weiler, Joseph, and Stone Sweet, Alec (eds.) (1998), *The European Court and National Courts—doctrine and jurisprudence: legal change in its social context* (Oxford: Hart Publishing).

Smismans, Stijn (2004), 'EU Employment Policy: Decentralisation or Centralisation through the Open Method of Coordination?', *EUI Working Paper* LAW 1/2004 (Florence: European University Institute).

— (2005), 'How to be Fundamental with Soft Procedures? The Open Method of Coordination and Fundamental Social Rights' in Gráinne de Búrca and Bruno de Witte (eds.), *Social Rights in Europe* (Oxford: Oxford University Press), 217–38.

Social Platform (2009), '5 Recommendations for an effective Open Method of Coordination on social protection and social inclusion' (Brussels: Social Platform).

Soriano, Leonor Moral (2003), 'How Proportionate Should Anti-Competitive State Intervention Be?' *European Law Review* 28(1) 112–23.

Staunton, David (2003), 'Social Inclusion in a Wider Europe. The Interaction between Indicators and National Plans: the Risks for National Policy Priorities and for the Determination of National Specific Research Priorities' in Michael F. Förster, Flip Maas and Bernd Marin (eds.), *Understanding Social Inclusion in a Larger Europe. An Open Debate.* Eurosocial Reports, Vol. 71 39–44.

Stewart, Kitty and Hills, John (2005), 'Introduction' in John Hills and Kitty Stewart (eds.), *A more equal society? New Labour, poverty, inequality and exclusion* (Bristol: Policy Press), 1–19.

Streeck, Wolfgang (1995), 'From Market Making to State Building? Reflections on the Political Economy of European Social Policy', in Stephan Leibfried and Paul Pierson (eds.), *European Social Policy: Between Fragmentation and Integration* (Washington D.C.: The Brookings Institute), 389–431.

Streit, Manfred E. and Mussler, Werner (1995), 'The Economic Constitution of the European Community: From "Rome" to "Maastricht"', *European Law Journal*, 1 (1), 5–30.

Syrpis, Phil (2000), 'The Integrationist Rationale for EU Social Policy', in Jo Shaw (ed.), *Social Law and Policy in an Evolving European Union* (Oxford: Hart Publishing), 17–30.

Szyszczak, Erika (2001), 'The New Paradigm for Social Policy: A Virtuous Circle?', *Common Market Law Review*, 38, 1125–70.

— (2006), 'Experimental Governance: The Open Method of Coordination', *European Law Journal*, 12 (4), 486–502.

Temple Lang, John (2005), 'Privatisation of Social Welfare: European Union Competition Law Rules', in Michael Dougan and Eleanor Spaventa (eds.), *Social Welfare and EU Law* (Oxford: Hart Publishing), 45–77.

ter Haar, Beryl (2008), 'Open Method of Coordination: A New Stepping Stone in the Legal Order of International and European Relations', *Nordic Journal of International Law*, 77, 235–51.

Trubek, David M. and Trubek, Louise G. (2005a), 'Hard and Soft Law in the Construction of Social Europe: the Role of the Open Method of Co-ordination', *European Law Journal*, 11 (3), 343–64.

— (2005b), 'The Open Method of Co-ordination and the Debate over 'Hard' and 'Soft' Law', in Jonathan Zeitlin and Philippe Pochet (eds.), *The Open Method of Co-ordination in Action: The European Employment and Social Inclusion Strategies* (Brussels: P.I.E. Peter Lang), 83–103.

— (2007), 'New Governance and Legal Regulation: Complementarity, Rivalry and Transformation', *Columbia Journal of European Law*, 13 (3), 539–94.

Trubek, David M., Cottrell, Patrick and Nance, Mark (2006), "Soft Law', 'Hard Law' and EU Integration', in Gráinne De Búrca and Joanne Scott (eds.), *Law and New Governance in the EU and the US* (Oxford: Hart Publishing), 65–94.

Tsakatika, Myrto (2004), 'The Open Method of Coordination in the European Convention: a missed opportunity?' in Lynn Dobson and Andreas Føllesdal (eds.), *Political Theory and the European Constitution* (London: Routledge), 91–102.

Unicef (2007), *Child Poverty in Perspective: An Overview of Child Well-being in Rich Countries* (Florence: Unicef Innocenti Research Centre).

Van den Bogaert, Stefaan (2002), 'Horizontality: The Court Attacks?' in Catherine Barnard and Joanne Scott (eds.), *The Law of the Single European Market: Unpacking the Premises* (Oxford and Portland: Hart Publishing), 123–52.

Visser, Jelle (2005), 'The OMC as Selective Amplifier for National Strategies of Reform: What the Netherlands Wants to Learn from Europe' in Jonathan Zeitlin and Philippe Pochet (eds.), *The Open Method of Co-ordination in Action: The European Employment and Social Inclusion Strategies* (Brussels: P.I.E. Peter Lang), 173–215.

— (2009), 'Neither Convergence nor Frozen Paths. Bounded learning, international diffusion of reforms and the Open Method of Coordination', in Martin Heidenreich and Jonathan Zeitlin (eds.), *Changing European Employment and Welfare regimes: the influence of the open method of coordination on national labour market and social welfare reforms* (London: Routledge), 37–60.

Walker, Neil (1996), 'European Constitutionalism and European Integration', *Public Law*, Summer, 266–90.

— (2002), 'The Idea of Constitutional Pluralism', *Modern Law Review*, 65 (3), 317–59.

— (2006a), 'EU Constitutionalism and New Governance', in Gráinne de Búrca and Joanne Scott (eds.), *Law and New Governance in the EU and US* (Oxford: Hart Publishing), 15–36.

— (2006b), 'Big "C" or Small "c" ', *European Law Journal*, 12 (1), 12–14.

Walker, Neil and de Búrca, Gráinne (2007), 'Reconceiving Law and New Governance', *Columbia Journal of European Law*, 13 (3), 519–37.

Wallace, Helen (2005), 'An Institutional Anatomy and Five Policy Modes' in Helen Wallace, William Wallace and Mark A. Pollack (eds.), 49–90.

Wallace, Helen, Wallace, William, and Pollack, Mark A. (eds.) (2005), *Policy-making in the European Union* (5th edn.) (Oxford: Oxford University Press).

Weiler, Joseph H.H. (1991), 'The Community System: the Dual Character of Supranationalism' *Yearbook of European Law*, 1, 268–306.

— (1997), 'The Reformation of European Constitutionalism', *Journal of Common Market Studies*, 35 (1), 97–131.

— (1999), *The Constitution of Europe* (Cambridge: Cambridge University Press).

— (2002), 'A Constitution for Europe? Some Hard Choices', *Journal of Common Market Studies*, 40 (4), 563–80.

— (2005), 'On the power of the Word: Europe's constitutional iconography', *International Journal of Constitutional Law*, 3 (2–3), 173–90.

Welshman, John (2010), 'From Head Start to Sure Start: Reflections on Policy Transfer', *Children & Society*, 24 (2), 89–99.

Wincott, Daniel (2003), 'Beyond Social Regulation? New instruments and/or a new agenda for social policy at Lisbon?', *Public Administration*, 81 (3), 533–53.

Wise, Mark and Gibb, Richard (1993), *Single Market to social Europe: the European Community in the 1990s* (Harlow: Longman).

Zeitlin, Jonathan (2003), 'Introduction: Governing Work and Welfare in a New Economy: European and American Experiments' in Jonathan Zeitlin and David M. Trubek (eds.), *Governing Work and Welfare in a New Economy: European and American experiments* (Oxford: Oxford University Press) 1–30.

— (2005a), 'The Open Method of Co-ordination in Action: Theoretical Promise, Empirical Realities, Reform Strategy' in Jonathan Zeitlin and Philippe Pochet (eds), *The Open Method of Co-ordination in Action: The European Employment and Social Inclusion Strategies* (Brussels: P.I.E. Peter Lang), 447–503.

— (2005b), 'Social Europe and Experimentalist Governance: Towards a New Constitutional Compromise?', in Gráinne de Búrca (ed.), *EU Law and the Welfare State* (Oxford: Oxford University Press), 213–41.

— (2008), 'The Open Method of Co-ordination and the Governance of the Lisbon Strategy', *Journal of Common Market Studies*, 46 (2), 436–46.

— (2009), 'The Open Method of Coordination and reform of national social and employment policies: influences, mechanisms and effects' in Martin Heidenreich and Jonathan Zeitlin (eds.), *Changing European Employment and Welfare regimes: the influence of the open method of coordination on national labour market and social welfare reforms* (London: Routledge), 214–45.

Zeitlin, Jonathan and Pochet, Philippe (eds.) (2005), *The Open Method of Co-ordination in Action: The European Employment and Social Inclusion Strategies* (Brussels: P.I.E. Peter Lang).

INDEX